WOMEN AND
THE DECADE OF
COMMEMORATIONS

IRISH CULTURE, MEMORY, PLACE
Oona Frawley, Ray Cashman, Guy Beiner, editors

WOMEN AND THE DECADE OF COMMEMORATIONS

—⁓—

OONA FRAWLEY, EDITOR

INDIANA UNIVERSITY PRESS

This book is a publication of

Indiana University Press
Office of Scholarly Publishing
Herman B Wells Library 350
1320 East 10th Street
Bloomington, Indiana 47405 USA

iupress.org

Manufactured in the United States of America

Cataloging information is available from the Library of Congress.

ISBN 978-0-253-05371-8 (hardback)
ISBN 978-0-253-05372-5 (paperback)
ISBN 978-0-253-05373-2 (ebook)

First printing 2021

CONTENTS

ACKNOWLEDGMENTS

THIS VOLUME WAS INSPIRED BY a series of keynote lectures, symposia, and roundtable discussions held at Maynooth University in 2016 as the university's centennial commemorations program. These public events aimed to diversify approaches to the decade of commemoration, focusing intentionally on "women and the decade of commemorations" as a corrective to the national conversation at that point, seeking to showcase the scholarly and creative endeavors of women working in an Irish cultural context and to initiate discussion about their counterparts of a century ago. Finally, they aimed to consider the ways in which the decade of *centenaries* had the potential to limit discussion and debate about events and commemorations perceived to lie outside of its remit, from the ways in which women in the North of Ireland contributed to the revolutionary period to the rights afforded to women in contemporary Ireland.

Scholars, writers, art practitioners, activists, and community workers attended and participated in a series of events throughout the year, generously funded by Maynooth University's Commemorations Committee and the Research Office at Maynooth University. The Department of Foreign Affairs' Peace and Reconciliation Fund's support meant that we were able to offer funding to postgraduates, independent researchers, and artists from across the island of Ireland, allowing for crucial exchanges between early career researchers, artists, community workers, activists, and established voices from an all-Ireland perspective. I am also most grateful to the Irish Research Council for generous funding under its New Foundations scheme, which allowed for the expansion of the original program and afforded the university the opportunity to host preeminent scholars from around the world. Thank you to Guy Beiner, Dominic Bryan, Maeve Casserly, Marie Coleman, Stef Craps, Graham Dawson,

viii ACKNOWLEDGMENTS

Martina Devlin, Jonathan Evershed, Roisín Higgins, Marianne Hirsch, Sinéad Kennedy, Stefanie Lehner, Sophie Long, Emily Mark-Fitzgerald, Laura McAtackney, Mary McAuliffe, Sinéad McCoole, Lucy McDiarmid, Eve Morrison, Conor Mulvagh, Maureen O'Connor, Emilie Pine, Ian Speller, Sonja Tiernan, Diane Urquhart, and Margaret Ward for fascinating, always thoughtful, and often provocative contributions. Heartfelt thanks to all of those who traveled to attend and participate in those seminars; your involvement is what made the series such a success.

Many Maynooth University colleagues were enormously supportive, too many to name. Thank you to all of my colleagues in the Department of English and particular thanks to Amanda Bent, Elaine Bean, Linda Connolly, Madhu Kambamettu, Tracy O'Flaherty, and Jennifer Redmond for their advice, assistance, and support in planning and coordinating the series. Several of the events were cohosted with the Irish Memory Studies Network; many thanks to Emilie Pine for her support and collegiality.

My sincere thanks to this volume's contributors, who, one and all, have been patient, enthusiastic, and wonderful to engage with during this project. Thank you to Jennika Baines at Indiana University Press, whom I am grateful to have the opportunity to work with once again, and to my series co-editors, Guy Beiner and Ray Cashman. Finally, my thanks to Donal, Caelin, and Oscar for their ongoing support and love, without which no volume could be completed. This volume is dedicated to the memory of my one-of-a-kind, loving mother, Maureen Frawley, feminist and role model.

WOMEN AND
THE DECADE OF
COMMEMORATIONS

INTRODUCTION

—៣—

NAMING NAMES

Countering Oblivious Remembering in the Decade of Commemorations

OONA FRAWLEY

THE SO-CALLED DECADE OF CENTENARIES, the Irish-government funded and promoted scheme marking the revolutionary period of a century ago, is now entering its final stages, providing the opportunity for analysis. The period that this commemorative decade marks includes World War I, the Easter Rising, the Revolutionary War, and the start of the Civil War, key events that have all contributed to and shaped myths that form the basis of the Irish state and of Northern Ireland. The same foundational myths have also been at the genesis of various crises that both spaces have endured since, so they are at the core of contested memory in an Irish context. Because of this, this decade's commemorations have been attended by much speculation and interest as to how, where, and with what perspective and consciousness events would be marked. As the island of Ireland approached a series of key centenaries in the 2010s, there was curiosity as well as concern about how the anniversaries would be commemorated: How would the marking of certain events by some groups avoid a celebratory tack that might be deemed offensive by others? What narratives would be promoted at national and all-island levels, and how would these conflict with or function alongside more local endeavors to commemorate? How would commemorations on this island relate to international commemorative contexts?

The initial launch of the Irish government's Decade of Centenaries program took place in 2012—early enough that voices immediately expressed concern that by the time key anniversaries would arrive the island would be in the grips of commemorative fatigue. The stated aims of the program, which in its initial iteration focused heavily on 1916, were to be "broad and inclusive," encompassing "the different traditions on the island of Ireland and aim[ing] to enhance understanding of and respect for events of importance among the population as a whole" (Decade of Centenaries 2012a). The program would "foster deeper mutual understanding among people from different traditions on the island of Ireland" (ibid.); a real effort was made, at Irish and British government levels, to use the moment to further reconciliation efforts, signaled by meetings between then prime ministers Enda Kenny and David Cameron as well as by the Northern Ireland Executive's commitment to oversee commemorations based on principles of "inclusivity, tolerance, [and] respect" (*Decade of Commemorations* 2012). The use of the term *centenaries*, rather than *commemorations*, signaled that it was a group of particular events that would be marked. Even when, as in the case of the British-Irish Parliamentary Assembly document cited above, the term *commemorations* was deployed, it was seen as being interchangeable with *centenaries*: "The Decade of Commemorations [is] also known as the Decade of Centenaries" (ibid.), the text begins. This kind of language indicated that official focus remained trained on major events such as the Battle of the Somme and the Easter Rising; under the program's remit, there would not be consideration of other noncentennial commemorations such as, for instance, the twentieth anniversary of the last closure of a Magdalene laundry in 2016, or the fiftieth anniversary of the Troubles in 2019. The government program sought, instead, to explicitly illuminate events of one hundred years ago and, as was much noted, stopped short of including the Civil War's conclusion by ending the official commemorative period in 2022.

The Decade of Centenaries project also made clear the prominent role played by and granted to historians and the seriousness with which "the past" and "history" continue to be taken in an Irish context; the "expert group" appointed by the government to advise on its centenary plans was composed almost exclusively of historians.[1] Significantly, the original membership of the expert group included only three women (of ten), later extended to four (of twelve); there was also only one committee member from Northern Ireland, and thus no attempt at gender balance in the Northern Irish representation.[2] The pluralist and inclusive intentions thus stood at odds with some of the realities of the program's oversight.

As commemoration is an engagement with the past the performance of which informs us of the present, there is a sense in which these details tell particular stories, which have become more significant as the decade has worn on. The fact that the *Decade of Centenaries* will close before the centenary of the Civil War's closure, for instance, reveals uncertainty about how to mark a period of "home-grown" conflict, one that continues to inform party politics on the island of Ireland and is profoundly marked by what Guy Beiner calls "goal-directed forgetting" (2018). These details also tell other stories, though, that suggest what I call "oblivious remembering"—which I conceive of not in contrast to Beiner's conceptualization of "goal-directed forgetting" but at a right angle to it. In 2012, when that initial expert group was formed, there was relatively little attention paid to its gender balance and not much public concern with the geographic spread of its representation; as we near the decade's close, however, there is an atmosphere of increased awareness of what we might broadly call women's issues in an Irish context, as well as an increasing uneasiness about what Brexit will mean for the future of Northern Ireland and the Republic's border. There is also an acute consciousness of the need for broader and more inclusive representation in public and social life.

As it was, the fact of the committee's composition chimed with a broader "story" that had long been narrated and would be subsequently challenged by the multitude of commemorations of this decade. As the decade of commemorations moved into its crucial opening phase, what became apparent was that, while there were individual projects underway drawing attention to women's roles in revolutionary Ireland—including by contributors to this volume—it was not a foregone conclusion that female experts in the contemporary moment would be involved in commenting on and analyzing Irish history and culture. This, I would argue, is because the Irish mnemonic context has long been marked by "oblivious remembering," which I define as a form of remembrance that lacks awareness of or dismisses the systemic biases present in its institutional and/or official approaches to the past. Projects such as 77 *Women* at Richmond Barracks, an exhibition and community art project that remembered women arrested and held at the barracks in 1916, often stood in contrast to the exclusion of female experts from the public forum in which the Irish past was analyzed. A Royal Irish Academy (RIA) series of "six high profile public lectures" promisingly titled "1916 as a Global Event," for instance, ran from early October 2015 to January 2016 and featured Professors Partha Chatterjee, Mark Finnane, Bill Nasson, and Jay Winter as well as journalist Fintan O'Toole.[3] While the RIA was by that time under the stewardship of its first female president in the distinguished historian Mary Daly, this did not, of course, excuse the blatant imbalance of the program, which lacked even one female speaker; nor would it have been solely the president's responsibility to take an entire organization to task for such programming. In response to not just the RIA's program but also other events with similar blatant gender imbalances, "Academic Manel Watch Ireland" started on Twitter (in September 2016) in order to call public attention to conferences and events to which few women had been invited as speakers; within days almost 250 Irish female academics had listed their areas of expertise under a request to "alert organisers of conferences/seminars/panels [that] you are a woman who is available to speak as a keynote & panelist" (October 8, 2016), since a common excuse was that event organizers did not know who to invite. Just as much historical focus on the women of revolutionary Ireland classed them as "exceptional" and out of the ordinary, it seemed that inclusion of female scholars as keynote speakers in the present and in certain places could also be "exceptional." It is telling, however, that only a few months later, by February 2016, the kind of exclusion and oblivious remembering seen in the RIA's program would no longer be tolerated: University College Dublin's major public conference for the centennial year, "Globalising the Rising: 1916 in Context," had a gender-balanced program that had nonetheless managed to engage "high profile" speakers;[4] my own institution, Maynooth University, ran 2016 commemorative events that focused on women's roles in the revolutionary period and their place in present-day Ireland.[5]

At least in part, this shift in atmosphere and expectation was due to Waking the Feminists, the response by female theater practitioners to the Abbey Theatre's commemorative program for 2016, *Waking the Nation*. As a national institution, the Abbey's artistic beginnings were clearly linked to the revolutionary period through its declared intentions to upend representations of the stage Irishman and to establish a national literary theater at a time when there was not yet, of course, a nation (see Maples 2011). The fledgling theater set out a stall for national drama with the production of plays like Lady Gregory and William Butler Yeats's *Cathleen Ni Houlihan* (in 1902), which saw a sold-out series of performances by Maud Gonne electrify Dublin's theatergoing population with a nationalist pitch that drew explicitly on the cultural memory of rebellion in Ireland. And, curiously, as an aspirational and then newly established nation sought to articulate a cultural and moral code of theater that distinguished itself from England's, it was often the performance of Irish womanhood—woman's virtue, role as symbol of the nation, role in the home—that became a site of debate and rupture.

This was seen and the Abbey's role in culture solidified only a few years into its tenure in the furor sparked by both J. M. Synge and Séan O'Casey's plays. Synge's *Playboy of the Western World* (1907) caused riots after his one-act drama *In the Shadow of the Glen* (1904–1905) had itself provoked a years-long war of words in national periodicals about the nature of Irish women following the lead character's forced departure into the Wicklow wilderness: objecting that no Irish woman would leave her husband (and failing to observe that Nora was evicted), Arthur Griffiths was famously provoked to proclaim that "Irish women are the most virtuous in the world" (Hogan and Kilroy 1979, 116), while James Connolly claimed that "young Irish wives, even when found in loveless wedlock with old men, do not act in the manner . . . [of] Mr. Synge's plot" (1904). Only a few years further on, O'Casey's *The Plough and the Stars* saw Yeats, enraged, taking to the Abbey stage, berating the audience for having "disgraced themselves again" for their response to a play that challenged comfortable notions of nationalism—a response that saw some of the widows of 1916 join the protest. From its earliest years, the theater thus played an important role in representing Ireland, particularly to itself, with that representation in the early years often linked directly to the performance of Irish womanhood.

Because of the place of the theater in Irish cultural history, there was a resulting strong expectation that the Abbey program would do justice both to that history and to the significance of the year. Launched on October 28, 2015, ahead of Ireland's centennial year, the Abbey's *Waking the Nation* program brought forth instead, however, an echo of Yeats's admonition from the Abbey stage, this time directed at the theater itself: for the program excluded female playwrights and directors and enraged a community. The theater likely had little reason to suspect what was about to happen—its own centennial celebrations in 2004 had included the work of only one female playwright, Marina Carr, even excluding the work of theater founder Lady Gregory (Madden 2004). When reaction was surprised and furious that the only work by a woman included in the *Waking the Nation* program was a monologue for children by Ali White, the Abbey was forced to apologize and rethink its programming, announcing a series of events that became known as Waking the Feminists. The event triggered an international response and, as the important research of Brenda O'Connell in this volume attests (chapter 13), led not only to the short-term gatherings of Waking the Feminists on the Abbey stage but to significant and longer-lasting initiatives.

As a result of Waking the Feminists, Ireland thus entered the key year of 2016 with a renewed consciousness of the role of women in commemoration and in Irish culture broadly conceived. The heated and sudden response provoked by the Abbey's programming decisions made it apparent that there was an energy and a mood in the country that had shifted and that Irish citizens, particularly women, were in no mood for weak excuses when it came to gender equality. What the Waking the Feminists episode suggested for me was that the cultural memory of women in the Ireland of a century ago was irrupting in the present, with many asking questions of what the State—which had been founded on principles of equality—had actually managed to achieve when it came to women's rights.

WOMEN AND IRISH CULTURAL MEMORY: THE EXAMPLE OF YEATS'S "EASTER 1916"

Closing in on one of the anniversaries most anticipated of all in this decade of commemorations, that of the Easter Rising, the island was thus furnished with an opportunity to reflect not just on history but on the larger notion of cultural memory in an Irish context and its implications for our present-day society. While there is a broad understanding of "history," notions of "cultural memory" are less understood and also rarely tacked down. Cultural memory, as I have defined it elsewhere, is a form of "remembrance amongst social groups that manifests itself in multiple forms and relies upon acts of narration" (Frawley 2010, 18). In contrast—though not in opposition—to history, cultural memory involves a consideration of why and how we remember what we remember—and, on the other hand, why and how we forget, as Guy Beiner's recent work documents (2018).

Irish memory studies has developed rapidly in the past two decades, with a particular acceleration in recent years that shows no sign of abating. Frameworks and methodologies of memory studies have proven useful in an Irish social context still dealing with contested versions of the past, and at times when the past—whether colonial or postcolonial—seems to continue to intrude in the present. This was particularly the case in the context of the sesquicentenary of the Famine in the mid-1990s, with the advent of the Northern Ireland peace process and the Good Friday Agreement in 1998, and amid ongoing revelations of church and industrial school abuse. In addition to a slew of important publications, the establishment of the Irish Memory Studies Network in 2013 at University College Dublin helped draw the parameters of the field, which has continued to grow during this decade of commemorations (Beiner 2007, 2018; Frawley 2010, 2011, 2012, 2014; Pine 2010, 2020 among others). Ireland is thus intensely marked by memory in the present. The lead-up to the centenary of the Irish Civil War and the Brexit negotiations' implications for Northern Irish identity and the Irish border mean that cultural memory continues to play a profound role in an Irish social context.

What I refer to as Irish cultural memory is neither monolithic nor monumental; instead—like any body of cultural memory—it is shifting and changeable. We have seen, repeatedly, that attempts to control cultural memory from the top down, to impose a single narrative or interpretation of the past, are likely to fail: as Roisín Higgins's work on the Easter Rising has convincingly demonstrated and as Guy Beiner's work on 1798 so comprehensively shows, commemorative plans might be made and initiated, but control of the message or its interpretation is regularly impossible, as cultural memory is responsive and changes over time (R. Higgins 2012; Beiner 2007, 2018). Thus it becomes important to consider not only what official commemorative narratives are but the commemorative environment more broadly. What stories are we telling ourselves? Who is doing the telling, and who is included in those stories? Conversely, who is not speaking, and who is excluded? How, in this key period, is the past being narrated to us—and which "us" is being addressed? What audiences have these stories found and reached, and what are their sources? What forms of narration are being deployed, and in what forums? And, crucially, what are the social contexts into which these narrations are inserted? The essays in this volume all explore these questions.

Commemorative practice is one of the most obvious lenses through which to view and gauge changes in cultural memory, since it is an opportunity to witness and observe memory performed. Cultural memory is a major determinant in how commemoration will be enacted; without the ongoing input of shifting cultural memory, commemorations would remain static and become irrelevant. Instead, what has tended to happen is that commemorative practice shifts and adapts to reflect the changing needs and aims of a given society, responding to politicized or other attempts to either support or suppress memory; in the latter case, memory can go underground, only to later reemerge as "forgetful remembrance" (Beiner 2018). The Easter Rising, one of the centerpieces of this decade of commemorations, met many of the conditions that scientific and social work on memory suggests makes an event memorable: it was unexpected by large segments of the population and gave way to great change; it involved considerable trauma and marked a watershed moment in individual lives as well as for the broad population who had not been directly involved but whose existence was shaped by its impact; it was a moment, arguably, that reflected a coming-of-age or emergence into self of the Irish State; and elements of its remembrance, particularly in relation to women, have been underground for most of the past century.[6] The fact that the Rising operated on the basis of what Beiner calls "prememory" (2018) and what we might think of as a schemata of the memory of rebellion in Ireland meant that it drew additional strength from other events: it was itself, in a sense, a commemorative act, for the brave and all of the "dead generations" that Patrick Pearse described (Pearse 1915, 72). "Ireland," as Guy Beiner has argued, "is deeply troubled by evocative memories of its past, not least 1916, which inhabits a mythic time and space reverberating with resonances that range far beyond the events of that year" (2007, 366). This meant that, in many ways, the Easter Rising was primed to become a "memory crux" at which the past would be debated and entered into dialogue with (Frawley 2014). Part of that ongoing attempt to enter into dialogue with the past is seen, viscerally, in 1916 commemorations.

What has made the Easter Rising all the more memorable, of course, is the commemorative practice associated with it. Commemorations, like other ritual practices, are attuned to our cognitive needs and evolve to ensure their relevance and remembrance.[7] By way of opening up the themes of this volume, I would like to consider a particular commemorative response to the Rising that manages to encapsulate some of the ways in which cultural memory functions. We have firsthand accounts of the Rising written from memory, but I want to look briefly at a text that manages to be at once a private memorial account of the Rising and its aftermath—a "personal" memory—and one that asserted itself as a public commemoration of the event and has become a "cultural" memory aligned with the sense of women's roles in the revolutionary period and, by implication, in Irish culture. Yeats's "Easter 1916," I want to suggest, manages both to record a memorial response to a major historical event from the individual perspective and, in its transition into the public mind as a representation of that event, also comes to signify distinctions between memory and history, especially as they coalesce around the idea of women's roles in Ireland.

Significantly, Yeats was not in Dublin at the time of the Rising and had to make do with reading newspaper reports and awaiting correspondence from friends. Yeats wrote letters himself in response, expressing his "bewilderment" (to sister Lolly), and, ten days after the event, confessed that "I have been a good deal shaken by Dublin events—a world one has worked with or against for years suddenly overwhelmed. As yet one knows nothing of the future except that it must be very unlike the past" (in Foster 2003, 46). What becomes evident is that "Easter 1916" is a poem of memory. It was composed in retrospect, governed by the gaze of a man who needs to reassess his past understandings of people, place, and events now that the present had erupted so forcefully as to rend the continuum on which we think of ourselves as operating. Importantly, Yeats was also at a physical distance, so that, as he began to compose his mind, he was working with the memory of Dublin and not a series of images before his eyes. Just as when he composed "The Lake Isle of Innisfree," Yeats gazes inward and backward to grasp at memory, to reinvent it: the poem intended as a memorial is written on memorial terms.[8]

Gradually moved to shock by the events that followed the Rising, Yeats drafted the poem within several weeks. If initially he deemed the Rising a "tragic business" that might interfere with the work of the Abbey Theatre (to Lady Gregory, April 27, 1916; Yeats 2002, InteLex 2934[9]), he was moved to see the Rising as something much bigger, primarily through correspondence with the two women who had profound influence on him at that time, Lady Gregory and Maud Gonne (see Pethica 2016). On May 11, he wrote to Lady Gregory:

> Cosgrave whom I saw a few months ago in connection with the Municiple Gallery project [*sic*] & found our best support has got many years imprisonment & to day I see that an old friend Henry Dixon—unless there are two of the name—who began with me the whole work of the literary movement has been shot in a barrack yard without a trial of any kind. I have little doubt there have been many miscarriages of justice . . . I see therefore no reason to believe that the delicate instrument of Justice is being worked with precision in Dublin. I am trying to write a poem on the men executed; "terrible beauty has been born again." If the English conservative party had made a declaration that they did not intend to rescind the Home Rule Bill there would have been no rebellion. I had no idea that any public event could so deeply move me—& I am very despondent about the future. At the moment I feel that all the work of years has been overturned all the bringing together of classes, of the freeing of Irish literature & criticism from politics. (May 11, 1916; Yeats 2002, InteLex 2950)

Yeats's letter to Gregory shows how his thinking of the Rising was enwrapped with his personal links to individuals and the effect of knowing people who were arrested and killed. He shows concern at the injustice of their mistreatment and execution and also believes that, had the House of Lords acted differently and not failed to sign the Home Rule Bill passed by the House of Commons in 1912, the entire rebellion could have been avoided; this is an explicit discussion of people and politics—a more extended discussion ensues in the letter about England's situation in European politics—into which is embedded the poet's own emotional response. Despite his ambivalence about the Rising's necessity, he was at work on the poem within weeks, compelled to it. At this early stage he had a version of his refrain, though with a less active form of the verb—the present perfect "has been." Yeats has already likened the impact of the Rising to that of a major life event—a birth, despite the fact that the event marked so much death—and has already settled on the key phrase "terrible beauty," indicating that the poem will be not a celebratory commemoration but a complex and ambivalent one.

When completed, the poem was privately printed[10] and circulated among friends—a mere twenty-five copies were made, dated September 25, 1916. Compare this to the one thousand printed copies of the Proclamation of the Irish Republic and it becomes clear that the poem was intended initially as a relatively private document. "'Easter 1916' is an elegy," Denis Donoghue notes, "a song of loss; as such, it is supposed to issue in a cry of sorrow for the dead. And so it does. But there is more in the poem than that cry, and some reluctance to utter it" (Donoghue 2018, 52). The reluctance is evident in the fact that Yeats refrained from offering it for publication for over three full years: a remarkable length of time. Yeats opted not to include the poem in the Irish edition of *The Wild Swans at Coole* (1917) as originally planned, and later declined to include it in the expanded English edition of that book in 1919 (Crotty 2016, 12; Yeats 1919). There are numerous prospective reasons for this holding back. There is the possibility, noted by many critics, that Yeats lacked the stomach for entering into the nationalist fray (see, for instance, R. Higgins 2012) or, more generally, the difficulties that he perceived in relation to the poet's responsibility with regard to war (see Brearton 2000, 45–82). It is also feasible that Yeats recognized the ambiguities in the poem as potentially incendiary; and the fact that Gonne found it to be an inadequate response to the Rising may also have hit its mark. "No," she wrote him, "I don't like your poem, it isn't worthy of you & above all it isn't worthy of the subject" (November 8, 1916; Jeffares and White 2008, 333). A proper commemorative poem, for Gonne, would have been one that "our race would treasure & repeat" (November 8, 1916) and that contained as well the kind of emotive demand for action that Yeats and Gregory had—arguably naively enough—written into *Cathleen* the previous decade.

The reluctance to publish the poem relented, as Patrick Crotty convincingly argues, only when the political situation in Ireland had worsened considerably:

> A decision finally to release the poem into the public domain had already been taken when Yeats made what Conor Cruise O'Brien called "probably the boldest [political act] of [his] career." By October 1920 "Easter 1916" was scheduled for inclusion in *Michael Robartes and the Dancer*, which would be published, as planned, by the Cuala Press early in 1921. Yeats elected to bring his lyric's debut forward, however, and to make an event of it, preferring a widely read British political journal to an Irish "slim collection" as the forum for the poem's unveiling. In Ireland the War of Independence / Black and Tan War was approaching its climax in October 1920, as, in Britain, was the Brixton Prison hunger strike of the Lord Mayor of Cork, Terence MacSwiney. Yeats, along with Irish public opinion in general and liberal opinion in Britain, was deeply disturbed by the Black and Tan atrocities sanctioned as "reprisals" by the British Prime Minister David Lloyd George. (Crotty 2016, 12)

When the poem was published, it appeared twice in close succession, first in the *New Statesman* on October 23, 1920, and then in *The Dial* in November

1920. While Yeats is regularly remembered as among the more conservative of twentieth-century Irish writers, both of these periodicals were left-leaning: the *New Statesman* was, of course, founded by members of the socialist Fabian society (with George Bernard Shaw's support) and had printed, six years prior to the publication of "Easter 1916," Shaw's lengthy essay, "Common Sense about the War" (1914)—which is as complex and multifaceted as Yeats's poem in its approach to divisive issues. Shaw, observing an early reluctance to "talk and write soberly about the war," begins by acknowledging that he had not "h[e]ld [his] tongue easily," and that "my inborn dramatic faculty and professional habit as a playwright prevent me from taking a one-sided view even when the most probable result of taking a many-sided one is prompt lynching. Besides," he continues, "until Home Rule emerges from its present suspended animation, I shall retain my Irish capacity for criticizing England with something of the detachment of a foreigner" (Shaw 1914, 3). While Yeats, even eighty years dead, would undoubtedly not appreciate the comparison to Shaw (and would likely banish me to the "objective" phase along with Shaw as a result), I think it worth noting that, in contrast, Yeats had less difficulty in holding his tongue but otherwise was, like Shaw, drawn in this case both to the "many-sided view" and to the critique.

The *New Statesman* took care to publish this kind of work. "Easter 1916's" first public outing here, at a delicate moment following the devastation of World War I, is pointed: it makes it impossible to read the poem as a simple nationalist text. Yeats's poem appeared in an edition that included, "from a correspondent in Ireland," an article on "The History of Reprisals," as well as an essay on "The Pall of Indifference," positioning his text among others that were taking politically left stances. *The Dial*, with its historical association with American transcendentalism, was, by 1920, a preeminent, radical, and modernist literary publication; it was similarly an unlikely venue for nationalist rhetoric, and the poem appeared in a volume with work by George Moore and T. S. Eliot, among others. These were not obvious venues for a commemorative poem marking the birth of a nation—and the poem's placement in them by Yeats demonstrates "Easter 1916" ultimately refusing that position.

It is only in subsequent years that the poem became an official kind of marker for the nationalist cause, with interpretations latching on to the refrain and certain lines and ignoring others—as, for instance, in its deployment in the 1966 commemorations, when the refrain *only* became part of an official program of events and served as the title of a commemorative poster distributed by a newspaper, depicting a burned-out General Post Office (GPO) with the words bannered above it. It is interesting that the refrain is focused on, since, of course, refrains exist to drive words and phrases into memory: Yeats uses the refrain to powerful memorial effect, even if with unintended results. One has only to google the phrase "a terrible beauty" to see the many iterations of the phrase in book titles, newspaper headlines, film names, documentaries, romance novels, and so on—it is a series of three words that have become inextricably linked to the Rising as an act and as the precipitator of a nation's establishment, which is an extraordinary fate for any poem's refrain but especially for one that took such an ambivalent position on what had happened.

Yeats's poem has thus stepped into the mythologies of the Rising. What this background shows is that while "Easter 1916" was not necessarily *intended* as an act of official national commemoration, its subsumption into commemoration and into broad cultural memory allows it to act in an official capacity and to perform some of the task of rewriting Ireland's narrative. In such a process, Jenny Edkins notes, "deaths are retrospectively claimed by the nation" (2003, 95), and, since Yeats's poem does elegize the dead, it is not difficult to see how the poem could be co-opted for nationalist purposes. The poem famously describes individuals—"that woman," "this man," "this other," "this other man"—without naming names. The rebels are initially denied monikers, though notably it becomes possible to identify each individual because of the details supplied:

> That woman's days were spent
> In ignorant good-will,
> Her nights in argument
> Until her voice grew shrill.
> What voice more sweet than hers
> When, young and beautiful,
> She rode to harriers?
> This man had kept a school
> And rode our wingèd horse;
> This other his helper and friend
> Was coming into his force;
> He might have won fame in the end,
> So sensitive his nature seemed,
> So daring and sweet his thought.
> This other man I had dreamed
> A drunken, vainglorious lout.
> He had done most bitter wrong
> To some who are near my heart,
> Yet I number him in the song;
> He, too, has resigned his part

In the casual comedy;
He, too, has been changed in his turn,
Transformed utterly:
A terrible beauty is born. (Yeats 1997, 85–86, lines 17–40)

It is a curious tactic, because to withhold the names is to withhold the assignation of "hero" and defies traditional poetic commemorative tradition; the poem initially insists on a kind of anonymity, albeit one that can be deciphered by those in the know—though Yeats might have been aware of the movement, following World War I, to commemorate the "unknown soldier."

When Yeats finally names names, at the close of the poem, they become a roll call for memorialization and not for the rebellion more generally: *some* of the dead will be memorialized. Countess Markievicz, with her "ignorant good-will" and "shrill" voice, goes unnamed to the end, since she was not martyred through execution, and so her presence is an absence; she is consigned by the poem to an explanatory footnote. This elision of Markievicz's name chimes with the general sense of how the Rising came to be held in cultural memory for the best part of the century, as an overwhelmingly male rebellion, an act of machismo in line with other such nationalist acts that had failed in preceding centuries. Markievicz's unnaming—her oblivious remembrance—echoes, of course, the photoshopping of Elizabeth O'Farrell out of the famous photo of the surrender with Pearse in what has become an oft-repeated symbolic example of the ways in which women have been removed from the frame of the Irish past. The century's pattern of thought about the Rising would not have changed, necessarily, had Yeats thought fit to include a woman's name among his roll call of national heroes; the absence of any women's names did indicate, however, the way in which memory would function in relation to the event.

Markievicz is not *absent* from Yeats's version of 1916, or entirely absent from earlier histories of Ireland—just as Elizabeth O'Farrell's feet remained in the original image of surrender. But Markievicz's presence is codified in certain ways: through that unnaming and through a characterization that undermines her womanhood by stressing the change that her nationalist commitment has wrought—she is no longer young or beautiful, no longer in possession of a "sweet" voice (unlike McDonagh, whose "sweet" nature arguably feminizes him). Markievicz is, as critics have remarked over the years (i.e., Butler Cullingford 1996), defeminized in this way. Her presence is thus codified through a dogged emphasis on her "extraordinary" status, which indicates that "ordinary" (McCoole 2003) women were limited in taking up their places in the annals of Irish history, literature, and culture, as much recent scholarship makes clear.

Iwona Irwin-Zarecka points out that "social forgetting" functions as a "*noticed absence*" (1994, 116), and in those early years—from within the social atmosphere that urged Yeats to unname her—Markievicz, and women more generally, were such a "*noticed* absence" in Irish history: allowed to participate in their capacity as guardians of memory but not included on a national or otherwise wide scale as the newly formed state set about establishing restricted roles for women.

Irwin-Zarecka argues that "*Documenting* an absence from collective memory is distinct from tracing its origins and transformations. . . . Finding out what has been excluded from the record produces more predictively powerful results than other types of inquiry into the framing process" (1994, 117). Beiner's most recent work on *Forgetful Remembering* serves as a model for what is often referred to as historical and cultural "recovery" work but is sometimes, in fact, a matter of listening to what has been said, as Beiner notes in the closing pages of his book: it is a matter of expanding our idea of what source material consists of and to whom we are willing to listen. This kind of work—the kind of work so strongly represented in this volume—is, in many ways, a self-reflexive exercise, one that demands a move away from oblivious remembering to a more critically aware remembrance that is actively inclusive. I would argue that there is a distinction to be drawn between the kind of "forgetful remembrance" that Beiner's work documents and the obliviousness that comes from structural inequalities of the kind, for instance, that has meant that women have so often been excluded from history and commemoration on this island as elsewhere. So while appreciative of the social usefulness of forgetting that Beiner's study demonstrates and also aware of the dangers of saturation in what Emilie Pine calls the "memory marketplace" (Pine 2020), I am also cautious and wary that such forgetfulness, or accepting the idea that we have seen excessive commemoration, might push us backward. My concern would be that, were we to agree that there is an excess of memory, an excess of commemoration, it would be the more marginalized voices and perspectives that would be the first to go. Since there has never been an "excess of commemoration" for any but a select few in Ireland, I would be more inclined to encourage the glut of memory, to open the door to all of those voices that have been, traditionally and historically, unheard.

It is the tack of recovery that has been so successful in an Irish context since the 1980s, when, in the decade following the women's movement, scholars began to publish the kind of work that not only documented but began to fill in those gaps. From the groundbreaking work of scholars like Margaret Ward, Maria Luddy, Margaret McCurtain, Gerardine Meaney, and many others, a substantial body of critical work has been amassed and is being constantly built on, as, for example, in Lucy McDiarmid's wonderful *At Home in the Revolution*

(2015) and the ongoing work of all the scholars who have contributed to this volume, whose work opens up the material culture of women of this period and their position both in Ireland and further afield, challenging us to change narratives and to remember differently.

Markievicz herself has gained in prominence as the decade has advanced. Paul Muldoon's "1916: The Eoghan Rua Variations" (published in the *Irish Times* on March 27, 2016) includes a direct mention of her in the opening of the fifth sonnet in the sequence: "I've watched Countess Markievicz striding through the oaks / where our aspirations turn out to be pigs in pokes." This echoes the start of Yeats's poem—"I have seen them"—but the effect of the contraction is to take the formality away, to remove the distance, which Yeats clearly felt while writing his poem. And rather than avoid names in the collection published as *Rising to the Rising*, Muldoon uses them regularly. Markievicz returns in part 7: "'Leave your jewels in the bank,' / the Countess told the girls. 'The only thing worth / wearing's a revolver.' It seems she shot one officer point-blank" (Muldoon 2016c). If Markievicz was left out of Yeats's poem because she had not died, she is used by Muldoon precisely because she had lived, her speech making her present in a different kind of memorialization, a bringing back to life through direct speech. Markievicz has been present in this decade in other ways, too: in July 2018 her portrait was presented to the House of Commons to mark her historic election to the British parliament, the first woman to be so elected (though she did not, of course, take up the seat). Markievicz was also the subject of an exhibition at the National Gallery of Ireland: "Countess Markievicz: Portraits and Propaganda" sought to illuminate the life and image of a woman historically eclipsed by the images of the men she fought alongside and was timed to correspond to the centenary of Irish women receiving the right to vote (in 1918). After a dearth of biographical attention, these past few years have also seen two new biographies as well as a book on Markievicz and her sister, Eva Gore-Booth. These activities, alongside many other regional and local endeavors during the decade of commemorations—such as the staging of Gore-Booth's *The Death of Fionovar* in Cork in 2015—suggest that there is a possibility of finally moving away from a dominant narrative of the nation's founding and the revolutionary period that saw women sidelined: to extend the narrative and to name names.

WAKING THE FEMINISTS, GLOBALLY AND NATIONALLY

The official Decade of Centenaries program has run parallel to key events both within Ireland and outside of it that have also had an impact on Irish consciousness. Though cultural memory was far from exclusively national in the period of a century ago, memory in the present is determinedly transnational, as recent studies have shown (De Cesari and Rigney 2014; Tornquist-Plewa, Bernsand, and La Rosa 2017)—it is also transcultural (Bond and Rapson 2014). There is a sense in which the Irish commemorative environment of this decade has been unquestionably informed by events outside of Ireland, and not just through engagement with other national commemorations to mark the centenaries of, for instance, the Battle of the Somme or the Gallipoli landing. Commemorations do not take place in a frame in which they reference only each other, but they occur in broad social contexts—and wide, even global, questions concerning women's rights have had an impact on our commemorative agendas as have had Brexit and the ongoing lack of a sitting government in Northern Ireland.

Only two weeks before the Abbey's announcement of *Waking the Nation*, for instance, then first lady of the United States Michelle Obama delivered a searing speech in response to revelations that presidential candidate Donald Trump had bragged, on camera, about his inappropriate and sexually abusive treatment of women: "This is not something that we can ignore," Obama said (2016). Obama's speech was prescient, preceding what was to end up as a torrent of comparable revelations as part of the #MeToo movement, which, in a now-global climate of outrage about sexual predation and the start of a Donald Trump presidency, took root in Ireland as elsewhere. While #MeToo had been founded by activist Tarana Burke in 2006 (Brockes 2018), it exploded on social media in October 2017 following a *New York Times* investigation into film producer Harvey Weinstein's long-rumored patterns of intimidatory practices, sexual harassment, and sexual assault (Kantor and Twohey 2017). While initial media reports focused on Hollywood revelations, the #MeToo hashtag rapidly spread far beyond that community and references to well-known or powerful men; it became, instead, a worldwide sign of resistance and reclamation of self in the aftermath of abuse.

The sense of an urgent need to speak out, to be heard and believed about abuse, came to an Ireland only approximately three decades into a process of dealing with revelations of its own particular and historical forms of abuse. Since the 1980s, there have been nearly continuous admissions regarding the abuse of children and women at the hands of the state in a variety of state-run institutions. #MeToo as an idea and as a movement has thus had a peculiar kind of resonance on this island, where the *Report of the Commission to Inquire into Child Abuse* (the *Ryan Report*) published its shocking findings as recently as May 2009, and where disclosures continue to be made about the scale of abuse and violence in industrial schools and mother and baby homes, where unmarried women were often placed and had their children removed from them.[11] While the aim here is not to suggest that instances of contemporary sexual assault in Hollywood are comparable to long-term abuse of numerous kinds at government-sanctioned institutions, #MeToo nonetheless has political and social power in the present to influence how we interpret and react to that long-term abuse. At present, at the urging of groups such as Justice for Magdalenes, which has fought for the rights of women forced to live and work in laundries in Ireland during the twentieth century, and in large part because of the independent research of Catherine Corless, who doggedly pursued information about the Tuam Mother and Baby Home, the Irish government is carrying out an investigation into mother and baby homes. The Decade of Centenaries program, as it went on, opened up its focus with the *Decade of Centenaries: Second Phase Guidance, 2018–2023*, thus extending the period of reflection to include the Civil War's end; it also relented in its focus on events of a century ago to fund other commemorative projects and events, including "1916 Home 2016," which "respond[ed] to the 20th anniversary of the closure of Ireland's last Magdalen Laundry. Papers consider[ed] how we commemorate the history of women and how their bodies were treated during the revolutionary period and, later, by the Irish State" (Irish Humanities Alliance 2016).

Specific cultural and historical situations of the Irish twentieth and twenty-first centuries have interacted, in other words, with a broader context—with a global, media-driven surge that urged women and survivors of abuse to come forward. Interestingly, this movement coincided with a new adaptation for global television of Margaret Atwood's dystopian novel *The Handmaid's Tale* (1985), which presents a world in which women have been utterly stripped of freedom and are used for breeding purposes—the costumes for which have been used by feminist protests around the world, including in the United States (Hauser 2017), Australia (Mary Ward 2018), and Ireland ("Pro-choice Campaigners" 2017)—and which provoked the wry headline "Women of Ireland to Watch *Handmaid's Tale* to Escape Grim Reality" in the satiric online news platform Waterford Whisperers (2018). That these international events and contexts have an impact on Ireland demonstrates how much current history has the potential to be shaped by transnational and transcultural women's movements that take root through unofficial forums such as social media; for instance, there were reports of higher-than-usual calls to the Rape Crisis Centre in Ireland following #MeToo, and rape trials in Ireland are thought to be influenced by the movement as well (Gallagher 2019). The response to and impact of movements such as #WTF, #MeToo, and #Ibelieveher—a hashtag that emerged on Twitter in response to a high-profile rape trial in Belfast in 2017 in which all of the accused were acquitted[12]—were all the more profound for Ireland in 2018 for, while the country marked the centenary of women's suffrage, it was also facing a key vote in relation to women's rights. On May 25, 2018, Ireland voted to repeal the Eighth Amendment to the Irish constitution (which had recognized the rights of the "unborn"), paving the way for the legal provision of safe access to abortion. The result came after a hard-fought grassroots campaign that repeatedly reminded people of just how many women's lives had been endangered and lost because of the amendment, which has prevented doctors from acting to save the lives of pregnant women. At such a moment, when bodily autonomy has been granted to Irish women through democratic vote, it was perhaps the centenary of Irish women's suffrage that had more resonance than any other (see the significant work of Kennedy, chapter 14 this volume). Jenny Edkins reminds us that "when we are less immediately involved we can more readily participate in, and perhaps challenge, practices of remembrance" (2003, 23). In this sense, the distance from events of a century ago and the distance of women from Irish history—by virtue of having been written out, silenced, and prevented from participating in the operations of the state for so long—have perhaps functioned as an enabling fact in the present.

As time passes, performed commemorations and the sites of memorials must not just evoke symbols: "It is no longer sufficient to evoke a recognised narrative symbolically: the story has to be explicitly told" (Edkins 2003, 124). The kind of story narrated by this decade of commemorations is being "explicitly told" not just through official and state commemorations but also through the work of activists, artists, scholars, and critics whose work continues to inform strands of women's movements in Ireland. Their work is no longer being patently ignored, but there are still voids to fill and still distance to be covered. As recently as May 2018, in a sign of the continuing importance granted to history in an Irish context, Irish President Michael D. Higgins launched *The Cambridge History of Ireland*, making an impassioned plea for an ongoing commitment to historical research, teaching, and support: "A knowledge and understanding of history is intrinsic to our shared citizenships, [and] to be without such knowledge is to be permanently burdened with a lack of perspective, empathy and wisdom" (M. Higgins 2018b). The project for which the prestigious launch took place, however, contains the work of only 28 female researchers out of the total 102, indicating that, however much change has taken place, more is required. Current projects, which include the work of established as well as up-and-coming scholars, continue the work of rewriting narratives, challenging commemorative practices, and encouraging others to contribute to a shifting landscape of Irish social studies.

Out of the explicit recognition that some of the significant commemorations of this period will not have been the ones that have been the most covered by media or those that received the most funding, this book marks "women and the decade of commemorations" rather than the "decade of centenaries," having sought not only to highlight work that concerns women in either the Ireland of a century ago or the Ireland of the present but also to privilege women's scholarship in an attempt to redress what has been a long-standing imbalance. What remains to be seen is whether our reinsertion, in this decade of commemorations, of absent voices, lost stories, and subverted histories into the national narrative will stick and become part of cultural memory in Ireland. The fiftieth anniversary of the Rising functioned as a narrative of modernization (R. Higgins 2012); the ninetieth anniversary marked a self-congratulatory Celtic Tiger-era display of hypermasculinity in its militarism. We can only hope that the commemorations of this decade have marked out a space that sees women permanently lifted out of the footnotes and brought into the text. That this is happening is in large part due not only to the work of committed scholars but also to the amount of new primary source material available, from census data to the military archives, which provides new windows into lives that have been obscured or are simply unknown. As part of my own ongoing research, I was recently able to access my grandmother's military pension archive, including a page that has stayed with me. Following her death, one of my aunts was required to complete a form, which contained the typeface "His Name" for the deceased; my aunt duly crossed this out and wrote "Her," highlighting the need to be prepared to revise and challenge the terms of the past as they are presented to us. Commemorative activity is always a reflection not of the past but of the present, and, just as Yeats's poem offers insight into a culture unprepared to acknowledge in full the contributions of women, the ways in which we mark the decade of commemorations similarly reflects our cultural views: perhaps the events of this decade will be remembered not only for the laying of wreaths and the pageantry of the official commemorations but for the waking of the feminists—some of whom have been awake already for a long, long time.

NOTES

1. Critics have noted that historians were privileged over anthropologists, sociologists, political scientists, and literary critics, for example (see Bryan 2016).

2. The original 2012 committee was chaired by Dr. Maurice Manning, with the support of Dr. Martin Mansergh; the committee members were Mary Daly, Francis Devine, Diarmuid Ferriter, Leeane Lane, Sinead McCoole, John A.

Murphy, Eunan O'Halpin, and Gearóird Ó Tuathaigh. In addition to the gender imbalance, there was a notable absence of expertise other than that of historians. The current committee remains the same, except that Gearóird Ó Tuathaigh has stepped down and Gabriel Doherty, Mary Harris, and Éamon Phoenix were appointed. The original committee did not have any representatives of historians working in universities in Northern Ireland nor any whose work specifically covered Northern Ireland. Éamon Phoenix is based in Stranmillis College, Queen's University Belfast, and Mary Harris's work also considers the conflict in Northern Ireland. This suggests that, as time has gone on, the need for further inclusion of Northern Ireland has been recognized. Available at http://www .decadeofcentenaries.com/expert-group/.

   3. The sixth lecture, to be delivered by the preeminent historian Keith Jeffrey, who passed away in February 2016, was canceled. Available at http://centenaries .ucd.ie/events/1916-as-a-global-event/.

   4. Available at http://centenaries.ucd.ie/wp-content/uploads/2016/02 /Globalising-the-Rising-Conference-Program-FINAL-05-06.02.16.pdf.

   5. Available at https://mucommemorations.wordpress.com/2017/02/02 /women-and-the-decade-of-commemorations/.

   6. Research suggests that events and ideas persist as long-term memory in the individual mind if they fulfill certain criteria: we are more likely to remember events that happen during the ages of fifteen and twenty-five because that period is one that sees the emergence of independence and the individual self (M. Conway 1997; M. Conway et al. 2005); we are more likely to remember major life events because they happen infrequently and involve transitions: marriage, birth, death, emigration. Traumas of all kinds are more likely to be remembered (Scrivner and Safer 1988), alas, than their joyous counterparts, as are surprising and emotional events (Christianson and Loftus 1991). Rehearsal of events in memory—what we call "consolidation"—also helps move memory from working memory to longer-term memory (McGaugh 2000). The Easter Rising involved all of these elements.

   7. The cognitive anthropologist Harvey Whitehouse found that daily or weekly religious rituals were not particularly distinctive experiences and would not be remembered, in fact, were it not for the practice of repetition. Unusual rituals practiced much more rarely, Whitehouse found, and thus under the threat of being forgotten, had to be more extreme, marked by features that would leave their mark on memory; otherwise the ritual would be lost (Whitehouse 1995). While Whitehouse is concerned with memory for religious ritual, his research suggests that the rituals associated with commemorative practice are comparable: it is unlikely that people recall, say, the fifty-ninth anniversary of the Rising as strongly as the fiftieth, and it is likely that the centenary will have marked memory more strongly than other anniversaries. This is because, of

course, the "special" anniversaries will be marked with more extreme, and more abundant, ceremonies.

8. It is, curiously, almost the opposite of Coleridge's famous dictum for the composition of poetry: not emotion recollected in tranquility, but what proved to be the illusion of tranquility recollected in a moment of profound emotional uncertainty.

9. Letters cited by accession number.

10. By Clement Shorter, the British literary critic and journalist.

11. More information available at "Justice for Magdalenes," http://jfmresearch .com; https://industrialmemories.ucd.ie. The independent research of Catherine Corless, which revealed the scale of death at the Tuam Mother and Baby Home, became international news when the *New York Times* ran a harrowing feature in late 2017 covering the story, available at https://www.nytimes.com/interactive /2017/10/28/world/europe/tuam-ireland-babies-children.html.

12. #Ibelieveher emerged during revelations of the so-called Belfast rape trial of early 2018, during which two members of the Ulster rugby team, who had also played on the Irish national rugby team, were ultimately acquitted, along with two other men, of rape, sexual assault, exposure, collusion, and perverting the course of justice. In a period during which commemorations, in spite of engaged efforts, have tended to take place in either Northern Ireland or the Republic, the Belfast rape trial provoked protests across the island, despite the fact that the jurisdictions are distinct.

A native New Yorker, OONA FRAWLEY received her PhD from the Graduate School and University Center and held post-doctoral fellowships at Trinity College Dublin and Queen's University, Belfast. Since 2008, she has lectured at Maynooth University, where she is an Associate Professor. Oona is author of *Irish Pastoral: Nature and Nostalgia in 20th Century Irish Literature* and editor of the four-volume *Memory Ireland* project (2010–2014), among other books. Her debut novel *Flight* (Tramp Press, 2014) was nominated for an Irish Book Award and led to her being named one of "the stars of post-crash Irish fiction" by *The Guardian*; she has recently completed a new novel, *My Amygdala, Charging*, and is at work on another.

ONE

—ᴍ—

REMEMBERED FOR BEING FORGOTTEN

The Women of 1916, Memory, and Commemoration

MARY MCAULIFFE

IN THE PAST, CRITIQUES OF gender and commemoration focused on the "absences" or marginalization of women from historical narratives or memorial performance. Critiques, however, should focus not just on these "absences" but also on how what is commemorated is made visible—and by whom. Gendered discourses of sacrifice, patriotism, and the masculine nature of heroic republicanism mean certain observations on the gendered memory of the 1916 Rising can be made. As noted by Karen Steele, Irish women's republican activism during the 1916 Rising as well as the subsequent War of Independence and Civil War, which was "shaped and encoded by gender norms," prevented "both comrades and enemies from noticing their political agency and effectiveness in the struggle for Irish liberty," resulting in the elision of much of what the women said and did from contemporary and subsequent historical accounts and commemorations (2010, 58). Women who participated in the Rising are made semi-visible, in mainstream narratives, through the very specific categories of carer and nurturer, and, post-Rising, this gendered narrative was expanded to include women as official mourners and keepers of the heroic male patriot flame. Women's militancy, on the other hand, has been invisible, censored, or noted with the understanding that militancy remained unique to a small number of "extraordinary" women. Women such as Countess Markievicz or Margaret Skinnider[1] have been encoded as unfeminine, and their behavior, as it was dictated by extreme or unusual circumstances, was considered temporary. These "unfeminine" women, even if lauded for bravery, could be set aside as unusual, and, therefore, once the "acceptable" women's nurturing and caring roles are mentioned, no other experiences need be considered. This constructed, safe, and passive image of

22

the women of 1916, which would dominate mainstream narratives, was set in place soon after the Easter Rising.

CONSTRUCTING THE GENDERED DISCOURSES OF 1916

In traditional histories, the years from 1916 to 1921 are regarded as most important in terms of republican propaganda; it is the period from the summer of 1916 to the end of 1918 that firmly established the gendered discourse that dominates received narratives of the Rising until, it can be argued, the present day. The lacuna of women's contributions in the mainstream narratives that emerge in republican propaganda can be perceived as a dismissal of the propaganda activism of republican women between 1916 and 1918. However, women historians[2] of the revolutionary period recognize the continuing importance of militant women, post 1916. As Margaret Ward has noted, in the months following Easter Week, "only the women remained free to consolidate the new mood and generate a new movement; it all depended on their energy and their commitment," so it was left to Cumann na mBan, the Irish women's paramilitary organization, to wage effective propaganda campaigns (1983, 118). This retrospective acclamation of the heroes of 1916, a constructed masculine "patriotic cult" of the Rising, developed very quickly and depended, as historian Peter Hart wrote, on the "flood of rebel memorabilia, of postcards, mass cards, song sheets, pamphlets, flags, badges, pictures, photograph albums, calendars and a host of mass produced items" (2000, 207). It was women who produced and distributed much of the Easter Week memorabilia, postcards, posters, and flags that commemorated the executed and imprisoned leaders of 1916; they also produced pamphlets that emphasized the loyalty owed by Ireland to the successors of the men of 1916, those men who were now leading Sinn Féin. A 1918 Cumann na mBan pamphlet declared that "not a week passes but some incident occurs in every part of the country which could be turned to account in driving home the lesson that the country must look to Sinn Féin for its salvation" (Novick 2002, 38). Women also submitted articles to newspapers describing the heroics and sacrifices of the men of 1916, positioning them as inheritors of a patriotic iconography stretching from the eighteenth-century heroes of 1798 such as Lord Edward Fitzgerald and Wolfe Tone through the myriad of nineteenth-century rebels.

This positioning of the male dead of 1916 in the chronology of the "glorious" patriot dead is evident in one of the most emotive occasions for republican propaganda post-Rising, the funeral of Thomas Ashe (see McAuliffe 2017). Ashe was one of the two senior surviving commandants of 1916 (Éamon de Valera was the other) and had commanded the garrison in Ashbourne. He had been court-martialed and sentenced to death, a sentence then commuted to life imprisonment; he was released as part of the general amnesty of 1917. Ashe was regarded as one of the most important, popular, and senior leaders of the Irish Volunteers. On release, he was determined to take advantage of an environment now more receptive to republican ideology, traveling the country and making seditious speeches in breach of the conditions of his release under the Defence of the Realm (DORA) regulation. Because of these activities, he was rearrested in August 1917 and imprisoned in Mountjoy Jail with dozens of other republican men who went on hunger strike to force the authorities to grant them "political prisoner" status. On September 25, 1917, Ashe suffered a heart attack while being force fed and died soon after being transferred to the nearby Mater Hospital. His funeral was deliberately planned, with Cumann na mBan help, to be one of the largest displays of republicanism since the Rising. As Michael Brennan of the East Clare Brigade of the IRA noted, "Ashe was given a national funeral which was probably the biggest and most impressive demonstration so far in our movement" (BMH 1,068, 29). Over nine thousand volunteers, eighteen thousand trade unionists, and members of the Irish Citizen Army and Cumann na mBan joined his funeral cortege from Dublin City Hall, where he had lain in state, to Glasnevin Cemetery.[3]

The cortege took a deliberately circuitous route to Glasnevin in order to pass sites associated with the patriot dead. At High Street, it passed Tailors Hall where Wolfe Tone and United Irishmen met prior to the 1798 rebellion; at Thomas Street, it passed the site of execution of Robert Emmet, whose failed rebellion in 1803 was still remembered in song and story. On the Quays, it passed the Four Courts, and, on O'Connell Street, it passed the GPO, both iconic sites associated with the 1916 patriot dead. It was noted that over "200,000 spectators and sympathisers thronged the route . . . roofs, windows, verandas—even lamp-posts, railings, walls, hoardings, trees, statues, and monument—every possible point of vantage was utilised by eager sightseers" (*Evening Herald*, October 1, 1917). The funeral cortege was filmed and shown around the country—and in the footage numerous members of Cumann na mBan, as well as Irish Volunteers and other militant groups, are seen marching in tight formation behind the hearse.[4] The message was that Ashe, now in his turn, joined the masculine pantheon of martyred patriots for Irish freedom. If executed signatories of 1916 and Ashe in 1917 were now firmly emblematic of the sacrifice of republican men, it was the widows and mothers of 1916, especially the widows of the executed signatories, who quickly became effective emblems of the sacrifices of women. A gendered concept of sacrifice was used in these propaganda campaigns, and it fell on fertile ground. In a culture already attuned to the concept of the heroic male fighting and dying for a passive, waiting Mother Ireland, images of the dead, mostly young male patriots of 1916 and Ashe, good looking, tall, the only militarily successful 1916 leader, reenforced the relationship between militant nationalism and masculinity. Republican womanhood, on the other hand, with the odd exception, had, in the propaganda, a more passive image.

One potent example of this passive image is the series of photographs reproduced in the *Catholic Bulletin*.[5] In December 1916, its editor, J. J. Reynolds, commissioned these photographs of the widows and orphans of the dead signatories of the 1916 Proclamation. Áine Ceannt, Muriel McDonagh, Lillie Connolly, Agnes Mallin, and Kathleen Clarke were photographed in widows' weeds, several of the women surrounded by their young orphaned children.[6] Hanna Sheehy Skeffington, widow of the murdered Francis, was photographed with her son Owen, while Nannie O'Rahilly, whose husband The O'Rahilly had been killed in the vainglorious charge up Moore Street on Easter Friday as the GPO garrison prepared for their retreat, was photographed with her four sons, one of whom, Rory, had been born in July 1916, three months after his father's death. Agnes Mallin also held a baby, Moira, born four months after the Rising and her father's execution. In particular, the poignant and romantic image of Grace Gifford resonated. Gifford was the fiancée of Joseph Plunkett, a poet, a journalist, a member of the Irish Republican Brotherhood, one of the planners of the Rising, and a signatory to the Proclamation. The couple were to marry on Easter Sunday in 1916, but, as the Rising broke out, their nuptials were postponed. After the surrender, Plunkett was court-martialed and sentenced to death. On May 3, 1916, Gifford was brought to Kilmainham where she and Plunkett were married in the prison chapel and granted ten minutes alone in his cell a few hours before his execution. The story of the 1916 rebel and his true love was widely publicized, with articles about their marriage appearing in Irish, English, and American newspapers. The fact that Gifford was an accomplished artist, political cartoonist, and activist in her own right was rarely mentioned. As noted by Brian Murphy in his study of the importance and impact of the *Bulletin*, "Few could remain unmoved by the pictures of children, many mere babies, surrounding their mothers" (1989, 75). These widows, sweethearts, and mothers of the Rising leaders became emblems of the nation, the ever patient, expectant, and sacrificing Mother Ireland; they were potent but passive symbols of the sacrifice of their men.

The *Bulletin*, as Clair Wills notes, was very important in molding the growing post-Rising support for the rebels' ideologies (2009, 110–116). Unlike other more radical or ostensibly republican publications, it was not heavily censored under the DORA regulations.[7] It was, as Sinn Féin historian P. S. O'Hegarty later admitted, one of the papers that helped "make the Rising acceptable to a majority in Ireland" (Ó Drisceoil 2012, 58). Editor J. J. O'Kelly understood that the "first stage of recession of Easter week into history" was important and determined that the *Bulletin* would be in favor of the heroes of 1916 (B. Murphy 2012, 48). The *Bulletin*, he wrote, would eventually be searched by students of history for "material that will enable them to place in its true perspective *the lives and the methods and the motives of the men* of Easter Week" (ibid., my italics). The "subtle mix of historical narrative and propaganda" in the *Bulletin* urged the Irish public toward support of the formation of a republican Sinn Féin by 1917 (ibid., 51–52). The *Bulletin* kept to the forefront of its readers' minds a narrative of the sacrifice of the "men of 1916." With its laudatory obituaries and its twenty-three photographs of the widows and orphans of the men of 1916, the *Bulletin* helped normalize and gender the patriotism of those who fought and died in the Rising. These hagiographic images and sketches of the male heroes and their grieving but proud widows showed a nonthreatening, acceptable republicanism, gendered in a respectable discourse of sacrificial male patriot and passive, keening, grieving woman. This, as Wills notes, reassured the initially skeptical public that the "rebels were not German stooges but Irishmen and Catholics, who devoted themselves to their nation" (2009, 111–112). The sacrifice of the widows, and of the wives and mothers of the thousands of imprisoned Volunteers, was swiftly constructed as one of stoicism, loyalty, and emotional suffering.

WOMEN AND THE FIRST COMMEMORATION, 1917

The first anniversary of the Rising in April 1917 was vital in the ongoing republican propaganda campaigns, but, with many of the male leaders in prison, constrained under DORA or on the run, it was, again, the political women who were central to organizing commemorative events. That April the *Bulletin* and other publications produced a glut of writings replete with the "hazy symbolism of the sword, righteous flame and Mother Ireland . . . hagiographical portraits of individual [male] insurgents emphasising their devotion to God and the Irish nation" (Wills 2009, 115–116) · However, when women were mentioned in these articles, the focus was on their roles as caregivers, nurses, and assistants. As Ireland was still under martial law in 1917 and physical acts of commemoration were banned, it fell to the republican women, despite their traditional representation in the media, to attempt illegal but emotive commemorations at the Rising outposts. According to Helena Molony, one of the organizers of that first commemoration, the women "intended to run up the flags again in all these positions and to get out the proclamation, and proclaim it again, and to try to establish the position that the fight was not over, and that the Republic still lives" (BMH, WS 391, Helena Molony, 42). This action was left to the "extremist group" in Liberty Hall, "women, including Jinny Shanahan and Winnie Carney" (ibid.). With some help the women managed to get the tricolor up a flagpole at the GPO the night before the date chosen for commemoration—which was Easter Monday, April 9, rather than the actual anniversary of the Rising, April 24.

Molony and her comrades also commemorated James Connolly with a major event at Liberty Hall on the first anniversary of his execution, May 12, 1917. A large scroll was created that bore the words "James Connolly Murdered, May 12th, 1916." Rosie Hackett described what happened: "Miss Molony called us together Jinny Shanahan, Brigid Davis and myself. . . . Getting up on the roof, she [Molony] put it high up, across the top parapet. We were on top of the roof for the rest of the time it was there. We barricaded the windows. . . . Thousands of people were watching from the quay on the far side of the river. It took the police a good hour or more before they got in, and the script was there until six in the evening, before they got it down" (Rosie Hackett, BMH WS 546, 10–11). In these first commemorations, as in all subsequent commemorations until the late twentieth century, it was the ideologies, activism, and sacrifices of the male heroes of 1916 that were central to the commemorative narrative. The flags, the emblems, and the reprinting and reposting in the city of the Proclamation "would become part of the battle for legitimacy not just between Republicans and the State, but between Republicans themselves; and women would adopt the mantle of guardians of the ideals of the Rising" (R. Higgins 2016b, 51). Nowhere, in any of these commemorations, was the role of women at the forefront. For republican ideologies to take root, it was important to focus on Pearse, who had proclaimed the Republic, on the sixteen men who had been executed, on the men still in prison for their republican activism: and it was thus important to consign the role of women to auxiliary or marginal status. The resulting narratives did not go unnoticed by some of the republican women in the years after the Rising. Senior activists such as Jennie Wyse Power and Hanna Sheehy Skeffington campaigned long and hard to gain executive roles in the Sinn Féin, which was now the political wing of republicanism. The aim, in having these roles at senior level in Sinn Féin, was to hold the party leaders to the promise of equality, as included in the Proclamation.

Because of the outbreak of the War of Independence and subsequent Civil War, the first formal commemoration of the Rising did not take place until

1924, when the Cumann na nGaedheal-led Irish Free State organized a military commemoration at Arbour Hill, where most of the executed men of 1916 are buried. Due to the divisions of the Civil War and since Cumann na mBan had, for the most part, rejected the Anglo-Irish Treaty, very few republican women took part. In fact, of the relatives of the signatories still living, only Agnes Mallin, widow of Michael, agreed to participate. In the 1930s, after Fianna Fáil came to power, commemoration became more about gaining political capital and legitimacy from the legacies of 1916. In 1934, de Valera, as head of the government, had Kathleen Clarke (widow of Tom Clarke) and Mary Margaret Pearse (sister of Patrick) prominently involved, symbolizing the sacrifice of the men of 1916, and so conferring legitimacy on his government. But women's part in commemorative events during this era remained marginal and purely symbolic, as did any commemoration of the part they played in 1916. In her study of commemoration and 1916, Roisín Higgins acknowledged that, during the fiftieth anniversary in 1966, "discourses on freedom were concerned with the national question and economic inequalities and were not translated into gender issues"; nor was the historical position of women during the Easter Rising discussed in terms of contemporary women's roles or position in society (2012, 82–83). Kathleen Clarke's offer to serve on the commemoration committee was tellingly declined at a moment when the women of Old Cumann na mBan saw themselves "as guardians of the republican conscience rather than representative of the interests of women," as Margaret Ward has argued (cited in R. Higgins 2012, 84). As the country moved further in time from the Rising, representations of women, as Louise Ryan wrote, were "contained within the conventional narratives of grieving mothers or passive, nameless victims" (2004, 47). More than most, it is in the person of Elizabeth O'Farrell that the nature of that gendered memory and historical amnesia was embodied.

REMEMBERING NURSE O'FARRELL: ELIZABETH O'FARRELL

In a letter to Patrick Pearse, commandant of the 1916 rebel forces, dated April 29, 1916, the British commander of the crown forces in Dublin, General Lowe, wrote that "a woman has come in and tells me you wish to surrender" (*Irish Independent*, April 21, 1965, 3). That woman was Elizabeth O'Farrell, commonly referred to in narratives of the Rising, and more particularly in those of the surrender, as Nurse O'Farrell. One of the most prominent and poignant images in these surrender narratives is of O'Farrell, "a pretty, pale girl," walking under fire toward the British positions to offer the surrender of the rebel forces on Saturday, April 29, 1916, assuring her place, albeit a gendered place, in the history books (Good 2016, 111). The *Catholic Bulletin*, in 1917, included descriptions from both O'Farrell and her lifelong companion, Julia Grenan, of her role in the surrender (E. O'Farrell 1917; Grenan 1917). O'Farrell describes the series of instructions she delivered to Lowe from Pearse, and from Pearse to Lowe, over a number of hours on that Saturday. In her own recounting, the woman who had made a choice to commit her life to militant separatism is evident. She recalled that she delivered her request to the first senior British officer she met, stating that "the commandant of the Irish Republican Army wishes to treat with the commandant of the British forces in Ireland." When, rather disparagingly, he asked if she meant the "Sinn Féiners," as the insurgents were now being called by the public and the Crown Forces, she corrected him, stating, "No, the Irish Republican Army they call themselves and I think that is a very good name too" (*Bulletin*, April–May 2017, 30). This exchange demonstrates a woman quite aware of who she was fighting with, and why. She continued negotiating with the British until, at about 3:30 p.m. that afternoon, she accompanied Pearse up Moore Street to General Lowe, where, standing by his side, she watched as he handed over his sword and surrendered. The moment of surrender was preserved in a famous photograph, with Pearse facing General Lowe and his aide-de-camp, while half-hidden beside him was Elizabeth O'Farrell. Artist Sinéad Guckian reimagines the famous photo in a painting that, instead, provides a fuller view of O'Farrell. (See Figs. 1.1 and 1.2.)

Who was this woman standing beside the commandant of the Irish Forces at one of the central and iconic moments of the 1916 narrative? Elizabeth O'Farrell was born in Dublin's City Quay in 1883 to Christopher Farrell, a dock laborer, and his wife Margaret. With Julia Grenan by her side, O'Farrell was, from the early 1900s, involved in activism. On leaving school, she got a job in a printing house, while her work as a political activist also began. Initially a member of the cultural nationalist organization the Gaelic League, she went on to join the militant, separatist, and feminist cultural organization Inghinidhe na hÉireann around 1906, and later, in 1908, the militant feminist organization the Irish Women's Franchise League (IWFL). O'Farrell was, in common with many of her generation, men and women, motivated by the three significant movements of early twentieth-century Ireland: the national moment, the women's movement, and the labor movement. In 1911, she joined the newly formed Irish Women Worker's Union (IWWU) and, in 1913, was part of the Dublin Lockout strike. In 1914, she joined the newly formed women's nationalist group, Cumann na mBan, and it was here, in common with most Cumann na mBan

Figure 1.1. 1916 Surrender, April 29, 1916. (Image courtesy of the National Library of Ireland, Irish Political Figures Photographic Collection, NPA POLF234.)

Figure 1.2. Her Surrender, 2016. (Image courtesy of artist Sinéad Guckian.)

members, that she received her initial training in first aid. When the Rising broke out on Easter Monday 1916, O'Farrell and Grenan were among the first women to join the insurgent general headquarters at the GPO on O'Connell Street. There, during the week, they served in several roles: as couriers and message carriers, as arms smugglers between outposts, and, as the fighting intensified, performing nursing and caring duties in the GPO. O'Farrell's political chronology of militant feminist and separatist activism led directly to her involvement in 1916.

However, in the mainstream narratives of 1916, women's political agency in choosing involvement in militancy from an ideological standpoint was often invisible or denied. As her comrade-in-arms Helena Molony later complained, it seemed that men were "unable to believe that any woman [could] embrace an ideal, accept it intellectually, feel it as a profound emotion and then calmly decide to make a vocation of working for its realization" (BMH, Helena Molony, WS 391). For O'Farrell and many of the women of 1916, their involvement was as political and as ideologically motivated as that of the men of 1916. They were not there because they simply followed their brothers, husbands, lovers, or fathers into battle; they were there because they were committed to the ideal of an Irish Republic in which they had full and equal citizenship, as promised in the Proclamation of 1916. The "pretty and pale girl"[8] who negotiated the surrender for Pearse in 1916 was in fact a thirty-two-year-old seasoned political activist who knew why she was there. As the photograph of the surrender was taken, O'Farrell made another decision, one that she admitted she later regretted. In retelling the story of that moment, she explained her decision: "If you examine the photograph of Pearse surrendering to General Lowe, you will notice the shoe and dress of a nurse on the far side of Pearse. She told us that when she saw a British soldier getting ready to take the photo, she stepped back beside Pearse so as not to give the enemy press any satisfaction. Ever after she regretted having done so" (*An Fiolar* 1958). Because she stepped back, in the original photograph O'Farrell is only visible from the knees down, and her gray coat with the white nurse's apron underneath is also visible. However, subsequent treatments of the photograph removed even this evidence of O'Farrell, with her gray coat being manipulated to make it seem as if Pearse was wearing a long coat. This was, as one commentator noted, "an editorial decision . . . Pearse was the important figure, Elizabeth wasn't" (Loughrey 2016, 5). This excising of O'Farrell from the iconic image has become a popular symbol of the airbrushing of the women of 1916 from the narrative, a willful act of amnesia about the role of women. However, it is perhaps the significance of the naming of O'Farrell as

Nurse O'Farrell that was more effective at airbrushing the more complicated and integral histories of the women of 1916 from mainstream Easter Rising and broader revolutionary narratives.

Nurse O'Farrell is often the only woman mentioned, often the only individual woman (other than the outlier and "extraordinary" woman Countess Markievicz) in histories of Easter Week. The image of the nurturing, caring, and passive nurse, the helpmate of the patriot male, dominates the gendered representations of 1916. Nurse O'Farrell, the kind, caring, reliable auxiliary, is an unthreatening representation of the women of 1916. In a report of her death in June 1957, she is described as "Pearse's envoy" and the nurse who "attended the wounded and the dying" during Easter Week. Her own political activism and ideologies, before and after the Rising, were not mentioned. However, another photograph exists, reputed to be of O'Farrell, a studio photograph taken prior to the Rising. In this image, the woman is standing facing directly at the camera, in a military uniform, holding in her right hand an unholstered gun, probably a C96 "Peter the Painter" semiautomatic gun.[9] It is telling that this woman is dressed in a more masculine Volunteer-style uniform, holding a weapon.[10] Here is a Cumann na mBan woman in a very different guise: this self-constructed image shows a woman with agency, an ideologically committed, fervently militant Cumann na mBan woman, in stark contrast to that of the nurse and caregiver. This photograph of the uniformed, armed woman is at odds with subsequent memoirs of O'Farrell; however, it is the image and title of "nurse" that remains central to memories of most of the women of 1916. For their male comrades, it was the care offered by the women that resonated in their memories. Irish Volunteer Fintan Murphy, who was stationed at the GPO during Easter Week, sang the praises of the "gallantry and goodness . . . of that brave band of women . . . who tended and cared for us during the week," although he did also admit that "some of them [were] risking their lives in crossing the street to our outposts there and [were] all ready and willing to undertake dangerous missions to other commands and elsewhere" (BMH WS 373 Fintan Murphy, 4). Emphasizing the nurturing and caring role of the women of 1916, the Catholic *Bulletin* of 1917 noted that they "looked after the needs of the men under arms, they nursed the wounded, they soothed the suffering and it was they who softly breathed the last prayer into the ear of the dying" (*Catholic Bulletin*, 1917). The women—their activism, ideological commitment and militancy disregarded, and their key role in reorganizing and propagandizing the republican movement in the following years forgotten—now became the "girls" who helped in the revolution.

"THE FORGOTTEN HEROINES OF THE EASTER RISING"

Eithne Coyle, an important Cumann na mBan activist during the War of Independence and Civil War, noted that she and her comrades were largely dismissed in narratives of Irish revolutionary history: "It is a curious fact that women as women got a very meagre place in the pages of history. And Irish history, I am sorry to say, is no exception to the rule" (Shighle Humphreys Papers [UCDA], P106/1226[1]). In the initial post–Civil War period, amid a backlash against those who had opposed the Anglo-Irish Treaty, the narrative of the women of the revolutionary era was of "unmanageable revolutionaries," those "furies" in Cumann na mBan who had voted by a majority to reject the Treaty and the setting up of the Irish Free State.[11] W. T. Cosgrave, the president of the Free State Executive, condemned those women who were anti-Treaty as "neurotic girls [who] are among the most active adherents to the Irregular cause" (G. Foster 2015, 33). The Sinn Féin historian P. S. O'Hegarty described republican women who had participated in revolutionary activism as "'practically unsexed,' animated by 'swashbuckling and bombast and swagger' and utterly incapable of understanding the complexities of politics" (Pašeta 2013, 7). "'War,' he wrote, 'and the things war breeds—intolerance, swagger, unwomanliness—captured the women, turned them into unlovely, destructive-minded, avid begetters of violence'" (O'Hegarty in Connell 2017, 104). Women like Coyle and O'Farrell, implacable in their opposition to the twenty-six county Irish Free State, were regarded as unhinged, unwomanly, and a real threat to that new State. Imprisoned during the Civil War and, after the cessation of violence, deliberately marginalized by the masculinist, conservative, Catholic ideologies of the new State, the contributions of women to 1916, other than that of the benign, respectably feminine nurse, began to disappear from official, mainstream narratives. It was inconvenient for the historical narrative that the committed Republican, the armed, militant feminist, Elizabeth O'Farrell, voted against the treaty, sided with the anti-Treaty Republicans during the Civil War, and for the rest of her life, rejected the legitimacy of the State formed in 1922. However, the whitewashed, passive, unthreatening figure of Nurse O'Farrell could, briefly, make an appearance in the Easter Rising story—with her simple white flag, her long nurse's coat, and her red cross.[12] And, as quickly as she enters the narrative, she exits; she exists only for those days of care in the GPO and the journey up Moore Street with her white flag. Once her moment is over, in history as in the photograph, she, along with most of the women of 1916, was quietly and effectively airbrushed from memory.

As the State moved further away from the events of Easter Week, there were attempts to collect histories and memories of the Rising. In 1947, the Bureau of Military History was established "to assemble and coordinate material to form the basis for the compilation of the history of the movement for independence from the formation of the Irish Volunteers on 25 November 1913 to 11 July 1921" (McGarry 2011, 26).[13] About 1,770 statements were collected from members of the Irish Volunteers, the Irish Citizen Army, the Irish Republican Brotherhood, Sinn Féin, and, of course, from Cumann na mBan. However, women's contributions comprised less than 10 percent of the Witness Statements, reflecting, as Ferghal McGarry notes, "contemporary assumptions about the relative importance of their contribution" (ibid., 28). O'Farrell, still refusing to recognize the State, also refused to participate in the Bureau of Military History interviews; nor, indeed, she did she apply for a military pension. Where the women were remembered in the male-centered narratives it was as the "loyal and courageous" girls of Cumann na mBan who "rendered heroic service . . . carried despatches, nursed the sick and wounded, [provided] clothing . . . and there were women and girls [outside of Cumann na mBan] who kept many a long vigil, who cooked and washed and provide shelter" (O'Donoghue in Ryan 2004, 48–49). The dominant memory of the women of 1916 and of the War of Independence had become, effectively and quickly, a gendered memory of wives, mothers, widows, nurses, and carers.

REMEMBERED FOR BEING FORGOTTEN

From the 1980s, the historiography of women and the Rising (and the following years of violence through to 1923) has been one of constant recovery, rewriting, and reiteration. Over forty years of research and writing on women and the revolutionary era, 1900–1923, mainly by women historians and researchers, has led to a real richness of scholarship.[14] Yet, in 2016, many articles appeared in the mainstream Irish media that emphasized the need to look again for "The Forgotten Heroines of the Easter Rising" (*Irish Times*, January 28, 2016). At the end of one such newspaper article detailing the activities of women such as Linda Kearns, Dr. Kathleen Lynn, Elizabeth O'Farrell, Julia Grenan, Ella Webb, and Margaret Huxley, the author noted that "we compound the original neglect by failing to remember them as we mark the creation myth of our state. . . . By remembering their role in the road to the Republic, the commemoration in 2016 could mark the start of a whole new inclusive chapter in our nation's story" (ibid.). The implication here, as in many other media pieces, was that 2016 would and should mark a turning point in including women's contributions to the narrative of the Rising. This is not the first time that decades of women's history and women's history writing was dismissed in the mainstream media. In an interview with the journalist Ronan McGreevy, Colin Teevan, the creator of the RTÉ drama *Rebellion* broadcast in 2016, said he "had not been aware of just how many women took part in the Rising" and that he was astonished that "some 50% of the population had their stories airbrushed out of history" (*Irish Times*, January 11, 2016, 3).

Bernice Harrison reviewed the RTÉ documentary *Seven Women* in similar language in "Rising from Obscurity: The Women Airbrushed Out of History." Narrated by Fiona Shaw, *Seven Women* explored the roles played by seven women in the Rising: Countess Constance Markievicz, Margaret Skinnider, Helena Molony, Louise Gavan Duffy, Leslie Price, Aoife de Burca, and Elise Mahaffy. "Knowing," she wrote, "that the reclamation of women's roles in the Rising is one of the big stories of this centenary commemoration," Harrison tuned in to get their stories. The documentary painted a "picture of the women's seriousness and commitment," which "makes their airbrushing out of history—Markievicz excepted—so frustrating" (*Irish Times*, March 26, 2016, 8). In this and other articles on the women of 1916 and commemoration, which appeared throughout 2016, there were two notable trends: first, almost every writer or journalist comments on women's airbrushing out of history, and, second, they remark that the 2016 commemoration will, assuredly, mark a moment when this airbrushing will end. This truth, of women forgotten and now, suddenly, remembered, remains unchallenged. As Una Mullaly wrote in March 2016, "I'm sure some people might feel that the role of women in the Rising is overstated . . . [but] isn't it sad that many women's stories didn't get the attention they deserve until now" (*Irish Times*, March 28, 2016).

All of this begs the question as to why, after forty years of scholarship on women's roles in the revolutionary period, the male-centric narrative and the concurrent airbrushing of women and the work of women historians remain so lodged in public memory? In April 2014, the Women's History Association of Ireland (WHAI), with funding from the Department of Arts, Heritage, and the Gaeltacht, organized a three-day public history event to commemorate the founding of Cumann na mBan. As part of these events, on April 2, 2014, the president of Ireland, Michael D. Higgins, marked the contribution of Cumann na mBan women at a special ceremony at Glasnevin Cemetery, at which wreaths were laid at the grave of Elizabeth O'Farrell and at the Sigerson Memorial.[15] The following day, a two-day international conference on Cumann na mBan began and was hosted by the WHAI at the National Museum, Collins Barracks. The range and breadth of research on Cumann na mBan and on militant, suffrage, and labor women of the early twentieth century demonstrated a vigorous interest in and research on the women of the revolutionary decade. In 2016, during the commemorations of the Easter Rising, the public interest in women's roles and contributions was visibly heightened by several funded public history projects.[16] Yet even as all this research on the women of 1916 complicates and broadens their roles, there remains some unease with moving away from traditional narratives. Complaints that a "gender agenda" favored by feminist historians, which serves not to correct but to exaggerate the role of women, were aired by some members of the public, often on social media. However, the fluctuating frameworks of a contemporary society more attuned to feminist activism, women's equality and achievements in the public sphere are less accepting of the nurse narrative then preceding generations.

With the opening of new archives, and especially with digital access to archives, scholars are delving deeply and producing more nuanced analyses of the roles and contributions of women to 1916. Upwards of three hundred women are now known to have taken part in the Rising, and their activism and politics are now seen in all their complexity. These women's contributions are far broader: yes, they served as nurses and first aid assistants but also as couriers, message carriers, intelligence gatherers, gunwomen, snipers, and military leaders—in roles understood, by most historians, as integral and vital to the history of the Rising. However, the intractable nurse narratives, the guardian of the patriot flame image, and the forgotten women stories prove difficult, still, to shift from public consciousness. These narratives were embedded in public consciousness soon after the Rising, initially developed and circulated by activist women themselves to propagandize the republican ideologies that motivated the patriot dead. Later, male writers, historians, and commentators usefully positioned women within a framework acceptable to a masculinist, conservative state, and it is these narratives that continue as dominant memory tropes. Widows and nurses are not generally the stuff of national narratives, but the ongoing understanding of the more militant contribution of women is, inexorably, challenging and changing that narrative of 1916. Commemoration cannot ever be separate from contemporary sociopolitical and cultural events, so 2016 also reflected contemporary politics, where gender equality within Irish society continues to be as contested as the place of women within the 1916 narrative. However, women's histories, as they are uncovered, will continue to challenge and question the myths and histories of 1916, broaden the role played by women, complicate our understanding of 1916, and question what constitutes an authentic past as well as expose the processes by which a gendered narrative was constructed and historicized.

NOTES

1. Both Countess Markievicz and Margaret Skinnider were, in subsequent histories, most noteworthy in 1916 for their militancy. Both served with the Irish Citizen Army at the Royal College of Surgeons outpost in 1916, where Markievicz was second in command to Michael Mallin. Both were associated with guns and violent incidents during the Rising. Markievicz was later accused of killing an unarmed Dublin Metropolitan policeman, while Skinnider was wounded leading an armed assault on a Crown Forces sniper during Easter Week. In 2016, one of the stories of the women of 1916 that received much attention in the media was the fact that Skinnider was denied a military pension in 1924 because of her gender.

2. Examples include Margaret Ward 1983; Sinéad McCoole 2003; Louise Ryan and Margaret Ward 2004; Ann Matthews 2010; Senia Pašeta 2013; Lucy McDiarmid 2015; Mary McAuliffe and Liz Gillis 2016.

3. The Ashe family were persuaded not to take his body back to his native Kinard, County Kerry, for burial. A republican funeral in the style of that held for the old Fenian O'Donovan Rossa to Glasnevin provided the resurgent republicans with a propaganda coup. The *London Daily Express* commented that Ashe's death had made one hundred thousand Sinn Féiners out of one hundred thousand constitutional nationalists.

4. The Ashe funeral was filmed by the General Film Supply Company as part of their *Irish Events* newsreel. See Condon 2008.

5. The *Catholic Bulletin* was first published in 1911 as *The Catholic Book Bulletin: A Monthly Review of Catholic Literature*. It was a family magazine with popular appeal and an estimated circulation of ten thousand to fifteen thousand. One of the few magazines to escape censorship after the Rising, articles sympathetic to the nationalist cause appeared between May and December 1916.

6. Áine Ceannt was the widow of Éamonn Ceannt; Muriel McDonagh was the widow of Thomas McDonagh; Lillie Connolly was the widow of James Connolly; Agnes Mallin was the widow of Michael Mallin; and Kathleen Clarke was the widow of Tom Clarke. All of these men had been signatories to the 1916 Proclamation. Hanna Sheehy Skeffington was the widow of Francis, who had been executed by British troops at Portobello Barracks during the Rising.

7. DORA, or Defence of the Realm Act, passed in August 1914, after World War I began, and gave the military powers to devise regulations in the interest of "the public safety and defence of realm." In Ireland, this meant the powers were used to curb and censor nationalism and republican publications.

8. Interestingly, in an account of her activities during Easter Week in an obituary, published in the *Irish Press*, Wednesday, June 26, 1957, she was described as "big and blond and fearless."

9. This image recently came up for sale at Adam's Auctioneers Salerooms in Dublin (2018) and was credited to photographer Thomas Tyndall, Dublin 1916. In this, she is wearing a military uniform, which was a coat of Volunteer tweed, with four pockets, dark green cuffs, and a leather belt. She is also wearing a slouch hat, more typical of that worn by Irish Volunteer or Irish Citizen Army men. She also seems to be wearing the recommended haversack as the leather straps are visible on her shoulders. The Mauser C96 she is holding, which the Irish Volunteers referred to as "Peter the Painter," proved lethally effective in close-quarter street fighting during Easter Week.

10. While the most famous studio images of a female 1916 rebel photographed in uniform and holding a gun are those of Countess Markievicz, in recent years studio photographs and other photographs of Cumann na mBan women, in uniform and holding guns, have surfaced. Self-constructed images of militancy were probably more common than previous thought.

11. Éamon de Valera said of the women of Cumann na mBan, "Women are at once the boldest and most unmanageable of revolutionaries" (in Margaret Ward 1983, viii), while P. S. O'Hegarty called the anti-Treaty Cumann na mBan women "'furies' who were helping perpetuate violence and unrest" (in Ryan 2004, 48).

12. Ironically, in 1916, O'Farrell was not actually a trained nurse, but she did, later, become one; in 1921, she trained as a midwife and began a long and well-remembered career in Dublin as a midwife and member of the Irish Nurses and Midwives Organisation.

13. The deliberate dates chosen meant that the Anglo-Irish Treaty, the treaty debates, and the subsequent Civil War were all excluded from the remit of the bureau.

14. These include Margaret Ward's groundbreaking *Unmanageable Revolutionaries: Women and Irish Nationalism* (1983) and *In Their Own Voice: Women and Irish Nationalism* (1989); Rosemary Cullen Owens's *Smashing Times: A History of the Irish Women's Suffrage Movement 1889–1922* (1984); Mary Jones's *Those Obstreperous Lassies: A History of the IWWU* (1988); Ruth Taillon's *When History Was Made: The Women of 1916* (1999); Sinéad McCoole's *No Ordinary Women: Irish Female Activists in the Revolutionary Years* (2003); Louise Ryan and Margaret Ward, *Irish Women and Nationalism: Soldiers, New Women and Wicked Hags* (2004); Rosemary Cullen Owens's *A Social History of Women in Ireland, 1870–1970* (2007); Cal McCarthy's *Cumann na mBan and the Irish Revolution* (2007); and Ann Matthews's *Renegades: Irish Republican Women, 1900–1922* (2010). As 2016 approached, several critically well-received books dealing with women, nationalism, and revolution appeared, including Senia Pašeta's *Irish Nationalist Women, 1900–1918* (2013); Sinéad McCoole's *Easter Widows* (2015); Lucy McDiarmid's *At Home in the Revolution: What Women Said and Did in 1916* (2015); and Mary McAuliffe and Liz Gillis's *We Were There: 77 Women of the Easter Rising* (2016).

15. As then president of the WHAI, I delivered a memorial lecture on Cumann na mBan to the gathering at Glasnevin (McAuliffe 2014), available at http://www.decadeofcentenaries.com/cumann-na-mban-centenary -commemoration-glasnevin-cemetery-wednesday-2-april-2014/.

16. These include the *77 Women of the Easter Rising Project* (book, quilt, and exhibition) at the newly restored and reopened Richmond Barracks and the traveling exhibitions of the *Women and the Rising*, developed by historian Sinéad McCoole. Sligo Field Club held an all-woman conference on "Ireland's Women" at Lissadell, in County Sligo, childhood home of Countess Markievicz. These and other projects throughout the year, north and south of the border, whetted the appetite of a public eager to learn more of women's involvement in the Rising.

MARY MCAULIFFE lectures in Gender Studies at University College Dublin and specializes in Irish women's and gender history, and is a past president of the Women's History Association of Ireland. She is author with Liz Gillis of *We Were There: 77 Women of the Easter Rising* (2016), which was selected as Dublin Public Libraries book of the 2016 commemorative year. Her biography of Margaret Skinnider was published by University College Dublin Press in March 2020, and she is now undertaking research on the gendered and sexual violence suffered by women during the Irish War of Independence and the Civil War.

TWO

—⚅—

UNITY OF UNIONISM?

Gender, Covenant, and Commemoration

DIANE URQUHART

DESCRIBED AS A "NATION OF women," the establishment of the Ulster Women's Unionist Council (UWUC) in 1911 was pivotal in both the history of unionism and Irish women's political activism (*The Spectator*, July 13, 1912).[1] Dedicated to the defeat of home rule, this organization developed into the most sizable female political association in Ireland, and its membership figures, peaking in the early decades of the twentieth century when the third home rule crisis was at its zenith, have never been matched. This period also witnessed the growth of a defiant, introspective process of "Ulsterisation" and militarization within unionism (Jackson 1989, 326).[2] This was epitomized by "Ulster Day" on September 28, 1912, when both the Solemn League and Covenant and its female equivalent, the Women's Declaration, were signed in a public pledge to support physical-force unionism. Yet these foundational texts for the unionist movement and their recent centenary also raise questions regarding the gender inclusivity of the unionist movement.

The emergence of women in unionist politics was explained by the political and legislative context of the late nineteenth century. Female unionist politicization was, in part, a response to the perceived threat that home rule posed from the 1880s. Despite the restricted powers defined for an Irish parliament in the first Home Rule Bill and its quick Westminster demise in 1886, the Gladstonian conversion to home rule and resultant Liberal split reframed the constitutional question.[3] The first formal assembly of women resisting home rule subsequently emerged in the Liberal as opposed to the Tory fold. Moreover, its founder was not a member of the aristocratic elite who would later lead the female unionist movement but a Presbyterian middle-class feminist.[4] Isabella Tod's establishment of a branch of the London-based Women's Liberal

Unionist Association in Belfast in 1886 was indicative of the political realignment that home rule caused on both a personal and a party level. Tod, fearing that hard-won feminist reforms and economic progress would be the casualties of home rule, primarily focused on the unionist cause for the remainder of her life.[5] Tod's deserved oratorical reputation led her to be embraced by the Ulster Liberal Unionist Association, a body born from the Liberal home rule party split. Tod was the sole female representative on a speaking tour with a male Ulster Liberal Unionist delegation, where she was acknowledged as rendering "valuable service to the Unionist cause on English and Scotch platforms by her persuasive eloquence and wonderful grasp of the question in all its bearings" (*Irish Times*, December 9, 1896). Tod's inclusion was, however, exceptional: for most women, resisting home rule in this early phase of the unionist campaign meant conducting auxiliary work. Petitioning, demonstrating, fundraising, and canvassing for unionist candidates formed the kernel of female unionist work, but this accustomed the electorate to women's presence and politicized formerly "quiet and non-political women" who were still disenfranchised (comment of Mrs. Spotswood Ash of Bellaghy, *Belfast News-Letter*, October 10, 1894). This work also broadened the domestic vistas of many middle-class women and took them, in some instances, not only out of the home but also out of Ireland to work in English and Scottish constituencies.[6]

The unionist opposition to Gladstone's second Home Rule Bill of 1893 was more populist than that of 1886.[7] Mass public demonstrations, such as the Belfast convention of 1892, characterized much of the campaign, and gender roles became more fixed within the augmenting unionist movement.[8] Despite the earlier acceptance of Tod in Ulster Liberal Unionist ranks, women were excluded from the convention to "dampen any suggestion of frivolity." Tod reacted to this marginalization by organizing a female committee to hold a *conversazione* in Belfast on the day preceding the convention. Tod navigated the restrictive gender terrain by describing this as a "social gathering," but it was a mixed-sex assembly that attracted an audience of several hundred. Her address was characteristically candid and unashamedly political: home rule was depicted as "the furnace of revolution" to which "Ulster raises its voice of solemn warning" (Lucy 1995, 55–56). Tod revived this tactic to counter the prescribed gender roles in 1894 when her "At Home" was held in the public setting of Belfast's Elmwood Hall and addressed by H. O. Arnold-Foster, the Liberal Unionist Member of Parliament (MP) for West Belfast (*Belfast News-Letter*, October 10, 1894).

In addition to Tod's efforts, considerations of women's political place were inadvertently furthered by the strictures of the Corrupt and Illegal Practices

(Prevention) Act of 1883. Amid a raft of electoral restrictions, this legislation forbade the payment of political canvassers in an attempt to level the political field. A further extension of the male electoral franchise in the following year made the need for a new source of unpaid and volunteer political labor acute. To the Conservative and Liberal parties, women held the solution to this legislative and democratic conundrum: the conservatives' Primrose League and the Women's Liberal Federation were founded in 1883 and 1886, respectively, and the Women's Labour League followed in their wake in 1906. A Ladies' Committee of the southern unionist body, the Irish Unionist Alliance, was active in the 1890s, while small local women's unionist associations were active, established in various parts of Ulster in the early twentieth century: in North Tyrone from 1907 and Derry from 1909.[9] However, the inauguration of the UWUC in January 1911 established a centralized and permanent association.[10] Like earlier female unionist incarnations, the UWUC's foundation was politically inspired. The Parliament Act of 1911 reduced the power of the House of Lords to a two-year veto. Any future legislation, including forthcoming home rule bills, could no longer be defeated outright by the upper house, which, with an built-in Conservative majority, had been a former unionist sanctuary.[11] The third home rule bill, the Government of Ireland Bill, was consequently only deferred for two years in 1912; this marked the beginning of the Ulster crisis (see Boyce and O'Day 2006).

For Julia Talbot of Mid-Armagh Women's Unionist Association, "Nothing but the sense of a great danger" could mobilize a female movement (*The Spectator*, July 13, 1912). Post-1911, women's unionism developed into a cross-class, pan-Protestant, popular body of "Liberals and Conservatives, women in favour of suffrage for women, and women opposed to it, Tariff Reformers and Free Traders, Presbyterians, Wesleyans, Methodists, and members of the Church of Ireland. Socially, . . . membership runs through the whole human sisterhood" (Letter from Julia Talbot of Mid-Armagh Women's Unionist Association to the editor, *The Spectator*, July 13, 1913). The organization's popularity was also bolstered by leadership from Ulster's aristocratic elite who were connected to unionism by blood and marriage. For example, the spouse of the UWUC's first president, Mary Anne, 2nd Duchess of Abercorn, was a unionist MP for County Donegal from 1860, the leading spokesman for unionism in the Lords from 1895, and first president of the Unionist Association of Ireland. The UWUC's second and most influential president, Theresa, 6th Marchioness of Londonderry, as a leading political hostess, had the moniker of "Queen of Toryism,"[12] and her sociopolitical connections allowed a local Ulster organization to act on a much wider stage (UWUC

Annual Report, 1920, Public Record Office of Northern Ireland [hereafter PRONI], D/2688/1/3).

Although elite-led, the rank and file of the female unionist movement was, as in much of the political associational culture in late nineteenth and early twentieth-century Britain, middle class in social origin. These were women with the prerequisite economic freedom to participate in political life. The UWUC's ruling body, the Executive Committee, reflected this by not only meeting on weekdays but also during normal working hours, which precluded working women's involvement. However, many working-class women joined the various female unionist associations that were established throughout Ulster. By the end of 1911, thirty-two branches of the UWUC had a collective estimated membership of 40,000–50,000. Two years later membership figures of between 115,000 and 200,000 members were cited. These figures are supported by the en masse campaign waged under the UWUC's aegis: by September 1913 10,000 leaflets and newspapers were sent weekly to Britain (UWUC Executive Committee Minutes, May 14, 1914 [PRONI, D/1098/1/2])[13] and an estimated 25,000 women greeted Carson on his first visit to West Belfast in 1913, which was believed to be the largest assemblage of women in Ireland's history (UWUC Annual Report, 1913 [PRONI, D/2688/1/3]). Contemporaneous comments from unionist women aver to an understanding that this political mobilization was not only new but also "means the rising of a people.... For though Irish-women have for a long time carried on useful charitable undertakings, this is a very different matter from attending public meetings, being 'heckled,' or ... canvassing" (Letter from Julia Talbot of Mid-Armagh Women's Unionist Association to the editor, *The Spectator*, July 13, 1912).[14]

The role that the UWUC defined for itself was distinct from that of men. This embedded the gendered space allocated to unionist women and reflected the innate conservatism that characterized the organization: there was "an underlying gendered understanding of how they are positioned by that identity within the national project" (R. Ward 2006, 74). However, seeking to work by means of "gentleness, tact and quiet influence" in an ancillary organization that was formed to complement, rather than rival, the work of male unionists was strategically astute. This stance reassured many women becoming politically active for the first time (*Belfast News-Letter*, January 24, 1911). The UWUC's remit was also strictly defined. Any fears that this might be a feminist body seeking female enfranchisement were swiftly bedded as the organization had the defeat of home rule as their sole purpose: "Our workers speak only on the maintenance of the Union, and on no other subject whatever" (*The Spectator*, July 13, 1913).[15]

Although a self-confessedly auxiliary association, the UWUC augmented the array of anti–home rule arguments beyond the standard religious, economic, imperial, and constitutional rationale. Their gendered rhetoric encompassed the sanctity of the home and portrayed female politicking as an extension of women's maternal and protective duties to the extent that members of the UWUC were known as the motherhood of Ulster.[16] This also made unionism appear germane to many women's lives:

> If our homes are not sacred from the priest under the existing laws, what can we expect from a priest-governed Ireland . . . let each woman in Ulster do a woman's part to stem the tide of Home Rule . . . the Union . . . meant everything to them—their civil and religious liberty, their homes and children . . . once the Union was severed there could be no outlook in Ulster but strife and bitterness. . . . Home was a woman's first consideration . . . in the event of Home Rule being granted, the sanctity and happiness of home life in Ulster would be permanently destroyed. (Minute book of Lurgan Women's Unionist Association, May 13, 1911 [PRONI, D/3790/4])

With a heightened sense of political crisis, en masse mobilization, and a waning faith in Westminster's ability and, at times, desire to defeat home rule, Ulster unionism became more introspective, militant, and militaristic (see Fitzpatrick 1996). The possibility of constitutional protest turning violent was also openly acknowledged by the unionist leadership and conscious efforts were made to maintain order to present a favorable public image to the English and Scottish electorate. "Ulster Day" on Saturday, September 28, 1912, coordinated by an all-male committee, provided one of the most striking examples of this dual process as unionist men and women signed the Ulster Solemn League and Covenant and Women's Declaration, respectively.[17] With foundations in the Old Testament and Scots-Presbyterian application in the sixteenth and seventeenth centuries, the Solemn League and Covenant was "a powerful political statement" of Ulster unionist intent (Mansergh 2017, 159). Pledging civil disobedience and a physical-force response if home rule was introduced, "this was not a benign text . . . it was nothing less than treason" (McGaughey 2012, 44). In embracing only those who were Ulster-born, the covenant and declaration were also exclusionary; southern Irish- or British-born unionists could not sign.

The covenant also excepted women as they remained disenfranchised. Like Tod in the earlier unionist movement, women had to negotiate gendered boundaries to be allowed to sign a separate document: the Women's Declaration. The variation in name was significant. While the male covenant suggested "an alliance" and a "binding commitment" (Mansergh 2017, 160), the Women's Declaration was an expression of dutifulness. The declaration's shorter text, although having words like "calamity" in common with the covenant, enshrined women's place within unionism—they would "associate themselves" with men as part of a wider protest against home rule (Urquhart 2001, 68). This text was not, however, of the UWUC's making. Rather, like the covenant, it was drafted by the Ulster Unionist Council's (UUC) Thomas Sinclair. Although the UWUC Advisory Committee was permitted to comment on it, it is not clear if they did so. The final text was also subject to UUC approval. Theresa Londonderry's "Ulster Day" speech also had to be sanctioned by the unionist second-in-command, James Craig. However, this should not obscure Theresa's agency: Craig commented, with considerable relief, that it struck "the right note," adding "of course, none of us would have ventured to alter a word without submitting it again for her approval" (Urquhart 2007, cited 105).

Women were also required to make separate arrangements to set up signing stations for the declaration throughout Ulster, but there was undoubtedly more collegiality at a local level than this suggests. Many of the agents responsible for collecting the signed declaration forms also collated the covenant. Furthermore, although claims have been made that women were denied the right to sign "beneath the illustrious dome of City Hall" in Belfast (McGaughey 2012, 46), female signatures were collected at this venue (*Illustrated London News*, October 5, 1912) and others including sixty in Belfast alone, local town halls, court houses, unionist clubs, schools, church halls, and temperance, mission, and orange halls throughout Ulster. Outdoor venues like church grounds, which were used in Raphoe in County Donegal, for example, were also common and aver to the unease in some clerical circles that unionist belligerence aroused. Some also signed in their own homes, and areas like Ballymena in County Antrim saw house to house collections, which further highlights the intersectionality of the private and public realms.[18]

The number of signatories to these documents provides one of the best examples of the scale of unionist opposition, the comparative strength of women's unionism in Ulster, and the credence of the UWUC's campaign: a total of 228,991 women signed the declaration in Ulster (UWUC Executive Committee Minutes, January 16, 1913 [PRONI, D/1089/1/1]) compared to 218,206 male signatories to the covenant (Stewart 1967, 66). Collectively, an estimated three-quarters of Ulster's non-Catholic adults (over the age of 16) signed these respective documents (David Fitzpatrick, Ulster covenant conference, King's College, London, September 6, 2012). A British covenant and declaration was also signed by those of Ulster birth in England and Scotland and this, in consequence of the lower number of women's political associations that were sympathetic to unionism, attracted more male signatories than female—19,162 men signed in comparison to 5,055 women. With the British and Ulster signatories combined, 237,368 men and 234,046 women signed their respective documents.[19] Even though the text of both documents was reproduced by the press (*Belfast News-Letter*, September 30, 1912), as McGaughey notes, the press coverage was biased toward the covenant and the "manly authority . . . [of] Protestant Ulstermen's siege mentality" that it encompassed: "The news coverage intentionally emphasized embellished depictions of unionist men who would protect their homes and their land against the forces of 'the other,'" although those in the latter category diverged from the British government to Irish nationalists. "The daily deixis of the homeland" thus crossed "the divides of gender," but the sacrifices to be made varied: men would give their lives (R. Ward 2006, 74); women their husbands and sons (Yuval-Davis and Anthias 1989). In addition, heightened emphasis was placed "on the men's covenant, rather than on the total number of signatories . . . [which] left masculine agency as the main force in defeating Home Rule" (McGaughey 2012, 42, 48). By comparison, although some sections of the press admired "the resoluteness and strength of conviction that proved how fully they realised the gravity of their action and the seriousness of the crisis in which they are called upon to take an active part," of both male and female unionists, women were still deemed "the gentler sex." Thus, although the "noble part" played by unionist women was commended (*Belfast News-Letter*, September 30, 1912), they were portrayed as immobile, "standing loyally by 'their menfolk' in this crisis" (*Northern Whig*, September 30, 1912). Ultimately, the press claim that "Ulsterman—aye, and Ulster women, too—will not deviate from the path marked out for them" (*Belfast News-Letter*, September 17, 1912) had a broader, if unintended, resonance.

The symbolic gesturing of the covenant and declaration were underscored by the fact that these documents were never presented to the government. Unionist plans for a provisional government in September 1913 signaled another move away from Westminster reliance. Constitutional means looked increasingly inadequate to defeat home rule. The formation of the Ulster Volunteer Force (UVF) in early 1913 signaled a formal move to militarism and a fuller engagement with unionist masculinity (see Bowman 2007). The UWUC helped administer the UVF Nursing, Driving, and Signalling Corps, drafting training schemes, organizing instruction classes in first aid, and securing medical equipment and supplies for UVF medical units that were established throughout Ulster in preparation for civil war. Some women were also involved in intelligence work, deciphering police messages, for example, and a small number were involved in gunrunning. This was an important, if partial, prewar realignment of gender roles, but a sense of stoicism prevailed on the question of civil war. That was never answered, as the outbreak of World War I changed the unionist course. This also provided another stark reminder of women's place within unionism; they were not consulted on the unionist political truce that was declared on the outbreak of the war in August 1914.

During the war, the focus of the UWUC changed to recruiting, supporting military conscription, dispatching comforts and assembling military dressings, and fundraising for the armed forces and their families, with particular support for the 36th Ulster Division and the UVF hospital in Ville de Pau, Cabinet du Maire in France, whose running they financed from 1914 to 1916.[20] Although most seemingly accepted that the change in the UWUC's priorities was dictated by wartime conditions, the question of home rule and the uncertainty of the postwar situation, with the third home rule bill passed but suspended, led them to instruct soldiers in unionism (UWUC Advisory Committee Minutes, January 2, 1917 [PRONI, D/2688/1/7]), but this work required the sanction of the UUC.[21] Such duality was again apparent early in 1916 in the aftermath of the Easter Rising, when it was feared that continuing to abide by the truce would be counterproductive and allow a republican advance.[22]

The 1918 Representation of the People Act, granting the electoral franchise to women over the age of thirty while the war waged on, caused a similar reassessment. The truce remained formally in place, but the UWUC registered women's voters, electioneered, and instructed the new female electorate on how to cast their votes (UWUC Executive Committee Minutes, June 18, 1918 [PRONI, D/1098/1/2]).[23] They also supported women standing for local government but not for parliamentary election where "men candidates were preferable" (ibid., January 25, 1921). This can partially be explained by the organization's innate conservatism; it had never advocated votes for women, but neither the unionist leadership nor the UUC encouraged female parliamentary candidates. Edward Carson expressed this position when advising a UWUC meeting "in choosing candidates to choose the man who they thought would best represent their views" (*Northern Whig*, February 7, 1921). Over a decade later, although the UWUC stated that "it would be helpful to the Unionist cause if more women would come forward to local government and town council work" (UWUC Executive Committee Minutes, January 26, 1931 [PRONI, D/1098/1/2]), employed female trainee political organizers in their headquarters, and funded scholarships to train women in politics, economics, and citizenship, they did not openly promote female candidates for election to the Northern Ireland parliament or Westminster.[24]

To measure the significance of women's enfranchisement solely in terms of the number of women who were elected to parliament overlooks the fact that possessing a vote gave women a new political import. The impact of the Representation of the People Act was readily apparent as unionist leaders gave the women's council permission to reorganize and continue as a separate organization. The vote also augmented the confidence of the UWUC as it issued an uncharacteristically vehement appeal, demanding a definition of their status within the unionist movement and representation on the UUC. This all-male body gave representation to the Apprentice Boys and Unionist Clubs in 1911, leaving the women's council as the only mass unionist organization outside of its ranks. It justified their exclusion on the basis that only voters could sit on the council. The UWUC requested representation from 1916 but after female enfranchisement this transmuted into a demand: "What is the position of the Ulster Women's Unionist Council? It has none—we are nothing. . . . [We] realise many anxieties, difficulties, and dangers . . . have to be faced by the Men with regard to the Vote for Women, and its possibility on future elections. But . . . we have not been treated as comrades. . . . We must have more power for immediate action . . . let us stand out now for the rights and liberties of the Ulster Women's Unionist Council" (UWUC Minutes, June 18, 1918 [PRONI, D/1098/1/3]). The UWUC was subsequently granted twelve representatives on the UUC in 1918. This was under 3 percent of the 40 percent representation that the UWUC felt would be fair (although they would have been content with 10–12%).[25] However, a joint committee of male and female unionists was established in the same year to coordinate work between these two bodies, but there was no question over which was the dominant partner: the UWUC was not consulted over the partition of Ireland and the six-county configuration of the new Northern Ireland.

The UWUC is still in existence today; it is, therefore, a lone survivor from the proliferation of women's political associations that were established in early twentieth-century Ireland. Political meetings and the dissemination of propaganda continued in the interwar period, and female unionist papers like *Northern Ireland: Home and Politics* (1925–1927) highlighted the continued combination of domesticity with civic affairs.[26] This was also apparent in the efforts of the UWUC to politically educate women and girls, holding classes that combined education with entertainment and defining women's interests as family, housing, education, and social services and, therefore, distinct from those of men. Although an intrinsically ancillary and conservative organization, the size of the UWUC and the scale of its activities are an effective illustration of the degree of political interest that many women had years before they possessed the right to vote. Indeed, some suffragists sympathetic to the unionist cause emphasized the liberating effects of women's unionism in politicizing women and providing an effective counter to antisuffragist claims that women were neither politically interested nor able (*Irish Citizen*, February 7, 1914). The UWUC of the early twentieth century is also the largest female political force in Ireland's history: membership of the suffrage movement, for example, peaked at an estimated thirty-five hundred, while Cumann na mBan's membership was about twelve thousand women at its height in 1919. The women's council made a significant contribution to the strength of popular unionism, and its espousal of unionist principles, although having much in common with male unionists, was not a mere imitation. The fact that many women remained members of the UWUC, not just over years but decades, alludes to a deep sense of political obligation and sometimes fear. They were not seen as the political equals of men; nor did they want to be. Their work enshrined women's distinct place within unionism and removed the domestic containment of many women's lives.

The UWUC is not, however, popularly known. In 2006, the *Irish Times*, reflecting on the ninetieth anniversary of the 1916 rising, noted that its commemoration tended "to forget about one important group of participants—women" (*Irish Times*, March 20, 2006). The same charge would not be leveled in the rising's centenary commemorations a decade later. By comparison, in Northern Ireland the "memorial landscapes" of both unionist/loyalists and nationalist/republicans "privilege male interpretations of the past (and therefore, present)" (McDowell 2008, 335). The 2012 centenary of Ulster Day thus offers an opportunity for analyzing women's place in the decade of centenaries and in unionism more broadly in a province where the male commemorative narrative still predominates. It is, however, hard to locate a definite tradition of female unionist commemoration, and, where it is apparent, it did not always follow the same path as their male counterparts.

Ulster Day, deemed "a date never to be forgotten in the annals of the Imperial Province" in 1912 (*Belfast News-Letter*, September 30, 1912), was commemorated in the year after the signing of the covenant and Women's Declaration. Yet the synoptic collectivism of the male document quickly emerged: "Covenant Week" in Ulster was referred to by the press (*Drogheda Independent*, September 6, 1913). The wartime political truce subsumed unionist commemorations, but, on the first anniversary of Ulster Day since the armistice, the *Derry Journal*, although not an impartial observer, presented a starkly contrasting depiction to the unionist euphoria of 1912: in Belfast's Ulster Hall the commemoration "fell very flat ... [with] even the rendering of 'Dolly's Brae' and similar airs ... failing to arouse much spirit in the gathering" (*Derry Journal*, October 1, 1919). "Covenant Week" also contracted to "Covenant Day" (*Irish Independent*, August 9, 1919). This highlights the reactive nature of commemoration: it is "an invocation of the past in the present; a negotiated tension between remembering and forgetting" (Graff-McRae 2010, 1). As events, commemorations are shaped, and often simplified, by how those in the present choose to remember *their* history (F. O'Toole 2013, 154–161; Hobsbawm and Ranger 1983, 1–2). Although religious commemorative services were held and a joint male and female unionist message was sent to Carson in 1919, postwar malaise and partition's mounting momentum, which threatened the province-wide promise of Ulster Day, took their toll. In the month preceding the fiftieth commemoration in 1962, there was again no surety about Ulster Day's allure: "No one can tell what popular appeal the celebrations will make, . . . or whether the people, who have so long been urged to 'Remember 1690' can be persuaded to remember 1912" (*Drogheda Independent*, August 16, 1962).

Ulster Day's commemoration was also closely associated with the Orange Order. The fiftieth anniversary in 1962, for example, saw sections of the press ask "how far the Orange Lodges will succeed in getting their members out to parade" (*Drogheda Independent*, August 16, 1962). Questions were also raised regarding the advisability of holding an event with such divisive potential: "After being interred for fifty years the corpse of the Covenant [was] dragged from its unholy grave to help the Unionist propagandist." The role of this commemoration was also queried: "Unionists are divided as to whether it is a good thing to have a Covenant celebration at all, very pertinently wondering what there is to celebrate in a community where the grim spectre of mass unemployment stalks to-day as threatening as . . . in 1912. [There is] Widespread public ignorance of what the Covenant was and what it achieved. . . . Most people know nothing . . . about the Covenant, and almost all had no interest in it" (*Ulster Herald*, September 8, 1962).[27] This was confirmed by a *Northern Whig* poll on the covenant: 49 percent of a random sample knew nothing of it, 35 percent had heard of it but did not know what it was, while 16 percent were well informed. In response, the pro-unionist *Whig* published an explanation of the covenant and reprinted its text, but not that of the Women's Declaration. There was also controversy on the role that UVF units might play in the event and the political statement that would make to a wider population whose enthusiasm for this commemoration was far from assured (*Drogheda Independent*, August 16, 1962). An estimated fifty thousand subsequently marched to commemorate the fiftieth anniversary of Ulster Day, but there was also public protest: the National Unity Council condemned the commemorations (*Donegal Democrat*,

October 5, 1962). Throughout the furor, the Women's Declaration was over-looked and male and Orange mobilization continued to dominate the com-memoration. In 1987, for example, "Thousands of Orangemen attended parades in Belfast . . . to commemorate" the seventy-fifth anniversary of the covenant (*Irish Independent* and *Irish Press*, September 28, 1987) while concurrently rejecting the Anglo-Irish Agreement (see Aughey 1989). Moreover, there was seemingly no mobilization of the Women's Orange Association; this remained male commemorative topography.

The Orange connection was also evident in the Unionist Centenary Com-mittee, chaired by Belfast's Orange grand master. Meeting from 2009, it deter-mined six events for unionist commemoration in 2011: the Balmoral review in Belfast of April 1912 when Conservative leader Bonar Law's address to the crowds and joint pledge with Carson to "Never under any circumstances . . . submit to Home Rule" provided part of the inspiration for the covenant and declaration that followed five months later; Ulster Day of September 1912; the establishment of the UVF in January 1913; the UVF gunrunning of April 1914; the 36th Ulster Division march in Belfast in May 1915; and the Battle of the Somme in July 1916. This marking of largely militaristic and masculine events disregarded the UWUC's establishment in 1911, and such a selective gaze inti-mates Berger's notion of ways of seeing (1973). Indeed, although members of the Orangewomen's Women's Grand Lodge were involved in the Centenary Committee, the latter acknowledged that its consultation process saw "young people, female, politicians and religious people involved but not enough" (www .unionistcentenaries.com).

The centenary of Ulster Day in 2012 was organized by the Orange Order and the Centenary Committee, which took the text of the Solemn League and Covenant as its mission statement; there was no engagement with the Women's Declaration. Carson's signing of the covenant at Belfast's city hall was reenacted, but the most popular focus of the commemoration was a six-mile march through Belfast to parliament buildings in East Belfast on September 29, 2012. Feeder parades converged to bring an estimated thirty thousand people together, but this was more of an engagement with the Orange parading tra-dition than with unionism per se. It was consequently "celebrated mostly by unionists, but not the wider pro-Union base . . . [and was] seen as [an] almost exclusively Protestant celebration" (*Belfast Telegraph*, September 29, 2012).

The week preceding the centenary revived the apprehension and tension that engulfed the fiftieth and seventy-fifth anniversaries: protests, violence, arrests, and riots occurred particularly in Belfast over subsequent nights. St. Patrick's Catholic Church in Donegall Street in North Belfast and St. Matthew's Catholic

Church on the Newtownards Road in East Belfast were sites of marked violence. As a result, the Northern Ireland Parades Commission restricted the 190 Orange Bands on the Ulster Day centenary parade to play only sacred music when passing these churches, but, as one North Belfast resident remarked, "nobody can work out what type of hymn that was" played outside St. Patrick's: "The minute they passed the church, a number of bands reverted to playing the Sash and clearly broke the restriction." Such triumphalism was also apparent in East Belfast with incidents reported to the Public Prosecution Service (www .bbc.co.uk/news, September 29, 2012).

In 2012, although women marched alongside men and a discernible Orange women's presence was apparent, it was hard to decipher any official involvement from the UWUC. Rather, this body celebrated a centenary of a different event: their foundation in 1911. Whether this was a deliberate distancing from the Orange dominance of Ulster Day's commemoration is hard to determine, but the UWUC was not listed as a stakeholder on the Unionist Centenary Committee. In commemorating the establishment of their organization, the UWUC held a thanksgiving service at St. Patrick's Cathedral, Armagh, and a reception and dinner at parliament buildings in Belfast, referring to their organization as an effective enabler of female politicization.

The covenant is often used as generic shorthand for both the male document and the female declaration. Indeed, the combined male and female figures are regularly cited for the covenant alone, which subsumes the dynamic and scale of the Women's Declaration (*Irish Times*, August 3, 1979). In 2012, the BBC news website also reprinted the text of the covenant but not that of the Women's Declaration (www.bbc.co.uk/news, September 27, 2012). The Ulster-Scots Community Network 2012 pamphlet, *Understanding the Ulster Covenant*, aimed to mark the centenary and explain the event but also reproduced the text only of the covenant and in twenty-seven pages made just two references to the number of women who signed the declaration (Ulster-Scots Community Network 2012, 4, 21).

The signing of the Women's Declaration was, therefore, a significant event for female unionists but not a seminal one for the UWUC. The foregrounding of the male covenant, despite the numerical superiority of the female declaration, reflects the association between unionism and the gender constraints of patriarchy. The continued dominance of that narrative and the selective remembering of Ulster Day also supports Kearney's view that "the enemy of genuine commemoration is not complexity but certitude" (Richard Kearney, *Belfast Telegraph*, July 16, 2016). The marginalization of women in the unionist movement, which Ulster Day and its commemoration reflects, is also apparent in the level of female unionist representation both locally and nationally, which is consistently the lowest of all the main political parties (Tonge 2014, 200). Unionist women are also popularly perceived to "make the tea, they stay in the background . . . women are raised to be the home-makers, the house-keepers, and all of that" (Tonge 2014, cited on 191). The unity of unionism has, therefore, yet to be attained.

NOTES

1. Letter from Julia Talbot of Mid-Armagh Women's Unionist Association to the *Spectator*'s editor. For an official history of the UWUC, see Kinghan 1975. See also Urquhart 2000; 1994, 93–123; 1996, 31–40.

2. The term *Ulsteria* was also applied to this process.

3. Liberal premier W. E. Gladstone introduced the first Home Rule Bill to the House of Commons in April 1886. The bill proposed the establishment of an Irish legislature with restricted functions but was defeated in the commons in June 1886.

4. This aligns with Pašeta's suggestion that feminism underpinned much of women's nationalist activity; see Pašeta 2013.

5. Tod died at the age of sixty in 1896. In the early 1890s, although Tod focused on unionism, she was still involved with the temperance movement, Victoria College in Belfast, and bodies such as the Society for the Prevention of Cruelty to Animals and Belfast Peace Society. See Brown 1998; Armour 2004.

6. Members of the UWUC also worked as "unionist missionaries" in Britain, cooperating with the Conservative Primrose League, the Women's Protestant Union, and the Women's Amalgamated Unionist and Tariff Reform Association to update electoral registers, address meetings, and canvass. Between April and May 1914, fifty-six UWUC members left their homes to conduct this type of work, with the time spent away from home varying from four days to five weeks. Twenty-six women were based permanently in England and Scotland at the height of the third home rule crisis, 1913–1914.

7. Gladstone introduced the second Home Rule Bill in January 1893. It passed its third reading in the commons with the repeated use of closure but was subsequently rejected by the House of Lords in September 1893.

8. Unionist women also petitioned in increasing numbers. One of the largest female petitions contained close to twenty thousand signatures and was conveyed to parliament in 1893 in a carriage belonging to Theresa, 6th Marchioness of Londonderry, a future UWUC president (Kinghan 1975, 8).

9. The North Tyrone association was under the presidency of the Duchess of Abercorn. Londonderry was under the Marchioness of Hamilton. Both associations electioneered, fundraised, distributed propaganda, and updated electoral registers.

10. The Association of Loyal Orangewomen of Ireland also revived and had twenty-five branches including ten in Belfast and one thousand members by 1919.

11. The Liberal government of H. H. Asquith introduced the Parliament Act of 1911.

12. Mary Anne, 2nd Duchess of Abercorn, was the first president of the UWUC and retained this position from 1911 to 1913. She was succeeded by Theresa, 6th Marchioness of Londonderry, who was president from 1913 to 1919. Theresa Londonderry was a patron to the unionist leader, Edward Carson, and the Tory leader, Andrew Bonar Law. She was replaced by Rosalind, 3rd Duchess of Abercorn, who was president from 1919 to 1922. She was succeeded by Lady Cecil Craig, later Viscountess Craigavon, who was president from 1922 to 1942.

13. Unionists saw some by-election successes. For example, Leith Burghs in Scotland was won for unionists in 1914 for the first time since 1832.

14. On unionism becoming popular for the first time in its history, see Jackson 1990.

15. The UWUC was likely following the lead of the Primrose League, with Theresa, 6th Marchioness of Londonderry, representing a key example of cross-organizational membership. James Craig and Edith, 7th Marchioness of Londonderry (a member of Fawcett's National Union of Women's Suffrage Societies [NUWSS]), are examples of unionist suffragists, but Craig did not appear on a suffrage platform from 1910 and Edith's activities were English based. The suffrage paper, the *Irish Citizen*, was also critical of unionist and nationalist women. In a front-page article, it declared UWUC members as "servile party women" and later averred to the organization's "slavish attitude . . . to toady for the men . . . [and] display . . . crawling servility . . . [they] deserve nothing but contempt" (*Irish Citizen*, February 7, and April 11, 1914).

16. This influenced the female nationalist organization Cumann na mBan's rhetoric; see C. McCarthy 2014.

17. Although souvenir copies of the Women's Declaration use the term *Covenant*, this was rarely used by the UWUC. Instead, to differentiate between the male and female signatories, the UWUC consistently uses the term *declaration* and I have followed their lead.

18. Some of the more unusual signing stations were a vacant shop in Carrickfergus and Portrush skating rink in County Antrim.

19. In 1914, a British covenant and women's declaration, organized by Lord Milner and the British League in Support of Ulster, were signed by two million.

20. The UWUC financed the running of this hospital until the end of 1916 when the French authorities decided to move the hospital nearer to the war front and provide the necessary financial support for its operation.

21. See, for example, Richard Dawson Bates to Theresa Londonderry, January 3, 1917 (PRONI, D/2846/1/1/8/65).

22. On unionist reactions to the 1916 Rising, see Jackson 2018.

23. This was perceived as fundamentally important work; £5,000 was expended on preferably female electoral canvassers and inspectors at a time when the council was experiencing some financial difficulties because of many of its local associations failing to pay affiliation fees during the war.

24. In the period from 1921 to 1972, six unionist women sat in the Northern Ireland Parliament: Dame Dehra Chichester (later Parker), MP for Londonderry City and County, 1921–1929, and South Londonderry, 1933–1960; Julia McMordie, MP for South Belfast, 1921–1925; Anne Dickson, MP for Carrickfergus, 1969–1972; Bessie Maconachie, MP for Queen's University, 1953–1969; Dinah McNabb, MP for North Armagh, 1945–1969; and Margaret Waring, MP for Iveagh in County Down, 1929–1933. On Parker, McMordie, and Waring, see Urquhart 2000, 175–198. See also R. Ward 2006, 117–118. Despite the lack of official backing, some, like Parker, McMordie, and Waring, were active members of the UWUC.

25. From 1918, delegates of local unionist associations could also be represented on the UUC (one representative was granted for every three hundred members). The wives of unionist MPs, peers, and senators were made ex officio members. Therefore, by 1923 there were 133 women on the UUC and in the interwar period women made up between one-quarter and one-fifth of UUC members. In 2000, there were 34 UWUC members on the UUC in comparison to 850 men.

26. An earlier female unionist publication was *Ulsterwoman*, which ran from 1919–1920.

27. See Northern Ireland House of Commons debates, December 18, 1962, vol. 699, cc 1081–3. By 1969, unemployment in Northern Ireland was twice the UK average.

DIANE URQUHART is Professor of Gender History at Queen's University, Belfast, and Fellow of the Royal Historical Society. A graduate of Queen's University, Belfast, she is a former postdoctoral fellow of the Institute of Irish Studies at Queen's and has worked as a researcher for the Women's History Project. She has published extensively on Irish women's history, gender, and politics, including *Women in Ulster Politics, 1890–1940* (2000), *The Ladies of Londonderry: Women and Political Patronage* (2007), *Irish Divorce: A History* (2020), as well as five edited/coedited international collections.

1916 AND AFTER

Remembering "Ordinary" Women's Experiences of Revolutionary Ireland

LAURA MCATACKNEY

UNDOUBTEDLY, THE CENTENARY OF THE Easter Rising was the first high point during the "Decade of Commemorations" in Ireland (Decade of Centenaries 2012b). This is due to its perceived role in initiating the end point in the long process of gaining partial Irish independence from Great Britain in 1920–1921. In response to this centenary, it is appropriate to assess not only what we know about the period in terms of the women involved but also how public memory of women has been altered by the form and scale of commemorative events that took place in 2016. Including the latter perspective is important. In order to better understand how the past is reconceived through time, we need to acknowledge that big anniversaries are significant. Commemorative periods open up public interest in events that are otherwise generally considered closed to societal interpretation, and they allow what we know of the past to be reconfigured beyond the realms of academic discourse. Therefore, we need to delve into the broader questions of why women were remembered so prominently in 2016 and how these new insights and interpretations may alter public memory moving forward. To answer these questions, this chapter will move beyond viewing women solely through the prism of a historian's backward gaze to incorporate the contemporary context of 2016. This reflexive dual focus is especially important as we consider how our memory of the Rising may fare as we move into the more difficult commemorations linked to the War of Independence (1919–1921), partition, and ultimately the Civil War (1922–1923) and its aftermath.

1916 IN 2016

Researchers of Irish history have long acknowledged that commemorations of historical events are as much to do with the contemporary understanding (and uses) of that past as they are about what actually happened during the events being commemorated (including M. McCarthy 2005; Ó'Grádá 2001). The edited volume by Mary Daly and Margaret O'Callaghan (2007) on *1916 in 1966* has been particularly explicit in revealing this truism with regard to how the Easter Rising was commemorated on its fiftieth anniversary in 1966. In particular, Daly and O'Callaghan have shown how the contemporary relevance of the Easter Rising directly related to how "official" Ireland felt about its place in the world, especially its more confident relationships with Britain and the then European Economic Union. The commemorations of the Easter Rising in 2016 have been no less impacted by its contemporary context. Indeed, some commentators have noted a future-focused tone adopted by "official" Ireland in communicating the Rising to the nation and especially the diaspora. The future-focus has been interpreted as a deliberate mechanism to allow a more detached, upbeat "celebration" that reveals a comfort with this aspect of the past, in contrast to the traditional memory of the Easter Rising being rooted in tragedy associated with a failed military insurrection (including Downes 2016). In this respect, the deliberate and very noticeable inclusion of women both as extraordinary individuals and as a mass of undistinguishable "ordinary women" (borrowing Sinéad McCoole's 2003 phrase) has a strong contemporary relevance.

During the 2016 commemorations, there were innumerable articles in the national and international media commenting on the newly discovered importance of women's roles in 1916, which had hitherto been ignored or sidelined in the public domain (if not historians' publications). These commentaries have not all been positive, however; the vast majority have uncritically emphasized a need to publicize the names and actions of women who played their part and deserved to be remembered. So important were women to how we framed the Easter Rising on its centenary that we now need to remind ourselves that their inclusion was not inevitable, nor did it seem probable even a few years before. Journalists such as Una Mullally have noted that this emphasis on women reflected current organizational realities—especially an increasing involvement of women in the hierarchies of the creative and governmental spheres that oversaw the commemorations (2016). This structural issue is important because one cannot disconnect the media interest in the women of 1916 from the number of commemorative events and memorialization processes that were discussed, promoted, and attended because of funding by the state or by state-funded bodies. For example, substantial renovations of Richmond Barracks in Inchicore, Dublin, were funded €3.5 million by Dublin City Council and the Department for Arts, Heritage, and the Gaeltacht in time for the Easter Rising commemorations (Dublin City Council 2014). The current website for Richmond Barracks makes an explicit connection to "The Women of 1916 and the Irish Revolution" as one of its core themes, with projects including an annotated list of seventy-seven women processed through the barracks for their involvement in the Rising (Richmond Barracks 2020b). However, when the refurbishment was announced in 2014, the role of women was not even mentioned in the press release. There was a much more generic, indeed male-normative, perspective on the history of the site presented: "The leaders of the 1916 Rising were interned and court-martialed within the barracks before being transferred to Kilmainham Gaol. It was also from here that soldiers, including the poet Francis Ledwidge, were transported to fight in World War 1" (Dublin City Council 2014). Clearly, there were changes in both the personnel and the public discourse between 2014 and 2016 to refocus the heritage perspective of Richmond Barracks from a normative history of the site to one that explicitly engaged with the previously marginalized roles of women.

As critics like Mullally noted, the involvement of women in positions of influence at the organizational level of the commemorations, up to and including Heather Humphreys as Minister for Arts, Heritage, and Gaeltacht from July 2014 to November 2017 in the Republic of Ireland, played an important role in facilitating the emergence of gendered perspectives. The prominence of contemporary gender activism should also be noted, as well as the ways in which this activism has taken different forms across the island of Ireland. It was evident, especially in the Republic of Ireland of 2016, that the interest in women and their roles one hundred years ago became strongly entwined with the activism and advocacy of the contemporary women's rights movement. In the Ireland of 2016, there were ongoing and highly public debates about the enduring impact of the eighth amendment to the Irish constitution, which was added in 1983 to ensure that the life of the unborn fetus be legally held as an equal with that of the mother. Such an amendment prohibited any form of abortion unless the woman's life was in imminent danger. Debate surrounded whether this amendment should be repealed to ensure various forms of abortion could be made legal. Having the repeal of this amendment as a focus allowed for strong interconnections to be made between women's rights and activism of the past and that of the present. These interconnections were not so clear cut or evident in Northern Ireland, where the Easter Rising does not act as a unifying commemorative event and where lack of access to abortion does not have one focal point like the eighth amendment. (In Northern Ireland, the absence of abortion provision, despite abortion's legality in the rest of the United Kingdom, had been due to the consensus of a cross-party, socially conservative political class; changes to the law at the end of 2019 mean that abortion in the first twelve weeks of pregnancy became legal as of spring 2020.) The connections made between women's agency in publicly fighting for their rights in 1916 and 2016 in the Republic of Ireland were especially explicit in the iconography and wordplay of the #Repealthe8th movement, which has utilized images and slogans such as "Rise and Repeal" to unambiguously connect their struggle to the historic independence and suffrage movements (e.g., J. O'Sullivan 2016).

The role of women was elevated during the centenary of the Rising to a level previously unseen. While the temporal nature of these commemorations has been noted, especially in the popular press, the spatial dimensions of the focus on women during the commemorations have not been so thoroughly dissected. Women were a focal point of a largely uncomplicated, societal commemoration in the Republic of Ireland; in comparison, in Northern Ireland any elevation of women remained within the nationalist community, who commemorated the Easter Rising, while the unionist community focused on World War I's Battle of the Somme. Both events had centenaries in 2016 and have long been articulated by their communities as key blood sacrifices proving their oppositional nationalist ideals. As such, they are both important but are also diminished in scale and impact by being sectional concerns. In Northern Ireland, new stories were located and circulated about women involved in the Rising (including those of sisters Elizabeth and Nell Corr from East Belfast [Monaghan 2016]), exhibitions were mounted about women connected to 1916 who had some connection to Northern Ireland (including *Con and Eva*, which presented the relationship of sisters Constance Markievicz and Eva Gore-Booth from their family papers residing in the Public Record Office of Northern Ireland [PRONI 2016]), and there was little contention among the traditionally left-wing republican communities in the North that it was appropriate to actively remember women. However, the story of the Easter Rising does not have strong spatial links to Northern Ireland due to the events of the Rising being centered on Dublin and the desire for freedom from Britain being an ongoing and contentious issue in Northern Ireland (Brewer 2016). Dublin and Belfast are separated by more than one hundred miles, and how the events and personnel of the Rising, including women, are remembered shows marked differences. This chapter starts by dissecting high-profile public art projects that were intended to promote gendered perspectives as a form of memory making to examine how able they were to complete such a role in the long term.

PUBLIC MEMORY AND WALL MURALS OF
EASTER RISING WOMEN

The first extant mural I discuss was created by the famous West Belfast mural painters Danny Devenney and Marty Lyons and was unveiled at the busy inter-section of Beechmount Avenue and the Falls Road in nationalist West Belfast on the same weekend as Mothering Sunday (March 30) in 2014. The context of this mural is important: the fact that it appeared two years in advance of the Easter Rising commemorations and still remains a number of years after its creation, in a prominent location, indicates the significance of the contents to West Belfast republicans and the wider community. Political wall murals are a well-known feature in working-class, urban communities in Northern Ireland (McAtackney 2011), and, for this mural to be painted by such esteemed artists, placed in such a prominent location, and retained for so long is as significant as its contents. One could suggest the link made between remembering historical female republicans and Mother's Day is clichéd in assuming that women are primarily mothers. However, the date was also intended to tie into the founding of the women's group Cumann na mBan on April 2, 1914.

Stylistically, this mural is representative of the types of murals we find relat-ing to historical revolutionaries of this period in Belfast, which, in general, contain few depictions of women in comparison to men. The contents deserve special attention to locate the nuances of the many messages included in it. The foreground of the mural has the figurehead of the already well-known exceptional woman Countess Constance Markievicz, who dominates the right-hand side of the composition and is the only individualized figure in the image. The left-hand background is filled with a large group of rank-and-file women marching in uniform, regimented, faces covered, and lacking indi-vidualization. Stylistic clues—including the differences in clothing—indicate there is a conflation being made between two groups of women: the anony-mous female revolutionaries of the Rising and the anonymous women of the IRA in Northern Ireland from "the Troubles" (ca. 1968–1998). Alongside the rather anachronistic connections being made between the two forms of female revolutionaries, there is accompanying text that states "Ní saoirse go saorise na mban" (literally "no freedom without the freedom of women"). This is a strik-ing claim to make if we examine it alongside the realities of how women were treated across Ireland since Markievicz took part in the Easter Rising and from partition to the present day. Not only has access to abortion continually being subverted in the jurisdiction of Northern Ireland, and has only just been intro-duced in the Republic of Ireland, but also, for stepping outside their proscribed roles, women suffered mass institutionalization in laundries and mother and baby homes throughout the island during the twentieth century up until the late 1990s (Smith 2007). While such a mural intends to be a celebration of women, and while one composition cannot address the nuances of gendered inequalities in the one hundred years between the Easter Rising and today, it misrepresents in a variety of ways. The continual overfocus on the figure of Countess Markievicz as often the only identifiable women portrayed in such murals implicitly reinforces the idea that she was an anomaly and the only woman of note actively involved in the Rising. The text's reiteration of 'saoirse' may reflect the aspirations of the women involved in the period but clearly it is not reflective of their treatment and experiences thereafter. Furthermore, this image perpetuates two long and parallel traditions in representations of women in conflict in Northern Ireland: beyond the exceptional figures (such as Markievicz) women are anonymized and/or communalized to the extent that they are little more than passive symbols. In contrast, men are more likely to be cast as active agents due to their frequent depiction as heroic, individualized roles (see McDowell 2008).

A second important mural to deal with these issues was a well-publicized, temporary piece of public art erected on the gable-end wall where South Great George's Street meets Dame Street in central Dublin. The mural appeared as a media sensation overnight in time for International Women's Day (March 8) in 2016 (Mulhall 2016). While it was not a painted mural—rather the artist Gearóid O'Dea created the image before it was scanned, digitally reproduced, and temporarily attached to the wall—it was monumental and dominated this busy intersection while it remained in situ. The image was called "Le Chéile I nGruaig" ("Together in the Hair") and was hailed at the time as being "amazing" (Barry 2016) in representing three women—Constance Markievicz, Grace Gifford, and Margaret Pearse—from the revolutionary period. The image itself was not only striking due to the scale and unusual representation of the women—joined by their hair but separated by their looking in various directions from the composition—but also due to the spatial connection. A campaign-oriented mural by a different artist, Joe Caslin, appeared on the same wall the previous year in the form of a monumental printed image of a same-sex couple embracing. It was famously erected on the wall overnight in April 2015 in the run-up to the Republic of Ireland's referendum on gay marriage (Barry 2015). The recent history of activism attached to the wall clearly reinforced the importance of the placement of the image, as was noted by many of the media reports (with some reports even misrepresenting the two images as being from the same artist). However, despite the media interest—and unwavering support—for the form and message of this mural, there are a number of issues with the representations that should be noted.

The primary problem with this mural is the fact that of the three women chosen by O'Dea to represent the Easter Rising, two were not participants and one is already extremely well known. While we know at least seventy-seven women were processed through Richmond Barracks due to their active involvement in the conflict, Grace Gifford and Margaret Pearse were not among them. On his inspiration for choosing these characters, the artist states: "Margaret Pearse gave her son, Patrick to the Rising [in fact, she 'gave' two sons, as William was also executed]. Her sacrifice might have been greater than his, her sense of loss more enduring. She had to witness the Civil War, and see an Ireland emerge that fell far short of the Rising's ideals" (Barry 2016). This is a noble thought, but one that reaffirms women in the role of passive victims, mothers and bystanders in Irish history, and a sentiment that also forgets that Mrs. Pearse became an influential politician in her own right in the years after the Rising. Of Grace Gifford-Plunkett, O'Dea notes: "[She] was a political cartoonist. Her husband Joseph was executed in Kilmainham Gaol on the day of their marriage. His execution began to turn the public in favour of the rebels" (ibid.). While there are no historical inaccuracies in this statement, it fails to acknowledge the fact that Grace was not active in the Rising but rather inspired by those events to become active in the War of Independence and Civil War, and she was imprisoned by the Free State during the latter conflict. Indeed, her sister, Nellie, was involved in the Rising but was not represented in the mural. Both Margaret Pearse and Grace Gifford-Plunkett are represented in this mural merely as conduits for the experiences and tragedies of men. In contrast, one can have no such critique of the inclusion of the ubiquitous Countess Markievicz, the only woman who commanded troops and who was court-martialed as a leader of the Rising. However, the representation of the countess is unusual and the artist's explanation makes it problematic: "Countess Markievicz is the icon. She is often depicted as a revolutionary [fi]gure [sic] . . . but I wanted to portray her in contemplative passivity" (ibid.). The wish to make an active combatant—who famously chose to present herself in a modified version of a paramilitary Irish Citizen Army uniform for the Rising (Barber 2016)—in an almost unknown form in order to emphasize her "contemplative passivity" is almost beyond comprehension. However, it does reinforce the conservative tradition of representing women as passive in conflict rather than portraying what Fionna Barber has noted were Markievicz's deliberate attempts to "undermine the status and power invested in more normative representations of aristocratic women" by her choice of dress (Barber 2016, 8).

Both these murals demonstrate how popular attempts at portraying women involved in the revolutionary period in the very different contemporary contexts of Belfast and Dublin have unintentionally, and undoubtedly without malice, skewed the realities of those histories in different ways, in keeping with their spatial and temporal context. Interestingly, all these compositions were designed by men who, although sympathetic to emphasizing women's roles in the past, are clearly not intimately aware of the critiques of the representation of women in conflict and the implicit messages these compositions communicate (see Johnson 1994, for example, on the eliding of women's experiences of the 1798 rebellion). In Belfast, the commemoration of the women of Cumann na mBan conflates the rank and file not only with the exceptional female figure but also with more contemporary women involved in conflict. In Dublin, the interest in remembering women does not involve those who have been newly discovered or who were even active in the Easter Rising. The exceptional is again the focus. The emphasizing of the already well-known exceptional women with "new" women presented as passive conduits for male actions and/or anonymous rank-and-file foot soldiers may have longer-term repercussions. Constance Markievicz was one of the few women involved in the Easter Rising who was already well known before the centenary so the use of her image does not significantly alter public memory of women from the Rising. In contrast, the focus on newly discovered passive women, or women being used as representatives of men, limits the potential for the focus on women in 2016 to translate into meaningful incorporation of women into the canon of Easter Rising narratives and actors. How do we try to implant new, meaningful narratives into the public domain? How do we ensure the incorporation of the realities of women's roles and experiences as we move through the decade to the more difficult histories of the revolutionary and early Free State period? One way is to continue completing historical research, using the newly digitized and opened public files, collating, and publishing the sometimes complicated, usually dark, often partial, stories of ordinary women active in extraordinary times.

ORDINARY WOMEN AND THEIR EXTRAORDINARY EXPERIENCES

As already noted, the website of Richmond Barracks in Dublin contains a list of seventy-seven women who were involved in the Easter Rising (Richmond Barracks 2020a). Most of those named were ordinary women actively involved in the conflict and whose names were not retained in public memory but have appeared in official historical records. Although this list is very welcome in bringing information about a group of largely forgotten women into the public domain, it also highlights inherent issues in locating women involved in conflict such as the Easter Rising. First, it reveals that our knowledge of ordinary women's involvement in this period is largely restricted to those who appear in our public records, which means they were recorded because they came to the attention of the authorities through either arrest or imprisonment. This can only ever represent a small percentage of the women who were actually "involved," and, while this is an issue across the gender spectrum, it particularly impacts women, as their roles were often hidden and later downplayed in the aftermath of conflict. Margaret Ward, in her seminal publication *Unmanageable Revolutionaries* (1983), discussed how our knowledge of women's often more hidden but essential roles during this period, such as maintaining networks, passing on messages, and providing safe houses, was directly related to whether the men in power decided to publicly acknowledge them. She noted that many men failed to state for the record the role women played, and those high-profile men who did often reinforced the idea that women were supporting and maintaining the fighters, thereby continuing the tradition of "man the leader and woman the auxiliary" (1983, 194). Second, the very nature of the types of public records associated with ordinary women focuses our attention on "snapshot" histories, moments in time that are recorded with varying levels of detail and with particular agendas. They infrequently provide us with a narrative thread that reveals the trajectory of how women's involvement changed over time and what, if any, were the consequences for ordinary women choosing to step outside the societal norms and be involved in an armed conflict.

Third, the timely focus on women from 1916 during the centenary has allowed us to question the highly gendered nature of not only Irish history but the writing of Irish history, especially how few women are remembered in terms of their contributions to Irish politics and society. This invigorated public focus on women in the commemoration of the Rising has been paralleled and enabled by academic discourse. Alongside the various books specifically focused on women that have been painstaking researched in time for the centenary (including Margaret Ward 2017; Ann Matthews 2012, 2010; Sinéad McCoole 2015), there has also been an uneven if notable expansion of attention paid to women in more general histories (especially R. Foster 2014), although this is not universal (edited volumes such as Grayson and McGarry 2016 lack any specific chapters on women). While this is to be commended, there is the need to heed caution as to how much inserting the stories of some women from the Rising reflects the involvement of women throughout the period. With the more challenging commemorations to come, especially of the Civil War in

2022–2023, we are in danger of allowing the more difficult and women-involved conflicts to fall off the end of the commemorative cycle. This could be a major issue in terms of incorporating into public memory a more historically nuanced view of women's involvement in the revolutionary period.

Civil Wars are always painful for the nation to remember, but this is precisely why they must be included. One need only view the imprisonment figures for women during the Easter Rising and compare them with those of the Civil War to see the greater knowledge of women's roles as the period progresses: seventy-seven from the Rising to at least six hundred in the Civil War (Matthews 2012). There is also a need to acknowledge that as the sporadic violence of the revolutionary period escalated, women became embroiled in conflict whether they wished to or not. This was not only because violence increasingly moved from the formal engagements of soldiers to attacks at night that permeated households but also because of the massive social changes brought about by World War I and the Rising. In the context of long-term guerilla warfare, women learned they could play more active roles because enduring ideas of propriety appeared to guard them from the harsher treatments men faced. The ambiguity of their traditional distance from conflict but potential for involvement at this time meant that on all sides they were viewed with suspicion. Through the War of Independence, women acted not only as subsidiary helpers but also as active combatants, and the significance of their roles made them targets. Ann Matthews has argued that from the War of Independence (1919–1921) onward, there existed an effective "war on women" (2010, 266–283). She interprets this deliberate policy as a repercussion of the unsettled politics and heightened militarization of the period but also as a reaction to the ambiguities brought into play by the changing roles of women in wider society (Matthews 2010, 12). Through the War of Independence and Civil War, women, especially non- elite women, were actively targeted for verbal, physical, and sexual attack, often as surrogates for their male relatives and friends (Connolly 2019; Matthews 2010; McCoole 1997), and this went largely unreported.

The Irish Civil War (1922–1923) became the first period in which women were imprisoned en masse for political reasons in modern Irish history. This is problematic for Irish people and historians to remember because it was the newly independent Irish state, not the British forces, who were the first to treat Irish women en masse as political prisoners. The incarceration of the estimated six hundred women imprisoned throughout the course of the Civil War created a problem for these new civilian forces, not only in terms of where they housed the women but also how they dealt with adverse public reaction to the mass internment of women. I have written previously on the evidence for gender-related violence perpetrated on women imprisoned during the Civil War (McAtackney 2016) and the problems of locating evidence for this due to the enduring taint of the offense being connected to the victim rather than the perpetrator. However, on bringing together a collection of implicit hints and explicit statements from letters, memoirs, and entries in autograph books, it is clear that women were targeted for physical and sexual assault while imprisoned—mirroring many of their experiences outside—and most did not report these offenses. The combination of uncomfortable truths around the mass imprisonment of women during the Civil War, the need to address the scale of sexual violence that undoubtedly occurred from all sides, and the repercussions on the lives of ordinary women afterward, makes commemorating this period difficult. However, it is imperative that we do remember it because this is precisely the period when the newly fledged independent state gained its taste for interning "unmanageable" women that would become an enduring feature. The possibility that commemoration fatigue will be used to pardon us from the later, more difficult, centenaries is something academics must ensure does not occur. The best way to do this is to present the stories of those "ordinary" women whom we have hitherto forgotten.

BRIDIE HALPIN, 1902–1987

The rest of this chapter focuses on the story of one such "ordinary" woman. It is a (partial) narrative of the life of Bridie Halpin, which is selective and incomplete due to the piecemeal survival of documentary and other sources about her. It reflects the fact that as an ordinary woman she intruded into few official documents; she published no memoir, nor were there any biographies written about her. Her story, as brought together through these sources, can be located because of existing public records, newly released government online archives, and the unusual and unexpected survivals of a personal archive and other materials and records that mainly connect her documented life to a short but eventful period as a political prisoner. This story focuses on the Civil War experiences of Bridie, because the five months she was held as an anti-Treaty republican have produced most of the accessible documents relating to her life. They do not detail her experiences of the Easter Rising because, in common with many women who were imprisoned during the Civil War, she was a child (14 years old) when the Rising occurred and, therefore, was not an active combatant. However, she was inspired to become involved in republican politics in its messy aftermath, and the Civil War was her period of most publicly acknowledged activity. Her story is the story of "ordinary" women during, and after, the revolutionary period.

Bridie Halpin is significant in her insignificance. As one of the ordinary women of revolutionary Ireland, we should know more about her in order to better understand the everyday experiences and lived repercussions of conflict, especially through the lens of gender. She was an Irish woman born in 1902 into a working-class family living in a tenement in central Dublin. The 1911 census show us that on April 2 she was nine years old and lived with her parents and four siblings (she was the second youngest) at 4 Nicholas Street. The house was a shared dwelling separated into nine contained residences; the family lived in one room. She was still living at that address when she graffitied the wall of a cell in Kilmainham Gaol in April 1923 with the words: "Up Dublin / Bridie Halpin / No 4 Nicholas St / Christchurch Dublin."[1] In contrast to the elite women we know about from the Easter Rising, the narrative of Bridie Halpin speaks not only to the everyday and ordinary but to the specific experiences of being a young working-class republican woman in early twentieth-century Ireland.

Bridie was imprisoned during the Irish Civil War and she was released in its aftermath. She remained in Dublin until she emigrated to Canada in 1937, at age thirty-four, to work at the De Havilland aircraft factory in Toronto. Later, she moved on to New York City in 1946 at the age of forty-three. She died fifteen days before Christmas in 1987 at the age of eighty-five. She was unmarried but had been the matriarch of her extended Irish American family; she provided support and housing for many of her extended family who migrated from Ireland. Before she died in December 1987, they thought she was simply "the typical spinster aunt of many an Irish family in Ireland" (McCormack 1988). The reason we know all these details is because Bridie's family made a discovery when they were going through her belongings after her death. Under her bed, they located a suitcase of papers revealing that she was a forgotten woman of revolutionary Ireland, a fact that they decided to publicize. They donated many of her papers to archives in Ireland.

Using some of the papers located in that suitcase—official documents and other related materials—we are able to piece together Bridie's involvement in, and experiences of, the Irish Civil War as well as in its aftermath. The Prisoners Location book (CW/P/01/01) kept at the Irish Military Archives reveals that she was sent to Kilmainham Gaol on April 16, 1923, and was then transferred to the North Dublin Union (NDU) on April 27, 1923. The diary of the governor of the Kilmainham Gaol and the NDU, Timothy O'Neill, shows that she was released, with seventy-four other prisoners, on Friday, September 28, 1923 (CW/P/o6/o4). Her imprisonment at the NDU throughout this period is confirmed, as her name and usual address appeared in "List 1" of "NDU Prisoners" (CW/P/o5/o8). There are some curious inclusions in the official paperwork she kept in her suitcase. There is a detention order signed by the Minister for Defense, Richard Mulcahy, dated to August 8, 1923, which appears to actually relate to the detention of an "Eileen Colgan" (in thick black ink) but also has "Bridie Halpin" in lighter ink above it. As Bridie had been in the prison system since April 1923, this piece of paper appears to officially relate to Ms. Colgan, and it is unclear how and why Bridie's name was added; maybe she added it herself to create a memento of incarceration (Halpin 1923c)? No other details are provided from official public records.

We do not know her experiences of the notorious removal of female prisoners from Kilmainham Gaol to the NDU, eleven days after she arrived. From surviving memoirs, official records, and letters, we know quite a lot of detail about the removal of women from Kilmainham Gaol to the NDU in April 1923. The intention to move the majority of the women between Kilmainham Gaol and the NDU was revealed to them on the same day the move was to take place. This was not coincidental; it occurred against the backdrop of a hunger strike undertaken by Mary McSwiney and Kate O'Callaghan reaching a critical stage. The women's response to the news was to barricade themselves into their cells to prevent their removal. This action in turn led to a series of raids in the middle of the night when they were forcibly, often violently, removed under the cover of darkness. The surviving firsthand accounts tell of the women being violently processed, individually, by male CID officers (the Criminal Investigation Department was an armed, plain clothed, police unit that operated during the Civil War) and members of Cumann na Saoirse (lit. Group of Freedom), who were the newly formed, pro-State, breakaway group from the women's organization that most of the prisoners belonged to, Cumann na mBan (lit. Group of Women). There exist a number of firsthand accounts that confirm the brutality and sexualized nature of these attacks. This includes a letter by Mary McDermott, which was smuggled out of the North Dublin Union and published by the *Daily Herald*. She claimed: "I was assaulted ... by four women employed by the Free State. My dress was taken off, because I resisted. . . . The prison adjutant, a man at least six feet of heavy build, knelt on me while the women assaulted me, beating me about the face and body with my own shoes. . . . I fainted. . . . On my recovering consciousness I found myself outside in the passage among drunken soldiers lying in a semi-nude state, my clothing saturated with water"

(McDermott 1923). The forced searching of women in the disorientation of the night was a deliberately humiliating and sinister act. It facilitated the violation and conquering of the physical body of the female prisoner (following Aretxaga 1997) in the name of the state and in doing so shamed the majority of women into silence. In all, seventy women were dragged from their cells and processed over five hours in one night, and most only hinted at their experience even to themselves (see McAtackney 2016); we can only assume Bridie was one of those women. She left no record of the event behind. Margaret Ward has claimed the women of Cumann na Saoirse were central in facilitating and initiating "sexual abuse in some attacks" (1995, 194).

We do get other glimpses into the more mundane aspects of Bridie's experiences of imprisonment due to her keeping a number of papers from the time. This includes four letters (one from Bridie to her brother Leo and the rest correspondence from friends to Bridie, including two from fellow female prisoners). Furthermore, two autograph books survive, one shop-bought and the other handmade. (Autograph books were relatively inexpensive, mass-produced books of blank paper popularly circulated in the late nineteenth to mid-twentieth century to allow friends to write messages, often used at transitional times.) The letters and autograph books provide an interesting insight into the life of imprisoned, twenty-one-year-old Bridie. Clearly the NDU, in particular, was horrifically inadequate in housing the women, with one correspondent noting in the autograph book, "My jail experience is written in letters of fire across my brain Bridie never to be effaced" (Cosgrove 1923). From her own autograph book, Bridie references the awful conditions at the NDU in a short poem: "Bridie Halpin No 3786 / Arrested by CID / Brought to Oriel House then to Kilmainham Gaol from that to the NDU Starvation Camp / Released ??? / We've for no lights in the Union now hurro / hurro / We've got to go to bed in the dark and then / We all can sing like larks and will sing / Starvation out of hearts on this Free State" (Halpin 1923a). However, Bridie does not communicate these hardships to her brother Leo when she writes to him three days before her release on September 25, 1923. Rather she uses most of the letter to ask about their family and friends, writing in a carefree tone about how much she enjoys playing games: "We have all sorts of games here we always play Rounders every day. We had a match on Sunday and our side won, up us" (Halpin 1923b). Clearly, different types of experiences were being shared with different communicants and those that hinted at the darker experiences of imprisonments were kept for those who shared those experiences rather than worrying family members and friends on the outside.

The papers from Bridie's suitcase extend beyond her period of imprisonment, and, in some ways, they are just as important in revealing the realities of
women's lives after the taint of being a political prisoner on the losing side of
a Civil War. One badly faded document relates to Bridie relying on the Dublin Republican Prisoners Employment Bureau (DRPEB) in order to locate
employment. The paper dates from July 16, 1924, and summons Bridie to "report
at Bureau at once for work" (DRPEB 1924). The existence of such a bureau, and
the fact that Bridie was registered with it, indicates the difficulties of gaining
employment for those who were working-class, ex-republican, women prisoners in the early Free State. One has to wonder if the continued privations of
being an ex-republican prisoner eventually led to her migration in her thirties
to work in the factory in Canada.

We know from the newspaper report detailing the contents of her suitcase that more papers were found than now reside in Kilmainham Gaol
Archive—including personal Christmas cards from Éamon de Valera (McCormack 1988). However, there are two significant letters that date from her life
in New York that are retained in the archive. These letters date from 1949 and
1976, and they originate from two famous Irish republican women who were
mother-in-law and daughter-in-law—Maud Gonne MacBride and Catalina
Bulfin MacBride. Although the letters were nearly thirty years apart, they were
alike in reminiscing with Bridie about their times together in prison during the
Civil War while reaffirming their enduring commitment to Irish republicanism in the contemporary moment. The letter from Catalina thanked Bridie
for her "list of prisoners" and then added to Bridie's reminiscence of a "Fancy
Dress Ball in the [North Dublin] Union" including "Annie O'Farrelly as Robert
Emmett I also remember the job she had to get the flour out of her hair—she
had 'powdered' her hair in the style of his period . . ." (Bulfin 1976). Maud
Gonne MacBride's letter focused less on the past and more on the present
and the future. She noted their shared and enduring interest in Irish politics,
referring to the need for American help "to help us free our 6 still occupied
counties" (MacBride 1949), as well as sharing family stories of marriages, ill-
nesses, and her own precarious health (she noted she was eighty-one when the
letter was written). Perhaps most poignantly in the context of trying to piece
together Bridie's story and why so few people knew it before she died, Maud
starts her letter with questions: "We were all so glad to hear from you—I often
wondered where you were. How do you like America? And are you enjoying
life? You say so little about yourself. . . ." This reticence in talking about herself,
even to the women she shared Civil War confinement with, whom she kept
in contact with for decades after her imprisonment, was also mirrored in the

memories of her family. In the newspaper article that publicly presented Bridie's suitcase, the family discussed knowing of her involvement with founding a choral society, dancing at Feis, and even being a one-time officer of the Dublin society, but their repeated, unanswerable question was: "Why didn't she ever say anything?" (McCormack 1988).

CONCLUSIONS

For Irish commemorations, 2016 was an important year, due not only to the centenary of the Easter Rising but also because of the overdue communication of the long-marginalized roles of women from this period. In what often seemed like a celebration of women, there was widespread public, media, and academic attention to the stories of many women who were both active combatants (such as Constance Markievicz) and symbols of male sacrifice (such as Margaret Pearse). While emphasizing the roles of women in the Rising is important, this chapter advises a note of caution in how we move forward through the more difficult final years of the decade of commemorations. Having examined how and which women from the Rising are being selected for public memory, it is clear that the stories of ordinary women, and meaningful engagements with new narratives, may not be substantial enough to be retained in future public memory.

This chapter presented the largely unknown story of Bridie Halpin, a working-class Irish republican woman who (like many women of this period) came to the attention of the authorities during the Civil War rather than the Rising. Her story did not start and stop with imprisonment, and, through her retention and curation of her own papers, it was evident that she left Ireland but maintained correspondence with her old confidants while performing the role of a cultural but apolitical Irish woman in New York. Bridie's partial and fractured story reveals that the experiences of women in this period should not be condensed to "snapshot" moments. Their imprisonment should not be the only focus of research, as evidently it sometimes had enduring repercussions—in creating friendships but also in forcing many women to leave. While we have been led to believe that 2016 was the year forgotten women were found, over fifteen years before the centenary, Louise Ryan (2002) revealed that newspapers publicized women's roles, often negatively, throughout the period. The highly influential press of the revolutionary period often contained information on women being arrested, convicted, imprisoned, and denounced in their notices, editorials, and articles. These women were not unknown, but many were ordinary and were undoubtedly marginalized and shamed for their transgressive roles in conflict. Ryan argues that later obscuring of the range and variety of female roles can be partially attributed to feminist scholars being uncomfortable with the active role some of the women held in military affairs (2002, 221). However, I argue that this loss of public memory may also relate to discomfiture in remembering the Civil War at all and especially the role the authorities played in imprisoning, mistreating, and targeting women. It is vitally important that they not be forgotten a second time, and that means exploring the full range of their experiences and role in the Civil War—no matter how unsavory—and the Irish state's treatment of "ordinary" women afterward.

NOTE

1. This graffiti was recorded during the course of the Kilmainham Gaol Graffiti Project, 2012–2014, www.kilmainhamgaolgraffiti.com.

LAURA MCATACKNEY is Associate Professor in Sustainable Heritage Management at Aarhus University, Denmark. An archaeologist by training, her current research uses contemporary and historical archaeological approaches, and its heritage implications, to explore areas as diverse as material barriers in post-conflict Northern Ireland, female experiences of political imprisonment during the Irish Civil War and the material remnants of Danish colonialism on St Croix, USVI. She created and maintains a website on female experiences of imprisonment during the Irish Civil War (McAtackney 2014).

FOUR

—◊◊◊—

WOMEN OF THE RISING IN AUSTRALIA

Memory and Commemoration, 1916–2016

DIANNE HALL

IN APRIL 1936, MAY O'CARROLL carried her faded green Cumann na mBan uniform on her arm as she laid a wreath inscribed with a quote from Sean Mac-Dermott: "Ni siochaim go saoírse. No peace until freedom." The ceremony in Sydney's Waverley Cemetery, on the other side of the world from Dublin's General Post Office (GPO), was organized by the Sydney-based Hands Off Ireland Organization to commemorate the twentieth anniversary of the 1916 Rising. O'Carroll laid the wreath at the monument that had been erected by Sydney's Irish community on the centenary of the 1798 rebellion and dedicated to "all who died and suffered in Ireland in 1798" (*Catholic Press* [Sydney], April 16, 1936, 21). Eighty years after the 1936 ceremony, at an event held at Melbourne's Celtic Club at the centenary of the Rising, Dublin-born Melbourne resident Maeve O'Leary movingly spoke about her grandmother, Lucy Agnes Smyth, who had been in the GPO during the Rising (O'Leary 2016). Having moved far away from Dublin and without any physical connection with the places of the Irish revolutionary period, these women and many others found different ways of remembering individual women and their part in the fight for Irish independence. While women veterans were living in Australia, their presence at commemorative events staked a claim of memory of the other women who had fought alongside them. But, for the majority of Australians, who did not know even one of the small number of Irish women veterans of the revolution who settled in Australia, newspapers, speeches, and group events were the only conduits to the history of these women. Over the course of the twentieth century, these avenues weakened, but, in the years leading up to the centenary, the wider spread of information through social media and easier international travel meant links between women in the diaspora and women in Ireland have

74

become stronger. In examining the ways that the memory of women's involve-ment in the Irish revolution waxed and waned in Australia, this chapter traces these commemorative threads during the hundred years after the 1916 Rising.

THE IRISH IN AUSTRALIA IN 1916

By 1916, a significant percentage of Australians were of Irish descent or birth. The long journey to Australia meant that only small numbers of Irish emigrants were able to travel so far, usually preferring the shorter and cheaper journey to England, Scotland, or North America. After the period of forced migration of convicts from Britain and Ireland, successive Australian colonial governments were well aware of the disadvantage of distance in attracting settlers from the United Kingdom and had initiated various subsidies and financial schemes to encourage the white population they believed they needed for British settle-ment to succeed in the Australian colonies. Irish people proved to be very adept at utilizing these schemes and by the time the six colonies joined together to form the nation of Australia in 1901, the Irish, their children, and their grand-children formed approximately a quarter of the total settler population. While the raw numbers of Irish migrants were small compared with those who trav-eled to North America, the Irish and their descendants formed a much higher proportion of the Australian settler population, making their presence par-ticularly important to the developing nation (P. O'Farrell 1986, 23, 63). By 1916, immigration to Australia from Ireland had slowed to a trickle as the subsidies had ceased and new restrictions on immigrants' health and economic status put additional barriers in place. In the 1920s and 1930s, there continued to be a much smaller number of migrants from Ireland arriving in Australia (Malcolm and Hall 2018, 337–339).

During the later nineteenth and early twentieth centuries, most Irish Aus-tralians supported the push for home rule as proposed by the Irish Parliamen-tary Party. They had learned about the situation through extensive speaking tours by men such as John and William Redmond in the 1880s, and they had been generous donors to the cause through home rule clubs. So, when the news of the Rising broke in Australia in May 1916, it was met with shock and disbelief by most. Newspaper editors had difficulty sourcing accurate information about the events in Dublin because wartime government restrictions had slowed the flow of news in general, which, combined with the dearth of eyewitness reports from Dublin, meant that there was often little that was new to be given to the Australian news reading public (see Hall 2020). But lack of timely reports did not deter the world's press in their widespread coverage of the events, and there were plenty of international news outlets from which Australian editors sourced stories. In the first weeks after the Rising, Australian papers received most of their reports from news cables via the English or American papers, such as the *New York Times, Chicago Tribune*, or the London *Times* (Overlack 1997). Reporting in the mainstream press in Australia, therefore, reflected these international sources and was initially hostile to the rebels, often using descriptions of women fighting to emphasize the unauthorized nature of the rebellion. One of the main news articles of the *Brisbane Courier* on May 1, 1916, stated, "Free fighting occurred in Jacob's biscuit factory between loyalist women and rebel women who were trying to get food into the rebel garrison" (*Brisbane Courier* [Queensland], May 1, 1916, 7). The picture of unnaturally violent women on both sides was spread throughout many newspapers in Australia.

It was not in the general descriptions of women, though, that most newspaper writers were interested. The human stories of the tragically widowed sisters Grace and Muriel Gifford and the "stormy petrels of Ireland," Constance Markievicz and Maud Gonne, dominated the headlines and women's pages whenever the women of the Rising were mentioned.[1] Australian newspapers were keen to find some local angle on the story of the Rising, and, in almost every Australian state in June and July 1916, papers published an eyewitness account of the Rising by a Melbourne doctor, Cecil McAdam. McAdam had been staying in the Shelbourne Hotel and had a view over St. Stephen's Green, where Markievicz was second-in-command. McAdam reported that he had been told by others that she had shot six of her men who had refused to obey orders. She was also described as a malevolent force who led other women astray.[2]

Australians eager for knowledge of the course of the struggle for Irish independence gathered their information mostly from the Catholic press, published in every state. These newspapers, many under the direct control of the Catholic hierarchy, devoted considerable print space to news from Ireland. They certainly carried more news of Irish activist women than the mainstream press, but even in these newspapers the stories followed familiar patterns: Irish women were either grieving widows or selfless help maids to the fighting men. In October 1916, the Sydney *Catholic Press* carried a long narrative about Moira Regan, "Irish Girl Rebel" and "friend and fellow worker" of Joseph Plunkett, Patrick Pearse, and Thomas MacDonagh. It is a lively account that included a brief outline of the work of Cumann na mBan in "doing the work that was before them," cooking, cleaning, and using rifles when needed (*Catholic Press*, October 16, 1916, 19). However, more attention was always paid to the grieving widows and mothers. Young widowed Muriel MacDonagh was presented as a pathetic figure among the widows of the executed leaders. In December

1916, an interview with her, conducted by American journalist Eileen Moore of Chicago's *New World*, was reprinted in the Sydney *Catholic Press*. Moore emphasized both Muriel's vulnerability and her youth; she had "a pathetic appearance in her deep mourning, with her three-and-a-half-year-old son, Donagh, clinging to her skirt. She is transparently pale, with copper-coloured hair and blue eyes. Her eyes have an appealing look" (*Catholic Press*, December 28, 1916, 18). The pathos of Muriel and her very young children was only increased when Australian readers were told she had died in 1917 of a heart attack while swimming. Reports of the grieving widows and female family members of martyred Irish republican men continued in the immediate aftermath of the Rising. In Melbourne in 1919, the *Advocate* published a short article titled "A Mother of Martyrs" about Margaret Pearse, the mother of executed Patrick and Willie, and illustrated by pictures of her two sons. Included in the article was a letter by Margaret Pearse prefaced by the comment, "How Irish mothers suffer and suffer gladly" (*Advocate* [Victoria], November 1, 1919, 12). When two anti-Treaty republican women activists toured the eastern states of Australia in 1924–1925, they tailored their message to suit the political climate in which they found themselves. Using tact and clever speechmaking, they managed to raise over £8,000 in just four months of intensive touring. Kathleen Barry, member of Cumann na mBan and sister of executed student and IRA member Kevin Barry, and Linda Kearns, veteran nurse who had been active in 1916, crafted a careful message of helpful Irish femininity that avoided as far as possible mention of their activist roles in the Irish revolution (Hall 2019). They did this by always emphasizing their roles as grieving sisters, willing helpers, and nurses of wounded men whose mission now was to assist the families of republican prisoners.

After the mid-1920s, the Australian Catholic presses' coverage of women's revolutionary activities settled into memorialization based initially on obituaries and then on reviews of biographies. One of the first and most prominent in both cases was Constance Markievicz. Many mainstream newspapers as well as the Catholic press announced her death in July 1927. In its obituary, the Adelaide Catholic *Southern Cross* newspaper described the presence of government troops at her burial and gave a brief history of her life (*Southern Cross* [South Australia], July 22, 1927, 11). Another Adelaide newspaper aimed at a general audience was more imaginative, with Markievicz described as "typically Irish in her sympathy for the oppressed"; "her spirited attacks on police had little effect other than to land her in police court" (*Observer* [South Australia], July 23, 1927, 47). The deaths of other women activists were noted over the years that followed, usually with their obituaries highlighting their association with one or more of their male comrades or relatives as well as their membership of Cumann na mBan.[3]

Irish Australian groups with links to Irish republicanism, such as the Hands Off Ireland Organization and the Irish National Association (INA), were the main avenues of memorialization of Irish revolutionaries throughout the twentieth century. The INA is the longest surviving of these organizations (P. O'Farrell 2005). Albert Dryer founded the INA in Sydney in 1915 and branches were established in Melbourne, Brisbane, and Adelaide (Collins 2013, Reid, Kildea and McIntyre, 2020). He modeled the INA on the Gaelic League by promoting Irish cultural events in tandem with fundraising for Irish American Fenian organizations and, after 1916, in support of Irish republicanism (Dryer 1956). After the 1920s, the INA held annual commemorations for the 1916 Rising often with concerts and fundraisers for republican causes in Ireland.[4] Funds coming from events such as these encouraged Archbishop Daniel Mannix and Éamon de Valera to support the fundraising tour of Kathleen Barry and Linda Kearns later in 1924. In Melbourne in 1926, the INA hosted two events to commemorate the Rising with a young Arthur Caldwell, later Australian Labor Party politician, giving an address to mark the tenth anniversary (*Advocate*, April 29, 1926, 23). The Hands Off Ireland Organization in Sydney held regular commemorations of the 1916 Rising during the 1930s at the 1798 memorial at Waverley Cemetery.[5] The 1936 commemoration when May O'Carroll presented the wreath at Waverley was unusual in that it highlighted women's roles in 1916.

During the 1920s and 1930s, when memories of the revolutionary period were fresh, there were also commemorative events by other groups, such as commemorative concerts held annually during the 1930s at Cathedral Hall in Fitzroy, Melbourne.[6] Major anniversaries like the one in 1936 were marked by other Irish Australian groups, such as the memorial celebrations of the men of Easter Week by the James Connolly branch of the Irish National Foresters association, one of many mutual assistance organizations in Australia (*Advocate*, May 13, 1926, 23).[7]

As well as attending events organized by local associations and groups, Irish Australians also read of reports of the commemorative events in Dublin in the Catholic press and, to a lesser extent, the mainstream press. The Australian press reported the Dublin commemorative parades and rallies in 1932, after Fianna Fáil's electoral victory (*Southern Cross*, April 1, 1932, 17). The rioting associated with the twentieth anniversary in 1936 was likewise reported throughout Australian mainstream press (e.g., the *Chronicle* [Adelaide], April 16, 1936, 46), while the Catholic presses gave a wider and more nuanced coverage of the ceremonies (e.g., the *Advocate*, May 7, 1936, 11). This was not surprising, as the mainstream press relied on international news agencies, principally from England, for their coverage. Catholic presses such as the *Advocate* published their reports a week or two after Easter and were sourced from correspondents in Dublin.

Both mainstream and Catholic presses reported the 1966 jubilee commemoration of the Rising in Dublin. Most of this coverage concentrated on the histories of the executed leaders, while little was noticed about the women. The Melbourne *Age* printed a long article by prominent Irish Australian Niall Brennan on the history of the Rising (Brennan 1966). As well as noting the preparations taking place in Dublin for the Easter parade, in the weeks prior to Easter, the Melbourne *Advocate* printed a full-page review of the 1966 *Capuchin Annual*, which included reprints of its 1916 edition. Dublin bookseller John W. Wright advertised souvenir publications about the Rising in the Melbourne *Advocate* on the regular Irish news page, and the *Advocate* also reprinted a history of the Rising from the "Wolfe Tone Annual" (Dublin) commending the bravery of Elizabeth O'Farrell, Una Carney, and Sheila Grennan of Cumann na mBan. The jubilee was celebrated with commemorative dinners and events held by many Irish social and political organizations such as the Irish Amateur Athletics Association in Melbourne and the Connolly Club (*Advocate*, April 7, 1966, 9; April 21, 1966, 27). The Waverley Cemetery commemoration in Sydney was attended by six survivors of the Rising and several Labor party politicians (see R. Higgins 2012, 197–198).

WOMEN VETERANS OF THE IRISH REVOLUTIONARY PERIOD IN AUSTRALIA

Newspaper coverage and commemorations by Irish Australian groups of the 1916 Rising and the revolutionary period did not give a great deal of attention to the women activists, apart from the occasional mention in brief histories of the Rising and in obituaries and reviews of biographies of the most well-known women. An exception was Cumann na mBan, which had small branches in both Melbourne and Sydney in the 1920s. The more active Cumann na mBan was in Sydney, and, after its establishment in 1919, the group held regular dances, concerts, and whist nights until the late 1930s (Whitaker 2018). They kept abreast of events in Ireland, particularly concerning women, and in November 1922 sent a cable to W. T. Cosgrave protesting about the treatment of Maire McSwiney (*Advocate*, November 30, 1922, 27). One of the first actions of Kathleen Barry and Linda Kearns when they arrived in Melbourne in late 1924 was to establish the Kevin Barry Cumann na mBan. However, this group did not survive for long after Barry and Kearns left Australia (Hall 2019).

Attending events such as those of Cumann na mBan or other Irish organizations gave people a chance to share news of events in Ireland that had not appeared in the newspapers. Some of this was communicated through formal talks, such as those given by Father Michael O'Flanagan and J. J. O'Kelly in 1923 and by Barry and Kearns during their tour in 1924–1925 (Whitaker 2016a, 208–211; Finnane 2013). Other Irish veterans residing in Australia also gave talks and were able to provide more information about women's activities and also their fate after the peace. Maire McKee, a member of Dublin Cumann na mBan and sister of Dick McKee, the IRA commandant executed by the British in 1920, spent a number of years in rural Victoria recovering her health after being on hunger strike when in prison during the civil war period. She had known Kathleen Barry in Ireland and kept in touch with her during and after Barry's tour of Australia.[8] McKee gave a talk about the Dublin Cumann na mBan to the Melbourne group in June 1925 (*Advocate*, June 4, 1925, 17).

Only a small number of women, like McKee, had been active in the Irish revolution and moved to Australia. One study of emigration after the revolutionary period has concluded that most of the activists who emigrated in the 1920s went to the United States, with only an estimated 2 percent traveling the much longer journey to Australia (Malcolm and Hall 2018, 332; see also G. Foster 2017, 744–747; Whitaker 1996). While it is likely that further research in the Military Archives and Pension files will reveal more individuals who settled outside of Ireland in the 1920s and 1930s, the overall proportions are unlikely to vary from this initial survey. The journey to Australia was long and expensive, so without subsidies, incentives of employment, or existing family connections, it is likely that many potential emigrants would not have chosen to travel the distance. Of the women who did emigrate to Australia, some maintained links with Irish Australian political organizations and participated in the commemorations of 1916.

The archives of the Military History Bureau indicate that only a few women veterans applied for pensions or medals from Australia. It is likely that there were more eligible women who migrated but did not apply, either because they did not know of the scheme or because they remained unreconciled to the Free State government (Coleman 2018; Morrison 2009). As well as the women who made applications, statements to the Military History Bureau sometimes mentioned former Cumann na mBan members living in Australia. For example, in his statement to the Military History Bureau, Michael Healy noted that former Cumann na mBan member Susan Ryan, from Loughrea, was living in Australia (MAI, BMH, WS1064). Phyllis Morkan, in her statement, described how a Miss Harvey came to Manchester from Dublin to help with the needs of the prisoners arrested after the Rising and subsequently transferred to Knutsford Gaol. Morkan noted that Miss Harvey later moved to Australia and was working as a nurse there (BMH WS210).

The numbers of Irish revolutionaries living in Australia applying for pensions was always small. Among the records currently released, there were twenty-four men and three women who applied for military pensions based on activities in the Rising and War of Independence and a further seventy-six men and three women who applied for service medals. Applications for pensions and medals show that women living in Australia needed the right combination of information about the processes and stamina to continue bureaucratic communications over such a long distance. Margaret Leonard, née Fleming, first applied for a pension in 1934, having heard about the new guidelines for the scheme from her brother-in-law in Sligo. Margaret Fleming was originally from Killarney, County Kerry, and, while working as a teacher in Liverpool, had joined Liverpool Cumann na mBan. Fleming returned to Dublin during Easter Week in 1916 and then delivered dispatches to Athlone. After her release from Mountjoy Prison in 1923, she moved to New South Wales in 1924, where she lived until her death in 1946 (Margaret Leonard, BMH pension file WMSP 34 Ref. 45593). Nora Douglas, née O'Sullivan, was a member of Cumann na mBan in Cork who moved to Australia in 1926 because she had been advised to move to a warmer climate after suffering ill health from her time in service (Nora Douglas, MSP34 Ref. 35989). Her sister, Mary McSweeny, also a member of Cumann na mBan, remained in Cork and had initiated inquiries about pensions on behalf of herself and Nora in 1934 (Nora Douglas, MSP34E615). Margaret Campbell, née O'Brien, originally from Bantry, County Cork, did not apply for a pension but successfully applied in 1960 for medals for her service in Cumann na mBan (Military medals file, MD 34701). While both Margaret Leonard and Nora Douglas were told of the scheme by relatives in Ireland, others may have found out through newspaper reports in the Australian Catholic media or through their association with Irish political or social groups. Certainly, the INA were well aware of the Military History Bureau's activities as Albert Dryer sent through a detailed report of INA activities in 1956 (MilitaryWitness statement, BMH WS 1526).

Some women were obviously very proud of their experiences during the revolutionary period, keeping memorabilia and attending memorial functions.

May O'Carroll, née Gahan, had been an active member of Cumann na mBan in Dublin in 1916 and continued in active service until 1923. She too moved to Australia for her health, which had suffered during her revolutionary service, her imprisonment, and her subsequent difficulties gaining work to support her young family (May O'Carroll, Military pension file, WMSP 34 REF10326). She, her husband, and their young children moved to Liverpool in 1924 and from there to Sydney via New Zealand in search of a fresh start, remaining in Sydney until her death in 1988. O'Carroll kept in her home her medals, uniform, and a framed engraving of the 1916 leaders at the GPO. She and her husband, John, were interviewed in 1954 for the *Australian Women's Weekly* when their daughter, Cathleen, won a prestigious violin scholarship. While the musical talents of Cathleen and their other children were discussed, the main focus of the article was on the memories of O'Carroll's time fighting for Ireland. O'Carroll herself told the reporter, "I was a rebel in those wild, wonderful exciting days and I nursed many fighting Irish men who fell foul of a bullet" (Patrick 1954).

Applying for a pension or medals was itself an act of memorialization, particularly for those who lived so far from Dublin. Margaret Leonard, in her application for a pension, mentions difficulties in remembering the names and addresses of people who could verify her actions and, at one point, says that she has only recently heard from someone in Dublin who was able to tell her the married name and address of one of the women she mentioned (Military pension file, MSP 34 45593). In 1938, Nora Douglas was asked to give more details of her service in addition to her original application. In doing so, she commented that she had not kept records and "would have to trust my memory" (Military Pension file, MSP3435989). Pensions were paid for life, so these women needed to keep in contact with the Irish government departments responsible for payments. Throughout her life until her death at the age of ninety-eight in 1998, Douglas queried deductions and notified changes of address and bank details (Nora Douglas, 34E615). Twenty years after 1916, May O'Carroll also had to remember and document the necessary information for the long application process, with lists of names, dates, and contacts for those who had been her superiors while she was active in Cumann na mBan. For O'Carroll, the incentive to apply for the disability and service pension was great, as the O'Carroll family had limited financial resources for much of the 1930s and 1940s while their large family was young. O'Carroll, both personally and through a solicitor in Dublin, sent several letters and cables to the department, and her daughter, Eileen Markievicz O'Carroll, also sent a letter protesting at the length of time the process was taking to approve her mother's application. The process of application meant that for O'Carroll, and the children who assisted her, the active remembering of her activities was very important (Doctor's certificate and letters in WMS SP34 REF10326). When the pension was finally back paid to cover a hiatus in payment, O'Carroll for the first time was able to buy a small house in Sydney, which secured her family's financial stability.

Throughout her life, O'Carroll attended commemorations of the 1916 Rising at the Waverley Cemetery, and, in 1966, she traveled to Dublin at the invitation of the Irish government to participate in the fiftieth anniversary commemorations (Whitaker 1996, 418). May O'Carroll's family held the memory of her revolutionary activities dear, although it is likely that she did not discuss many of the details of what she had witnessed (see Whitaker 1996). When one of May O'Carroll's daughters, the gifted concert cellist Maureen O'Carroll, died in 2012, the obituary, written by Maureen's own daughter, Leora, noted that, as "a child of two Irish revolutionaries who had fought for Irish freedom," she had refused to play "Rule Britannia" at one concert (*Sydney Morning Herald* [New South Wales], September 25, 2012; O'Carroll 2019). As part of the 2016 centenary, another of May O'Carroll's granddaughters, Cathy Dunn, wrote about O'Carroll in an article for the INA and also attended the centenary commemoration at Waverley Cemetery with her father, O'Carroll's son, Sean (Dunn 2017). For the O'Carroll family, personal memory and public commemoration was an important part of their lives and connections with Ireland.

The small numbers of Irish activist women who settled in Australia made their own peace with their experiences, some joining commemorations over the years and others probably content to settle into their new lives far from Ireland without reminders of their tumultuous pasts. For some Australians without direct family memories of revolutionary women, memorialization has also been important. From the 1960s, some Irish Australians whose forebears had emigrated generations before became interested in the political situation in Ireland, particularly with international coverage of the onset of the Troubles (Malcolm and Hall 2018, 340–343). They then looked into their own family's Irish backgrounds and discovered female relatives who had taken part in the Irish revolution. Australian-born activist, politician, and writer Phil Cleary met his relatives Marie and Nellie Cleary when he visited Dublin for the first time in the 1970s. Both women had been imprisoned during the Civil War and Cleary later researched and wrote of their lives and time in prison, drawing on autograph books, diaries, and other historical records (P. Cleary 2000). His own memories of these women were from when they were elderly, but he added to these memories through his own historical research, filling in the gaps of family knowledge and memory.

In the years leading up to 2016, interest in the women of the revolutionary period grew among the Irish diaspora in Australia. The centenary of the 1916 Rising was commemorated in Australia by a wide range of activities, many of which were sponsored by the program administered by the Irish government through the 1916 commemoration fund (Embassy of Ireland, Australia 2020). As part of these events, the national public broadcaster, Australian Broadcasting Commission, interviewed well-known comedian and satirist John Clarke about his relative Kathleen Fox. Kathleen was an art student in Dublin in 1916 and witnessed Constance Markievicz's surrender and arrest at the College of Surgeons. She then created a remarkable painting of the event, sending it for safekeeping to New York. New Zealand–born Clarke, who had been interested in his Irish family history for some time, had been delighted to find out more about Fox and spoke vividly on a number of public occasions about her life and her connections with the Rising.[9] For Clarke, the family connection with the Rising gave him an avenue to further explore the history of Irish women in the revolutionary period.

By 2016, the public campaigns of Irish women historians and activists, such as @womenof1916, to acknowledge and remember the women of 1916 in the centenary events was widely known among Australians interested in Ireland. One of the first commemorative events of 2016 was the annual BrigidFest lunch held at the Celtic Club in Melbourne. BrigidFest began in 2004 to honor Irish and Irish Australian women, and the annual event attracts a diverse audience of Irish Australians, Irish migrants, and Australians interested in Irish women's history and society. In 2016, BrigidFest hosted Maeve O'Leary as their speaker, and she spoke about her grandmother, Cumann na mBan member Lucy Agnes Smyth. Smyth had been in the GPO with James Connolly and had escaped with other women, completing the hazardous journey along Moore Street to evacuate the wounded.[10] There was a great deal of interest in learning about the history of the women of 1916 on that warm February afternoon in Melbourne. Some of the audience already knew a great deal of the histories of these women; however, many others commented that they did not and were angry that this history had been omitted from what they had learned about the 1916 Rising.

CONCLUSION

By 2016, memories of the women of 1916 and the Irish revolution had moved through several interlinked cycles among the Irish diaspora in Australia. These memorializing cycles operated within the specific Australian diasporic context. The distance between Australia and Ireland led to immigration of far fewer

Irish revolutionary veterans than in countries such as the United States or the United Kingdom. This meant the memorializing of Irish women revolutionaries in Australia was almost completely reliant on media reports and public events held by Irish organizations. Most of the mainstream newspapers in metropolitan and regional centers sourced their international news from news agencies or from larger newspapers in the United Kingdom and the United States. This allowed swift coverage of distant events, but it also meant that the reports of Dublin Rising, and commemorations in 1936 and 1966, were all similar to each other. Just as the international press gave limited coverage to the women activists, so too did the mainstream Australian press. In general, Catholic newspapers were more sympathetic to the aims of the Irish revolutionaries and had more eyewitness reports. They did not, however, have significantly wider or more detailed coverage of the women activists. In the years after the Rising, the Catholic press published obituaries of many of the women activists, often republished from Dublin and UK papers. However, these were often brief. When the biographies of women like Constance Markievicz and Maud Gonne appeared, usually media published reviews, again often sourced from international news outlets.

Diasporic connection with Ireland often starts with individuals' personal memories feeding into communal memorial activities through social and political organizing. In Australia, while some of the few women veterans' memories were shared publicly, more often they were kept fairly private. For these women, the application process for Irish pensions and service medals required codification of memories into lists of dates, of actions, and of names and addresses of those providing verification of service. Living in Australia made this more difficult due to disrupted connections with those still living in Ireland, the distance, and disruptions in postal services.

While some of these women joined Irish Australian organizations, they were always a tiny minority. Most of the membership of Irish diasporic groups in the twentieth century were either born in Australia of Irish parents or had migrated as children. As the twentieth century wore on, personal connections with Ireland faded and the numbers of these organizations dwindled after World War II (McConville 1987, 108–117). It was through these groups that many Irish Australians had received their news of events in Ireland. In the immediate aftermath of the Rising, events organized at Easter through Irish Australian organizations kept up a cycle of memory through annual concerts and commemorative events, though few seem to have mentioned the women of the Rising. The exceptions were those events organized by Cumann na mBan in Melbourne and Sydney, which did occasionally report that their speaker had been a member of Cumann na mBan in Ireland. Cumann na mBan in Australia, though, was relatively short lived, with the Melbourne Cumann collapsing in acrimony in the mid-1920s; the last mention of the Sydney group's activities was in the 1930s.

By the beginning of the twenty-first century, the veterans of the revolutionary period living in Australia had died. Some of their families continued to write and talk about them when the occasion arose, and the centenary commemorations were welcomed by several who spoke and wrote about their family members' experiences. They were joined by more recent arrivals from Ireland who told stories of the activities in Ireland of their own mothers, aunts, and female relatives. Other Irish Australians whose relatives had left Ireland long ago were inspired to research their own family history and found Irish women who had some role in the Rising and the revolution. The emotional connection John Clarke described when he talked of his relative Kathleen Fox was not based on personal or even family memory, but on a reconstructed history that connected him to the stirring events in Irish history (J. Clarke 2017).

The interconnected cycles of individual, familial, and community memory in Australia of the women of the Irish Rising drew in more people as the centenary of 1916 approached. Social media and faster travel means that the distance between Australia and Ireland is no longer such a barrier to sharing information as it was when May O'Carroll, Nora Douglas, and Margaret Fleming arrived to build new lives in the 1920s. Immediate connections with historians and feminists in Ireland agitating for increased recognition of the role of women in revolutionary Ireland meant that more Irish Australians became aware of the histories of these women. This historical memorialization joined with the threads of personal and familial memories to form a more detailed and holistic picture of Irish revolutionary women and their Australian connections.

NOTES

1. See some of the instances: Maud Gonne described as a "stormy petrel" in *Bendigo Independent*, May 23, 1918, 7; and Countess Markievicz as a "stormy petrel" in *Advertiser* (Adelaide), March 3, 1919, 9. See also Hall 2020.

2. This story was repeated almost verbatim in, among many other papers, the *Bendigo Independent* (Victoria), June 16, 1916, 7; *Kalgoolie Western Argus* (Western Australia), June 20, 1916, 4; *Darling Downs Gazette* (Queensland), June 21, 1916, 6, and is also cited in Overlack 1997, 191.

3. Charlotte Despard, *Newcastle Sun* (New South Wales), July 23, 1939, 4; Hanna Sheehy Skeffington, *Advocate*, August 7, 1946, 7; Ada English, *Southern Cross*, June 30, 1944, 9. Lillie Connolly, *Southern Cross*, March 18, 1938, 12.

4. For example, funds raised from a concert in May 1924 were sent to the Prisoners Dependents Relief Fund; see *Labor Daily* (Sydney), May 8, 1924, 3.

5. *Catholic Freeman's Journal* (Sydney), April 25, 1935, 23; *Catholic Press*, April 21, 1938, 17, *Catholic Press*, March 28, 1940, 24.

6. *The Age* (Victoria), May 9, 1933, 8; *Labor Call* (Victoria), April 19, 1934, 6; *The Age*, May 22, 1935, 15; *Advocate*, May 7, 1936, 11; May 6, 1937, 23; May 5, 1937, 27; April 24, 1946, 21.

7. For the Irish National Foresters in Australia, more information is available at https://collections.museumvictoria.com.au/articles/2772, accessed June 5, 2020.

8. Maire McKee, Quambatock, Victoria, to Kathleen Barry Moloney, February 2, 1926, Kathleen Barry Moloney Archive, University College Dublin Archives, P94/67.

9. More information is available at https://www.abc.net.au/radionational /programs/archived/booksandarts/the-arrest-of-countess-markiewicz/7270200, accessed June 5, 2020. Val Noone had spent many hours talking with Clarke about his Irish family before John Clarke's death in April 2017: see "John Clarke, and a Link to the Easter Rising," *Tintean*, April 13, 2017, available at https:// tintean.org.au/2017/04/13/john-clarke-and-his-irish-antecedents/, accessed June 5, 2020.

10. More information available at https://brigidfest.wordpress.com/previous -years/. Maeve O'Leary has published accounts of her grandmother, "Smyth Nursed Connolly and Helped the Wounded under Fire," January 28, 2016, available at https://www.herald.ie/opinion/smyth-nursed-connolly-and-helped -the-wounded-under-fire-34402393.html and https://www.youtube.com/watch ?v=qHvH7l_k94c, accessed June 5, 2020.

DIANNE HALL is Associate Professor of European History at Victoria University, Melbourne. Dianne has an international track record in the histories of gender, violence, memory, and religion in Ireland and the Irish diaspora, especially in Australia. She has previously held research positions at Queen's University Belfast and the University of Melbourne. She is working on a book-length study of gender and war in Ireland, with Elizabeth Malcolm, with whom she recently published *A New History of the Irish in Australia*. Her current research interests are in the long histories of children and war in Ireland, Scotland, England, and Australia. Dianne is one of the editors of the *Australasian Journal of Irish Studies*.

FIVE

—ɯ—

"SICK ON THE IRISH SEA, DANCING ACROSS THE ATLANTIC"

(Anti)-nostalgia in Women's Diasporic
Remembrance of the Irish Revolution

SÍOBHRA AIKEN

IN 1936, BESSIE CAHILL WAS tasked with supplying the Department of Defence with names and addresses for all Cumann na mBan veterans associated with the Ballymacelligott District Council in North Kerry. However, it was nearly impossible to locate such data for the Keel Branch, "as the majority of them have imigrated [*sic*] and the others have changed their addresses" (July 7, 1936, Cumann na mBan Nominal Roles [hereafter CMB]/116). This external and internal migration affected all Cumann na mBan branches to varying extents: in Newtownmanor, County Sligo, the appointed verification officer lamented that "a number of them are married and gone away that I don't know their present address" (CMB/49), while, in South Down, only six of the twenty-strong membership of the Warrenpoint Branch could be named or located (CMB/60). Levels of emigration prove startling in some rural coastal areas. In Dungloe, County Donegal, Ventry, County Kerry, and Beara, County Cork, between 60 percent and 70 percent of Cumann na mBan members had emigrated by the mid-1930s (see Aiken 2020b).

The substantial displacement of people following the Irish revolution (1916–1923), particularly of women, has little place in the hegemonic state-sanctioned commemorative history of the period. This is perhaps best understood as evidence of the "active forgetting," to use Aleida Assmann's terms (2008, 98), of certain aspects of the past that were at odds with the state-building project of the fledgling Free State. Rather, the highly competitive revolutionary commemorative culture of the 1920s and 1930s was dominated by "heady stories of heroism, honour and brotherhood" that circumvented the more controversial, divisive, and violent aspects of the War of Independence (1919–1921) and Civil

War (1922–1923) (Flanagan 2015, 7, 22). Typical of such post-conflict nationalist remembrance, the actual experiences of women were converted into symbolic, romantically conceived significance; women's militant activism was submerged by the weeping widow "Mother Ireland" trope or occluded by the allegorical figure of the patriotic, yet always ancillary, Róisín Dubh (see Gillis 1998, 10; Young 2009, 1779).

Yet, paradoxically, the documentation of the absence of these emigrant women in the 165 Cumann na mBan Nominal Rolls, which were released online in 2014, serves as an aide-mémoire to their existence. As Guy Beiner outlines, for all its power, "official commemoration was not able to totally wipe out the deviant narratives of remembrance," which Michel Foucault designated as "counter-memories" (Beiner 2007, 305). Since the beginning of the decade of centenaries, various scholarly and public endeavors have successfully reinscribed many previously elided women's voices into the narrative(s) of the revolution. The phenomenon of displacement and emigration among female activists, however, demands more sustained critical attention.

On a local level, large-scale emigration poses a problem for social remembrance as it disrupts "the social frameworks" that Maurice Halbwachs outlines as essential for supporting collective memory (1992, 38–40). Who remembered Cumann na mBan in Allihies on the Beara Peninsula after nearly all its membership had relocated to America and Canada? How does a community remember when it no longer exists in the geographic place of origin? Drawing on an array of disparate narratives—including letters, memoirs, and fictional self-representation—this chapter aims to recuperate a number of the "counter-memories" of female revolutionary émigrées in order to consider the mechanisms and spaces available to women for coming to terms with the past within diasporic communities. Furthermore, it explores how these memories of revolution can oscillate between nostalgic and anti-nostalgic remembrance and how nonconventional forms of memory, such as Kathleen Hoagland's autobiographical novel *Fiddler in the Sky* (1944), can offer more complex readings of women's diasporic remembrance than first-person testimony.

Exile has historically functioned as "the nursery of nationalism" (Lord Acton, cited in Brundage 2016, 9), yet emigration also problematizes nationalist beliefs in its severing of one's patriotic ties to the nation. While the significant decline of the southern Protestant population has sparked much historical debate (see Hart 1998; Bielenberg 2013; Fitzpatrick 2013a), historians have been slower to document the post–Civil War emigration of IRA veterans (see Hanley 2009; G. Foster 2012, 2015; Wilk 2014). Recent studies on the flight of de Valera's "Wild Geese" have largely glossed over the emigration of female republicans, thus emulating the long-established narrative of exile that centers on involuntary, generally male, exiles whose emigration is attributed to the wrath of the British colonial system (see Miller 1988). This forced exile narrative belies the reality that between 1871 and 1971 the majority of emigrants who left Ireland were young single women, a demographic trend that went against the grain of general European emigration patterns (Travers 1995, 148). The striking scholarly neglect of these women's experiences continues to be addressed (Diner 1983; Nolan 1989; Ryan 2001b; Whelan 2015; Trew 2016; Redmond 2019), but questions remain regarding how this masculine trope of exile complicates the memory making of female activists.

The prevention of emigration was one of the key aims of the broader nationalist movement. The First Dáil, established in January 1919, issued a decree banning emigration without written sanction (*Dáil Éireann* 1920) and the Irish Volunteers later denounced emigration "as desertion in the face of the enemy" (cited in MacCarthy 1953). From the early twentieth century, cultural nationalist movements shared an anti-emigration agenda. Patrick Pearse claimed that it was the obligation of all Gaelic Leaguers—a movement from which a great many of Ireland's future revolutionaries were to emerge—to protest against the "emigration terror" (1903, 3). This discourse was highly gendered, and women feature heavily in the widespread anti-emigration diatribes of the period. Popular anti-emigration short stories typically focused on the treachery and selfishness of rural female emigrants as well as the moral, spiritual, and physical decline awaiting them in the seedy underworld of the diasporic city (see Aiken 2018, 97–99). Within this context, it is perhaps unsurprising that the assistance of Cumann na mBan was considered "imperative" in stemming the tide of emigration (Letter from Séamus Fitzpatrick 1920, cited in Furlong 2009, 82). Indeed, potential emigrants were directly targeted by the IRA; some were "relieved of their passports" (Daly 1953, 38), while others were ordered to be "removed from cars and trains" (Fitzgerald 1954, 6).

Such drastic measures were perhaps thought to be temporary. Seán O'Faoláin remembered in 1953 that many had hoped "that once we got a native government we would soon put a stop to all that" (1953, 140). In contrast, the establishment of the Free State coincided with a renewal of emigration to the extent that the IRA imposed a blanket ban on emigration, with the chief of staff of the IRA Frank Aiken writing that the "emigrant who could earn a livelihood at home and yet leaves is a deserter" (University College Dublin Archives [hereafter UCDA] p104/2561, n.d.). However, the economic reality soon vanquished this political rhetoric. Writing to the chief of staff during her Australian tour, activist and revolutionary Helena Molony emphasized the helplessness of the situation and the necessity of incorporating these "deserters" into the republican movement: "Frank, there are a lot of our men here who emigrated and people have asked me how they should be treated. I've explained that of course they deserted my country but that as the conditions were terrible it was only weakness—though bad weakness—and that now they're here they ought to be encouraged to work here. If they're turned down they'll be lost forever and lots of them are very keen to work" (November 9, 1924, UCDA p69/37 [112]). The IRA thus jettisoned their anti-emigration policy in July 1925 on the condition that IRA members who emigrated put themselves on the Foreign Reserve List to be available for duty abroad (G. Foster 2012, 213). At least two women were included on this list to provide intelligence, namely Celia McDonald and Emily McMahon, who were associated with the North Mayo Brigade and supposedly employed as nurses in London (Letter from Adjutant General to Adjutant North Mayo Brigade, August 4, 1923, UCDA p69/167 [10]). The splintered and numerically weakened post–Civil War Cumann na mBan continued to protest against widespread emigration and tended to lay the blame at the foot of the Free State government, thus perpetuating the long-established "involuntary exile" trope. Writing in the republican weekly *An Phoblacht*, the president of Cumann na mBan Eithne Ní Chumhaill (Coyle) lamented that "tá fir agus mná, buachaillí agus cailíní, ag éalughadh as Éirinn gach lá do nochtann an ghrian a geob os cionn uisce na mara" (Men and women, boys and girls, are escaping out of Ireland every single day that the sun rises over the sea) ("Cúis na Saoirse" *An Phoblacht*, January 10, 1931).

Despite such public anti-emigration pleas, private correspondence and memoirs demonstrate a deeper understanding of the complex motivations for emigration. Many republican women found themselves in dire straits in the aftermath of the conflict and suffered for their political stances, regardless of which position they took on the question of the Anglo-Irish Treaty (see McAuliffe 2018a). Anti-Treaty women were particularly targeted. The six female Teachtaí Dála (members of the government ministry) who rejected the treaty were scapegoated for the slide to Civil War, and over 681 anti-Treaty women were interned between 1922 and 1924 (C. McCarthy 2014, 227; Matthews 2010, 257; McCoole 2015, 244–265). Even after the conflict, republican women were denounced from church podiums and found themselves in precarious economic positions. Despite her condemnation of emigration, Eithne Coyle understood the realities; she recalled that after her release from prison, "I had none [a job]. Nor could I find any" (cited in Mac Eoin 1980, 158).

Máire Comerford, one of the most prominent Cumann na mBan activists, was less sympathetic to emigrants. In a letter to fellow journalist and activist Molly Flannery, she bemoaned that Ireland was "a nation of people that all want white-collar jobs; it [emigration] is the penalty of too much intelligence wrongly directed" (Molly Flannery Woods Papers). However, Comerford's letter may reflect the sacrifices she made to stay in Ireland. She famously ran her own poultry farm in an effort to eke out a living:

> I was one of the few who managed to stay in Ireland when thousands left. The Republicans were in abject distress and poverty. I had left Dublin and was living on a hill in Wexford. I didn't have any money, but I had credit in the shops because I had belonged to people who were able to run bills in shops. The shopkeepers wouldn't believe I had no money. It was very useful to me because only for that I wouldn't have survived. I had less and less contact with anybody else because every Republican had a very long period of being boycotted. You couldn't get any employment associated with the state at all without signing an oath of allegiance, and we wouldn't sign that. (cited in Griffith 1998, 314)

But Comerford was actually one of the many republicans to flee to the United States after her release from Cork jail in early 1924. The republican movement arguably used the preponderance of single female emigrants as a veil to conceal their activities, and women often delivered messages across the Atlantic: Mimi Plunkett traveled alone from Liverpool to New York in March 1916 with a coded message for John Devoy, while Min Ryan made the same unaccompanied journey a number of months later ("UK Incoming Passenger Lists"; "New York, Passenger and Crew Lists"). Anti-Treaty Cumann na mBan activist Kitty O'Doherty similarly couriered $50,000 in a body belt from her adopted home in Philadelphia to Eamon de Valera in the summer of 1922 (O'Doherty 1999, 61). While publicly condemning emigration, IRA chief of staff Frank Aiken sardonically wrote to Comerford in January 1924 asking, "Have you got a Ford over there? I suppose you have and that it is your closest friend?" (January 9, 1924, UCDA p69/37 [124]).

Comerford's own recollections reject any romanticization of emigration. Years later, when composing her memoir, 'The Dangerous Ground'—which she contends went on paper not "hot from memory" but *well churned and tested*"—Comerford presents her exile as embodying the final tragedy of the Civil War ("Draft introduction to a book entitled The Dangerous Ground" 1956, UCDA LA18/1; emphasis in original). In fact, her memoir ends with a poignant reflection on her arrival in New York and the fractured sense of self engendered by her displacement and falsified identity:

> Bhí am uafásach agam ag iarraidh gabháil i dtír ón Aquitania. Bhí an turas dona go leor mar le hainm bréige is le pas bréige bhíos an-leasc meascadh le daoine. Ní mór dom a rá fúm féin gur lú go mór mo chuid imní faoina raibh

i ndán dom as a bheith ag tréigean na hÉireann agus mo chuid comrádaithe
ar an stailc ocrais ba mhó riamh. . . . Bhí an Conradh ina bhrat trom fliuch
anuas ar thine dhearg ár ndíograise. An tír deighilte; rí Shasana ina rí orainn;
ár gcalafoirt ina seilbh acusan; ár bpoblacht thaibhseach ina spreas; áilleacht
ár n-aislinge smeartha; feall ar iontaoibh na marbh agus mise, anois thar na
bóchna i Meiriceá ar thóir cabhrach. (M. Comerford 1990, 10)

I had a terrible time trying to disembark from the Aquitania. The journey was
fairly awful as with my false name and false passport, I was very reluctant to
mingle with other people. I must say that my own worries about what was
in store for me for abandoning Ireland were diminished in the knowledge
that my comrades were on the largest hunger strike ever. . . . The Treaty
was a heavy wet cloak which extinguished the red flames of our ardour.
The country divided; the King of England ruling over us; our ports in their
possession; our honourable Republic reduced to nothingness; the beauty of
our dream smutted; the trust of the dead betrayed; and I, across the sea in
America, searching for help. (my translation)

This concluding section is missing from the extant unpublished English-
language version of Comerford's memoir held in the University College Dublin Archives, but her memoir was translated into Irish by an unnamed trans-
lator under the title *Lasamar Ár dTinte* (*We Lit Our Fires*) and serialized in
the Cork-based monthly *Agus* between 1981 and 1990. Like many republican
women, Comerford chronicled her experiences with a sense "that their experiences were worth remembering" (Paséta 2013, 1). However, the fact that Comerford's memoir was never published in English and that the Irish version has
been omitted, to date, from any historical study is a reminder of the cultural,
historical, and even linguistic conditions governing silence and remembrance.
Furthermore, it highlights what Assmann refers to as the distinction between
"actively circulated memory," which keeps the past present "as the canon,"
and the "passively stored memory," which preserves the past "as the archive"
(2008, 98). While there are a number of autobiographies by male IRA veterans
that detail their experiences of emigration (S. O'Connor 1970; Lennon 1971;
J. Comerford 1980; Murphy 1998; Flannery 2001)—including J. F. O'Connor's
appropriately titled *An Irish Civil War Exile* (1989)—there are far fewer published autobiographies by women, thus restricting their stories to the "passively
stored memory" archives.

Memories of female emigrants, therefore, must be excavated from "the
archive" and are frequently no more than fragmentary traces. The online availability of the Cumann na mBan Nominal Rolls and the Military Service Pension
Files allow for invaluable insights into the stories of many emigrants, who, unlike

Comerford, may never have returned to Ireland nor produced memoirs. That said, the 165 nominal rolls do not reflect the true extent of emigration. Despite instructions from the Department of Defence to supply addresses for all members, in many cases locations are simply not provided. When they are, female emigrants' names are frequently followed by fleeting scrawls—"America," "gone away," "somewhere in America," or "in foreign lands"—suggesting the perceived finality of such emigration. Nevertheless, the nominal rolls do provide the names of over two thousand women who emigrated to the United States, England, Canada, Australia, New Zealand, and even to China, thus opening the possibilities for further research (see Aiken 2020b).

This emigration resulted from various, often complex, personal situations and was frequently driven by hopes for a better life abroad. In his account of a trip around Ireland in the immediate aftermath of the Civil War, *The Road Round Ireland* (1926), Pádraic Colum recounts his visit to the Moynihan family in the midland town of Aughnalee. The Moynihan brothers had been active in the IRA. However, Colum is particularly fascinated by the daughter of the house, Brighid, who seems more connected to America than to her homeland:

> Brighid was a capable girl who regarded things gravely. She was going to America in a while. I asked her if she was sorry to leave home, and she said no. Her brothers and sisters were there; she was going amongst her own—"New York is full of Aughnalee people." The newspapers on the settle were American, and the photographs in the room above had come from America also.... She had no need to leave the country, for she could get a dowry that would make her a good match; still she had no wish to settle here. (Colum 1926, 26–27)

"Aughnalee" is undoubtedly a fictional place-name. But intriguingly, "Aughnalee" is also the setting for Colum's 1905 play *The Land*, which sets up emigration as an alternative for women to life in "a farmer's house" (1905, 46). The protagonist, Ellen Douras, is dismissive of the folly with which the local girls speak about visiting fine American theaters, but reveals her true attitude when she discovers her own prospect of emigrating: "I can see what I longed to see. I have a chance of knowing what is in me.... No one ever brought me such news before" (1905, 31). While the play could have been understood by theater-goers as representative of the anti-emigration agenda, Colum later clarified, after his own emigration to the United States, that his intention was indeed to illustrate that emigration was not solely driven by economic necessity but rather motivated by "the lack of life and the lack of freedom" in Ireland (1916, vii). The similarities between Brighid and Ellen's motivations to emigrate two decades apart point to how post-independence emigration built on generations of chain migration and was often tied to women's personal aspirations.

Just how, then, did the events of the revolutionary period affect emigration? United States immigration records show that Matilda Dudley, then captain of the Garnish Branch Cumann na mBan, County Cork, made her way to Fall River, Massachusetts, at the height of the Civil War in December 1922, accompanied by her sister Maggie ("New York, Passenger and Crew Lists"). But how can we ascertain if her emigration was a result of the political split or tied to economic, familial, or personal ambition? The conspicuous absence of the Irish revolution in Gaeltacht autobiographies points, perhaps, to the fact that, as illustrated by Séamus Ó Grianna in his novel *Tarngaireacht Mhiseóige*, coastal communities had more pressing concerns than the color of the soldiers' uniforms (Ó Grianna 1959, 64). In October 1922, a small fishing boat carrying thirty intending emigrants from Dingle landed in Cobh after being at sea for five days in a desperate attempt to get around rail and road disruptions (Doyle 2008, 207). A report from the *Cork Examiner* titled "Kerry Emigrants: A Trying Journey to Cobh" notes that their plight was "pitiable in the extreme" but also suggests that the passengers were "nearly all women" (*Cork Examiner*, October 23, 1922, 5).

Nevertheless, a number of sources suggest that women's political activism many have informed, or at least hastened, emigration. Female republicans were even threatened with emigration, as occurred in Sligo during the War of Independence when members of Cumann na mBan "were taken out during the night and ordered to be shot or to leave the country" (Sara Bomar to Secretary of the Pensions Board, November 1939, CMB/47). Applications for Military Service Pensions further illustrate how politics was often combined with social and economic factors. Margaret Leonard (née Fleming), after being arrested in Liverpool and interned in Mountjoy Jail, emigrated to New South Wales in 1924 where she had a brother who was a priest (Whitaker 2016b, 183). She euphemistically claims that her own political activity and her husband's IRA membership "compelled" them "for obvious reasons to leave" (Letters to Secretary of the Minister of Defence, December 1, 1934, MSP34E8493). Mary Agnes Davin, who lost her sight in one eye in an attack by the Black and Tans, refers to "personal reasons" and pressure from her family to emigrate to New York (Sworn Statement made before Advisory Committee by Agnes Mary Davin on the June 26, 1936, no. 16824. MSP34REF16824), while Katty Hicks (née O'Driscoll) "had to borrow her fare to America," owing to her impoverished state subsequent to years of keeping an "open purse" for the IRA (Letter from Seán Ó Driscoll to the Department of Defence, April 21, 1936. MSP34REF16920). Equally, Mary

Lytle claims that it was a combination of political and economic factors that led her to relocate to Manhattan with her children via Canada in 1926: "I was a widow with two other children to educate and support and in our part of the country it was considered dangerous to be seen working for me even if I paid good wages. We never recovered from the financial loss and in the end were forced to sell out and try to make a new home here" (Letter from Mary Lytle to the Department of Defence, August 30, 1934, MSP34REF58239).

Yet, in the same way that the Famine is rarely presented as the cause for emigration in nineteenth-century Irish–North American fiction (Janssen 2018), it may have been easier to rewrite memories of emigration into the greater nationalist narrative of exile than to admit economic penury, especially when applying for a military pension. Public obituaries also emphasize politically motivated emigration, such as that of Cumann na mBan's Nora Brosnan McKenna, who died in Queens, New York, in 1996, and whose family's wholesale emigration is ascribed to "their Republican beliefs" (Lenehan Nastri 2016). However, another account prepared by the McKenna family, in 2000, details the practical reasons for Brosnan's emigration from her native Castlegregory, County Kerry: "Her family was very poor, and the forge had nearly closed down. All of the young people had begun to entertain thoughts of leaving Ireland for America" ("The Nora McKenna Story," Kilmainham Gaol Collection, 20MS-1D46-27).

Despite the emergence of new archival material, scholars of women in the diaspora point to the various challenges of accessing the stories of female activists. Anne-Maree Whitaker recently stated that "finding information about the later lives in Australia of Easter Rising veterans can still be problematic" (2016, 182). Íde B. O'Carroll pointed to similar challenges when gathering interviews for her oral history *Models for Movers*: "I searched high and low for women who had emigrated to America after being active in the Easter Rising of 1916, the Irish revolution. . . . I was convinced that some of these revolutionaries must have emigrated to America. I had almost given up hope of finding someone with this history when Mike McCormack wrote a piece on Dubliner, Bridie Halpin, for the *Irish Echo* newspaper on 2 April 1988" (1990, 42). McCormack's article, "Aunt Bridie—A Woman of Ireland," was written just a few months after Halpin's death in December 1987. After sorting through her personal papers in her New York apartment, Halpin's nephew discovered she had been interned in Kilmainham (McCormack 2015). A booklet she stitched together when imprisoned reveals the idealism of her youth, with one excerpt reading, "Never fear for Ireland, for she has soldiers still. Up Us!" (O'Carroll 1990, 42). While Halpin corresponded privately with Maud Gonne and received Christmas cards from

Eamon de Valera, she never told her family about her past (N. O'Sullivan 2007, 167). Sinéad McCoole opens her book *No Ordinary Women* with Halpin's story, which seems to epitomize the silence of revolutionary women (2003, 13).

It proves difficult to trace the later lives of the emigrant women named in the nominal rolls, which is further complicated by the fact that most women changed their names when they married. Miss Peg Daly, "the principal Cumann na mBan girl in Kildare town" (Dunne 1957, 17), emigrated to Los Angeles in 1926 after being imprisoned during the Civil War (Matthews 2010, 263)—as did many ailing veterans seeking recuperation in a warmer climate (Wilk 2014). A 1930 census return places her on South La Fayette Park Place as a domestic servant and lists Peg's language as Gaelic ("Los Angeles, California, 1930, Census Return"). For want of sources, this small assertion of national identity from a Kildare, and mostly likely English-speaking, native is possibly the only available archival trace that *might* hint at Peg's revolutionary background.

The culture of shame surrounding emigration, exasperated by nationalist anti-emigration rhetoric, may also have engendered such long-standing silences. Writing to Sinn Féin Teachta Dála Mary MacSwiney from Coffeyville, Kansas, a Mrs. Ellie Ferrick attempted to justify her emigration, thus illustrating how women's self-representations were mediated through such perceptions of shame: "What on earth will I do with [Daisy?]. I am really worried about her you know Mary McSwiney, we would never leave our own beloved Ireland if there was any future there for them, she is making it very hard for us and almost insists on going home" (UCDA [ca. 1926] p482/123 [2]). Ferrick's reference to Daisy's insistence on returning to Ireland seems to tactfully counterbalance any accusation of a lack of patriotism.

Cork Cumann na mBan activist Annie Crowley Ford's poignant autobiographical account—self-published by her son Daniel Ford under the title *When I Am Going: Growing Up in Ireland and Coming to America, 1901–1927* (2014)—also hints at the shame of emigration. Crowley recalls her friend Tom Barry's somewhat judgmental comment to her, as she boarded the tender in Queenstown, that he "would rather live on one meal a day in Ireland than three in the United States" (Crowley Ford 2014, 870). Crowley displays similar anti-emigration sentiments and claims that she loathed the idea of going to America after her fiancé Pat Ford: "It was the last place I wanted to go, so I broke off our engagement and told him to take back his ring" (2014, 842). However, Crowley's attachment to her homeplace broke after her brother, Billy, took his own life. She set sail for Boston in 1927 to join Pat, as she "foolishly thought if I went far away from home I would forget, but no matter how many miles you go, you always take your grief with you" (2014, 852). In a conclusion to her memoir, written shortly before her death in 1968, after a troublesome marriage and a rather itinerant life in Massachusetts, New Hampshire, and Arizona, she laments the instability of life in the United States. During the Civil War, Crowley writes that "we didn't have a moment's peace. They were always raiding us, any time of night or day they would sneak up to the house" (2014, 803). However, life in the United States proved more restless still: "There was always a sense of security in our life at Kilnahone [County Cork]. We never had to worry about moving. The place was our own, and in all my years in the United States I never felt that sense of security, on rainy nights the feeling of warmth with the rain pelting against the windows and the rain dripping against the house and the rustle of the leaves in the ash trees" (2014, 919).

Despite such sorrow and even regret, a number of women remained highly active in the republican movement among the diaspora and, given the slow retreat of women from the political sphere in post-independence Ireland, may have even gained greater visibility outside of Ireland. Nellie Hoyne Murray was hospitalized after being on hunger strike during the Civil War (Connolly O'Brien 1981, 55). She later served as secretary of the Los Angeles Council of the AARIR (American Association for the Recognition of the Irish Republic) and as an officer on the Peter Murray Council for twenty five years ("Mrs. Nellie H. Murray [obituary]," *Los Angeles Times*, May 1, 1955, 74). Her colleague Máire McKee, with whom she established the underground republican newspaper *The War Bulletin* (O'Mullane 1951, 12), emigrated to Australia, where she made headlines as "A Staunch Worker for Ireland's Cause" and was celebrated by the leaders of Melbourne's Irish community on her eventual return to Ireland ("Miss Máire McKee Farewelled," *The Advocate* [Melbourne] April 1, 1926, 17). The annual Pearl Flannery Humanities Award is awarded by the New York organization Cumann na Saoirse in honour of Cumann na mBan member Pearl Flannery (née Egan). Flannery was well-regarded—not only due to her husband's notoriety for gun-running and as a founder of Irish Northern Aid— but also on account of her active participation in the greater New York Irish community. Despite the anti-emigration mandate of the national organization, in 1926 the local "B" Company of the IRA in Mullinahone held an "American Wake" of sorts for Pearl's mother, Mrs. Egan, on her emigration "in appreciation of the services rendered by herself and family in the cause of Ireland's freedom" ("Left for America—Mullinavat and District Notes," *The Kilkenny People*, January 30, 1926, 6). Over the years of her residency in the United States, Pearl was further recognized at numerous events in her adopted home, such as at a dance held in her honor by the New York County Tipperary National and Benevolent Association (*The Irish People* [The New York] February 23, 1985, 12).

Whereas Flannery and her husband's political beliefs were celebrated in Irish America, this social role would have been comparatively diminished had she remained in her native Tipperary.

Furthermore, for a number of these women, rather than being repressed, memories of Cumann na mBan activism were recalled in order to scaffold later life events. Bridget Dirrane, born in 1894 on Inis Mór in the Aran Islands, emigrated to Boston in 1927. Complicating the forced-exile narrative, Dirrane remembers her excitement at joining the many revolutionaries and neighbors from the islands who had made for the New World before her: "The whole business of emigration from Aran and Ireland was not that traumatic an experience for me. I didn't mind leaving the native sod at all because quite a number of the volunteers from the troubled times had been deported or had emigrated and General Mulcahy (God rest his soul) helped me in every way, by giving me a lovely testimonial and vouching for me. I also wanted to continue my nursing care abroad, and besides, there were so many Aran people in Boston including my future husband, Ned Dirrane" (Dirrane 1997, 46). Echoing the case of Pearl Flannery, Dirrane's memoir, *Woman of Aran*, indicates the social status afforded to women in the diaspora who were known for their political activism at home. Having been outside of Mountjoy on the day that Kevin Barry was executed, Brigid recollects how she relived these memories: "It was a dreadful time but years after, as I passed by Irish taverns in Boston or sat with Irish people at a sing-song or concert and heard Kevin Barry sung, I was proud to have been there that day" (ibid., 42). While Dirrane is frank in her acknowledgment of the violence of the revolution, her somewhat sentimental recollection of Barry's death points to the possibly heightened influence of nostalgia on diasporic communities, which Andreas Huyssen attributes to their "tenuous and often threatened status within the majority culture" (2003, 149). While nostalgia is often seen as escapist or regressive, Oona Frawley writes that nostalgia functions as "a safety mechanism designed to bridge past and present for cultures as they experience change" (2005, 3). Indeed, Dirrane fuses her memories of her Cumann na mBan days to her later service as a nurse during World War II, thus demonstrating how emigrant memories are reconfigured through transcultural contact: "I found myself working for the Military Airforce and was sent on a mission to take care of American soldiers down in Mississippi near the Gulf of Mexico. . . . It was my duty to care for and prescribe medication for the sick. Believe it or not I drilled the same as I did many years before with Cumann na mBan" (Dirrane 1997, 61). Autobiographical memory can also be integral to the construction of self-identity, particularly in a diasporic context, as memory, rather than place, becomes key to identity formation. Sister Joseph Teresa

O'Sullivan was purportedly imprisoned in Kilmainham during the Civil War and subsequently became a nun in Kenya. Her zeal and commitment to "changing the system" was associated with her revolutionary background. As Sister Columbiere Kelly recounted: "It was one of the great blessings of my work to work with her. She was ex Cumann na mBan and she wasn't afraid of anything. She was a pioneer feminist. When she arrived here, girls weren't educated. The parents kept them at home. But Sister Teresa ran after them and brought them to school. She was a great mathematician and was very tough in insisting that all that mattered was girls' education. She was marvellous" (cited in Coogan 2015, 543).

However, a number of accounts demonstrate that while women's public memories are often mediated through the nostalgic longing for the heroism of the revolution, private forms of remembrance can be at odds with such nostalgia. In an overt display of her nationalism, May Gahan O'Carroll named her children who grew up in Bexley North, Sydney, after Irish republican figures, including Countess Markievicz, Eamon de Valera, Robert Emmet, Peadar Clancy, Liam Mellows, and Seán Heuston ("There Is Harmony in This Home," *Australian Women's Weekly*, January 1954, 11). She was front and center at the twentieth anniversary of the Rising in Sydney and "carried on her arm an old tattered uniform of dark green, as worn by the Cumann-na-mBan (League of Women) during the Easter-week rebellion" ("Irish Memorial," *Sydney Morning Herald*, April 13, 1936, 2). In 1941, O'Carroll's speech about her continued hopes for Irish independence in the context of World War II was printed in *The Catholic Freeman's Journal*: "We are with our motherland in any action she takes in this war, neutral or belligerent, and we who pass on leave our children after us to pick up the sword and carry on where we left off until Éire is free from north to south and east to west, as the late Seán MacDermott told us in 1916, there can be no peace till freedom" ("Easter Week Recalled at Waverley," *Catholic Freeman's Journal* [Sydney] April 17, 1941, 23).

Despite O'Carroll's public glorification of the revolution, her application for a Military Service Pension demonstrates just how memories are conditioned by the expectations of the intended audience. O'Carroll was imprisoned after the Easter Rising for her role as a "basket girl" and later participated in a number of hunger strikes during the Civil War (File on May Gahan O'Carroll, Kilmainham Gaol Collection 20MS-1B53-10). She was one of a number of women who assert that they emigrated to Australia on the advice of their doctors in order to treat neurasthenia, or what would now be termed post-traumatic stress disorder. This was not uncommon in the aftermath of the revolution, and the IRA made exceptions for veterans to emigrate to warmer climates on medical grounds (Wilk 2014, 27). However, in line with the highly gendered medical understandings of the time, women were not only more likely to be diagnosed with nervous conditions—which were routinely connected to gynecological health—but women's treatment was also more focused on rest and isolation than men's, which often centered on social reintegration (see Aiken 2020a).

When filing her pension application, O'Carroll was "extremely aggravated by the Irish Government's apparent indifference" to her activism and subsequent ill health (Letter from W. G. H. Cable to the Department of Defence, MSP34REF10326). She was further vexed that she only received an E grade (a D grade was the maximum awarded to women) and that her annual pension would not even cover the costs incurred by her recourse to the Dublin-based solicitor, Mr. Dixon, to process her application. The upset caused by the application process led to Mrs. O'Carroll undergoing medical treatment for at least five weeks, according to her daughter Eileen Markievicz (Letter from Eileen Markievicz O'Carroll to Mr. Dixon, August 21, 1935, MSP34REF10326). A newspaper interview with the O'Carroll family in the *Australian Women's Weekly* in 1954 sums up the disjunction between Mrs. O'Carroll's public national pride and her personal distress at being exiled from, and let down by, the country to which she dedicated her youth: "'I was a rebel in those wild, wonderful, exciting days, and I nursed many fighting Irishmen who fell foul of a bullet,' she said, her eyes moistening with tears. . . . 'But Australia is my country now,'" ("There Is Harmony in This Home," *Australian Women's Weekly*, January 1954, 11). O'Carroll's interview frustrates the idea that nostalgia for a romanticized past could function as a supportive bridge into the future by signaling a clear break from that past and asserting her new national loyalties. O'Carroll's fellow Australian émigré Margaret Fleming also complicates the anticipated nostalgic yearnings often associated with the diaspora. In her initial letter to the minister of defense, Fleming wrote that, "like many previous exiles who came out here, we found a haven" (Letter to Secretary of the Minister of Defence, December 1, 1934, MSP34E8493). As her application was delayed, however, her narrative began to increasingly comply with the established victim exile narrative: "I regret to say that we did not find this Sunny Land much good except for Sydney [*sic*] climate" (January 23, 1939, MSP34E8493). In a later letter, she even wrote that she would return to Ireland for good if a position could be found for her (December 17, 1939, MSP34E8493).

The only full-length published autobiography of a Cumann na mBan emigrant is Bridget Dirrane's memoir, which was dictated to and compiled by Rose O'Connor and Jack Mahon, employees at St. Francis Community Nursing Unit in Galway, when Dirrane was already 103 years old. The various unseen hands involved in producing Dirrane's autobiography complicate the legitimacy of a literary contact between the author and reader, which Philippe Lejeune referred to as "le pacte autobiographique" (1975). Given the complex circumstances in which such "autobiographical" texts are produced, there has been a turn within the field of memory studies to consider non-conventional genres or subgenres of life writing "as routes into cultural memory" (Saunders 2008, 332). To date, there has been little scrutiny of such non-conventional life writing, including fictional self-representation, in studies of the revolutionary period, despite Tom Dunne's contention that "if all history is a form of fiction, so too, all literary fictions are a form of history, and constitute indispensable historical evidence" (Dunne 1987, 3).

The virtually overlooked novel by Kathleen Hoagland, *Fiddler in the Sky*, published by Harper and Brothers in the United States in 1944, offers a far more complex treatment of female emigration during the revolutionary period. While Hoagland's edited poetry volume, *1000 Years of Irish Poetry* (1947), has been widely reprinted, the novel has received no scholarly attention. But Hoagland's novel very much supports Aidan Arrowsmith's contention that in the context of the Irish diaspora, "life writing is not more real than fiction and, indeed, that confused, second-generation experience is often evoked far more successfully via fiction's heteroglossic quality than by the more monological mode of much life writing" (2012, 17). Although Hoagland did live through the period in question, and as such is not strictly "second generation," the novel incorporates elements of what Marianne Hirsch calls "postmemory," in that the omniscient narrator has access to inherited or secondhand memories and thus "bears witness" on behalf of the family as a whole (2012, 4–5).

The novel traces the impact of the Easter Rising and revolutionary period on the young Pegeen Brendan in a small community in the west of Ireland and documents the political and economic implications of the revolution on the Brendan family, ultimately resulting in Elizabeth Brendan fleeing with her five children to the United States "in continual fear that politics or the Brendans [her in-laws] might reach out to hinder their departure" (285). The novel also addresses a number of social taboos scholars struggle to locate in curated state archives: sexual violence is hinted at through the women's best efforts to organize entertainments for the British soldiers "to keep them out of harm and away from the servant girls" (62); Pegeen's mother is treated for postnatal depression; and domestic violence, cloaked behind alcoholism, threatens throughout the novel. Moreover, the novel illustrates how emigration arises from the intersection of family politics, bankruptcy, alcoholism, and domestic violence exacerbated by the turmoil of World War I and the Irish revolution.

The minute details and use of historical dates in Hoagland's novel frustrated contemporary reviewers who questioned the distinction between fact and fiction: "Although the book is presented as fiction, it is undoubtedly historical in setting, and it is hard to believe that Mrs. Hoagland's characters are entirely creations of her imagination. It is easier to assume that the book must be at least partly autobiographical, for, like Pegeen, the heroine of the story, the author was born in Ireland and came to America with her family while in her 'teens'" (Walker 1944, 17). Another reviewer, in *The Cincinnati Enquirer*—which refers to it as a "remarkable first novel"—equally observes that "there is some parallel between the author's life and that of her protagonist, Pegeen Brandon [*sic*]. Pegeen grew up in Ireland of the transition period between revolutions, the years of World War I and the early twenties. In her teens she came to America, as did Miss Hoagland, escaping the convulsive birth pangs of Éire" (Lindsey 1944, 5).

Kathleen Hoagland—then Kitty Dooher—hailed from Ballina and, like the protagonist, fled from Ireland during the War of Independence with her mother and four siblings. In the novel, the father, hotelier James Brendan, brings forward a legal objection on March 31, 1920, to his wife's intended emigration, which results in a number of stressful weeks for the family before they finally board a ship in Queenstown on a Friday morning under the cover of darkness. Immigration records of the Dooher family suggest that the fictional scenario directly matches their own experiences: Mary E. Dooher emigrated from Queenstown on the Kaiserin Auguste Victoria on Friday, May 28, 1920, with her own five children, Kitty, John, Evelyn, Murdock, and Gerald ("UK Outward Passenger Lists").

In an interview in the New Jersey newspaper *The Record*, Hoagland further elaborates on the connections between the novel and her own experiences and details the family's struggles in integrating into the community of Bergen County in New Jersey. More revealing, however, are Hoagland's ambiguous comments on the family's reasons for emigrating. In a statement marked by ellipsis, she recounts, that her father "[although] a wonderful man . . . got in with a fast crowd, you know, and she [her mother] had to leave . . . It was a lovely life, really, except for that; we had hotels in the country, and my father ran horses . . . a lovely life, but . . ." (Toolen 1982, C19). That Hoagland's father's personal troubles are evaded in the interview while the fictional father's alcoholism is detailed in full in the novel suggests that, as Leigh Gilmore argues, such trauma is often more successfully rendered in narratives that swerve from conventional forms of autobiographical narrative (2001).

Further reporting in *The Record* conveys Hoagland's devout patriotic fervor: she claims she protested against the Black and Tans in Dublin as a child ("Irish Seeress to Visit Mall," *The Record*, June 28, 1970, 25). She also had fond memories of her second cousin Taoiseach Liam Cosgrave (1920–2017), and claimed the Cosgrave boys could "talk politics in a barroom at 3" (Litterine 1973, 60). She also prided herself on being behind the plans to repatriate writer Ernest Boyd's body after his death in New York in 1946 ("Ashes to Ashes," *The Record*, September 23, 1966, 60). In contrast, the novel is largely condemnatory of the "fanatics" of Sinn Féin, as the local nationalist community turns against Elizabeth Brendan for her entertainment of British officers. Mrs. Brendan's cousin Shaun Fitzhugh—who, like Liam's father the eminent politician W. T. Cosgrave (1880–1965), was sentenced to death for his involvement in the Rising—attempts to persuade her from emigrating, asking "Why should you take the boys and money from Ireland? Every boy and every penny will be needed to make Ireland's freedom possible" (227). Ultimately, the family are chaperoned by British "Spike Island officers" to the tender to ensure their departure is not thwarted by "Sinn Féiners."

Even though Hoagland recalls that the family had a "lovely life" in Ireland, the novel is far from romantic. Indeed, it is largely characterized by an anti-nostalgic impulse that emerges, as Emilie Pine notes in the context of contemporary Ireland, when the past is no longer "a welcome break from the demands of the present" (2010, 8). The small town of Tirawley—in stark contrast with its etymology of "Tír Álainn" (Beautiful Country)—is crippled by social divisions; the district of Bournah is populated by impoverished laundrywomen, "half-fed" fighting dogs, and "close-cropped" children "marked with ringworm" (5). Emigration, in the opening of the novel, is presented as engendering insanity as the police "strapped and manacled" the town's mentally ill, including a woman who "hasn't been right in the head since Bridgie went to America" (7). Yet, emigration is also a necessary escape. The novel's concluding passage is characterized by the protagonist's relief as the family catches their final glimpse of the Irish shore:

> "Thank God, *that's* the last of Ireland, Mamma!"
> "I hope I have done right, pet," Elizabeth said.
> "You have, Mamma!"
> Pegeen could not bear to see the green now. She got up and made her way to the prow of the liner. Standing there, alone, she looked into the distance of the ocean; a gray mist was over the water. The ship seemed to shudder with delight as it plowed ahead faster and faster, leaving the land behind it. The girl's eyes were full of tears, she brushed them away. Tomorrow ... America! (294)

Is Hoagland's fictional testimony any less authoritative than Máire Comerford's memoir, which Comerford also acknowledges is subject to the mechanics of memory, "churned and tested"? Hoagland's final passage points to a less received narrative of female emigration that emphasizes not only female solidarity but also the sense of liberation, and even empowerment, that emigration could provide. This final passage is redolent of Nora Kilduff's terse account of her emigration to New York in April 1923 ("New York, Passenger and Crew Lists"). Active in the revolution in her native Ballyhaunis, County Mayo, Kilduff recalled being "sick on the Irish Sea, but then dancing across the Atlantic"; a comment that, according to family lore, suggests "freedom from drudgery" (Brian Kilduff Hughes, message to author, January 30, 2019).

When Hoagland's novel was published in 1944, it also contributed to the production of cultural (post)memory. This evokes the broader question regarding the intergenerational transmission of memories of the revolution, which merits further study. In her autobiography *Children of the Far-Flung*, Geraldine O'Connell Cusack relates that her mother, Nellie Taaffe, who emigrated to New York from Banteer, County Cork, was, like many others, reticent about the revolutionary period: "Nellie was, to all outward appearances, the most gentle of souls; soft-spoken, kind and generous to a fault, with never a harsh word for anyone. But beneath that gentle exterior was a steely resolve. Few in America knew anything about her early days with Cumann na mBan in the hills of north Cork" (2003, 19). These silences may explain why Maeve Brennan, after her mother Úna's death, struggled to understand the revolutionary background of her quiet "homemaker mother" in New York, even wondering whether her father pressured her mother into using the Gaelicized version of her name (Bourke 2004, 232). Eileen O'Faoláin appears to have been more open with her daughter Julia, who recounts that she "confided snippets of her personal history. . . . Some of which went back to the Troubles, which had petered out a year or so before first Seán, then she herself, left for Boston" (O'Faolain 2013, 12). Yet, Julia O'Faolain's novel *No Country for Young Men* suggests there is no escape from those "snippets" of memory for the succeeding generations. The character of Sister Judith experiences years "of almost catatonic silence" (1980, 192) in the aftermath of the Civil War; for her, "memory was a bog" defined by its "power of suction" (ibid., 12). However, the contemporary characters of the following generation unconsciously mimic the plot of their forebearers, thus illustrating the cyclical nature of family history.

While the retreat into the domestic sphere and sidelining from politics of republican women under the Free State is much debated, the dual aspect of this retreat has yet to be fully considered: that female republicans experienced both inner exile (as second-class citizens) and external exile (through emi-gration) in the twilight years of the Free State. This chapter goes some way toward redressing this question and suggests that diasporic memories of the revolution are composed of a complex interplay of nostalgia and anti-nostalgia that often left behind a strong legacy of silence and even denial in later genera-tions. In fact, in the course of researching for this paper, as I trailed through the Cumann na mBan Nominal Files county by county, I recognized the name of the adjutant and later secretary of the Cumann na mBan Passage West Branch in County Cork: Nellie Stuart (1898–1985). Nellie was an older sister of my great-grandfather. She spent much of her life in the domestic service on the Lower East Side of Manhattan; I had grown up hearing of the generous packages and dollars she sent home, making her nieces and nephews feel like "millionaires." While family lore suggested that the Stuart brothers "ran away to the U.S. to get safe from the Black and Tans," Nellie's revolutionary background was never integrated into family memory. Furthermore, the two older brothers, Tom and John, emigrated in 1927 and 1924, respectively, after British forces left Ireland ("New York, Passenger and Crew Lists, 1820–1957"; "US Census Records 1930").

Not only was Nellie's revolutionary background expunged from family stories, memory was also distorted to conceal the complexities of the Civil War. Nellie's story serves as just another reminder of the discomfort evoked by female activism and a further example that the glorification of war and exile was reserved for male combatants. For Richard Kearney, these unconscious transgenerational memories form "repressed wounds" that "scar the psyche and return to haunt us again and again" (Kearney and Gallagher 2017, 26). If catharsis can be achieved through narrative, the recovery of such lost memories is perhaps one of the most crucial aspects of this decade of commemorations.

SÍOBHRA AIKEN recently completed her PhD at the National University of Ireland, Galway. A former Fulbright Scholar, her publications include *The Men Will Talk to Me: Ernie O'Malley's Interviews with the Northern Divisions* (Merrion Press, 2018), *An Chuid Eile Díom Féin: Aistí le Máirtín Ó Direáin* (Cló IarChonnacht 2018), and articles on Irish-language literature, the Gaelic Revival and Irish Revolution.

SIX

—ᴍ—

"NO CONSCRIPTION NOW! OR AFTER THE HARVEST"

Remembering Women and Anti-conscription
in Ireland and England

SONJA TIERNAN

ON COMMONWEALTH DAY IN 2015, the British secretary of state for communities and local government Eric Pickles addressed a large crowd at Memorial Gates on Constitution Hill in London. Pickles's speech overtly celebrated the actions of commonwealth soldiers, which, he maintained, have an "enduring relevance to modern Britain." He proclaimed that "in both world wars millions of soldiers from across the Commonwealth fought side-by-side, defending the values of freedom and liberty, and defeating the dark forces of tyranny and oppression" (Pickles 2015). If the remembrance of British activities during World War I becomes a patriotic celebration of this kind, there is little room in such commemorations to recognize that millions of men were compelled or forced to fight on behalf of Britain and her allies in World War I.

This chapter discusses an area that national commemorative events have failed to appropriately observe: those who campaigned against war from 1914 to 1918 and worked against conscription of men into the British army, with a particular focus on the significance of women in anti-war activities. Women in Britain who campaigned against the war effort placed themselves in a particularly vulnerable and even dangerous situation. Speaking out against the war positioned these women in direct opposition to growing patriotic sentiment, the mainstream suffrage movement, and even the law. By tracing the activities of female peace activists during World War I, it becomes apparent that these women forged an unlikely bond between peace movements in Ireland and England during a turbulent time in Anglo-Irish relations. This connection challenges our views of anti-war campaigners and of connections between Irish and British feminists at this time. It is clearly evident from this research that female anti-war activists in England influenced an even more focused campaign against conscription in Ireland.

WOMEN AND WORLD WAR I IN BRITAIN AND IRELAND

Remembrance of World War I undoubtedly has a more contentious position in former territories of the British Empire than in Britain itself, something that is particularly evident in Ireland. Concerted efforts have been made in Ireland in recent decades to commemorate Irish men and women who supported the British war effort. The Irish government's official program for the decade of centenaries attempted to be "broad and inclusive ... to encompass the different traditions on the island of Ireland" (Decade of Centenaries 2012a). Unlike in Britain, the commemoration of World War I in Ireland is not overtly celebrated as patriotism. Rather, many seek to understand the complexity of Irish involvement in relation to the country's rebellious years. The initial surge of Irish men joining the British army can be partly attributed to John Redmond, leader of the Irish Parliamentary Party; Redmond was certain that Ireland would be rewarded with the implementation of home rule if Irish men supported Britain during the hostilities. The feminist campaigner Francis Sheehy Skeffington attested that in this way Redmond simply "sold Irish people to the British army for nothing" (in P. McCarthy 1915).

The reaction to men joining the army or refusing the call to volunteer was intrinsically different in Britain and in Ireland. This is most apparent in recruitment campaigns organized by women. The patriotic activities of women in Britain stretched to publicly humiliating men of military age who did not voluntarily join the army: a favored activity was to target young men not in uniform and present them with a white feather as a sign of cowardice. As early as October 1914, the English author Arnold Bennett penned a short story, titled "The White Feather: A Sketch of English Recruiting," for the popular American magazine *Collier's Weekly*, condemning the practice. The Women's Social and Political Union (WSPU) adopted an extreme patriotic stance from the onset of war, evident in their decision to rename the organization's journal *Britannia*, complete with the new slogan, "For King, for Country, for Freedom."

In contrast, the Irish women's organization Inghinidhe na hÉireann publicly humiliated Irish girls seen, as they described it, "walking through the streets with men wearing the uniform of Ireland's oppressor" ("Irish Girls," Inghinidhe na hÉireann handbill, Military Archives Ireland, CD119/3/1). Since the onset of the Boer War in 1899, Maud Gonne had organized teams of women to distribute leaflets throughout the main thoroughfare of Dublin city, in public houses, on trains, and on the streets. Leaflets implored "Irish girls [to] make a vow, not only that you will yourselves refuse to associate with any man who wears an English uniform, but that you will also try and induce your girl companions to do the same." Such anti-recruitment work was dangerous; soldiers often retaliated by lashing out with their belts and the women had to frequent disreputable areas where soldiers could be found, including the vicinity of the General Post Office, which was on the side of the road considered out of bounds for decent people.

Such opposing views of the war effort ensured an even more defined split between the feminist movements in Britain and those in Ireland and between unionist and nationalist women on the island of Ireland. The Ulster Women's Unionist Council supported the war effort from the war's onset and aided in recruitment drives. On the other hand, the views expressed in the pages of the *Irish Citizen*, the official organ of the Irish Women's Franchise League (IWFL), were decidedly and fervently anti-war from the outset. Editor of the journal Francis Sheehy Skeffington attacked the actions of Emmeline and Christabel Pankhurst, leaders of the WSPU. Previously, the IWFL had worked closely with the WSPU and had invited Christabel Pankhurst to Dublin on many occasions. In 1910, Christabel delivered a talk to a large audience at the Rotunda Concert Rooms. In her animated address, Pankhurst was forthright in her assertion that Irish women should dedicate themselves to the cause of suffrage for women first and home rule second. After the outbreak of war, Skeffington declared Christabel a hypocrite, writing in the *Irish Citizen* that she was "now advocating war first and suffrage second" (*Irish Citizen*, October 10, 1914). Skeffington later announced that "the woman who does not . . . discourage recruiting, has an imperfect understanding of the basis of the feminist movement. The woman who deliberately encourages recruiting is betraying that movement—though her name be Christabel Pankhurst" (ibid.).

Ultimately, the differences of opinion were based on the fact that it was considered patriotic in Britain to support the war effort and help with the recruitment of men, while in Ireland there was a risk of being considered unpatriotic if seen even associating with a man in a British military uniform. It follows that anti-war activities were driven by differing motivations. Therefore, connections between the anti-conscription movements of England and Ireland may at first appear surprising. Such activities in England predominantly rose out of pacifist idealism, while the anti-conscription movement in Ireland was, primarily, driven by a militant nationalist cause.

REBELLIOUS PACIFISM DURING A PRO-MILITANT AGE

From the onset of war, Eva Gore-Booth initiated a targeted campaign for peace, though she was an unlikely proponent of peace. Gore-Booth was born into a wealthy Anglo-Irish family in County Sligo: her landlord family owned one of the largest estates in the west of Ireland, and she was raised in the ancestral mansion of Lissadell House. The Gore-Booths were originally granted tens of thousands of acres of land in Ireland for their military prowess in defeating local Irish chieftains and for their loyalty to the English crown. Gore-Booth despised her heritage and rejected her background in early adulthood, moving to England, in 1897, to live with her partner, Esther Roper. Initially the women lived among the working classes, mainly Irish emigrants, in Manchester, where Gore-Booth helped form trade unions and improve social conditions for textile factory workers. In 1913, the couple moved to London. After the onset of war, Gore-Booth shifted her efforts from trade unionism to campaigning for peace. During the same period, Gore-Booth's older sister, Countess Markievicz, took an active role in the fight for Irish independence.

As an Irish woman living in England, Gore-Booth was at greater risk of appearing unpatriotic or, worse, labeled as a German sympathizer in the midst of anti-German hysteria. There were repercussions for people who expressed anti-war sentiments during World War I. When Ramsay MacDonald took a stance against declaring war and resigned as leader of the British Labour Party, he was subjected to a mass media attack. Newspapers described him as pro-German, with *The Times* announcing that "no paid agent of Germany has served her better than himself" (*The Times*, October 1, 1914). For a woman to voice opposition to war had further ramifications. Women were also labeled as ungrateful since, after all, millions of men faced death or mutilation in order to protect them.

Undeterred by such consequences, Gore-Booth signed an "Open Christmas Letter," in 1914, addressed to the women of Germany and Austria. The letter, orchestrated by British suffragist Emily Hobhouse, began: "Sisters, . . . Do not let us forget that our very anguish unites us, that we are passing together through the same experiences of pain and grief. . . . Though our sons are sent to slay each other, and our hearts are torn by the cruelty of this fate" (Hobhouse 1915, 228–229). The letter was signed by 101 British and Irish women, including the suffragists and trade unionists Louie Bennett and Helen Chenevix. Printed shortly after Christmas in a suffrage journal, it acted as a public call for peace and reconciliation between warring nations. Within two months of publication, 155 German and Austrian women responded with "warm sisterly greetings" (Oldfield 2003, 67). The significance of this contact between warring nations has been somewhat overlooked in commemorative events. While it has been the subject of academic research, it has failed to seize the public attention in the same way as what is now termed the Christmas truce.

The short, impromptu truce between opposing sides in the trenches on Christmas Day in 1914 is publicly celebrated: most recently, in 2014, the Christmas truce was reenacted for the Sainsbury's television advertisement in Britain. Made in partnership with the Royal British Legion, the advertisement focused on one English soldier and one German soldier who exchange Christmas greetings and a bar of chocolate during a short ceasefire on Christmas Eve 1914. As might be gauged from the ad, the event has been somewhat romanticized. Witness accounts show that while impromptu periods of peace happened in the run-up to Christmas 1914, this was normally for practical reasons, such as retrieving injured soldiers or dead bodies from outside trench areas. It was most certainly not an orchestrated attempt to broker peace between warring nations. The main reason for the ceasefire over the Christmas period in 1914 was to bury soldiers killed in a series of attacks known as the Battle of Givenchy. The battle lasted from December 18 to December 22, resulting in an immense loss of life, with over four thousand allied troops and two thousand German soldiers killed.

The ceasefire was used by many soldiers to exchange Christmas greetings, such as a group of Royal Dublin Fusiliers who met with German troops and posed for a photograph on St. Stephen's Day 1914 (Brigadier C.A.F. Drummond Collection, Imperial War Museum, Photographs Department, Call number HU 35801). However, not all troops complied in this way. It was far more likely for Irish men to fraternize with German troops rather than Belgian and French soldiers whose home countries were then occupied by German forces. Newspapers glorified such stories and carried illustrations of Christmas truces. The front page of a January 1915 edition of the *Illustrated London News*, for instance, was devoted to a full-page illustration of German and English soldiers meeting across the trenches, with the scene described as "the Light of Peace on Christmas Eve. A German soldier opens the spontaneous truce by approaching the British line with a small Christmas tree." Military commanders immediately issued orders that any soldiers initiating temporary times of truce with the enemy would be charged with treason.

INTERNATIONAL CONGRESS OF WOMEN

Civilians were also greatly restricted in their activities due to the introduction of the Defence of the Realm Act, which granted British authorities increased powers to regulate numerous aspects of life during the war. Ignoring any legal threat, Gore-Booth gave her first public anti-war speech in London in December 1914. Her talk, titled *Whence Come Wars?*, condemned the premise that men were fighting to protect their women and children at home. This idea was regularly reinforced through British recruitment posters, and such propaganda became increasingly more emotive. After a German bombardment on Scarborough in December 1915, a poster depicting a small girl holding a baby outside a bomb-damaged building was widely distributed. The caption implored "Men of Britain! Will you stand this? 78 women & children were killed and 228 women & children were wounded by the German raiders" (Prints and Photographs, Library of Congress Division, Washington, POS-WWI - Gt Brit, no. 39). In her speech, Gore-Booth insisted that if men were expected to go to war to protect women, "it would be intolerable to any high-spirited woman to be asked to buy her life and safety at such a price of suffering and death to others" (Tiernan 2015, 145).

Throughout her talk Gore-Booth blamed male politicians for the outbreak of World War I, since women had no political voice in the matter. The speech, later published as a pamphlet by the National Industrial and Professional Women's Suffrage Society, concluded that successive governments have told women, "'We can do quite well without you; men can manage the affairs of the world; we have no need of your assistance' [and so] men have had it all their own way. And now look what they have brought the world to" (Gore-Booth 1914). Gore-Booth's assessment—that if women had a political franchise the war would not have been instigated—was a fundamental feminist argument, based on the assumption that women were naturally peaceful and the key to successfully resolving the armed conflict.

This was echoed by many female pacifists at this time. In Holland, Aletta Jacobs called for an International Congress of Women to be held at The Hague in the Netherlands. Jacobs cabled suffrage organizations and individuals across the globe, stating: "We feel strongly that at a time when there is so much hatred among nations, we, women, must show that we can retain our solidarity" (in Oldfield 2005, 89). Within weeks the idea of an international congress gained momentum and a date was set to meet in April 1915. The prospect of the congress caused a split in the British suffrage organization, the National Union of Women's Suffrage Societies. Their president, Mrs. Fawcett, declared that until Germany and her allies were defeated it was "akin to treason to talk of peace," and no delegates should be sent to The Hague (Strachey 1931, 289). One hundred eighty women applied for exit permits to travel from Britain and Ireland across the Channel to neutral Holland; Hanna Sheehy Skeffington was one of the delegates chosen to represent Ireland. Margaret Ward describes Hanna's delight that Ireland was afforded the opportunity for independent representation rather than under the British banner (2016, 225). At the behest of the home secretary, Reginald McKenna, the Permit Office denied the travel request of the vast majority of the women, and days before the congress was due to meet, the British Admiralty closed the North Sea to passenger shipping, with the result that no delegates were permitted to travel from Britain or Ireland to The Hague.

One thousand and three hundred women from twelve countries did attend the congress. At the closing of the congress on May 1, resolutions were announced and envoys dispatched to heads of state globally. This mass meeting had an impact on world leaders, most notably the president of the United States, Woodrow Wilson, and retains influence on feminist peace movements to this day. The British media ridiculed the congress delegates as "'pro-Hun peacettes' who were going to 'pow-wow with the fraus'" (Cullen Owens 2012, 20). Only three British women attended the congress, and news of what occurred at The Hague was slow to reach women in England. Emmeline Pethick-Lawrence had been visiting in New York when the North Sea was closed, and she traveled to the congress with the American suffragist Jane Addams, who would become a recipient of the Nobel Prize in 1931 for her peace work. When Pethick-Lawrence returned to London, Gore-Booth organized a special meeting in London to provide a full account of the events, proceedings, and outcomes at The Hague to the women who could not attend.

The Congress of Women led to the establishment of the Women's International League of Peace and Freedom, a vibrant organization still actively working toward global peace today. Yet commemoration of the centenary of this significant event was mainly relegated to feminist organizations in 2015. A three-day conference was held at The Hague in 2015 by female peacemakers, and the Women's International League of Peace and Freedom led numerous local commemorative celebrations. It is disappointing that a supposed Christmas truce has gained more attention during the centenary of World War I than this international congress. Historian Helen McCarthy stresses that remembering the congress is imperative as it "can tell us a great deal about how power works and, in this case, why women remained peripheral to international politics and diplomacy for so much of the 20th century" (2015).

WOMEN AND THE NO CONSCRIPTION FELLOWSHIP

The British restriction placed on passenger shipping in the North Sea was a reminder that war was escalating across Europe with dire consequences. In May 1915, the threat extended beyond Europe when the passenger liner the Lusitania was torpedoed by a German U-boat on its route from New York to Liverpool. German authorities maintained that the Lusitania was carrying weapons and was, therefore, a legitimate target, but British authorities depicted the sinking of the Lusitania as a savage attack on civilians. The tragedy was used to incite anti-German feelings and became a prominent feature in military recruitment campaigns, especially in Ireland. The British Council for Recruiting in Ireland printed depictions of women and children drowning off their coast, with the caption "Irishmen avenge the Lusitania join an Irish regiment today" (*Join an Irish Regiment today*). Gore-Booth's friend Hugh Lane did not survive the Lusitania attack. In the aftermath of the tragedy, she attended a conference on the Pacifist Philosophy of Life at Caxton Hall in London that July, presenting a paper titled "Religious Aspects of Non-resistance." In the paper she explored how to resist the "appalling calamity of present cruelty and destructiveness of war" (Tiernan 2015, 148). The pacifist conference was an immense success. Gore-Booth impressed two noteworthy delegates, Bertrand Russell and Fenner Brockway, key players in the British anti-conscription movement.

Russell, a philosopher and an academic, objected to the war not on pacifist grounds but on the basis that Britain had entered into the hostilities out of a misguided foreign policy. As the war progressed, Russell became a significant voice of radical political objection. Brockway, a politician and anti-war activist, founded the No Conscription Fellowship. The organization offered support for men who refused to take up arms on moral, religious, or political grounds. Initially, only men who volunteered for active service were sent to war; military conscription had never been enforced in modern Britain and, therefore, few people thought it likely. However, from as early as 1914 Emmeline and Christabel Pankhurst actively called for enforced military service. At the suggestion of his wife, Lilla, Brockway published an appeal for conscientious objectors to contact him in the autumn of 1914. There was a huge response and the Fellowship was established. By the time that Gore-Booth met Brockway the organization was a thriving one. Initially, female membership was mainly confined to those related to conscientious objectors; however, this changed dramatically as the war progressed.

World War I had now been raging for just one year and already it had caused an enormous loss of life. The numbers of British soldiers at the front were declining rapidly. A compulsory national register taken across Britain in August 1915 revealed that two million eligible men had not yet volunteered for war service, compounding the argument for enforced military service. The Derby Scheme pressuring men under oath to enlist failed to gain a significant increase. Various bills went through the House of Commons from November 1915 and a proposed conscription bill did not exclude the possibility of the death penalty for those men who did not comply. Gore-Booth launched a media campaign to contest this issue. On January 20, 1916, the *Manchester Guardian* published her letter testifying: "With regard to the refusal of the Government to eliminate the possibility of the death sentence from the Compulsion Bill, may I point out that, as the bill now stands, if a man fails to convince a committee nominated by the local authority not only that he is a bona fide conscientious objector, but also that a conscientious objector ought to be exempted, he may pay with his life for the private militarist views of members of his district council." Conscription came into effect in Britain on March 2, 1916; less than four months later, enlistment was extended to include married men. If in the unlikely event a man was granted an exemption, he would be assigned a noncombatant post in the war service. Often the roles allocated involved extreme danger, such as stretcher bearer at the front. If a man failed to gain an exemption from a tribunal and still refused to take up war service, he would face a court-martial and, ultimately, a prison sentence. The process for gaining an exemption on conscientious grounds would prove to be particularly challenging. Over two thousand local tribunals and seventy appeal tribunals were established across Britain. Tribunal members were generally elderly middle-class men. The work was unpaid and seemed to attract enthusiastic supporters of war.

Although death sentences were not enforced, the death rate due to incarceration with hard labor was particularly high. It is estimated that sixteen thousand men refused to fight; records confirm that over six thousand of these were arrested ("Conscientious Objectors Information Bureau Reports 1917–19," Working Class Movement Library, Manchester, UK, ORG/NCF/1/C.). Seventy-three of those died after being incarcerated and a further forty suffered mental breakdowns. The high level of arrests depleted the male membership of the No Conscription Fellowship. Brockway was himself imprisoned on numerous occasions; by the time of the Armistice he was still being held in Lincoln Prison. As a result, women began to play an increasingly more important role in the Fellowship until, finally, they took over operations. The suffragist Catherine Marshall was appointed as secretary when her partner Clifford Allen was imprisoned. Marshall and other women oversaw a highly organized press department to expose the injustice and brutality of how conscientious objectors were treated. As part of their propaganda campaign, the fellowship launched a weekly newspaper, *The Tribunal*, in March 1916.

WOMEN AND ANTI-WAR PUBLICATIONS

Tribunals were open to the public, and, while journalists could have reported on trials, this was rare. The Fellowship thus established a system to monitor the activities of tribunals and appeals. Hundreds of volunteers, including

Gore-Booth, attended trials across the country, recording personal details of conscientious objectors, remarks made by tribunal members, perceived illegal activities, and the outcome of cases. These fastidiously recorded details were published in their journal on a weekly basis. Publication of such anti-war material was suppressed through a tight censorship code, and, due to the contents of the *Tribunal*, authorities made persistent attempts to discontinue the publication. The printer's offices were raided, and their printing presses dismantled; the National Labour Press was eventually shut down altogether for their involvement. The fellowship simply organized more printing equipment, at one stage buying a small handpress. The front page of their issue in April 1918 carried the headline, "Here We Are Again!!" celebrating the *Tribunal*'s survival and mocking the attempts of Scotland Yard to shut their operation down.

Authorities also turned their attention to the Fellowship offices on Fleet Street in London. During these raids, the official publisher of the *Tribunal*, Joan Beauchamp, was arrested. The general secretary, Violet Tillard, was sentenced to sixty-one days in prison for refusing to divulge the whereabouts of the printing equipment. Edith Smith was sentenced to six months in prison for printing an anti-conscription leaflet. Gore-Booth was undeterred by such criminal prosecutions. She dramatized a day in her role as a "watcher" at military tribunals for publication, describing a day spent in an "ugly airless room . . . haunted with memories of vain appeals and helpless protest" (Tiernan 2015, 155). The stark story, originally titled "At the Military Tribunal," was published by the National Labour Press as a pamphlet in 1917, with the same title as the Fellowship journal, *The Tribunal* (*Eva Gore-Booth Collection*, Pennsylvania State University Libraries, AX/B40/RBM/00139). Gore-Booth's account provided a rare glimpse into the oppressive process involved in seeking an exemption from war service. The pamphlet includes a poem, "Conscientious Objectors," on the cover, which concludes that tribunals are held "before six ignorant men and blind."

The pamphlet was a blatant condemnation of the government's war policy. It is not clear how Gore-Booth escaped arrest for this and other publications, especially since this pamphlet described numerous cases before the military tribunal with harrowing detail. She did not name those applying for an exemption or the tribunal members but wrote the accounts to incite sympathy for the individuals involved and to create disdain for the tribunal members. It was a brave move for Gore-Booth to identify herself as author of such a contentious pamphlet. As an Irish woman connected with the Irish nationalist movement, she was at risk of receiving a more severe sentence than her female colleagues in the No Conscription Fellowship. Significantly, this pamphlet was published only months after the Easter Rising.

EXTENDING MILITARY CONSCRIPTION TO IRELAND

Gore-Booth's sister, Countess Markievicz, was a prominent member of the Irish Citizen Army and took up arms, acting as second in command of a battalion during the Rising, which took place just weeks after conscription had been enforced in Britain. The British public were horrified that Irish people would plan a rebellion at a time when tens of thousands of British soldiers were being killed at the front. To add to English contempt, the Irish rebels were supported by Germany in their quest. At the center of the German organization was Roger Casement, who had traveled to Ireland in a German U-boat to oversee shipment of a large stock of German ammunition. Casement's plans were intercepted, however, and he was charged with high treason. It was Gore-Booth who instigated a lobbying campaign for his reprieve, a campaign so intense that British authorities were forced to launch an investigation days before Casement was due to be executed. Gore-Booth's campaign placed Britain's actions regarding Ireland under international scrutiny at a crucial time during World War I. The British prime minister Henry Asquith was then courting the United States to come to the aid of Britain and her allies. In 1916, an estimated twenty million people in the United States were of Irish descent. Gore-Booth used Casement's death sentence and subsequent execution to cause outrage in the United States. British authorities were now well versed with Gore-Booth's activities and a "personality file" was held on her and her sister by British intelligence at their Irish headquarters in Dublin Castle.

It is noteworthy that while her writings against conscription in England were based on pacifist ideals, Gore-Booth never condemned the militant actions of the Irish against British forces. In fact, her public speeches and political pamphlets at this time stressed that the Irish had no other option but to take up arms in their struggle for independence, a stance shared by many of her fellow peace activists in England. In the midst of campaigns for Irish independence, the recruitment of Irish men into the British army was a contentious issue. Due to the growing political instability in Ireland, the Military Service Act of 1916 excluded Irish men and various tactics were employed by the recruiting committee in Ireland instead. The German invasion of Belgium at the onset of war became a focus of propaganda campaigns imploring Irish men to avenge the invasion of a similar small Catholic country.

It is estimated that over two hundred thousand Irish men voluntarily joined the British army during World War I. The British government wanted more. In March 1918, the Irish Convention, established to resolve the Irish home rule issue, recommended the enactment of the bill under the condition that conscription would be extended to Ireland. On April 16, 1918, the extension of the Military Service Bill enforcing conscription in Ireland was announced: this new legislation would ensure that all Irish men between eighteen and fifty years of age would be forced to join the British army.

Members of the Irish Parliamentary Party walked out of Westminster in protest, and Irish MPs John Dillon and Joseph Devlin returned to Ireland to organize against conscription. A meeting was held in the Lord Mayor of Dublin Lawrence O'Neill's residence at the Mansion House and saw the formation of the Irish Anti-Conscription Committee, which included members from Irish nationalist and trade organizations including Dillon, Devlin, Eamon de Valera, and Arthur Griffith. The committee developed an anti-conscription pledge: denying "the right of the British government to enforce compulsory service in this country, we pledge ourselves solemnly to one another to resist conscription by the most effective means at our disposal" (Mitchell and Ó Snodaigh 1985, 42). The Irish bishops were quick to support the anti-conscription movement and addressed the issue at their conference in Maynooth, agreeing that this pledge would be taken at the door of every church around the country before mass the following Sunday on April 21.

WOMEN AND ANTI-CONSCRIPTION IN IRELAND

Political instability in Ireland again intensified as anti-conscription activities increased, including a general strike on Tuesday, April 23. This was the first general strike in Ireland, and it saw the country come to almost a complete standstill: government offices remained open but most businesses across the country closed, even schools shut for the day and where teachers turned up pupils did not (Yeates 2017, 6). Women would prove to be the main instigators behind such movement: the IWFL stepped into action and examined the situation in England. Enforced military service there meant that women had to take the place of male workers. This was often greeted with hostility in England, since men were concerned that women's low rate of pay would reduce their own wages and saturate the jobs market after the war. The Franchise League adopted a clever tactic, epitomized by a banner positioned on their premises in Dublin the day before the general strike. The banner warned: "Conscription! No woman must take a man's job" (Horne 2010, 180). A women's meeting was held in Dublin's Mansion House on April 27, with speakers from labor and nationalist organizations. A Women's Day Committee was established to oppose conscription under the direction of Alice Stopford Green. A Lá na mBan

(Woman's Day) was declared to take place on June 9, the feast of St. Colmcille, notably one of the three patron saints of Ireland. The event was widely advertised by leaflets and posters announcing:

No Conscription
Now! Or after the harvest.
No economic Pressure!
Lá na mBan.
The Woman's Day,
Sunday, June 9th.
For Home & Country.
IRISHWOMEN,
Stand by your countrymen
In resisting conscription.

The poster included a call for women to sign a pledge to this effect.

British authorities, in fear of this sudden and rapid growth of an anti-conscription movement, were keen to dismantle the organization. In a move that would backfire, British Intelligence claimed to have uncovered a Sinn Féin plot with Germany. Authorities began arresting lead members of the party and, by May 18, 1918, seventy-three Sinn Féiners were imprisoned in England without trial, including three women: Countess Markievicz, Maud Gonne, and Kathleen Clarke. There was no evidence of this "German plot" presented by the British authorities and this prompted Markievicz to describe the event as a "comic opera" (Roper 1987, 179). Markievicz wrote to her sister Eva Gore-Booth from Holloway Prison explaining that the imprisonments will "rebound on our oppressors. Myself I think it is about the best thing that could have happened for Ireland, as there was so little to be done there, only propaganda, and our arrests carry so much further than speeches." The arrests not only inspired a more effective propaganda campaign but also forged a significant connection between anti-conscription organizers in Ireland and those in England.

The Woman's Day convention went ahead as planned in June; however, the Women's Day Committee now joined forces with the IWFL, the Irish Women's Workers Union (IWWU), the International League, and Cumann na mBan to generate a huge turnout, signifying "that women's protest had become a fact of Irish political life" (Pašeta 2013, 242). Led by female trade unionists Helena Moloney, Louie Bennet, and Helen Chenevix, women from the IWWU, numbering nearly twenty-four hundred, gathered outside their headquarters on Great Denmark Street and marched on city hall where they were met by over seven hundred uniformed members of Cumann na mBan. At city hall women signed a pledge to resist the conscription of their countrymen. The highly successful event saw Irish women's organizations unite on this issue with over forty thousand signatures collected throughout the day in Dublin city and county alone. Thousands more women gathered around the country during meetings, processions, and gatherings where they also signed the pledge in huge numbers.

At their annual convention in September that year, Cumann na mBan made their stance on conscription clear. In their section outlining their policy for 1918–1919, they stipulated that they would continue:

> ... To organise opposition to Conscription along the lines laid down in the two Anti-Conscription Pledges, i.e.:
> Denying the right of the British government to enforce compulsory service in this country, we pledge solemnly to one another to resist Conscription by the most effective means at our disposal.
>
> (Women's Pledge): -
> Because the enforcement of conscription of any people without their consent is tyranny, we are resolved to resist the conscription of Irishmen.
> We will not fill the places of men deprived of their work through refusing enforced military service.
> We will do all in our power to help the families of the men who suffer through refusing enforced military service. (Minutes of the Cumann na mBan convention, September 28–29, 1918)

BRITISH AND IRISH ANTI-CONSCRIPTION MOVEMENTS COOPERATE

Meanwhile the key members of Sinn Féin remained in prison. The president of the party, de Valera, was a close friend and colleague of Markievicz and was incarcerated in Lincoln Prison. Because he was not convicted of any crime, he was afforded the rights of freedom of association with other prisoners. At the same time, Gore-Booth's friend and anti-conscription activist, Fenner Brockway, was also imprisoned in Lincoln. Gore-Booth had versed Brockway in the politics of Irish nationalism and he became an ardent supporter of the cause. The meeting of de Valera and Brockway was to have an influence on de Valera's anti-conscription campaign in Ireland. While in prison, he compiled a full outline of the proceedings of the conference at the Mansion House, and this was sent to Woodrow Wilson. The case was later published as a pamphlet titled *Ireland's Case against Conscription* by Gore-Booth's Dublin publisher, Maunsel Press (de Valera 1918).

Gore-Booth launched a propaganda attack at the heart of the British war effort, in England, opening a debate in the pages of popular newspapers. Her piece "The Ruin Preparing in Ireland" was published in the *Manchester Guardian* and received much attention (Tiernan 2015, 189). She began her testimony with the determined assurance to the people of England that in Dublin "a resistance to the death is being undertaken in a spirit of passionate revolt and religious faith which may turn Ireland into a nation of rebels and martyrs, but never into an army of conscripts." Gore-Booth (1914) described the position adopted by the IWFL by noting how "the women workers are pledging themselves not to take the place of a man who is conscripted."

In order to animate the determination of Irish women, Gore-Booth quotes an unnamed source who adopts an extreme stance:

> I am a farmer, I have farmed land all my life. Your government has demanded compulsory tillage and compulsory military service. That means that women must till the land. We will not do it. If my brother is taken he will not be taken alive, and I shall be left with farm and stock. I will do this. Neither crops nor cattle shall go to you. I will kill the stock; I will destroy the crop if I have to dig it up by the roots with my hands, and then I will take my rifle. I have used a rifle all my life, and I will take it and go out and fight and die.

Days later a man from Surrey replied to the *Manchester Guardian* exclaiming how "the striking letter of Miss Gore-Booth . . . compels all thoughtful men and women to pause. We English people want above all things to win the war, and we ask ourselves whether the conscription of Ireland against her will is not the way to lose it. We may deplore Ireland's action, but we cannot ignore it." Despite British efforts, forced conscription of Irish men into the British army was never legally introduced. Markievicz wrote to her sister explaining that "it wasn't talk blocked conscription: it was the astounding fact that the whole male population left at home and most of the women . . . would have died rather than fight for England, and they simply did not dare exterminate a nation" (Roper 1987, 195).

COMMEMORATING WOMEN AND ANTI-CONSCRIPTION

Although women were at the heart of the anti-conscription movement in Britain, undoubtedly women were also the key to the successful introduction of conscription there. In commemorative events in Britain, it is this compliant aspect of women that is celebrated. Women are now celebrated for taking up jobs vacated by conscripted men and for contributing to the war effort in their various roles as munition workers or in caring capacities. This is generally welcomed by historians of women's history for granting women their deserved place in the centenary commemorations. However, when commemorating Britain's role in what Pickles terms "defeating the dark forces of tyranny and oppression," the role of anti-war activists confuses the issue. Therefore, women's peace activities have been, in the main, overlooked in British commemorations.

Women are remembered for their work in blocking conscription in other parts of the British Empire during World War I, most notably in Australia. The introduction of conscription was put to a public vote in two separate referenda in Australia in 1916 and 1917. Women were the predominant organizers against the introduction of conscription, forming many organizations, including the Women's Peace Army and Sisterhood for International Peace. These two organizations successfully rallied against conscripting men into the Australian Imperial Force. The intrinsic role of women and anti-conscription is now celebrated in Australia and became part of their centenary commemorations. Individuals are applauded, including the youngest sister of Christabel Pankhurst, Adela, who moved to Australia in 1914 and became a vibrant anti-war activist.

By their complete lack of compliance, Irish women played a central role in overturning the extension of the conscription bill to Ireland. Although the proposal to extend the bill was only made in 1918, authorities could not foretell that World War I would end months later. Undoubtedly, the introduction of this bill would have changed the course of Irish history, perhaps drastically. Celebrating the work of female anti-conscription campaigners during World War I is less complex in Ireland than in Britain, due to differing ideals of patriotism. However, we should be keenly aware in commemorations that the women who drove this movement in Ireland did so for often complex reasons and cannot simply be labeled as nationalist or pacifist. Commemorating the centenary of the conscription crisis in 2018 provided a unique opportunity to celebrate how women in Ireland and England overcame political divides to work together for a mutual goal. The decade of centenaries in Ireland has rarely afforded us such opportunity.

In June 2018, Ireland witnessed many events in celebration of the centenary of Lá na mBan, mainly hosted by trade union movements. A banner celebrating the mobilization of women was draped across the Services, Industrial, Professional and Technical Union (SIPTU) headquarters, Liberty Hall, from Tuesday, June 5. SIPTU also hosted an event that included an impassioned reading of the original address to women who gathered outside the Mansion House by Sabina Higgins (wife of Irish president Michael D. Higgins). Mrs. Higgins addressed a public audience from the top of a nineteenth-century tram in period costume. On Sunday, June 10, 2018, a further event was held at Dublin city hall, where many women had signed their anti-conscription pledge one hundred years earlier. Across the country, historians, feminist campaigners, and politicians addressed events celebrating Lá na mBan and articles appeared in newspapers and magazines drawing some public attention. As vibrant and engaging as events were such commemorations, unfortunately, failed to ignite a larger national interest.

The year 2018 witnessed an impressive agenda of celebrations for the centenary of votes for women. A program launched by the Oireachtas, Vótáil 100, was particularly impressive. Female politicians and members of the Vótáil 100 committee—Senator Ivana Bacik, Senator Alice Mary Higgins, Senator Gabrielle McFadden, Senator Rose Conway Walsh, Deputy Fiona O'Loughlin, and Deputy Catherine Martin—are to be congratulated for overseeing an engaging and inspiring year of events. The importance of Lá na mBan remains undervalued as an event which, Mary McAuliffe notes, was a major propaganda coup for Cumann na mBan, with mass marches of women in local areas inspiring many more young women to join, "leading to an organisation of female voters in the upcoming 1918 general election" (McAuliffe 2018b).

SONJA TIERNAN is the Éamon Cleary Chair of Irish Studies and co-director of the Centre for Irish and Scottish Studies at the University of Otago, New Zealand. Sonja has held fellowships at the National Library of Ireland, Trinity College Dublin, the Keogh-Naughton Institute of Irish Studies at the University of Notre Dame, the School of Irish Studies at Concordia University and the Moore Institute at NUI Galway. Sonja has published extensively on modern Irish and British women's history, including a biography of *Eva Gore-Booth: An Image of Such Politics* (2012) and her volume *Eva Gore-Booth: Collected Poems* (2018), which includes a foreword by the president of Ireland, Michael D. Higgins. Her most recent book is *The History of Marriage Equality in Ireland: A Social Revolution Begins* (2020).

SEVEN

—⬥—

EMERGING FROM THE "HISTORICAL SHADOW"

Memory and Commemoration of Irish Women's Experiences in World War I

FIONNUALA WALSH

I began then a sort of journal of the war, to which I gave fanciful names. When I was writing it, I must have done it self-consciously, with an eye on posterity; that is my impression looking back on it. It might be very interesting if it was dug up, say in 2014, that is, if there are not myriads like it. . . . Looking back on my notes now—I decided to call it "A woman's notes on the Great War"—I find it intensely depressing. The prophecies that never came true: the rumors that were so soon dissipated: perhaps above all, the fact that these were written down in ignorance of how the war should still be dragging on, slaying and torturing, after three and a half years had gone by, makes the reading of these notes a dreary business.

Katharine Tynan, *The Year of the Shadow* (1919, 146)

AMONG MANY OTHER WOMEN IN Ireland and Britain, the poet and novelist Katharine Tynan kept a journal from autumn 1914, consciously recording the momentous events happening around her. She had future readers in mind, imagining it might be useful for historians, "if there were not myriads like it." She might have been surprised to learn one hundred years later how few such journals by women in Ireland remained, especially in the public domain. Her memoir *The Year of the Shadow*, initially completed in April 1918, is one of the few surviving wartime accounts by Irish women. Academic and public interest in such women's experiences is a relatively new phenomenon. Catriona Clear argued in 2008 that Irish women remained in the "historical shadow" of writing about women and World War I (Clear 2008, 160), echoing Keith Jeffery's phrase in 2000 that the involvement of Irish women in World War I constitutes a "historically hidden Ireland" (Jeffery 2000, 30). Although gender remains one of the most important categories for analyzing the impact of World War I in international scholarship, both gender and the war have until recently been given comparatively little attention in the Irish case. Ireland's women of World War I have been neglected at the expense of women active in the suffrage, nationalist, and unionist movements of the period. The centenary of World War I, however, has led to renewed attention on Ireland's war experience and an uncovering of women's stories.

Following the outbreak of war in August 1914, the Irish population mobilized to support the British war effort. Catriona Pennell's work has demonstrated that the response of the Irish population to the outbreak of war in the summer of 1914 resembled that of the British people. It was widely believed that British and Irish participation in the war was necessary to prevent a German invasion (Pennell 2012, 194–195). The *Lady of the House*, a Dublin women's magazine, asserted that the Irish people were asked to put aside grudges, to "forget old wrongs," and to give the "blood of those we love—in order to help a neighbor who trusted us" (September 15, 1914). As estimated 206,000 Irish men voluntarily served in the British Army during the war, including Patrick and Toby Hinkson, the two sons of Katharine Tynan (Fitzpatrick 2018). In a parallel service, thousands of Irish women became involved in activities to support the war effort. These included nursing wounded soldiers either on the home front or overseas, supporting Belgian refugees in Ireland, collecting sphagnum moss for surgical dressings, fundraising for specific regiments, and preparing parcels of food and clothing to send to Irish soldiers at the front or in the prisoner of war camps.

My analysis of the British Red Cross membership records reveals that more than thirteen thousand Irish women—comprising approximately 1.4 percent of the female population aged twenty to fifty-five—served under the wartime joint committee of the British Red Cross and St. John Ambulance Association. This was a similar percentage to British women, supporting Pennell's argument that the United Kingdom as a whole mobilized for the war effort.[1] Hundreds of Irish women also enlisted in the military auxiliary services created to free up men for armed service. These included the Women's Legion, the Women's Army Auxiliary Corps (known as the Queen Mary Army Auxiliary Corps after 1920), the Women's Royal Naval Service (WRNS), and the Women's Royal Airforce. A combination of a desire for personal fulfillment or economic independence with patriotic idealism motivated Irish women to join these organizations or to participate in other war relief work. This chapter focuses on women's lived experience of the war and how they conceptualized their wartime experience in later recollections before examining public commemoration of women's mobilization. The ways in which women's participation in the war has been remembered and commemorated in Ireland over the past century will be considered, linking the Irish case to international examples of commemoration of women in wartime.

WOMEN'S EXPERIENCES OF WAR

Uncovering women's voices has proved difficult. There are many fewer surviving accounts of women's experience of World War I, and so the history of Ireland's World War I, in both public history portrayals and academic scholarship, focuses almost exclusively on the figure of the male combatant. The relative lack of public interest in Irish women's war experience affected the archival record; in comparison to Britain, items relating to the war were less likely to be valued or donated to public bodies in Ireland. Consequently, there are relatively few surviving "ego documents" such as diaries, letters, and memoirs concerning domestic and social life on the Irish home front. The marginalization of the female voice is, however, also evident elsewhere. In her work on British and French women veterans, Alison Fell notes that post-war memories and cultural representations of war have prioritized a narrative with the male combatant in the central role (Fell 2018, 6). The British historian Lucy Noakes has rightly observed that firsthand accounts of grief or coping with "the wartime exigencies of family, work and shortages of food and fuel" are less likely to be memorialized than those of the male combatants: "When women write, or speak about these experiences, their voices often sound less confident, and quieter than men's" (Noakes 2001, 664).

The few surviving accounts of Irish women's memories of their wartime experience typically fit two broad categories: those that recall the war in positive heroic terms or others that focus on the loss and grief it created. Although the growing disenchantment with the war effort and the increasing polarization of Irish society in the second half of the war affected women's mobilization, for the most part their articulation of their experience closely resembles that of British women. In common with women in other combatant countries, Irish women experienced the war as change and transformation. Penny Summerfield's work on Britain has attempted to examine the gap between the historical evidence that gender relations were not permanently changed by the war and the emphasis in personal accounts of the emancipatory impact of war work and the significance of participation for individual lives (Summerfield 1998, 6). Those who emphasized the heroic narrative of contribution to the nation in its peril drew on popular culture such as film but faltered somewhat in describing women's immediate post-war lives when there was no available public discourse in which to place their experiences. Noakes has observed that women who remembered the war as a period of personal growth and freedom emphasized their wartime work and used language similar to that found in wartime propaganda (Noakes 2001, 670–671).

This is evident, for example, in the British Red Cross service record completed by Isabella Cleland from County Antrim after the war ended: "I was well pleased with the privilege of doing a little bit" (BRCA First World War service records: Isabella Cleland). Another Ulster woman wrote that "I first went when I could and did all I could" (BRCA First World War service records: Emilie Gilmore McCaw). Both these women were Ulster Protestants, for whom war service was conceptualized as an expression of unionist identity and loyalty to the British Empire. Cleland, for example, had signed the Women's Declaration protesting against the imposition of Home Rule in 1912 (PRONI Ulster Covenant 2020). Their war service took place within their communities, creating an associational environment that affirmed their mobilization.

Ulster Catholics also participated in war work, however, albeit in smaller numbers. The only account by an Irish woman among the Imperial War Museum oral history testimonies of war workers is that of Isabella Clarke, née McGee, a Catholic from Belfast. Clarke migrated to England and worked in White Lund munitions factory in Morecambe, Lancashire. Munitions work was one of the most significant features of women's wartime employment: it was well paid compared to domestic service and other traditional female employments. Five national shell factories were established in Ireland, two in Dublin, and one each in Galway, Waterford, and Cork, employing over two thousand people. Private firms also gained munitions contracts from the War Office with over £24 million worth of army contracts awarded to Irish firms. Most of these contracts went to Belfast, where thousands of women found work producing bombs, grenades, and shells for the army. There were much greater opportunities and higher wages available in the British munitions industry, however. Significant numbers of Irish men and women traveled to Britain seeking such work (Walsh 2017, 19–24). Clarke was just sixteen when she left Belfast after signing up for munitions work in England through the labor exchange. She later emphasized the economic motivation of the higher wages and the need to find some means of supporting her family.

Interviewed in 1976, she recalled the harsh effects of the work on her health. In common with many other munitions workers, she suffered ill effects from working with TNT, which damages the liver, causing toxic jaundice, evident in the yellow skin of such workers (Thom 2017, 61). However, when asked whether she had enjoyed her war work, Clarke was emphatically positive about it: "Yes, every minute of it, it was a very happy time. Well everyone was very happy. We were in work and the people we were in work with. Everyone was very happy to help you" (Interview by Ciaran O'Gallagher, June 1976; Imperial War Museum Oral History no. 774). Clarke's positive experience of her fellow workers was not shared by all Irish girls in English munitions factories, however. In an incident recorded in the diary of Gabrielle West, a supervisor at the Hereford factory, a group of Irish women were sent home from the factory in August 1917 following a fight among workers allegedly sparked by the Irish girls singing Sinn Féin songs. West's account is mentioned in several British histories of women wartime workers and is often the only reference to Irish munitions workers, giving the impression that conflict between Irish and British workers was the norm. Incidences of deliberate antagonism by Irish workers, such as that described in West's account, were, in fact, rare, and Clarke's experience was likely more representative of the majority of Irish migrants who assimilated into the British workforce (Walsh 2017, 25).

Reminiscences of their war experience as a pleasant period are common in the oral history testimonies of women munitions workers. They focus on the camaraderie of the work and the sense of purpose and fulfillment gained from it, something perhaps absent from the remainder of the women's working lives (Woollacott 1994, 209). Clarke's interview was recorded sixty years after the war, and thus the intervening years and nostalgia likely colored her reflections. Summerfield argues that such local and personal accounts are influenced by the broader societal narratives, "the conceptual and definitional effects of powerful public representations" (Summerfield 1998, 15). Deborah Thom has also cautioned that the interviews of munitions workers in the Imperial War Museum were derived from a presupposition of the significance of their wartime experience to their later lives (Thom 1998, 19). Clarke's interview nevertheless gives an insight into the experience of Irish munitions workers in Britain and her positive recollections offer a corrective to the trope of the unruly Irish worker whose politics prevented assimilation.

Similar emphasis on personal fulfillment can be found in Emma Duffin's reflection on her experience of wartime nursing, also completed toward the end of her life. Duffin, an upper-class Belfast woman, served in France with the St. John Ambulance Association. In her unpublished 1967 memoir, she wrote:

> It had been a hard life but a great experience, never to be regretted. We had seen great suffering, but greater courage. We had learnt to take responsibility and to act on our own when required. . . . We had learnt the value of comradeship and

that class could be ignored, an orderly could be a friend as well as an officer, a patient could be a brother. To me some of those men are more dear than those I met perhaps a year or so ago. I can never forget them, and many I know will remember me. I am indeed their "sister" in both senses. (Parkhill 2014, 17)

Duffin had outlined her motives for enlisting to serve with the St. John Ambulance Association in a letter to her mother in May 1915: "I think it is the right thing to do, you will feel that you are being of some use, and it makes me independent till the end of the war anyway, and I daresay I will get to like the work, everyone seems to, it will certainly be interesting" (May 22, 1915, Public Records Office of Northern Ireland [PRONI], D2019/9/3/a). Similarly to Cleland, Duffin was from an Ulster Protestant family and so her sense of the "right thing to do" was likely influenced by the focus on war service among her community. Her brother was an officer in the British Army and her sisters all participated in the war effort in some form or another.

Duffin's account also makes clear her desire for independence and personal fulfillment. These were all important factors, particularly in sustaining relief work beyond the first few months of the war. Wartime nurses enjoyed a sense of pride in their handling of their duty, the companionship of working with others, and a feeling that their lives had meaning and purpose (Donner 1997, 688). This was evident in the case of Marie Martin, a Catholic woman from Belfast who served overseas with the British Red Cross. Her letters from France and Malta to her mother reveal the sense of self-worth she gained from receiving praise from the matron, and the enjoyment she found in being able to dispense medical advice to her relatives. She found the work difficult but wrote home to her mother after a month in Malta that she could "stand anything and everything to feel I am of use and doing a certain amount for all these poor men who are suffering to save us from ruination" (Walsh 2020, 55).

One of Martin's colleagues in Malta was another Dublin Catholic, Iza Mahony, who like Martin and Duffin had a brother serving in the British Army. Mahony's diary reveals a strong sense of duty to her nursing work but also suggests that the war offered a relief from a more mundane existence at home. She noted the day she left Dublin for overseas service as "the beginning of a new career for me." Although the pay provided to volunteer nurses was paltry, the arrival of Mahony's first pay packet generated excitement: "Great day. Got our first pay. First money I ever earned" (Mahony family papers, Diary of Iza Mahony, September 1, 1915, to March 3, 1916).[2] Sharon Ouditt has suggested that British voluntary nurses, epitomized by Vera Brittain, whose memoir of the war became a best seller in the 1930s, found themselves "suddenly released from the passive, chaperoned Edwardian existence characteristic of provincial female life" (Ouditt 1994, 31). Arthur Marwick argues that a conscious awareness of their contribution to an essential war effort brought a new "self-consciousness and a new sense of status" to the middle- and upper-class women involved in war work (Marwick 1967, 99). Marwick's conclusions have been critiqued by scholars such as Alison Fell, however, who highlights the limited and temporary nature of wartime progress in women's emancipation and the prewar roles performed by many women in the public sphere (Fell and Hallett 2013, 186). Nevertheless, many of the women involved recognized the emancipatory potential of war service and welcomed the distraction from their otherwise restricted lives.

Another Ulster nurse, Catherine Black from Donegal, has more in common with what Summerfield describes as the "stoic" response. Although these women came from similar social backgrounds and participated in the same types of war work as those who adopted the heroic narrative, "stoic" women attributed different meanings to their war work, more typically seeing it as a necessity rather than an opportunity and the war as an unwelcome intrusion into their personal lives (Summerfield 1998, 92). Noakes has noted that "memories of death and fear, loss and grief tended to take precedence in their recollections over memories of challenge, change and autonomy" (Noakes 2001, 671). Reflecting on her nursing experience in France two decades after the war ended, Catherine Black was conscious of its significance in her life. She wondered how she endured her time with the Queen Alexandra Imperial Military Nursing Service in France, finding it only possible to contemplate it at all from the distance of twenty years: "You could not go through the things we went through, see the things we saw and remain the same. You went into it young and light-hearted. You came out older than any span of years could make you. But at the time you did not reflect on it much or on anything else. You did not dare to" (Black 1939, 95).

The significant emotional toll of the war is also evident in Katharine Tynan's memoir and that by the Countess of Fingall, Elizabeth Burke-Plunkett. Tynan anticipated the lingering effects of the war: "We might emerge from underneath the scourge, but our backs would still be bloody" (Tynan 1919, 298). Born into a Dublin Catholic family in 1859, Tynan was well known in Irish literary circles. During the war, she lived in Claremorris in County Mayo, where her husband, Henry Albert Hinkson, served as a magistrate. A moderate nationalist, she supported Ireland's involvement in the war but over time "weariness of it and longing for it to end overcame all other feelings" (187). Although not involved in the Red Cross, Tynan's wartime life was preoccupied by the conflict. She published four collections of poetry on the war, including the immensely popular collection *Flower of Youth* in 1915. The title poem, originally published in the *Spectator* in December 1914, offered comfort to the families of the lost soldiers. She also wrote various poems dedicated to the memory of the fallen sons of friends and engaged in continual correspondence with soldiers themselves and bereaved families (O'Neill 1987, 90). The enlistment of her own two sons in the British Army when they came of age brought her great distress, mingled with pride: "On the last day of 1914 I had finished up my little diary with 'Lord my heart is ready!' I do not know why I wrote it. I never thought then that the War would last long enough for the boys to go" (Tynan 1919, 179). The family had lived in England for many years and consequently the outbreak of rebellion in 1916 created pain and sorrow for Tynan. She felt divided between her affection for England and her love for Ireland and struggled to accept the sudden "sharp bitter cleavage" between the two countries (204). Too much had been lost over the four years, and for her there could be "no rejoicing for the peace when it came" (298).

Elizabeth Burke-Plunkett similarly found it difficult to celebrate the 1918 Armistice: "I used to think and say, during the war, that if ever that list of dead and wounded would cease, I would never mind anything or grumble at anything again. But when the Armistice came at last, we seemed drained of all feeling. And one felt nothing" (Hinkson 1991, 386). A Catholic and a liberal unionist, Burke-Plunkett had served as president of the United Irishwomen, which focused on rural renewal and food production during the war, while also involved in the Irishwomen's Association, an organization devoted to preparing parcels of comforts to send to Irish soldiers in prisoner of war camps. She also led the Central Committee for Women's Employment, established in 1914 to help women who had lost employment due to the war. Burke-Plunkett, the wife of Arthur Plunkett, the 11th Earl of Fingall and the state steward to the administration at Dublin Castle, was a member of the landed gentry, a class that had suffered disproportionate losses in the war. She described how the "world we had known had vanished. We hunted again but ghosts rode with us. We sat at table and there were absent faces" (Hinkson 1991, 386). Of the 109 Irish peers who served in the war, 29 were killed or died of wounds sustained in active service (Beckett 2007, 446). The isolated, self-contained nature of the aristocracy meant that each casualty was taken personally by the whole community (Dooley 2001, 122). Many of the bereaved struggled in the aftermath, especially in Ireland where republican politics took center stage and war service became maligned.

COMMEMORATING IRISH WOMEN
PARTICIPANTS IN WORLD WAR I

In an influential article, F. X. Martin identified a "national amnesia" surrounding Ireland's participation in World War I and noted the disproportionate historiographic and public attention paid to the Easter Rising (1967, 68). In 1986, David Fitzpatrick noted the continuing gap in scholarship, observing that references to the war in Irish historiography tended to treat it as an external political event of little importance in the lives of ordinary people (Fitzpatrick 1986, vii). He recently corrected Martin's phrase to "historical aphasia," arguing that the problem was not forgetting the past but an inability to speak or write of the war (Fitzpatrick 2018, 257). Timothy Bowman attributed this perceived silence to the difficulty encountered by historians in separating the experience of World War I from that of the subsequent Irish revolution (Bowman 2014, 603). The participation of Irish men in World War I, occurring in parallel to the 1916 Rising and the burgeoning republican movement, represented unwelcome contradictions and complexities in the history of the founding of the Free State and subsequent Republic (Townshend 2004, 890).

Ireland's relationship to World War I is complex, however, and this narrative of national amnesia or aphasia risks being overstated. Armistice Day was marked throughout Ireland between 1919 and 1931, with Mass for the war dead said in Catholic churches in Dublin, for instance. Families mourned their own lost relatives by holding remembrance services, organizing parish memorials, tending to graves, and attempting to hold on to the memory of their lost loved one. As noted by Jay Winter and David Fitzpatrick, personal remembrance acts also had a public commemorative function, with headstones or in memoriam notices inviting the wider public to offer respect to the dead (Winter 1995; Fitzpatrick 2001, 184). While town memorials served a political purpose and were intended as reminders of sacrifice, they were also sites of mourning and reflection for family members of the casualties, who were typically buried far from home (Switzer 2007, 86).

Following the beginnings of the use of the poppy as a way of marking remembrance for the war dead in 1921, there was great popular demand for poppies from November 1922 in Ireland, prompting Annie MacSwiney, sister of the late republican activist Terence MacSwiney, to complain in 1928 "how the poppies fly in Ireland since the Free State came into existence—Union Jackery of every description foisted on the country" (Fitzpatrick 2001, 194). Thousands of Irish veterans took part in a parade in the Phoenix Park in 1929 that was attended by representatives of the Free State government. That year, however, the president of the Executive Council, W. T. Cosgrave, reminded a unionist senator that there remained "certain hostility to the idea of any form of war memorial" (Fitzpatrick 2001, 192). Nonetheless, in 1930 Cosgrave supported the proposal for a war memorial at Islandbridge, on the edge of Dublin city. It received financial support from the Fianna Fáil government in the 1930s and the official opening was planned for 1939, when the outbreak of war and the threat of conscription in Northern Ireland led to its postponement and eventual abandonment. In the context of World War II, Irish participation in World War I was recast as a "great mistake, a profound betrayal," and gradually allowed to disappear from the narrative of the history of the state (Boyce 2002, 201–202). Irish Republican paramilitary attacks in the 1950s, combined with lack of government financing for its upkeep and care, resulted in the memorial falling into a state of dilapidation. Restored in the late 1980s, the War Memorial Gardens were finally officially opened in 1988 (Jeffery 2000, 135).

Despite the abandonment of Islandbridge and the hostility among much of the public toward World War I, reminders of Irish men's military service were nonetheless visible around the country in the form of the village and church memorials to those who served in the war. Although much fewer in number and typically less prominently placed than those in Great Britain, they nevertheless exert a physical presence and a reminder of a history that could not be entirely ignored. Women's war experience, however, left fewer tangible traces and has more easily disappeared from the historical narrative. This is not unique to Ireland. In all former combatant countries, World War I memorials provide a "male-dominated vision of gender roles that either excludes or offers a highly restricted interpretation of women's contributions and experiences during the war" (Fell 2018, 21). In his work on commemorative practice in France, David Sherman argues that the role of commemoration was to "reinscribe gender codes" that had been disrupted by the war, a process involving the placing of men and women into a set of restrictive allegorical roles derived from prewar gender norms: "men were active, heroic, resourceful . . . women were grieving, suffering, emotional" (Sherman 1996, 84, 93). Some of these same tendencies appear in Irish cases. Catherine Switzer's examination of World War I memorials in Northern Ireland reveals that women appear in sculpture solely as allegories intended to represent "Peace" or "Victory." The most realistic representation is the "daughter of Erin" sculpture in Coleraine, depicting a shawled woman placing a wreath in remembrance. Women's wartime role as nurses or in the auxiliary services are typically absent from such memorials (Switzer 2007, 80). Women's primary commemorative function was as the bereaved mothers and wives of soldiers, representing the loss generated by the sacrifice of the heroic men in battle.

However, more dynamic roles are occasionally visible. Looking beyond the national or state memorials, it is possible to find commemorative discourse that places women within the "community of active citizens who served" (Fell 2018, 37). In the 1920s, some villages and local communities raised funds to erect war memorials and rolls of honor that marked the contribution of the entire community to the war effort rather than only the sacrifice of the dead, thus providing a space to commemorate those who had served and survived as well as those who had died. Catherine Switzer has noted the difficulties that local committees had in compiling the names for such memorials and the vexed decisions committees had to make concerning the inclusion and exclusion of names. Gender was just one of many contentious issues to be considered, alongside connection to the local area, date of death, and length and type of service (Switzer 2007, 124–126). These memorials did occasionally include the names of local women who had been in active service, providing recognition of their contribution. Nurses were most likely to be included, rather than members of the women's auxiliary military services such as the Queen Mary Army Auxiliary Corps, the Women's Legion, or the WRNS.

Killyleagh village in County Down, for example, produced a commemorative booklet in late 1918 that records the contribution of the entire community to the war effort. Rolls of honor for the various local churches were compiled in it, including the Presbyterian church, which listed the war service of two Red Cross nurses—Kathleen Heron, who served in Salonika, and Gwennie Moore, who served in France—alongside the ninety-six Presbyterian men from the parish who served with the British military (W. H. Martin 1918). Killyleagh was one of the few villages where women were represented on the war memorial committee—such committees typically being composed solely of men—and this may have contributed toward Heron and Moore's inclusion on the roll of honor. Indeed, the Killyleagh memorial scheme was led by the local Women's Work Guild (Switzer 2007, 62–63). Killyleagh was not usual, though: many Irish memorial plaques or commemorative booklets did not include the names of women who served. The exclusion of women from other rolls of honor was not always accepted with equanimity by women veterans. One woman, titling herself "A girl who has served," wrote to the *County Down Spectator* in November 1922 to protest the exclusion of women, arguing that memorials should include all those "who offered their lives for their country ... I hope the girls who donned the King's uniform will in no case be forgotten" (in Switzer 2007, 127).

The small number of Irish women who died in active service more frequently appear on memorials around Ireland, where they are presented as war deaths, aligning their sacrifice with that of servicemen. As was the case with men, many of the Irish women who died in active service are buried far from home, in England, France, Italy, Malta, Egypt, Palestine, and Salonika, giving greater importance to memorials on the island of Ireland as sites of mourning for their families. Although women's war service carried much less risk than that of men in the armed forces, at least forty-four women from Ireland died in active service between 1914 and 1918, while another thirteen died in 1919. The women who died were Queen Mary Army Auxiliary Corps officers, or professional and voluntary nurses and members of the Women's Legion, the Women's Royal Airforce, and the WRNS. Disease was a constant risk for those serving overseas. Many nurses also faced danger from shellfire while working in casualty clearing stations close to the front and from torpedoes while traveling overseas.

Ten Irish women in active service were killed when the mailboat RMS *Leinster* was torpedoed in the Irish Sea, the greatest loss of life of Irish women in enemy action. They included Josephine Carr, who has the dubious honor of being the only member of the WRNS to die in World War I due to enemy action. Born in Cork in 1899, she had recently enlisted with the WRNS to work as a shorthand typist. Carr was traveling on the *Leinster* en route to England for WRNS work and was with two colleagues from Cork, Maureen Waters and Lilian Barry, who both survived the sinking (Fletcher 1989, 23). Maureen Waters recalled afterward the moment of the torpedo collision: "The ship was standing upright almost, propeller in the air . . . I prayed as I never did before" (Newman 2014, 150). Carr's body, like so many of the casualties, was never recovered. She is, however, commemorated on the WRNS memorial in Plymouth. The other casualties included Clare McNally, a member of the Women's Legion, whose father had been killed earlier in the war. Her body was recovered, and her coffin was carried to the grave in Bohermore Cemetery in County Galway between two files of Connaught Rangers, her father's regiment (Newman 2014, 150).

Most of the Irish women casualties of the war died of disease contracted in active service. They include Iza Mahony, the Dublin Red Cross nurse. She was sent to France following her service in Malta, where she is believed to have developed tuberculosis. She died in Dublin after nineteen months of poor health (Mahony 2015). Others died far from home. Mary Agnes Doherty from Magherafelt in County Derry died from malaria and dysentery in Salonika. The daughter of a retired Royal Irish Constabulary policeman, Doherty was employed as a nurse in Dr. Steevens' Hospital in Dublin in 1914 when she volunteered with the Queen Alexandra Imperial Military Nursing Service.

She initially served in France, where she was awarded a Royal Red Cross and was mentioned in dispatches for her devotion to duty (*Irish Times*, December 9, 1916). In 1916, Doherty was transferred to Salonika, where she died aged twenty-eight. She was buried in the local Lembet Road military cemetery (Commonwealth War Graves Commission 2020).

Doherty was one of eighteen Irish women who died in the service of the Queen Alexandra Imperial Military Nursing Service. These eighteen women were named on a memorial placed in Arbour Hill Garrison Chapel in Dublin. At its unveiling in 1921, the Reverend C. A. Peacocke praised the nurses for showing "the highest qualities of womanhood" and suggested that the congregation should be inspired by the memorial's reminder of "a wonderful record of service, of character, of fortitude, of the highest and best gifts that God gave to man and woman" (*Irish Times*, November 7, 1921). This overtly militaristic language and didactic emphasis was common to commemorative practices for World War I nurses after the Armistice. Such commentary typically combined the traditional representation of nurses as icons of saintly womanhood with a discourse centered on tragic sacrifices for the nation or for civilization itself (Fell 2018, 40–41). The memorial plaque's sojourn in Dublin was short lived, however. In 1922, the Arbour Hill church asked St. Anne's Cathedral in Belfast to accept the memorial and since then it has remained in Belfast (Remembrance NI 2018). There is little surviving information on the memorial plaque's origins and the reasons for its transfer to Belfast, but the timing of the move suggests the impact of strengthened hostility toward Ireland's participation in World War I following the War of Independence and the outbreak of the civil war.

Some of the other women casualties are remembered in individual parish memorials. A memorial plaque at St. Mary's Catholic Church in Ballsbridge, Dublin, for example, includes the name of Iza Mahony, who grew up in the local area, together with the ninety-four men from the parish who died in the war. She is the only woman listed on the memorial plaque, with her name placed below that of the men and separated by a space. Her inclusion on the memorial was likely influenced by her father's role on the memorial committee. Mahony's brother Edmund is also among the names: he was killed serving with the Royal Munster Fusiliers (Mahony 2015). Although intended primarily as sites of remembrance and mourning for the bereaved families, these memorials have an important function in shaping the narrative of the war and what constitutes service. When women were included, it served as a reminder of their contribution and recognition of their efforts. Historians are now attempting to trace more such references to women participants, assumed for many years to be solely records of military service, and more recent memorials have expanded the definition of war service and war casualties.

CENTENARY COMMEMORATIONS OF THE IRISH WORLD WAR I EXPERIENCE

Popular attitudes toward Irish participation in World War I have undergone a transformation in the past two decades (Pennell 2017, 261–271). There are numerous organizations devoted to remembering Ireland's soldiers, such as the Royal Dublin Fusiliers Association and the Connaught Rangers Association, while the National Museum's permanent exhibition on military heritage includes a section on the role of Irish men and women in World War I. During National Heritage Week in August 2014, there were more than eighty separate events taking place around the Republic of Ireland that focused on Irish participation in World War I. The historian Catherine Switzer's work on memorials at the Somme noted the growth in public interest in visits to the battlefields and graves. Her interviews with visitors from the Republic of Ireland in 2009 suggested to her the emotional power of "rediscovered history," with respondents expressing "sadness at what these men went through and never recognized up to now" but also noting that while the men had been "forgotten in their own country for so long," this was "changing very quickly, at long last" (Switzer 2013, 204). While this focus was initially solely on the soldier figure, more recent commemorations have acknowledged women's involvement in World War I.

In a speech to mark the centenary of the ending of the war on November 11, 2018, Michael D. Higgins, the president of Ireland, reflected on the transformation of public understanding and how reticence to confront the reality of the war had been replaced by a "better appreciation of the experience of the war, not only for those in uniform but for civilians" (2018a). His deliberate inclusion of civilians reflects a broader recognition that military service was not the only World War I experience. One of the key features of the centenary commemorations has been the effort to develop an understanding of the impact of "total war." Recent international scholarship has demonstrated that the separation between the home and the battlefield was more permeable than previously thought, with emphasis increasingly placed on the constant interaction between soldiers and civilians, and the hardship endured by civilians in the face of severe food shortages (Jones 2013, 869). While the Decade of Commemorations has led to more academic interest and public engagement with Ireland's participation in World War I, unsurprisingly there has been a heavy emphasis on recovering the "hidden history" of the military service of men and especially on remembering the lives lost in the war. Effort has been made to compile a more concrete figure of the Irish fatalities and to put names to the statistics. County rolls of honor have been created, led primarily by Tom Burnell (2017). There have also been various local initiatives to arrange memorials to the dead and to mark the lost lives.

For example, in 2017 the "Weeping Window" poppy sculpture created by Paul Cummins was assembled at the Ulster Museum in Belfast, with each ceramic poppy intended to represent a lost life in the war (*Irish Times*, October 13, 2017). The French government presented a memorial cross to Glasnevin Cemetery in Dublin in 2016 to remember the men of the 16th Irish division who lost their lives in France in 1916 (*Irish Times*, November 13, 2016). In 2018, five Victoria Cross plaques were unveiled at Glasnevin to mark the extreme bravery of five Irish soldiers during World War I. These commemorative events were imbued with political significance. The poppy has long been a contested symbol in Ireland, north and south, largely in response to the actions of the British military in Northern Ireland during the Troubles. For many in Northern Ireland, Armistice commemorations are intrinsically linked to the Enniskillen bombing on Remembrance Sunday, November 8, 1987 (Longley 2001, 227). The designer of the poppy sculpture in Belfast, Tom Piper, acknowledged that the poppy was a "contentious symbol" but suggested that the sculpture offered an opportunity for people to "reimagine the symbols and reclaim them in a different way" (*Irish Times*, October 13, 2017). Glasnevin Cemetery has been more typically associated with the martyrs of the Irish revolution (Johnson 2003, 153–161). The site of famous impassioned oratories such as Patrick Pearse's lament over the grave of the Fenian Jeremiah O'Donovan Rossa in 1915, those interred in the republican plot include Thomas Ashe and Cathal Brugha, while Michael Collins is prominently entombed in the cemetery as well. Its central role in World War I centenary events is further evidence of attempts at shared inclusive commemorations.

While the general focus has remained on combatants, and specifically on casualties, women's experience has also received greater attention. Women have been included in recent community rolls of honor with their wartime service recognized as a parallel contribution to that of men in the armed forces. For example, the Kilkenny Great War Memorial Committee, founded in 2011, was determined to include the five women from the county who lost their lives in the war, alongside the 820 men (Kilkenny Great War Memorial 2011). There have been popular panel discussions of women's contribution to the war at the Dublin Festival of History and the Belfast International Arts Festival. The National Library of Ireland opened an exhibition on Ireland and World

War I in 2014 that has been updated annually with new material on each year of the war. It has included female experiences from the outset, drawing on documents such as the 1916 diary of Mary Martin and the papers of the Irish War Hospital Supply Depot. A handout produced by the library's education department for Leaving Certificate students asked them to reflect on "how the lives of women might have changed" over the course of the war and how men and women might have reacted to these changes (WWI Ireland 2014). Dublin City Library and Archive at Pearse Street held an exhibition in spring 2018 specifically on women and the war, showcasing items from their collections relating to women's participation in the war effort and their home front experience. An accompanying lecture series took place in Dublin City Hall in April 2018 (Dublin City Council 2020). The success and popular appeal of these endeavors reveals the public appetite and interest in women's war stories, which was unanticipated at the beginning of the centenary in 2014. When I began work on Irish women and World War I in 2011, I was constantly warned that there was not enough material, that women in Ireland did not experience World War I to any significant extent. This proved to be incorrect, and, indeed, it became clear that the war ought to be considered one of the defining events in the history of women in twentieth-century Ireland. By the centenary of the Armistice in 2018, it was widely accepted that any discussion of the war's impact and its legacies would include women, indicating a rapid transformation in attitudes and understanding.

This public interest is also apparent in the engagement of schoolteachers with the topic. The Department of Education and Skills in the Republic of Ireland and Department of Education in Northern Ireland, in collaboration with University College Cork, Mercier Press, and *History Ireland* magazine, have organized a school history competition since 2012 for both primary and secondary level pupils. Among the themes relating to the decade of centenaries is "women's history in Ireland during the revolutionary period" (Decade of Centenaries School Project Competition 2020. At second level the topic has been included in a new Junior Certificate history textbook, published by Mentor Books (McCaughey 2018, 428).[3]

Oona Frawley has noted that "what is remembered or forgotten does not remain constant, and nor does the amount of remembrance or forgetting" (Frawley 2010, xxi). This has relevance for Ireland's World War I history, which is evidently more complex than the narrative of national amnesia might suggest. While the state has had a conflicted relationship to this history, commemoration of the war has persisted in some form or another over the past century. It is worth reflecting on which voices and experiences have been emphasized or which have been marginalized. Ireland's war was not a solely military affair, with the war also having a profound and transformative impact on women's lives on the home front. The gendered nature of war commemoration and memorialization from the outset, however, obscures this history and emphasizes the combatant narrative. Women's voices are also more difficult to locate, and the few recorded memories are often situated within heroic narratives centered on the emancipatory impact of the war rather than the more mundane but perhaps more common everyday experiences of disruption, hardship, and loss. The surge of research and public interest prompted by the Decade of Centenaries has, however, led to a more nuanced focus on the experiences of ordinary people and on non-combatants, including women. A more inclusive approach has also been taken to the period that places Ireland's contribution to World War I within the wider context of the Irish revolution.

Women have featured prominently throughout the Decade of Centenaries, with a renewed scholarly and public emphasis on their roles in the Easter Rising and the War of Independence as well as World War I. The centenary of the granting of the franchise received significant attention in 2018 and several pioneering women's history texts have been reissued in response. Primary sources—such as the writings of the suffragist Hanna Sheehy Skeffington (Margaret Ward 2017)—have also been made more widely available, while projects such as the Letters of 1916–1923 have expanded the range of sources publicly available for examining everyday experiences during revolutionary upheaval (Letters 1916–1923 Project 2013). Fruitful interdisciplinary collaborations have been possible for scholars in Ireland and Britain, and there has been a significant growth in women's history publications. These provide a lasting legacy for the discipline and will spur future research. For scholars working on women's lives in this period, it is rewarding and instructive to witness both the transformation of public attitudes toward women's place in the centenary commemorations, and Ireland's role in World War I.

NOTES

1. I am grateful to the British Red Cross Archives (BRCA) for providing me with a database of all the Red Cross membership records from World War I, and to Daniel Purcell for his assistance with the data analysis.

2. My thanks to Hubert Mahony for making this diary available to me.

3. This inclusion resulted from a collaboration between the book's author Patsy McCaughey and the executive committee of the Women's History

Association of Ireland as part of an effort to improve the coverage of women's history in the volume.

FIONNUALA WALSH received her PhD from Trinity College Dublin in 2015. She subsequently has held a research position at the National Library of Ireland and an Irish Research Council Postdoctoral Fellowship in Trinity College Dublin. Since 2017, she has lectured in the School of History, University College Dublin. Her first monograph, *Irish Women and the Great War*, was published in 2020.

EIGHT

—ɯ—

COMMEMORATING A MISSING HISTORY

Tracing the Visual and Material Culture of the Irish Women's Suffrage Campaign, 1908–1918

DONNA GILLIGAN

THE YEAR 2018 MARKED A centenary since Irish women first received partial enfranchisement for the right to vote in general elections. The centenary commemoration prompted national remembrance and recognition through lectures, events, and discussions. The Irish suffrage movement has previously been absent from Irish written historical records. What of its visual and material records? Museum objects relating to Irish women's history have often belonged to the domestic or craft sphere rather than to political and national involvement. Prior to the 2018 commemoration, the subject of the Irish women's suffrage campaign was a topic that had not featured prominently in museum displays. Only a small number of public exhibitions dealing with this theme have taken place in Ireland over the past fifty years. These forms of commemoration have occurred as one-off events or temporary exhibitions rather than continued inclusions in permanent exhibitions as a part of Irish history. Research has shown that the majority of Irish museums do not hold any suffrage material in their collections, which has made it a historical subject that has rarely been dealt with through an exhibition format.

Work by the author has undertaken a detailed cataloging and assessment of surviving and non-extant visual and material culture associated with the second wave of the Irish suffrage campaign. An examination of the objects and images of the Irish campaign helps better materialize a section of national history that has previously been overlooked for discussion in Irish heritage institutions. Historical artifacts and visual representations act as witnesses to the past and can be introduced into the narrative to tell a more complete tale of the actions and complexities of the campaign and the people involved. Unlike the visual and material culture of the British and American suffrage campaigns, the combined objects and images of the Irish movement have not previously been examined as a whole. One of the reasons Irish suffrage objects have never been assessed as a group may be simply due to their quantity. Despite the fact that the Irish movement was considered proportionally equal in size to that of its British equivalent, only a relatively small collection of objects survive from this period. It would appear that the Irish national struggle for independence overshadowed the suffrage movement as a focus for collection and preservation. With this in mind, it is important to ask—how can museums commemorate this period without surviving material representation?

It could be suggested that the fact that very few objects survive for exhibition gives the misleading impression that suffrage was a small or unimportant movement in Irish history. Research expanding on the visual and material culture of Irish suffrage aims to fill in details of a neglected material past, and, ultimately, to provide a new contribution toward the commemoration of the Irish suffrage movement in the future. On a wider scale, the case study dealt with in this chapter hopes to stand as an example of the ways in which broader research in the fields of design history and material culture can contribute to better representation of women's history in interpretation, display, and exhibition within Irish museums.

INTRODUCTION

Research conducted by the author has sought to provide a commemoration of the Irish women's suffrage movement of the early twentieth century through an examination of the associated surviving and non-extant objects and images. This work explored what such aspects of the visual and material past can inform us about the Irish suffrage campaign, its participants, its activities, and its contemporary environment. Due to the small number of surviving objects from this period, research also examined the non-extant material referenced in primary sources as used and produced by Irish suffragists. This approach presented a broader understanding of the scale and actuality of the visual and material past of the movement. Research aimed to fully recognize the role that material and visual culture played in the Irish suffrage struggle and thus mark the scale and significance of this hidden history.

Due to its occurrence during a period of significant political and national upheaval in Ireland, Irish suffrage can be recognized as a distinctly individual form of the international suffrage campaigns. During the peak of the suffrage movement, Ireland was involved in events relating to the fight for Home Rule, World War I, the 1916 Rising, and the Celtic Revival cultural movement. Research parameters for this work focused on the period ranging from 1908 to 1918, covering the phase from the beginning of the second wave of Irish suffrage up to the granting of first partial female national vote in Ireland. Irish suffrage objects were cataloged and assessed in terms of form, design, and use in comparison with the objects recorded from the wider British and American suffrage campaigns. This approach evaluated similarities and differences, highlighted national or international influences, and examined whether the Irish movement reflected a specific national style through its material past.

Objects and images played a key role in international women's suffrage movements of the early twentieth century. The international movements of this period are widely recognized for their means of successful political promotion through branding and imagery (Tickner 1987; Crawford 2018; Garrett and Thomas 2019) as well as for their significant role in the development of consumerism (see Finnegan 1999). This impact may be seen in the mass-produced promotional material (see Florey 2013), the creation of a political uniform (see Rolley 1990), and the clever visual and material advertisement of their cause (Tickner 1987)—all of which served to actively promote and publicize their aim. Despite the fact that the Irish movement was considered proportionally equal in size to that of its British equivalent (Ferriter 2010, 174), research has revealed that only a small collection of objects survives from this period. The state repository of the National Museum of Ireland holds a collection of objects of a quantity of less than 3 percent of the comparative collection of the Museum of London.

When considering the survival rate of Irish suffrage objects, it is important to understand the scale of the Irish suffrage campaign. A second wave of suffrage activism emerged in Ireland in the early 1900s, headed by several young women who had benefited from advances in female educational opportunities. Developments on a more international scale, such as the formation of the radical English Women's Social and Political Union (WSPU), also influenced this second generation of Irish suffragists. The formation in 1908 of the Irish Women's Franchise League (IWFL) introduced a new native organization that followed the modern methods of suffrage campaigning heralded by the WSPU. The women behind the IWFL understood the complex political scenario of the Irish suffrage situation, where women from a colonized country struggling for independence fought for a vote in a British government. The following years saw the formation of a number of other Irish suffrage societies that differed in their approaches and alliances. Women involved in militant or radical activity were known as suffragettes, with the wider term of *suffragists* used to represent nonmilitant suffrage campaigners (as well as a broader term for women involved in the overall cause).

Records suggest that approximately thirty suffrage groups existed throughout Ireland between 1908 and 1916, with the number of Irish suffragists in 1912 estimated at "well over three thousand" (Cullen Owens 1984, 45). The early stages of this second wave of Irish women's suffrage saw Irish suffragists campaign passively for the inclusion of a female franchise clause on the upcoming Home Rule Bill. John Redmond, leader of the Irish Parliamentary Party, was openly hostile to women's suffrage as well as wary of embracing any issue that may have negatively affected the granting of Home Rule. The exclusion of women's suffrage from the Home Rule Bill in 1912 altered the course of suffrage protest in Ireland. The IWFL engaged in pronounced militant activity for the first time, carrying out a campaign of militant activity throughout the country during the period from 1912 to 1914. Many suffragettes served terms in Irish and English prisons as a result. In protest at their lack of a vote, they smashed the windows of government buildings, heckled politicians, carried out attacks on postboxes full of letters, and organized protest events that publicly advertised their dissatisfaction. In prison, the IWFL members campaigned to be treated as political prisoners and participated in hunger strikes in protest when their demands were not met.

This second phase of Irish women's suffrage saw a significant change in the methods and public visibility of the campaign. The new suffrage organizations of the early twentieth century created branding through the use of slogans and organizational colors, produced printed posters and handbills with their demands, and wrote political responses and articles for publication in newspapers and journals. The green and orange organizational colors of the IWFL became the recognizable Irish equivalent of the British WSPU suffrage colors of purple, white, and green.

Research by the author has initially uncovered approximately seventy surviving three-dimensional objects associated with the Irish suffrage movement. With the exception of archival material, this small group of objects exists as the only physical representation of an important political campaign almost ten years in length and involving thousands of Irish women. In comparison, 2016 saw the centenary of the six-day rebellion of the 1916 Rising in Ireland, for which hundreds of ephemeral objects had been retained and collected by museums and the public. This allowed for widespread exhibition of the associated material and visual culture of this event. It would appear that the Irish national struggle for independence has previously overshadowed the suffrage campaign as a focus for preservation and collection. The 2018 centenary of "votes for women" has thus offered an opportunity for new public focus and attention on the physical past of Irish suffrage.

The author's research aimed to address a number of specific objectives. It questioned what could be learned about the Irish suffrage movement from the examination and evaluation of its associated visual and material culture, contributing a new method of historical analysis to the current subject corpus. The aim of the research was not to retell the entire history of the Irish suffrage movement but rather to physically materialize its presence, influences, and choices during a defined period through analysis of its associated objects and images. Specifically, the work aimed at the examination of objects and images rather than archival sources such as letters, newspapers, and organizational records. The key primary sources for this research were the associated surviving objects and images, which were sourced and accessed through Irish museum and library collections and from private and public collections from both national and international contexts. Information on objects and the visual record was also obtained from primary sources such as contemporary newspapers, photography, magazines, and artwork such as political cartoons. Research examined the surviving and non-extant material through emerging themes such as objects of promotion and protest, graphic design, imagery, and suffrage dress. Surviving objects and images embody important stories of the actions and activities of those involved in the campaign and perhaps can be said to make a more immediate connection with a public audience interested in learning about the movement.

OBJECTS OF PROMOTION AND PROTEST

Suffrage badges served as an intrinsic form of propaganda and visual support in the women's suffrage campaign and played a role in a number of private and public events in contemporary Irish society. Such badges displayed the name and organizational colors or symbols of a suffrage group and often a general suffrage slogan. During food kitchen relief work throughout the 1913 Dublin Lockout, involved members of the IWFL deliberately wore their suffrage badges to distinguish themselves and to express the campaign's solidarity with the workers (Cullen Owens 1984, 77).

Primary records and a small selection of surviving examples show that a number of the Irish suffrage organizations deliberately chose Celtic Revival or nationalist-inspired symbolism and colors for their badges. The surviving badge of the Irish League for Women's Suffrage (ILWS) displays clear influence of this type. (See Fig. 8.1.) The ILWS badge features a gold "maid of Erin"

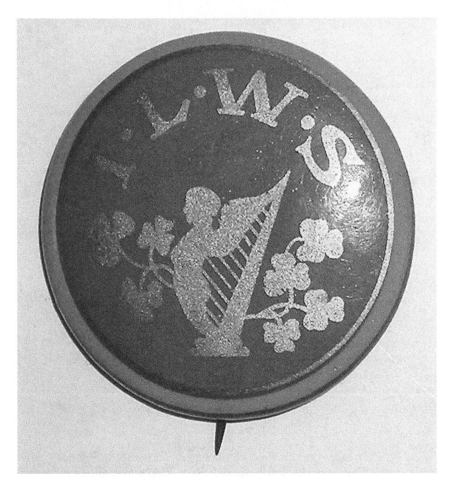

Figure 8.1. Celluloid membership badge of the Irish League for Women's Suffrage, circa 1911. (Image courtesy of Kenneth Florey, owner.)

harp on a green celluloid background. The harp is uncrowned, removing the imperial emblem usually placed on this symbol, and is fully strung, a visual detail often associated with republican ideals of independence and freedom (Morris 2004, 12–13). The harp is shown entwined with the national symbol of the shamrock. The ILWS was a London-based suffrage group whose choice of nationalist design would presumably have been a way to clearly differentiate both their allegiance and their nationality while outside their own country.

The provenance and use of certain Irish suffrage badges can be linked to Francis Sheehy Skeffington, a significant male figure in the Irish suffrage movement.

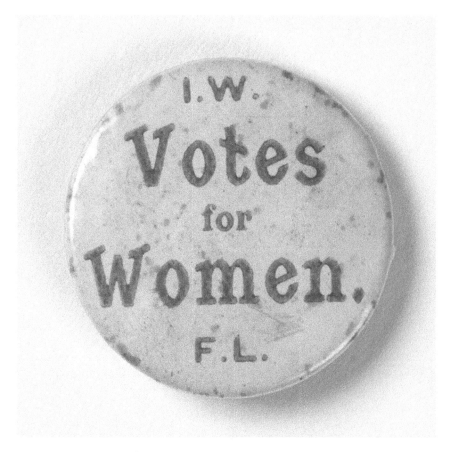

Figure 8.2. IWFL badge from the Sheehy Skeffington collection of the National Museum of Ireland, circa 1916. (Image reproduced with kind permission of the National Museum of Ireland.)

Husband of the IWFL founder and suffragette Hanna Sheehy Skeffington, he was a vocal and important player in the movement and one of the first male associate members of the IWFL (Levenson and Natterstad 1986, 24). From the beginning of the suffrage movement, Francis was known to always wear a "Votes for Women" badge in his suit lapel (Margaret Ward 1997, 19). One example of the surviving Irish suffrage badges is definitively known to have been worn by Francis. This has been ascertained through the involvement of the badge in a particularly tragic circumstance involving its owner. The badge in question is a white celluloid button badge, with the message of "Votes for Women" in simple green text, flanked by the acronym of the IWFL. (See Fig. 8.2.)

During the tumultuous events of the 1916 Rising, Francis was mistakenly arrested by British forces and executed by firing squad without trial at Portobello Barracks the following day (Levenson and Natterstad 1986, 89). Following Francis's execution, Hanna noted in a newspaper account that his signet ring and "Votes for Women" badge had been taken from his body as souvenirs by the soldiers who had executed him (Margaret Ward 1997, 159). Objects stolen from Francis's body were later restored to Hanna, and the records of the National Museum of Ireland note that this particular badge (see Fig. 8.2), initially taken from Francis's lapel, was also returned.

Flags and banners formed an important component of the visual promotion of the women's suffrage movement. Primary records reference the importance of flags and banners in the representation and demarcation of the individual suffrage organizations. Irish national flags were used by the campaign to head Irish contingents at mass suffrage rallies in London and as national identifiers of the speakers on speaking platforms at such events (C. Murphy 1989, 70). Protest banners were also used by the IWFL during events such as homecoming parades to celebrate the release of Irish suffragettes from prison. While the majority of the small group of surviving suffrage banners demonstrate simplistic homemade efforts, one surviving example is distinctly different to the former examples in terms of craftsmanship, materials, and design. This example consists of a superb embroidered green poplin IWFL banner with a decorative base fringe. (See Fig. 8.3.)

Hand-embroidered in orange thread to an extremely high standard of craftsmanship, the banner displays text in "Celtic" script, with decorative nationalist emblems. The orange and green color choices represent the organizational colors of the IWFL. The Gaelic script typeface of this banner, emulating the form of zoomorphic capitals and monastic script used in Irish early Christian manuscripts, spells out "Irish Women's Franchise League," with the opposing face depicting the Old Irish translation of the name: "Cumannact I gCóir Comhtruime (Comhthruime) na mBan." The English text side of the banner features a number of embroidered shamrocks. This banner can be viewed in use in a surviving photographic image depicting IWFL representatives at a mass suffrage rally in London in the first decade of the twentieth century. (See Fig. 8.4.) Tickner has commented that the mobilization of feminine needlework skills in the production of suffrage banners challenged that previously conceived aspect of femininity in the collective political enterprise (1987, 60).

Further examples of visual tools of protest and promotion for the Irish suffragists included sandwich boards with messages for "poster parades." The dispersal of handbills and the posting and wearing of posters also aided in the

Figure 8.3. Embroidered IWFL banner, circa 1908, from the Sheehy Skeffington collection of the National Museum of Ireland. (Image reproduced with kind permission of the National Museum of Ireland.)

visual promotion of the aims and work of the cause, and street pavements were regularly chalked to announce details of suffrage meetings and events (Margaret Ward 1997, 81). As an object of promotion, *The Irish Citizen* suffrage newspaper played a crucial role for the national suffrage movement. The newspaper helped distinguish the Irish suffrage campaign from the English movement, providing a specifically Irish vehicle and ambassador for issues of Irish suffrage and feminism (C. Murphy 1989, 76). Louise Ryan's research on the newspaper has shown the range of gender and political matters that were discussed within

Figure 8.4. Magnification of a Museum of London photograph (reproduced in postcard form) showing Irish suffragists with an embroidered IWFL banner at a suffrage rally in London. Dating to the period between 1908 and 1912. (Image reproduced with kind permission of Museum of London.)

its pages and the ways in which this media acted as a platform for advertisement and promotion of the Irish suffrage cause (Ryan 2018).

Suffrage promotion also took a more marketable commercial form, with promotional goods created and sold to raise funds for suffrage organizations as well as to spread knowledge of the cause. Advertisements in *The Irish Citizen* promoted "Franchise Tea" and promised that each purchase of the tea would fund a contribution to furthering the cause of women's franchise through financial support of the newspaper and Irish suffrage societies. Jessica Sewell's research

has shown that tea held a particular status in the international suffrage movement of the early twentieth century, symbolizing domesticity, class, femininity,
and modernity in its consumption and sale by the suffragists (2008). The sale
of suffrage label tea was a common feature of many suffrage organizations in
England and America (Florey 2013).

The fashion for suffrage-run or suffrage-associated tearooms was also
prominent in the United States (Sewell 2008) and Britain (Crawford 2000). A
surviving pamphlet in the collections of the National Library of Ireland adver-
tises meetings of the IWFL and suggests "a cosy tea in the Suffrage Tea Room"
in Westmoreland Street, Dublin. Tearooms can be seen to have provided a
civilized and relaxed forum for discussion, with the IWFL tearoom presenting
a domestic and socially respectable image of the militant suffragette organization. Despite a low survival rate of commercially produced promotional Irish
suffrage goods, documentary evidence suggests that such objects were indeed
produced and sold in Ireland. An advertisement for the 1913 Suffrage Week event
in Dublin—a week dedicated "to Suffrage propaganda" (C. Murphy 1989, 36)—
advertised the sale of a huge range of specialist suffrage items: "Suffragist Tur-
keys, Suffragist Sweets, Suffragist Flowers, Suffragist Toys, Suffragist Dolls,
and Suffragist Homes" (Ryan 1996, 110). Two surviving prototype examples
of "Suffrage Toys" were designed by the stained glass artist Wilhelmina Geddes (Gordon Bowe 2015, 88). Geddes, a member of the Dublin Arts and Crafts
glass workshop An Túr Gloine, was a contemporary and friend of the sculptor
and illustrator Sophia Rosamund Praeger. Praeger was involved in suffrage
graphic design and had set up a toy-making workshop in Holywood, County
Down, in 1915, for the Irish Women's Suffrage Federation (McBrinn 2009).
The sale of these toys is thought to have been used either to raise funds for
the organization (McBrinn 2009, 587) or as part of a war effort in Belfast on
behalf of the Irish Women's Suffrage Federation (Gordon Bowe 2015, 88).

THE MATERIALITY OF MILITANCY

A number of militant suffragettes in Ireland utilized a variety of domestic
objects in their acts of political militancy. These objects can be considered to
have significant object biographies because of their use and involvement in
militant suffrage acts and their role as witnesses to historical events. One of
the most notorious objects of protest associated with the Irish suffragettes was
actually connected to an English WSPU suffragette and would serve to damage
Irish suffragettes' public reputation and support following its use. On the visit
of English prime minister Herbert Asquith to Dublin in July 1912, an English

suffragette named Mary Leigh threw a hatchet into the carriage conveying Asquith and John Redmond around the city. The hatchet "skimmed between Asquith and Redmond and grazed the latter's ear" (Levenson and Natterstad 1986, 41). Particularly as Asquith had come to Dublin to publicize the Home Rule Bill and as the suffragettes had always been accused of attempting to derail the progress of the bill (Pašeta 2013, 77), this incident further distanced public support for the suffragettes' cause.

A public outcry resulted, with newspaper headlines such as "Hatchet Outrage" and "The Virago and the Hatchet" fueling the fires (Levenson and Natterstad 1986, 40–41) and providing an opportunity for specific groups of militant nationalists to physically exercise their hatred of Irish suffragettes, who were blamed for the attack (Margaret Ward 1997, 93). The "hatchet" incident would remain a memorable event in the minds of the public, which would go on to link the incident with Irish suffragettes and use it as a heckle during suffrage speeches (e.g., "Rival Meetings in the Phoenix Park," *Irish Times* August 17, 1912, 15; "'Suffragette' Meeting in Boyle," *Weekly Irish Times*, March 14, 1914, 6). The incident severely damaged public opinion of the Irish suffragettes, which significantly handicapped the progress of their cause.

Irish suffragettes participated in a number of acts of militancy that mimicked the form of acts being carried out by British suffragettes. Reports record a number of postbox attacks, militant acts that originated with the suffragettes in Britain whereby the government postal service was directly targeted for destructive protest (Margaret Ward 1997, 106). These events were often well organized, with a recorded attack in Dublin on December 16, 1913, carried out between 6:00 p.m. and 7:00 p.m. across the city and suburbs, destroying hundreds of letters and packages with a corrosive fluid (Century Ireland 1913). An attack detailed in *The Irish Times* gave details of the act: "Bottles containing corrosive fluid were dropped into boxes, and as they were uncorked, the acid poured over the letters and damaged very many. Around each bottle was wrapped some suffrage literature indicating the purpose of the 'protest'" ("Corrosive Fluid in Dublin Letter Boxes," *Irish Times*, December 20, 1913, 4).

The most militant of all of the suffragette activities in Ireland took place in the counties Antrim and Down (Margaret Ward 1995), carried out mainly by members of WSPU branches that had been established there (Crawford 2008, 269). Large-scale militant activity can be seen through a surviving object portion from Lisburn Cathedral, County Down. A fragment of stained glass from a window is a result of explosive material placed in the cathedral by WSPU suffragette Lillian Metge. The explosion badly damaged the chancel window from which this surviving glass fragment originated. Suspicion for the attack fell upon the militant suffragettes when in the aftereffects of the explosion "suffrag-ette literature 'danced in the air'" among strewn glass and masonry (Toal 2014).

Further material evidence of Irish suffrage protest can be seen in both the presence and the absence of census return forms from 1911. The 1911 census was boycotted in Ireland and Britain by a large number of suffragists, with the act of census resistance differing in practicality between Ireland and Britain. Unlike in Britain, the Irish census enumerators were policemen who could implement a large fine for resistance. This meant that it was not possible for Irish women to organize the type of mass-resistance public events that occurred in Britain. This resulted in women more commonly evading rather than resisting the cen-sus, staying with friends or camping in the hills and in empty houses (Margaret Ward 1997, 73). Thus, it must be acknowledged that several of these forms of protest objects are deliberately absent, as those women who participated in the noncompliance boycott would have remained unaccounted for in national records. Those suffragists that did not resist placed their protest in writing on the form, using the "Religion" and "Infirmity" columns to record their protest. As an example, a census form for the Manning family at Rathmines and Rath-gar East shows Susan Manning and a visitor to the house, Elizabeth Duggan, recording their religion as "Militant Suffragette," and noting their infirmity as "legally unfit to vote" (Census of Ireland 1911).

A surviving wooden speaking platform with a hand-painted "Votes for Women" plaque represents both a primary object of protest as well as an exam-ple of male support for women and suffrage groups in the Irish movement. (See Fig. 8.5.) Obtaining physical platforms from which to speak publicly at weekly outdoor meetings proved to be an ongoing challenge for a number of the suf-fragettes. At some of the early events, chairs were used (Cousins and Cous-ins 1950, 196), and at later events, lorries, benches (Margaret Ward 1997, 94), soapboxes (Sheehy Skeffington 1975), and even biscuit boxes were deployed (Margaret Ward 1997, 118). Due to common public hostility toward suffragettes, they found it increasingly difficult to obtain platforms or public locations of any kind when they traveled across the country to speak. Following the "hatchet" incident involving Asquith in 1912, firms would no longer consent to renting lorries to suffragettes (Margaret Ward 1997, 52).

To attempt to solve this ongoing problem the wooden portable platform seen in figure 8.5 was made for the IWFL by the husband of their member Dora Ryan (Margaret Ward 1997, 52). This tool proved a valuable asset for public speaking, and the presence of two further wooden IWFL platforms in the collections of the National Museum of Ireland show that the organization continued to build and use these portable items for public protest. Further male involvement in

Figure 8.5. IWFL portable speaking platform, circa 1912, from the Sheehy Skeffington Collection of the National Museum of Ireland. (Image reproduced with kind permission of the National Museum of Ireland.)

the female cause can be seen through a case study of one of the non-surviving objects utilized by the IWFL suffragette Margaret (Gretta) Cousins in an act of militant window breaking in 1913. Margaret's husband James's account of his creation of a militant object states:

> A request came to me to find the oldest umbrella in the house. Later I was invited to the council, not for words but for deeds. I had to entwine the stripped top of the umbrella with a strip of lead. I knew I was an accessory before a fact, but I had no idea as to what the fact was. I asked no questions, and got no information between then and my departure for school on cycle next morning, though the obvious tenseness in Gretta covered by a slightly enhanced cheeriness meant "God knows what." In the early forenoon of January 28, as I was giving a lesson in The High School, I heard a crescendo of cries of newspaper boys in the street, and when they reached the front of the school, on their way to the suburbs, I could hear them shout: "Suffragettes attack Dublin Castle," and smiled as the thought of the handle of an umbrella entwined with lead came into my mind. (Cousins and Cousins 1950, 206–207)

A report of the court proceedings in the *Weekly Irish Times* noted that three of the women who carried out the attack—Mrs. Margaret Cousins, Mrs. Margaret Connery, and Mrs. Barbara Hoskins—each used an umbrella to break a combined total of twenty panes of glass in the windows of the State Apartments and Prisons Board Office in the Upper Castle Yard. Contemporary newspaper records show that Cousins's infamous umbrella was later produced in court by the prosecution as an example of the means of destruction ("Police Court Proceedings," *Weekly Irish Times*, February 1, 1913, 1). The umbrella later reemerged in public after Cousins's jail sentence following conviction for this act, when a newspaper noted that it was waved in the air by IWFL suffragette Meg Connery on Margaret's release from Tullamore Jail (Margaret Ward 1997, 109).

IMAGERY, PAGEANTRY, AND DRESS

Specific visual symbols and imagery were often cleverly chosen in order to distinguish the Irish movement from its English counterpart, as well as to demonstrate the international role of the Irish campaign in the cause of women's franchise. The visual rhetoric of political cartoons and the power of imagery to mold or change public opinion were keenly understood by suffragists

(Sheppard 1994), and visual humor played a prominent role in both the suffrage and the anti-suffrage efforts. Contemporary cartoons could serve to present the suffragettes, and women's suffrage, in both a sympathetic and a critical or lampooning manner, depending on the publication or artist that had produced them. Cartoons also appear to have sometimes been published in individual forms, with examples of popular images first published in newspapers later sold in postcard form to the public (Curry 2012, 103). A number of the satirical cartoons of the period offer insights into the actions, dress, and public opinions of the Irish militant suffragettes. While a selection of the Irish images of the suffragette can be seen to have been influenced by the broader international movement (C. Murphy 2007), a number of the native examples also demonstrate specific national representations of identity, politics, and context, which differentiates them from their international suffrage counterparts.

A 1912 anti-suffrage cartoon from *The Lepracaun Cartoon Monthly* features an attractive, haughty young women being marched forward by a comically small round policeman, who looks at her in bemusement. (See Fig. 8.6.) The woman is dressed in affluent clothes, with a stylish hat on her head held in place by two prominent long hatpins. She carries a fringed handbag with the logo "Votes for Women," from which visibly extends a claw hammer, visually and inextricably linking the logo and tool of destruction together.

The rhyme below the cartoon reads:

Mary had a little bag,
And in it was a hammer,
For Mary was a suffragette,
For votes she used to clamour.
She broke a pane of glass one day,
Like any naughty boy,
A constable came along,
And now she's in Mountjoy.

The image identifies the militant suffragette as a well-dressed woman of middle-class status, demonstrating the dominant female class involved in the Irish movement (C. Murphy 1989). The juxtaposed presentation of the respectable, attractive, middle-class woman engaged in an act of civil disobedience and violence was a powerful contemporary image (Parkins 1997). The fringed handbag with the "Votes for Women" slogan carried by this woman may be simply a visual device to identify her as a fashionable woman and a militant suffragette. However, records also detail the presence of handbags with this slogan that were made in jail by suffrage prisoners such as Hanna Sheehy Skeffington

Mary had a little bag,
And in it was a hammer,
For Mary was a suffragette,
For votes she used to clamour.
She broke a pane of glass one day,
Like any naughty boy,
A constable came along,
And now she's in Mountjoy.

Figure 8.6. A 1912 anti-suffrage cartoon from *The Lepracaun Cartoon Monthly* showing the arrest of a militant suffragette. (Image reproduced with kind permission of Dublin City Council Libraries.)

(Margaret Ward 1997, 42). These bags were sold at suffrage fundraising fairs, so it is possible that the bag may also represent an actual contemporary piece of suffrage fashion and propaganda. The prominent appearance of the hatpins in the character's hat may potentially hold further visual symbolism. Contemporary international laws had recently enacted legislation regarding a defined hatpin length, partially due to the fear that larger examples of such items would be used as weapons against men (Gibson and Vanderveen 2013). Thus it could be speculated that the prominent hatpins in this cartoon may hint at the possibility of further physical violence by the suffragette, visually marking her as a threat to public safety.

The image of the hammer as a tool for breaking windows likely comes from reports of this activity in England, where hammers were a commonplace weapon for this act (Parkins 1997). The accounts that detail the Irish act of window breaking indicate that the Irish suffragettes used other implements such as a cherrystick (a wooden walking stick) (Margaret Ward 1997, 83) and an altered umbrella (Cousins and Cousins 1950, 206–207) to carry out their actions. The hammer, however, remained a popular associated image for the international suffrage movement. It features again as the tool of the suffragette in another cartoon from *The Lepracaun Cartoon Monthly* in May

When she gets it, what will she do with it?

Figure 8.7. Anti-suffrage cartoon showing a threatening militant suffragette from *The Lepracaun Cartoon Monthly*, May 1913. (Image reproduced with kind permission of Dublin City Council Libraries.)

1913, depicting a somewhat darker illustration of an Irish suffragette. (See Fig. 8.7.) This image shows a deviation from the common depiction of the middle-class suffragette, instead showing a masculine, angry woman with unrestrained hair in working-class costume. Her headwear possibly alludes to a Tyrolean hat, a masculine style associated with suffragist wear (Florey 2013, 145). She holds a hammer in one hand and leans impatiently on a ballot box, beneath which is shown a jug of paraffin and a fizzing bomb. Behind her the city skyline appears to be ablaze. Such images reference acts of suffragette militancy involving explosives—one such alleged incident in the same month of that year being the planting of a bomb in the ladies' lavatories of the Empire Theatre in Dublin. The Irish Times reported "a tin canister containing forty-two gunpowder cartridges was found in one of the lavatories. The cartridges were packed all round with cotton, which was saturated with paraffin oil, and a cotton cord, also saturated with oil and ignited, was connected with the contents of the canister" ("Bomb in the Empire Theatre," Irish Times, May 12, 1913, 5). In relation to the female vote, this cartoon's caption asks "When she gets it, what will she do with it?" implying a wariness of the women who would receive this right following their previous actions of civil disobedience.

Recognizing the important role of imagery in the successes of those critical of female suffrage (Tickner 1987, 16), suffragists commonly countered their negative portrayals with clever and attractive imagery of their own. Female artists, writers, and craftspeople featured prominently in the international suffrage movement, with organizations such as the Suffrage Atelier in England specifically established to create and distribute suffrage art that would promote and help the general suffrage cause (Atkinson 1997, 16). Irish suffragists countered their negative visual portrayals with clever responses in the same humorous format as their detractors. The participation of a number of women artists in suffrage propaganda offered the opportunity for women to market and publish their artistic skills in a manner that benefited their political cause, and the availability of such suffrage artists provided the Irish movement with a powerful weapon in their promotional arsenal. Certain Irish suffrage cartoons turned the tables on those who mocked the women and the aims of the movement. Two cartoons from The Irish Citizen by the artist Grace Gifford (née Plunkett), a supporter of suffrage and of the IWFL (O'Neill 2000, 11–12), are titled "Should men have the vote?" The cartoons display a drunk and disheveled middle-class man being steadied by a policeman (see Fig. 8.8a) and an unhappy male gambler turning out his pockets to show that he has lost all of his money (see Fig. 8.8b).

Figure 8.8a. Grace Gifford cartoons from the *Irish Citizen* depicting examples of male voters as gamblers and drunks. Male gambler cartoon from the *Irish Citizen*, June 14, 1913. (Images reproduced with kind permission of Special Collections, UCC Library, Cork University.)

Figure 8.8b. Male drunk cartoon from the *Irish Citizen*, May 17, 1913.

Figure 8.9. Christmas card designed by Sophia Praeger for the Irish
Women's Suffrage Federation. (Image reproduced with kind permission
of the Public Records Office of Northern Ireland [PRONI].)

A gentler and subtler form of persuasive cartoon can be seen in examples of the suffrage cartoons created by the Irish artist Sophia Rosamund
Praeger. Praeger was a champion of women in the arts, whose work as a
sculptor and illustrator was very highly regarded. In her commitment to
female emancipation, Praeger also designed posters and cards for suffrage
groups in Ireland and England and produced designs for the Suffrage Atelier (McBrinn 2009). One of the cartoons produced by Praeger for the Irish
Women's Suffrage Federation takes the form of a Christmas card for the
organization. (See Fig. 8.9.) This cartoon shows a dancing man in Irish-style

dress, watched by a pretty, modestly dressed woman seated on a stool and accompanied by a small, curly-haired child. The card's caption reads: "Nora: (Irishwomen's Suffrage Federation) 'Bravo' Shamus, you are learning to handle your feet a bit; but the boys can do none of the best jigs without the girls to help them."

Irish suffrage cartoons also displayed both broad international stereotypes of the suffragette and specifically Irish imagery and themes. A St. Patrick's Day themed cartoon from the March 20, 1915, edition of *The Irish Citizen* uses the visual metaphor of the myth of the saint driving the snakes from Ireland to present a suffrage message. (See Fig. 8.10.) Captioned "The Modern St. Patrick," the saint is shown as a suffragist wearing a "Votes for Women" sash, while driving out the snakes—all of which are identified as individual social ills by written titles on their bodies. As St. Patrick drives out "snakes" of "sham patriotism," "illiteracy," and "child labour," the rising sun behind him—a symbol common to Celtic Revival imagery (Morris 2004, 16)—announces the "emancipation of women," with the "slavery of women" setting beneath the water.

One of the most powerful suffrage propaganda cartoons was created by Ernest Kavanagh, a prolific Irish political cartoonist and suffrage supporter. This cartoon, titled "The Angel of Freedom" shows a winged depiction of John Redmond, leader of the Irish Parliamentary Party, using one foot to hold down an Irish female suffragist while displaying an unfurled message scroll in the other. (See Fig. 8.11.) The scroll declares "Hurro! For Liberty!!! No Irish woman need apply. No votes for women by order The New Liberator." The woman at his feet is unconscious and bound in ropes, a copy of *The Irish Citizen* newspaper by her side. Home Rule, represented by Redmond, is stamping on Irish women's suffrage (C. Murphy 2007). The cartoon demonstrates the hypocrisy of Redmond's stance, which argued for national emancipation while opposing the voting freedoms of Irish women (Curry 2012, 103). This was a powerful and successful protest cartoon for the suffrage movement, which made a bold public statement that garnered publicity and caused outrage and embarrassment among Redmond's supporters. The cartoon was later issued in postcard form by *The Irish Citizen* (ibid.).

Pageantry, theater, and performance were key parts of Irish suffrage commemoration and publicity. IWFL suffragette Hanna Sheehy Skeffington commented that "we made use, with feminine ingenuity, of many good publicity devices and stunts, and became a picturesque element in Irish life, the Irish being always glad of any new element, especially one that challenged and took sides" (in P. Reynolds 2007, 83). A number of recorded incidents and images

THE MODERN ST. PATRICK.

Figure 8.10. St. Patrick's Day cartoon from the *Irish Citizen* showing the saint driving snakes of social ills out of Ireland, while women's suffrage rises behind him. *The Irish Citizen*, March 20, 1915. (Image reproduced with kind permission of Special Collections, UCC Library, Cork University.)

give an insight into the importance of this aspect in relation to the publicity of the cause. In order to celebrate the release and homecoming of six IWFL members who had been jailed in England for suffrage protest, the organization staged a dramatic public reception on Christmas Eve in 1910. The released women were brought in open horse-drawn carriages on a parade through the city, led by a band marshal and flanked by IWFL members wearing organizational sashes of orange and green, as well as by male supporters bearing torches (Margaret Ward 1997, 72).

A feminist pageant featured as the highlight of the IWFL Daffodil Fête in 1914, which brought together participants and attendants from several nationalist and suffrage organizations. The pageant celebrated great women from history and was composed of a tableau vivant titled the *Feminist Tableau*

Figure 8.11. "The Angel of Freedom" cartoon from the *Irish Citizen*,
March 15, 1913, criticizing John Redmond's anti-suffrage stance.
(Image reproduced with kind permission of Special Collections,
UCC Library, Cork University.)

(Matthews 2010, 97). The pageant featured fifteen presentations, and among the historical women portrayed were Florence Nightingale, Sappho, the republican Ann Devlin, and the mythological tragic Deirdre (ibid.). The pageant also featured four separate presentations of Joan of Arc, which were deemed the most successful of the tableaux (Fitzpatrick Dean 2014, 81). Two of these portrayals were played by the nationalist revolutionary Constance Markievicz (Matthews 2010, 97). Joan of Arc was an international republican heroine as well as a feminist and suffrage role model (Tickner 1987, 209–210) and was thus suited for use as part of the symbolism for Irish female nationalists (Matthews 2010, 52). Markievicz played the Daffodil Fête role in a homemade suit of armor, made from either linoleum or cardboard that was "washed over with silver paint and on stage it looked just like a suit of armour" (Matthews 2010, 97–98). IWFL suffragette Margaret Cousins commented that the pageant "formed object lessons of what women had done in the past, and would act as an incentive to future deeds as great as those of earlier ages" (in Fitzpatrick Dean 2014, 80).

CONCLUSIONS

Research has collated an important collection of documentary sources and primary objects that have helped better materialize the objects and imagery of the Irish suffrage movement. The cataloging and discussion of these objects allows for a greater appreciation and understanding of the activities and scale of the Irish campaign, as well as a means of better cementing its place in national history. This research hopes to add further depth, information, and prominence to a neglected period of Irish women's history, adding to the discussion of Irish suffrage one century after the granting of partial female franchise. Approaching the history of the suffrage movement through a material and visual culture lens had previously been a technique carried out in relation to the British and American movements (Tickner 1987), but this had not been done for the Irish counterpart. Research hopes to have shown the importance and relevance of such objects and imagery to a part of Irish history for which little of either of these things survives today.

While much discussion here has been of "disappeared" or "invisible" objects, this does not diminish their importance and agency within the wider material and visual culture record. Considering the scale of and participation in the Irish suffrage campaign, few physical objects survive, which does not give a truthful indication of the spread and significance of the movement. With the exception of a small number of private and overseas collections, Irish suffrage material does not seem to have been maintained for historical or sentimental posterity. Limited response to a number of public appeals by the author have shown that objects do not appear to have been widely kept by members of the public, and the very sparse collection of suffrage objects from the museums and heritage centers across Ireland show that institutions have not engaged in significant contemporary or historical collection of this subject.

Recent decades have seen a significant rewrite and reinterpretation of gender within Irish history. With the centenary of the 1916 Rising, a number of historians helped rewrite the Irish revolutionary story to significantly include the women involved for the first time (McAuliffe and Gillis 2016; McCoole 2015; McDiarmid 2015). One hundred years after the original event, the significance and scale of female involvement was finally acknowledged in Irish history, a feat that had not been undertaken or achieved on a similar scale on any of the previous Rising anniversaries. The year 2018 presented another opportunity to write women and their important role back into national history. The Irish suffrage movement has long remained absent from popular Irish historical discourse, with the achievements and actions of the women involved often overlooked and forgotten over the space of a short one hundred years. This campaign is not currently marked by permanent inclusion in Irish museum exhibitions, and the few valuable historical publications dealing with this period have previously been out of print prior to the 2018 centenary, which provided the opportunity for the same reevaluation and reappreciation of suffrage history as has recently occurred in the history of revolutionary Irish women.

The year 2018 saw the inclusion of temporary exhibitions in approximately half a dozen Irish historical institutions and libraries to mark the suffrage centenary. Several institutions chose to commemorate the year through talks, seminars, and associated events due to their lack of relevant objects to display. In this Irish Decade of Commemorations, how should we consider and commemorate this period of women's history with only a limited number of the primary objects that marked its physical presence? Public appreciation and understanding of the importance of historical events is often only attached to actual material remains, which act as witnesses to the events. Laurent Olivier has commented that material remains retain the latent ability to provide new meanings, with material culture central to reassessment and understanding (2011). Worryingly, it could be said that the fact that very few objects survive for public exhibition gives the outward impression that suffrage was a small or unimportant movement in Irish history, which research has shown is simply not the case. Such restrictions for museum exhibition scope requires careful and considered forms of display, which has the ability to inform of the scale and importance of the material and visual culture, even if it is not present to view. Gaps in academic knowledge and the practical presentation of theory have previously led to the inclusion of empty display cases within exhibitions, which serve to symbolize an ethnic group or gender that is not clearly identified through the material record (Swain 2007, 215; Pearce 1995). Such a technique, where curatorial honesty acknowledges earlier omissions and gaps in a gendered or cultural section of the past, could potentially be considered as a means of discussion for the sparse material past of the Irish suffrage campaign.

This research hopes to contribute toward the record of a lost and neglected material past and, ultimately, to provide a new contribution toward the commemoration of the Irish suffrage movement in the near future. However, much work yet remains to be carried out on this subject, with future research contributing further to a more complete and thorough understanding of this theme. Suffrage history has garnered limited historical attention and appreciation over the past one hundred years. Commenting on a statement made by WSPU treasurer Emmeline Pethick-Lawrence that certain suffrage processional banners would "one day be historic possessions to the women of the country," Tickner laments that this has not happened, and considers the reasons why. She suggests that the decision of what objects become "historic" is often related to a question of power invested in particular discourses and institutions and the forms of knowledge produced by these (Tickner 1987, lx), an opinion following the views of Foucault (1972). Spender has argued that women need to reclaim and rediscover their role in history, to make the female past visible and real in order to avoid a repeat of the past patriarchal removal of women from the historical record (1982). With this in mind, such research as that presented here can be seen as an effort to materialize and make visible a section of the female national past in an attempt to solidify and mark its role in the wider historical record. Recent years have seen a pronounced international reexamination and discussion of the need for improved representation of women's histories in traditional museum exhibitions and historical narratives (Ashton 2017; 2018).

Ward has commented that new categories and new questions are needed in order to better understand the complexities of the female historical experience (Margaret Ward 1991, 22), and the evaluation and discussion of the Irish suffrage movement through an approach focused on material and visual culture may help meet this important need. The presented research argues that the Irish suffrage campaign offers a unique visual and material history in comparison to its British and American counterparts. While stylistic and material influence from British and American suffrage is clearly visible in a number of cases, the unique contextual circumstances of Ireland's campaign can be seen to be reflected within its native objects and imagery. Discussion and recognition of the material and visual past of the Irish suffrage period will hopefully contribute to an enhanced and more comprehensive understanding and commemoration of the national and historic importance of this period of Irish women's history.

DONNA GILLIGAN is an archaeologist, museum professional, material culture historian, and heritage educator. She curated *Print, Protest, and the Polls: The Irish Women's Suffrage Campaign and the Power of Print Media, 1908–1918*, at the National Print Museum, an exhibit that then traveled throughout Ireland (2018–2020). She specializes in work with historical and archaeological artifacts and museum collections, and provides heritage consultancy services to a wide range of organizations through her company, Scéal Heritage.

NINE

—⚞⚟—

IRISH SUFFRAGE

Remembrance, Commemoration, and
Memorialization

MARGARET WARD

OUR MEMORIAL LANDSCAPE IS PROFOUNDLY male, contributing to a gendered understanding of history that elides women's contribution, leaving the
historical record and cultural and material landscape to be defined and shaped
by male actors. If the specific nature of women's struggle for equality is not
recognized, acts of remembrance cannot be imagined. The task of retrieval
is not specific to Ireland, as "grand narratives" of history are constructed by
men, ignoring gender as a category of analysis and omitting all but the most
exceptional of women. This chapter explores how the feminist activism of the
past has been remembered and memorialized, particularly after the advent of
second wave feminism, when historians, to paraphrase feminist scholar Dale
Spender, "reinvented the wheel": "women are 'kept in the dark,' with the result
that every generation must begin virtually at the beginning and start again to
forge the meanings of women's existence in a patriarchal world . . . every fifty
years women have to reinvent the wheel" (1982, 13).

The focus is specifically on Irish suffrage and the centennial celebrations of
the 1918 Representation of the People Act, as a case study of a social remembrance of the past centered on women's agency. In acknowledging that gender
allegiance was not the only determinant in Irish feminism—which was influenced also by religion, class, and national allegiance—the concept of *social*
rather than *collective* remembrance is used in order to avoid what Guy Beiner
has described as otherwise "giving an impression of collective homogeneity"
(2018, 23).

The Irish suffrage movement was a vibrant and active one that existed from
1871 until the advent of the Representation of the People Act in 1918. By 1911,
groups were occupying physical space in Dublin's city center, with the Irish

Women's Franchise League (IWFL) in Westmoreland Street sustaining a meeting place, café, and library, and the Irish Women's Suffrage Federation establishing an office in South Anne Street. The suffrage newspaper the *Irish Citizen* was in existence from 1912 to 1920, publishing three thousand copies each fortnight during the height of the campaign in 1912–1914.[1] In Belfast the Irish Women's Suffrage Society had an office in Donegall Place and held forty-seven open-air meetings in 1912–1913 alone. But the ideas and activities of that generation were not transmitted to the next, and, consequently, feminists lacked a public, social memory of that past. When the fiftieth anniversary of the Representation of the People Act occurred in 1968, there was no "reinventing the wheel" because Irish feminism appeared to have neither a past nor a present as the historical focus remained tied to a nationalist narrative. In contrast, two years previously, the fiftieth anniversary of the Easter Rising had been celebrated extensively. Women such as Nora Connolly O'Brien, Kathleen Clarke, and Louise Gavan Duffy (who had played key roles in the 1916 period) were honored, but for the most part their testimony was less about their own contributions and more about the part played by male participants. It would take the advent of the second wave of feminism (which in Ireland did not arrive until the mid-1970s) and the emergence of feminist scholars to raise questions about female agency, thereby rescuing feminist activists from an undeserved obscurity.

A groundwork of empirical evidence was researched and published, demonstrating the significant contribution made by women not only to nationalist movements but also to the campaign for female emancipation. More recently, this process of historical recovery "gathered speed when feminist pressure was exerted as the postcolonial Irish nation prepared for centenary commemorations of the revolutionary years (1912–1922)" (Crozier-De Rosa and Mackie 2019, 5–6). The centennial commemoration of the 1916 Rising had been notable for its focus on women. New archival evidence highlighting the numbers of women involved in nationalist activities, coupled with the release of witness statements and applications for pensions for active service contributions, enabled women's own testimonies to be heard. Women were celebrated in local communities and by state actors for transgressing their normal roles through participation in armed uprising. However, while challenges in finding women within many archives exist, the difficulties are far more pronounced when it comes to women-led campaigns and movements. Were it not for suffragette Hanna Sheehy Skeffington, who maintained an extensive archive of suffrage literature and ephemera, which her family bequeathed to the National Library of Ireland, it would be impossible for scholars to do justice to the richness and complexity of the movement.[2] The recent digitization of newspapers and archives has also been transformative, enabling a greater scrutiny of sources and, consequently, more nuanced representations and interpretations.

MEMORIALS AND IRISH WOMEN

The absence of public memorials to women who took an active role in political struggle ensures their continued invisibility. While the recent centennial commemoration of 1916 saw a Dublin bridge (following public consultation) named after labor activist Rosie Hackett, the only woman to be honored with a public memorial prior to this was Constance Markievicz, dressed in the uniform of the Irish Citizen Army, whose bust on St. Stephen's Green, near the scene of her participation in the Rising, was unveiled by Eamon de Valera in 1932. His focus was not on the revolutionary aspects of her life but on the depiction of a philanthropist who had given up a life of privilege in order to work for the poor. There was no mention of her significance as the first woman to be elected to parliament nor of her role as the first female cabinet minister in Ireland (Sheehy Skeffington 2017, 300–302).

Some memorials to suffrage campaigners do exist. In April 1924, following the death of Anna Haslam, a committee was formed to collect funds for a memorial to her and her husband that included within its ranks militants and non-militants as well as unionists and nationalists: Lady Dockrell, the artist Sarah Cecilia Harrison (who had been the first woman elected to Dublin Corporation), Professor Mary Hayden, Senator Jennie Wyse Power, and Hanna Sheehy-Skeffington. The memorial chosen was a garden seat of Kilkenny limestone, sculptured by Albert Power and inscribed: "In remembrance of Anna Maria (1829–1922) and Thomas (1825–1917) Haslam this seat is erected in honour of their long years of public service chiefly devoted to the enfranchisement of women." In 1958, following her death, a long curved wooden bench dedicated to Louie Bennett was also placed in St. Stephen's Green, with an inscription to her companion Helen Chenevix added in 1963. Bennett and the Haslams were deeply critical of the use of militancy, and it could be argued that the choice of benches as a form of commemoration contributes to a representation of women's activism as primarily domestic, outside of the political sphere. Ireland's best-known suffragette, the militant Hanna Sheehy Skeffington, was the subject of many admiring obituaries after her death in 1946; however, plans for a memorial to her did not come to fruition. Only in 2005, with the erection by Duhallow's Women's Forum of a life-size statue in her birthplace of Kanturk, was she honored with a monument.[3] In the 1990s, Dublin Tourism had installed a plaque at 8 Airfield Road, Dublin (the house in which she and her husband

Frank had lived after their marriage), dedicated to the work of both: "Francis and Hanna Sheehy Skeffington Feminists, Pacifists, Socialists, Nationalists lived here 1903–1908." Margaret Cousins, cofounder with Sheehy Skeffington of the IWFL, has been remembered by a plaque outside her home in Boyle, County Roscommon. This was not, however, installed by an Irish body. It was unveiled by the president of the All-India Women's Conference on September 16, 1994, as a means of paying tribute to her work as an activist in India: "Born in this house 1878/Died in India 1954/Irish suffragette/Wife of Irish poet Dr James Cousins/Founder, in 1921, of the Women's India Association, Madras/ Co-founder in 1925 of the All-India Women's Conference/First woman magistrate in India (Madras 1923)."

A defining moment at the start of what became an extremely busy year of commemoration in 2018 was the dedication of a plaque to Hanna Sheehy Skeffington as one of the participants in the first act of suffrage militancy in Ireland. Significantly, the originator of this memorial was Micheline Sheehy Skeffington, granddaughter of Hanna and a feminist activist in her own right, who took the opportunity to frame the event in such a way as to emphasize its significance in challenging the gender and political inequalities that existed in colonial Ireland. In her application to the Commemorative Plaques Scheme, established to commemorate "people, organisations and events that have made a unique and significant contribution to the life or history of Dublin through outstanding achievement, distinctive service or significant community contribution," Sheehy Skeffington stated: "One of Hanna's most significant actions was the deliberate smashing of a window on the outside of Dublin Castle, the seat of British Government rule. For this she was arrested and imprisoned. In prison she went on hunger strike" (M. Sheehy Skeffington 2017). Micheline Sheehy Skeffington emphasized that she wanted to ensure that "[the] courage of the suffragettes was honoured on the centenary of women getting the vote. What they did and what they achieved is incredibly impressive. We have the vote today because of them. Power and privilege are never given up easily by any section of society, but things changed through women like Hanna taking a very public and often unpopular stance" (*Dublin People*, February 12, 2018). As the official plaque was not ready for the February 6 anniversary of the passing of the Representation of the People Act, a temporary plaque was erected, and the Lord Mayor of Dublin, Micheál Mac Donnacha, invited Micheline Sheehy Skeffington to re-enact her grandmother's window smashing and subsequent arrest. This was followed by a public reception in the Mansion House. There was a second ceremony on June 20, when full state recognition was accorded to suffragette militancy as President Michael D. Higgins officially unveiled the plaque: "Hanna Sheehy Skeffington/1877–1946/Suffragette/Smashed these windows/13th June 1912." The president's speech explored the history of women's activism in Ireland in considerable depth. In providing an unequivocal endorsement of the actions of the militants, he also acknowledged that the exclusion of women from historical narratives contributed to their omission from commemorative sites:

> It is a great honour, as President of Ireland, to join you all here today as we gather to honour those brave women of a century ago who dedicated themselves to the cause of equality for women. We gather particularly to commemorate the courageous act of resistance carried out by Hanna Sheehy Skeffington and her comrades, not far from where we stand today, one hundred and six years ago.
>
> . . . For far too long the historical contribution of Irish women in the struggle for emancipation, independence and equality and to our social life has been overlooked, and even, may I suggest, deliberately eschewed in what was a narrow historiography, one with a militaristic bias that could easily carry a chauvinistic bias. In the near century since the formation of an independent Irish state, the vast majority of monuments and streets of our towns and cities have invariably been dedicated to commemorating and valorising the actions of men. (M. Higgins 2018c)

In recognition of the part played by other Irish suffragettes, a list of all Irish women imprisoned for suffrage activities was then read aloud by members of the Galway Feminist Collective.

One other plaque in commemoration of suffrage militancy was erected in 2018. This again was an initiative of an individual, historian Rosemary Raughter, a longtime member of the Women's History Association of Ireland who has published widely on Irish women's history. On October 25, 1910, Hanna Sheehy Skeffington and Hilda Webb had heckled the chief secretary while he was on an official inspection of the dilapidated Greystones pier. Politicians had proven reluctant to meet activists and be questioned regarding their position on votes for women, and for this reason the militants had decided public protest was necessary. It was the first occasion Irish women had participated in organized heckling. A report in the *Irish Times* described the incident as an "amusing scene," adding that one of the women was heard to retort: "You would not hear our views, and so you have left us no alternative but to approach you in this way, and we shall do so every time you appear in public" (Raughter 2018). As the chief secretary did agree to an interview, the tactic of public confrontation became a common occurrence. In recognition of the significance of the occasion, the Greystones Archaeological and Historical Society in association with Greystones Municipal District and Wicklow County Council hosted an event that included the unveiling of a commemorative plaque and a reenactment of the incident by pupils of St. Brigid's National School:

25 OCTOBER 1910
ON THIS SITE, SUFFRAGETTES
HANNA SHEEHY SKEFFINGTON AND
HILDA WEBB CHALLENGED
CHIEF SECRETARY BIRRELL AS
THE OPENING MOVE IN THE MILITANT "VOTES FOR WOMEN" CAMPAIGN

MATERIAL CULTURE AND IRISH SUFFRAGE

The first public exhibition on Irish suffrage, curated by Rosemary Cullen and Andrée Sheehy Skeffington in 1975 in Trinity College Dublin, was accompanied by a booklet containing Hanna Sheehy Skeffington's unpublished memoir, *Reminiscences of a Suffragette*.[4] However, some of the artifacts listed in the exhibition catalog are no longer in the public domain. Jane Maxwell, curator of the Trinity College Dublin online suffrage exhibition *Violence Ridicule and Silence*, has brought this loss to public attention. In regretting that "even the figurine, which adorns the cover, has not made it into a public repository," she argues strongly that "permitting public access to any records of female endeavour is a vital act to prevent further erosion of 'herstory'" (Maxwell 2018).

An anthology of key extracts from the *Irish Citizen* newspaper was published in 1996, bringing to popular attention the wide range of issues and challenges confronting suffrage campaigners (Ryan 2018). However, it was not until 2008, with the centenary of the formation of the IWFL, that another commemoration of suffrage was organized. The National Museum of Ireland held a conference addressed by eleven leading scholars in Irish women's history. It was a landmark in being the first time Irish suffrage received formal recognition by an institution receiving state funding. An edited work on suffrage—*Irish Women and the Vote: Becoming Citizens*, with thirteen contributors—had been published in 2007, an indication of the increase in interest within academia (Ryan and Ward 2018). With the start of the formal Decade of Centenaries (1912–1922), the *Irish Times*, supported by the Department of Arts, Heritage, and the Gaeltacht, produced a supplement titled *How Irish Women Won the Vote*, with contributions from a wide group of historians of women's history (Crowe, Cullen, and McTiernan 2012). In the same year Belfast City Hall organized a public event on suffrage and the Speaker of the Assembly invited this author to address an audience of politicians at an event in the Senate chamber of Stormont. All these initiatives have been important in helping create some awareness of suffrage, but the impetus for most have been due largely to the initiatives of key individuals involved in suffrage memory recovery.

In 2016, anticipating the 2018 centennial celebrations of the Representation of the People Act, curator Donna Gilligan made a public appeal for suffrage memorabilia: printed ephemera, including postcards, Christmas cards, membership cards, flyers, handbills, and letters. In addition to this, the material culture of militant suffragettes can be said to include prison charge sheets, prison art and graffiti, and hunger strike medals. Objects used in militant protests could include chains for securement to railings, hammers and stones used to break windows, or weapons and damaging substances used in the public vandalism of items such as postboxes and works of art.

Gilligan contacted institutions across Ireland, Britain, and America, finding some suffrage material in private ownership but concluding that a total of seventy objects gathered after a two-year search was "not huge considering we're looking at a 10 year period." It was another example, Gilligan believed, "of women's history excluded from the national narrative, something we're still trying to fix 100 years later" (*Irish Examiner*, November 2, 2018). Gilligan would subsequently curate for the National Print Museum an extensive display of print ephemera, postcards, photographs, and newspapers, titled *Print, Protest, and the Polls: The Irish Women's Suffrage Campaign and the Power of Print Media, 1908–1918*; some of her research on these items is contained in this volume (see Chapter 8).

The Expert Advisory Group on Centenary Commemorations, providing guidance on the second phase of the decade (2018–2023), had recommended that the state "marks the centenaries of the passing of the *Representation of the People Act 1918* and the *Parliament (Qualification of Women) Act 1918* and acknowledges the significant contribution of Irish women in public and political life" (*Decade of Centenaries: Second Phase Guidance, 2018–2023*, 9). In response, a cross-party initiative of the Houses of the Oireachtas, Vótáil 100, was created to ensure parliamentarians could pay a comprehensive tribute to the women who had fought for the right to vote. During 2018, in collaboration with the National Museum of Ireland, Vótáil 100 hosted an exhibition of artifacts and images, *Votes for Women: Suffrage and Citizenship*, with a majority of artifacts on display donated by the Sheehy Skeffington family. As a result, the militant side of the movement was prominent. Items included the orange and green banner of the IWFL, embroidered by the women of the Dun Emer Guild; the portable platform made by the husband of an IWFL member, which women used throughout Ireland to speak at rowdy outdoor meetings; hunger strike medals; and the IWFL badge worn by Francis Sheehy Skeffington and taken from his coat after his death in 1916. Although the banner and the portable platform had been donated to the National Museum some years before, they had been in storage and not on display. A temporary display of these items in Collins Barracks was to remain in place until at least mid-2019, but there is no guarantee that they will not return to storage. What does this tell us about official attitudes toward women's struggle for citizenship if essential items of their material culture are not considered sufficiently important to warrant permanent display?

The existence of family members of activists, knowledgeable of the past activities of relatives, has been an essential feature in the preservation and valorization of suffrage activism. A large contingent of the Sheehy Skeffington family attended the Dublin Castle event. Karen Fitzgerald, the niece of Geraldine Laura Lennox—a suffragette from Cork who joined the Women's Social and Political Union (WSPU), lived in London and became a key aide of Christabel Pankhurst's—has used invaluable material left by Lennox to the family to highlight the political career of a woman who had been a significant figure in the British movement ("West Cork Suffragette Laura Will Always Be Remembered as a Hero," *Southern Star*, May 19, 2018; Fitzgerald 2018). The enthusiasm generated by the current focus on suffrage activism has been invaluable in encouraging families to consider the legacy of their feminist ancestors, but it is too late to have prevented the loss of much material discarded by families unaware of the importance of documents left by deceased relatives.

Other initiatives in the calendar of events to commemorate the role played by women in 1918 included exhibitions in archives, libraries, and museums and a wide-ranging symposium, *Political Voices: The Participation of Women in Irish Public Life, 1918–2018*, organized jointly by the National University of Ireland and Maynooth University, which brought together academics and activists, prompting discussion on the continuities between women's activism in the past and the challenges that remained for women in the present. At the end of the year a "Pop-Up Women's Museum" commemorating *Women in Politics and Public Life 1918–2018*, curated by the historian Sinéad McCoole, went on show in Dublin Castle before traveling to provincial venues in 2019.

SUFFRAGE, COMMEMORATION, AND MEMORIALIZATION IN NORTHERN IRELAND

For many people in Northern Ireland the Representation of the People Act has been a matter of complete indifference. The result of the 1918 election in the northeast was that the Irish Parliamentary Party and the Ulster unionists

remained political forces while Sinn Féin won only two seats, in Derry and
Fermanagh. It was a defining moment in what northern nationalists have perceived as their abandonment by Sinn Féin, heralding another step along the
road to partition. The fact that women were able to vote for the first time and
to stand for election was almost irrelevant, given the outcome. In a conflicted
environment, commemoration remains problematic.

A suffrage movement had existed in many parts of the North. In Belfast, the
Irish Women's Suffrage Society included militants with nationalist and unionist views, but this changed when the WSPU set up an "Ulster Centre," attracting so many members that the Belfast group was forced to dissolve. Northern
women now took part in a militancy that went far beyond smashing windows
of buildings associated with government or political parties. Their activities
included the burning down of a mansion associated with the Ulster Volunteer
Force and attacks on golf courses, racetracks, and churches: all targets viewed
as part of the male establishment and in keeping with the WSPU campaign in
Britain. The intention was to put pressure on the Ulster unionists, who had
reneged on a promise to grant women the vote in a secessionist provisional
parliament to come into existence in Ulster if Home Rule was granted to Ireland. Women in Dublin and Cork regarded this intrusion into Irish politics as
unhelpful, a manifestation of an imperial center/periphery relationship that
had always existed just below the surface of what was ostensibly a joint campaign. Christabel Pankhurst's instructions for Irish suffragettes taking part in
the great suffrage procession in Hyde Park in 1910 to dress as "Irish colleens"
was, Hanna Sheehy Skeffington had remarked, "a WSPU touch . . . we didn't
care much about," indicative of an arrogance regarding ownership of the movement and a desire by the English section to emphasize the strength of women
in the empire (Letter to Frank Sheehy Skeffington, July 24, 1910, Sheehy Skeffington MS 40,466/4, NLI).

Issues around national identity and the use of militancy have been raised
during this commemorative period in the North, significantly impacting on
commemorative events and influencing how women are memorialized. The
Ulster History Circle has erected plaques in Belfast to Victorian suffragist Isabella Tod in 2013, to suffrage militant Margaret McCoubrey in March 2016, and
in October of that same year, on the last home of Dr. Elizabeth Bell, a medical
doctor for Belfast Corporation, doctor to suffragettes in Crumlin Road Prison,
who also served a prison sentence in Holloway Jail because of her suffrage
militancy. The most notorious of local militants was Lillian Metge of Lisburn,
one of a group of four women arrested and incarcerated in Crumlin Road following an attempt in August 1914 to blow up Lisburn Cathedral. The Ulster

History Circle, despite requests, has refused to erect a blue plaque on the home of Metge, which is situated in close proximity to the Cathedral, on the grounds that she was mainly associated with violent activity, which they believe makes her ineligible for recognition.[5] The WSPU awarded Metge a medal to mark her hunger strike in Belfast Prison, and, by coincidence, the medal came up for auction in the summer of 2018. It was acquired by the Irish Linen Centre and Lisburn Museum, where it is now on display. It is the only WSPU hunger strike medal in any museum or collection on the island of Ireland. When the acquisition of the medal was announced, chair of Lisburn and Castlereagh City Council's Leisure and Community Development Committee, Alderman Paul Porter, commented that "although I do not agree with the methods Mrs Metge employed, the medal is a hugely significant addition to the museum's collection, and its acquisition marks an important chapter in the local 'votes for women' campaign. The attack on Lisburn Cathedral was the most militant attack in Irish suffragette history" (Lisburn and Castlereagh City Council 2018). In this case, commercial considerations appear to have outweighed other scruples.

Winifred Carney, a trade unionist, suffrage supporter, and the first woman to stand for parliamentary election in the North, was also a convinced republican and a woman who had taken part in the Easter Rising. In her role as aide-de-camp to James Connolly, she had been the first woman to enter the General Post Office and had been with the rebel leaders to the very end, subsequently serving time in Aylesbury Prison. Commemorations concerning Carney during 2018 further illustrate the divided nature of contemporary Northern society. The 1916 Relatives Association and the National Graves Association organized a wreath-laying ceremony at her grave in Milltown Cemetery, Belfast, on June 9, attended by the incoming Lord Mayor of Dublin (a Sinn Féin member) and by Deirdre Hargey, recently appointed as first female Sinn Féin Lord Mayor of Belfast. This author gave the graveside oration. In her capacity as Lord Mayor during this period of commemoration, Hargey took the opportunity to commission a portrait of Carney, inviting the Vótáil 100 politicians to the Mayor's Parlour in Belfast City Hall on the occasion of its unveiling. On a smaller scale, this was intended to replicate the visit of the Irish politicians to Westminster, when the portrait of Constance Markievicz was presented to politicians in the Palace of Westminster, as discussed below. Vótáil 100 politicians also visited parliament buildings, meeting with members of the Assembly Women's Caucus, a cross-party committee of members of the Legislative Assembly of Northern Ireland but (in the absence of an Assembly under an ongoing suspension) without power to initiate policy or to influence events.

The statuary in the grounds of Belfast City Hall reflects the long years of unionist dominance. Queen Victoria is the only female of prominence. An equality impact assessment was undertaken in 2012, the conclusion of which, in the words of Ciaran Beattie, Sinn Féin leader on the council, was that there were "too many statues of white, male, British, unionist, middle/upper class statues in Belfast City Hall grounds" (*Belfast Telegraph*, February 5, 2019). Suggestions were made for alternative statues that would reflect the city's increasing diversity. In February 2019, a Sinn Féin proposal for a statue of Winifred Carney was rejected at a meeting of the council. As a concession to unionist sensibilities, it was suggested that Carney's husband, former UVF member and Somme veteran George McBride, be part of the statue, as a way of mitigating its republican character. This was not accepted ("Winifred Carney Statue Row Divides Councillors," *Irish News*, February 4, 2019). The juxtaposition of Carney and McBride has been used often in the North as a means of enabling discussion and acknowledgment of Carney in a manner that does not offend unionist sensibilities. Thus, a stained glass representation of Carney installed in the Duncairn Arts Centre was complemented by a matching window of her husband. During the 1916 commemorations in the North, the BBC developed a website, *Voices 16*, that included Carney and her role as an active republican, but a separate site was also compiled, with a section devoted to the love story of Carney and McBride under the general title "Would You Have Married Your Enemy?" (BBC *Voices 16*, 2016).

Commemoration and memorialization in the North have often centered around the creation of wall murals adorning gable ends in nationalist areas. Constance Markievicz and Winifred Carney feature in many of these, which celebrate their activism as republican women. There are images of Markievicz as a founder of the Fianna na hÉireann and as an inspiration for the women of Cumann na mBan. Carney is an iconic figure, standing with Bobby Sands and Wolfe Tone in symbolically uniting Protestant, Catholic, and Dissenter. She is also portrayed in her role as a trade unionist. Neither woman has been portrayed in the context of suffrage. Carney's significance in contesting the Westminster election of 1918 and her later commitment to labor politics in Belfast remains overshadowed by her republican persona, making social remembrance problematic and collective remembrance impossible.

In the Republic of Ireland, a specific commemoration of Lá na mBan was held on June 9, 2018. This marked a pivotal moment when women from the labor movement, Cumann na mBan, and suffrage had come together throughout Ireland in a Women's Day intended to show opposition to the imposition of conscription. Women signed pledges of resistance in all the major towns except for Belfast, where the political situation was considered too delicate for such a demonstration. In the post-1916 period, considerable convergence existed between nationalist and feminist groups, which also served to illustrate the growing isolation of those in the North. Political harassment led many activists to leave the six-county area. Those who left were not only nationalists; the suffragette Lillian Metge moved to Dublin.

During 2018, official commemoration in the North, funded by the Department of Communities and organized by civil servants and external consultants in the absence of a functioning parliament, concentrated on the theme "Exploring Our Past Together," focusing on electoral reform, educating young people about the significance of the period, and hosting events to encourage a new generation of young women into political and public life. A Peace IV–funded project coordinated by Politics Plus organized a series of events in parliament buildings in which suffrage was a minor part and women in areas of public life not associated with politics—sports, Girl Guides, the media—were given prominence.

In 2015, the Public Record Office Northern Ireland (PRONI) had used its archives to develop a number of resource packs on suffrage, exploring its relationship with unionism, nationalism, and labor as well as highlighting campaigns of militants and non-militants. In 2018, PRONI held a series of seminars on suffrage, adding the contributions of speakers to its website. It also developed an online interactive "Suffrage Map" that plotted militant activity in Belfast and Derry (NIDirect Government Services 2020).

National Museums NI, lacking any suffrage ephemera, mounted a year-long theme titled "Hear Her Voice" in the Ulster Museum, which included a focus on female artists, feminist fashion, and a range of lectures on a suffrage theme. Other museums organized exhibitions and events, concentrating where possible on the contributions local women had made to public life and staying away from the explicitly political.

The Universities Ireland yearly conference of reflection on the decade was held in Belfast and titled "Votes for the People: 1918, Ireland's First Democratic Election?" Helga Woggon, biographer of Winifred Carney, provided an account of her election campaign in 1918 while Diane Urquhart highlighted the unionist reaction to the election. There have also been seminars concentrating on unionist attitudes to suffrage and the role played by Edith, Lady Londonderry, founder of the Women's Legion, in order to ensure a "parity" of attention to both sides of the political divide, despite the hostility of Ulster unionists to the suffrage movement and the fact that they did not support female candidates in 1918. Two women—Dehra Chichester and Julia McMordie—were elected as unionists to the first parliament of Northern Ireland in 1921 and, anticipating the forthcoming commemorations of the foundation of the northern state, their existence has already been highlighted in commemorative suffrage events. As Beiner so powerfully illustrates, "Territorial partition . . . introduces separate, mutually exclusive, memorial rituals," becoming "a framework for social forgetting" (Beiner 2018, 444). This is borne out by the controversy over the unionist refusal of a civic memorial to Winifred Carney and by nationalist disregard of the Parliament (Qualification of Women) Act 1918 and the part played by Markievicz and Carney in the election of 1918.

IRISH AND BRITISH COMMEMORATION OF CONSTANCE MARKIEVICZ AND THE 1918 ELECTION

The repercussions of the election of Markievicz were markedly different depending on whether the event was viewed through an Irish or a British lens. She was a prisoner in Holloway Jail during the election period (held as part of the "German Plot" arrests targeted at leading figures in the nationalist movement) and unable to take part in her election campaign or, indeed, attend the opening of the British Parliament, had she been so inclined. During the early part of 2018, there was speculation concerning whether the British government would choose to remember her victory. When Prime Minister May was asked if there would be a centenary celebration to mark the first woman to be elected, she deliberately did not mention Markievicz by name, replying instead in general terms: "I think it is important that we mark the centenary next year and recognise the role that women have played in this House and in their time in the area of public life." When the Irish online paper *The Journal.ie* persisted in querying the nature of the commemorations, a spokesperson from the House of Commons confirmed that Markievicz would feature, specifically in the *Voice and Vote* interactive exhibition to be held in Westminster during the summer of 2018 ("UK Government Will Commemorate the Election of Republican Countess Markievicz Next December," *The Journal.ie*, January 12, 2018). The election victory of Markievicz served to provide Irish politicians with a postcolonial moment to relish as it was decided that, as part of the joint British–Irish commemoration of a shared event, a photographic reproduction of the 1901 Szankowski portrait of Markievicz in evening dress would be gifted by the Vótáil 100 committee and presented by Dáil Éireann Ceann Comhairle Seán Ó Fearghaíl TD to the House of Commons speaker, the Rt. Hon. John Bercow MP. At the ceremony Ó Fearghaíl said it was "very appropriate" that the portrait should hang in Westminster to mark the 100th anniversary of her election: "This gifting also illustrates our shared historical and suffrage heritage and underlines the sometimes troubled, but overwhelmingly very positive links between our two countries." In reply, Speaker Bercow added that Countess Markievicz held a "unique place in British and Irish history" (Houses of the Oireachtas 2018). There were cries of horror from predictable voices, as some criticized a "distasteful" ceremony that highlighted a "convicted felon" (Gordon Lucy, Ulster-Scots historian, and Jim Allister, MLA for the TUV, in the *Irish News*, July 19, 2018), while Ruth Dudley Edwards condemned her as a "cold blooded killer" (*Belfast Telegraph*, July 20, 2018). These isolated opinions contrasted sharply with the evenhanded treatment of Markievicz in the Westminster exhibition. The portrait became part of the *Voice and Vote* exhibition before it was transferred to Portcullis House for public display as part of the Parliamentary Art Collection.

The curators of *Voice and Vote*, Melanie Unwin and Mari Takayanagi, took four years to gather material for an immersive experience that recorded the name of each of the 491 women who have been elected to the British Parliament. Their perspective was feminist as they reproduced mechanisms such as the grille or "Ladies' Cage" that had served to render women invisible within parliament, and their explanatory text regarding the Markievicz election result acknowledged her militant republicanism: "The only woman to be elected was Constance Markievicz, standing for Dublin St. Patrick's from her prison cell in Holloway. As a member of Sinn Fein she never took her seat in Westminster, but did take her seat in the first Dáil Eireann (Republican Irish Parliament established 1919)" (*Voice and Vote* Panel Text). An extract from the Markievicz election address accompanying her portrait could have concentrated on her plans for women in the constituency, but the curators chose instead to include her unambiguous avowal of resistance to British rule in Ireland: "Today we may hope that our road to freedom will be a peaceful and bloodless one; I need hardly assure you that it will be an honourable one. I would never take an oath of allegiance to the power I meant to overthrow" (*Voice and Vote* Panel Text).

Antoine Guillemette's study of commemorative practices devotes much consideration to those taking part in those practices. His conclusion is that "commemorations can be interpreted as expressions of the lively relationships people establish with the past, but also as a reflection of the socializing processes and the power structures existing between them" (Guillemette 2013, 19). The fact that images of the past can be used to legitimize the social order when national leaders are able to dictate the commemorative terms (22) was noticeable in Britain during the controversy surrounding which suffrage figure would feature in a statue to be erected in Parliament Square.

THE RIGHT KIND OF MEMORIALIZATION?
THE CASE OF MILLICENT FAWCETT

Controversy surrounding the erection of the statue to Millicent Fawcett, the first woman to be represented in Parliament Square, highlights the nature of political power and the "lively relationship" with the past experienced by many. Feminist campaigner Caroline Criado-Perez launched a petition, signed by 84,734 people, "to put a statue of a suffragette in Parliament Square to mark 100 years of female suffrage." It was subsequently announced that the proposed statue would not be a suffragette but the suffragist Millicent Fawcett. Some argued that the statue should have included several figures, in order to illustrate the complexity and diversity of the women's suffrage struggle. Others felt strongly that the decision was a deliberate attempt to write the militants out of history. Cultural historian Rachel Holmes linked the decision to the current state of political life in Britain: "This represents the kind of airbrushing of history that makes the fight for women's suffrage palatable in a contemporary context where populism of the nationalist right is tolerated and appeased but only so-called 'moderation' and 'gradualism' are allowed in support of the cause of greater equality. A new feminist statue is a great idea. Shame they picked the wrong feminist" (Holmes 2017). In a possible response to the critics, fifty-five women and four men were chosen to be represented on the plinth on which Fawcett stood. June Purvis, biographer of the Pankhursts, wrote with emotion to the press of her hope that the list would not include the name of Emily Davison: "She died after being trampled by a horse and does not belong under Fawcett's feet" (Purvis 2017). Davison is not included, despite her revered role as a suffrage martyr. Professor Julie Gottlieb of the University of Sheffield, historical adviser to the project, was instrumental in advising which suffrage campaigners would be selected. She believed this served to illustrate the collective nature of the struggle and that it would have "a profound and lasting impact on the framing of the story of women's political emancipation." She was also of the opinion that this representation of historical struggle would have an influence on the future fight for gender equality: "Anniversaries aren't just opportunities to look back and reflect. They're moments when we mobilise, when we think about how the past can powerfully inform the future" (University of Sheffield 2018). However, while Gottlieb clearly believed that this influence would be positive, Rachel Holmes echoed the views of a considerable minority in her contention that the political establishment had eliminated any radical potential that could have been drawn from the choice of subject for the statue: "I am far from naive enough to think that the Conservative Brexit establishment would, for example, have countenanced a memorial to . . . Sylvia Pankhurst. Pankhurst was not a suffragist but a full-blown, red-blooded suffragette—complete with the trips to prison and forced feeding also endured by her mother, Emmeline . . . Sylvia was a socialist and an internationalist—and no doubt far too rich for the blood of those running Britain right now" (Holmes 2017). When Prime Minister May came to deliver her speech at the unveiling of the statue, there were no uncomfortable reminders of women's past militancy. The leader of the British Conservative Party felt justified in making links between her experiences and those of the suffragists: "And, for generations to come, this statue will serve not just as a reminder of Dame Millicent's extraordinary life and legacy, but as inspiration to all of us who wish to follow in her footsteps" (Prime Minister Statement, published April 24, 2018).

Five Irish women are featured on the Fawcett plinth. Not all would have agreed with the nonmilitant approach of Fawcett, nor with her anti–Home Rule views. Anna Haslam was a contemporary and a close political ally, both women having similar views on suffrage and supported a continued union with Britain. Frances Power Cobbe belonged to an older generation, a campaigner against domestic abuse, a member of the London Society for Women's Suffrage, and someone who also would have agreed with the political views of Fawcett. However, the other three women—Eva Gore-Booth, suffragist, socialist, pacifist, sister of Constance Markievicz and the person credited with inspiring Christabel Pankhurst to become an activist; Charlotte Despard, founder of the Women's Freedom League, Irish republican and Communist, and Hanna Sheehy Skeffington, suffragette and Sinn Féiner—would surely have found their presence in this Westminster setting highly inappropriate, given that all three supported Irish independence from Britain and were not supporters of the National Union of Women's Suffrage Societies. While the decision to be "inclusive" is admirable, is it possible, in a postcolonial context, to emphasize "collective struggle" and the creation of "collective memories" without acknowledgment of the political environment that existed in the past? The history of British/Irish relations has helped shape commemoration of the suffrage past at the state level and that history has also influenced those involved "from below" in what is commemorated, with many expressing a desire for history not to be sanitized and made palatable for a ruling elite.

LEGACY

Suffrage commemoration has been driven by feminist activism, both from within academia and from without. We have seen how a limited form of memorialization in Ireland in the form of blue plaques recognizing the historical importance of people and/or places was achieved in 2018, and these plaques will remain as a permanent reminder of women's militant campaign for the vote. There will, at a future date, also be a permanent memorial to women, as the Irish State's calendar of events for 2018 promised "a symposium to explore development of a new monument to revolutionary women—the monument is intended to mark the role of women in the revolutionary period leading to the foundation of the state" (Centenary Programme of Events 2018). We do not know what form this will take, nor its intended location, but this is a historic and unprecedented commitment by the Irish State. State recognition of suffrage has also included temporary forms of memorialization, with displays of suffrage memorabilia and pop-up exhibitions but without any responsibility to develop a permanent site dedicated to the memory of women's activism. The official guide to the Pop-Up Museum urged visitors to "see what material has survived, in this once off opportunity to see this material gathered all in one place" (Centenary Programme of Events 2018). A women's museum—or, at the very least, a dedicated space to women housed in one of the national cultural institutions—would have been a fitting outcome and lasting legacy of the Decade of Centenaries. As an initiative to encourage a holistic and integrated representation of women's activism within feminist, nationalist, unionist, and labor movements, it could provide the stimulus for more complex forms of representation of the varied ways in which women have contributed to the political, public, and cultural life of the nation, past and present. Remembrance can be difficult and contested, but a living, dynamic memorial for the women of Ireland, created on an all-Ireland basis, could inspire a dialogue that is truly intersectional, not only revisiting the debates of the past but providing inspiration for the future.

NOTES

1. The pioneering text on the Irish suffrage movement is Rosemary Cullen Owens, *Smashing Times: A History of the Irish Women's Suffrage Movement 1889–1922* (1984). See also Cliona Murphy, *The Women's Suffrage Movement and Irish Society in the Early Twentieth Century* (1989).
2. See the Sheehy Skeffington Collection in the National Library of Ireland.
3. In March 2018, South Dublin County Council also agreed to name a new estate in Tallaght "Sheehy Skeffington Meadows." This was particularly appropriate as Hanna Sheehy Skeffington, when a councillor with the Dublin Corporation, had been active in supporting the building of new houses for the working class.

4. Andrée Sheehy Skeffington was the daughter-in-law of Hanna and a strong feminist in her own right, as a cofounder of the Irish Housewives' Association. The memoir *Reminiscences of a Suffragette* is reproduced in Margaret Ward 2017, 68–79.

5. Conversations with staff in the Lisburn Museum and with Dr. Myrtle Hill of the Ulster History Circle confirm this decision.

MARGARET WARD is a feminist historian and the author of groundbreaking and acclaimed books, including *Unmanageable Revolutionaries* (1983), *Maud Gonne: A Life* (1990), *Hanna Sheehy-Skeffington: A Life* (1997), and *Fearless Woman: Hanna Sheehy Skeffington, Feminism and the Irish Revolution* (2019). She is currently Honorary Senior Lecturer in History at Queen's University of Belfast and a board member of Libraries Northern Ireland. She is a former Trustee of National Museums Northern Ireland and a former Director of the Women's Resource and Development Agency.

TEN

—⚋—

TEA, SANDBAGS, AND CATHAL BRUGHA

Kathy Barry's Civil Wars

EVE MORRISON

ON JUNE 29, 1922, THE second day of the Civil War, as the provisional government forces shelled the Four Courts, Oscar Traynor, Officer in Command of the anti-Treaty Dublin IRA, ordered his forces to occupy buildings around the city, including the Gresham and Hammam Hotels on O'Connell (then Sackville) Street.[1] At least thirty women were involved in the initial occupation. They were ordered to leave after a couple of days; many left very reluctantly. "There was terrible excitement when the girls were told that they would have to evacuate," remembered one Hammam veteran.[2] According to Máire Comerford, who acted as a dispatch rider between the Four Courts and O'Connell Street that week, Eamon de Valera (who had refused to let women into Boland's Mills in 1916) discovered eighteen-year-old Elgin Barry hiding in a barrel, and then physically carried Kathy Barry, her older sister, out of the building.[3] In a letter to the latter written a few days later, Frank Henderson, adjutant of the Dublin Brigade, remarked: "I am afraid DeV was a bit rough with you on a certain occasion but as Von Hindenburg said 'orders is orders.'"[4] Most of the women eventually left under protest, and the Cumann na mBan contingent marched as a body down O'Connell Street (Andrews 1979, 234). Three women, however, did not go—Kathy Barry, Linda Kearns, and Muriel MacSwiney. They stayed with Cathal Brugha and a small number of men until the Hammam was surrendered.[5]

The small garrison held out until Wednesday, July 5. By then most of the occupied buildings were on fire. Brugha ordered everyone to surrender, but then famously charged down St. Thomas's Lane toward Free State troops on Findlater Place, where he was fatally wounded in the thigh. Kearns stopped him bleeding to death there in the lane by pinching his severed artery between her fingers, but he died two days later. Crowds of civilian onlookers lined the streets to watch the surrender (Dorney 2017, 92). Barry and MacSwiney were sufficiently well known to be spotted. The *Irish Independent* reported that they insisted on marching with the men to Amiens Street Station despite being "twice told that they could go home" (July 7, 1922). This was denied by the women. On July 12, 1922, *Poblacht na hEireann* carried a letter from MacSwiney stating that she and Barry had been arrested, then released a couple of hours later (Clifford 1996, 35). Barry later said the same, and as she was carrying the Dublin Brigade's funds under her clothes (given to her by Frank Henderson), it is unlikely that she willingly put herself in the hands of the authorities.[6]

In the immediate aftermath of the O'Connell Street fighting and in the months that followed, women were at the forefront of publicity and public activities surrounding Brugha's death. At the request of Caitlín Brugha (his widow), a Cumann na mBan guard of honor led his funeral procession on July 10, 1922 (Margaret Ward 1983, 185).[7] In August, Kearns and MacSwiney embarked on a fundraising tour of the United States (Ó Duigneáin 2002, 71–89). Their accounts of the O'Connell Street fighting and the death of Brugha were published in the *Irish World* (September 30, 1922).[8] In contrast to Sceilg's "Cathal Brugha—As I knew Him," the women made a point of paying tribute to the female activists involved in the O'Connell Street fighting (Ó Ceallaigh 1922, 485–496; 1942, 297–344). The involvement of Barry, MacSwiney, and Kearns in the Hammam occupation was well publicized at the time, and most of the women were interviewed and/or wrote their own accounts afterward, as did Comerford.[9] This chapter traces the Hammam women through various contemporary and retrospective sources, focusing particularly on Barry.

Some but not all IRA veterans were disinclined from the outset to mention the women present. Ernie O'Malley heard about the O'Connell Street fighting and Hammam occupation from Tom Derrig, who arrived in Blessington a couple of days later after anti-Treatyites retreated from Dublin. O'Malley included this bemused but not unkind description of the Hammam women in *The Singing Flame*, his Civil War memoir:

> When flames ate through the houses it was decided to evacuate O'Connell Street and a rearguard under Brugha was left to cover the retreat of the others. The girls had refused to leave. They recited the proclamation of Easter Week: "The Irish Republic is entitled to, and hereby claims, the allegiance of every Irishman and Irishwomen. The Republic guarantees religious and civil liberty, equal rights and equal opportunities to all its citizens . . ." Why, if the men remained, should women leave? The question was debated with

heat in rooms of burning buildings, under the noise of shells and the spatter of machine guns. Cathal Brugha had to exert his personal influence to make them go ... (O'Malley 2012, 169–170)[10]

O'Malley also interviewed several O'Connell Street veterans, including Barry and Comerford, in the late 1940s and early 1950s.[11] One of his interviewees, Ned O'Reilly, recalled Barry filling sandbags and helping put out a fire in the basement.[12] Todd Andrews's memoirs contained particularly vibrant sketches of the various Cumann na mBan members he encountered during the Civil War. He remembered Barry as a short-haired, fashionably dressed, lipstick-wearing "modern girl": "In the wilderness of West Cork," he wrote, "to be faced with such an exotic figure was as if we were seeing an apparition" (Andrews 1979, 281; Ryan 2002, 37–68). He was also unusually blunt in referring to Frank Aiken, Sean Lemass, and de Valera as "sexists," admonishing the latter in particular for failing to give the women who worked for him enough credit (Andrews 1982, 56).

Like most women involved in the War of Independence and Civil War, Barry's revolutionary activism combined political work, fundraising, and providing logistical support to the IRA. Cumann na mBan was an essential part of Sinn Féin's electoral machine by 1918, but with the exception of the Irish Citizen Army, women were barred from separatist nationalist military organizations (Pašeta 2013, 256). Women carried dispatches, did intelligence work, smuggled arms, and supplied food, clothing, and first aid. In common with many others in the independence movement, almost all of Barry's siblings were involved one way or another. She and her sisters as well as their brother Mick (OC of Carlow Brigade IRA) were all prominent activists, but the most well known of the family was her younger brother, Kevin, the young medical student executed in Mountjoy Jail on November 1, 1920, for his part in a Dublin IRA attack on a military party. Barry joined the University Branch of Cumann na mBan in 1920. Later, she was a member of the Cumann na mBan Executive, a Dáil Court judge, and, at various times, attached to the Dáil Departments of Home Affairs and Labour. In April 1922, she toured the United States with Countess Markievicz.

Barry worked closely with Liam Lynch (chief of staff of the anti-Treaty IRA), Oscar Traynor, and de Valera throughout the Civil War. Shortly after Brugha's funeral, Traynor sent her south to appeal to Lynch for funds. From then until late November 1922, she organized and maintained a special line of communication between Dublin and Lynch and was then ordered back to Dublin to reorganize the Irish Republican Prisoners Defence Fund (IRPDF).[13] In

1923, she was arrested in March and again in November and went on hunger strike.[14] The following year, she and Kearns toured Australia raising funds for the IRPDF (Whitaker 2016, 208–211).

Barry wrote two accounts of the Hammam occupation, and in later years commented on public commemorations and commemorative writings relating to Cathal Brugha's death. Her first account appears in a letter written in January 1923 to Jim Moloney, her fiancé, just a few months afterward; her only published account of the Hammam appeared in the *Irish Press* in 1932. Barry met Moloney, then Lynch's director of communications, in July 1922 in the Glen of Aherlow in County Tipperary.[15] Although Lynch knew Barry much preferred working as an IRA courier to organizational work, he sent her back to Dublin.[16] If he was trying to keep Barry and Moloney apart, it had the opposite effect to the one intended: "I really can't help it so here goes," Moloney wrote: "I have lost interest in everything since you left. I find it absolutely impossible to concentrate on anything... after half an hour's reading... [I hadn't] the remotest idea of what I had read... I have a terrific longing to live and meet you again. You don't mind me saying that you are the best girl I ever met. This is not flattery. I really mean it."[17] The pair remained in regular contact and were engaged by early January 1923. They married on September 5, 1924.

Their many letters, exchanged via clandestine twice-weekly couriers, documented their daily existence, their romantic lives, and the increasingly grim news of the war: the execution of republican prisoners; the deaths of Martin "Sparky" Breen (January 10, 1923) and Dinny Lacey (February 18, 1923); the arrests of Ernie O'Malley, Máire Comerford, Sighle Humphries, and Liam Deasy, OC of the First Southern Division, and the latter's subsequent appeal to the IRA to end the war (January 30, 1923). Barry was witty and well read, sending him George Bernard Shaw's play *Back to Methuselah*, which, he admitted, he did not much understand.[18] He read *Nash's Magazine* and Robert G. Ingersoll (the famous American nineteenth-century orator and agnostic humanist). She quoted Shakespeare, the poetry of Rudyard Kipling, Robert Burns, the Rubáiyát of Omar Khayyam, and the Bible.[19] Their letters record several attempts to communicate by telepathy (always unsuccessful), and both were sure that "Kev," the watchful ghost of Barry's brother, was keeping them safe.

The exchanges between Barry and Moloney capture the dominant mentalities and atmosphere of the time, both in terms of how the women in Cumann na mBan were viewed by others and also how they themselves understood their role. Republican women were being routinely attacked and humiliated by Free State politicians and the press during the Civil War (Ryan 2002, 221–222). Barry made several references to the negative rhetoric used against them in her letters.

In February 1923, she wrote: "Did you see Kevin O'Higgins' latest analysis of us 'hysterical young women who should be practising our 5 finger exercises or helping our mothers to polish the brasses.' Poor us. Squelched. And poor you irregulars. Goaded on by us. But poor Bridie Cole married to that thing. And poor him if some of the hysterical young women ever get a chance at him."[20] It was easy enough to dismiss the criticisms of "Staters" and the lurid headlines about "Amazons" in the British press. She was less immune to criticism from Moloney. In the letter in which he asked Barry to wear his ring, he commented on the Hammam occupation:

> I remember ... having a discussion with you about the O'Connell St. fight. I said that girls were more of a hindrance than a help in that fight. That didn't mean the help given in that fight by the girls didn't amount to much; instead, as I made clear to you at the time, if you remember, I meant that the presence of the girls in the buildings must have prevented our fellows from fighting to the end if they had no means of escape.... Tis very badly put but you'll see what I mean ... I meant it to disapprove of the men for allowing girls to remain in the building.[21]

Already in hot water for describing the ring as his "badge of ownership," Moloney showed no sign of understanding why this assessment might upset her.[22] In finding herself judged, challenged, and effectively dismissed by someone she loved, Barry experienced what was likely to have been a common predicament for women pushing the boundaries of what was considered acceptable female behavior at the time. Her letter in response to his was a mix of conflicted and conflicting sentiments, and her memory of their conversation was markedly different from his: "And to go back to the other episode you mentioned—your disapproval of me—all the horrid things you said that night. Among other things you told me I wasn't a woman at all so I decided if I ever got a chance when the war was over I'd vamp you and let you see whether I was not..."[23] She was still delighted to accept his ring, worried that his mother disapproved of her, and desperately afraid that he would be shot. Yet she was also clearly stung by his suggesting that the women had gotten in the way: "Now you may disapprove of me all you like for refusing to go when I was told but you mustn't disapprove of the men. And you can ask Jack O'Meara or Ned O'Reilly or Dan Keeffe if we hindered the fight or kept them from holding out as long as they would otherwise have done. The men were great—they were sports and let me do heaps of things."[24] Barry's description of how she, MacSwiney, and Kearns were eventually allowed to remain also gives a good indication of how controversial their actions were seen to be at the time:

By the way too your explanation of your attitude with regard to the Hammam is based really on a wrong impression. First of all, the men didn't allow us to stay. We just stayed. . . . Five of us were mean enough to let all the others be put out and to hang on ourselves and then refuse to go. So they held a Council of War and very skilfully selected the tactics which should dispose of each of us the best advantage. I was the last to be bullied into going. Dev kind of carried me across the room and then he put me down and turned round to see if there were any more neurotic girls. I crawled around a door and eventually around another—and stayed all night in a beastly dirty place. I emerged in the morning and some of the others had got in again—having stood outside the back door all night. . . . For the honour of your sex I must admit that three men knew I was in the building and didn't split on me.[25]

As Barry's letter indicates, not all of the men objected to the women's presence. Frank Henderson, for instance, admired Barry's pluck: "I was very glad indeed to have met you in the recent fighting and shall never forget the splendid way you 'carried on' all the time."[26] According to Barry, Brugha eventually relented. At one point, she confronted him, insisting that it hadn't been fair to "drive us all to mutiny in order to be let stay." Brugha acknowledged that the women's work at the Hammam had been a great help: "It wasn't [fair]," he said, "If I had to do it over again I'd let you stay without the mutiny." Nonetheless, Brugha remained uncomfortable with the situation: "I had to dodge Cathal all the time," Barry wrote. "He approved my making tea and Bovril, but not of me filling sandbags in my leisure moments."

The way Barry described, articulated, and understood her involvement in the Hammam reflects just how difficult it could be, in practice, for first wave feminists to demand equality without challenging a gendered understanding of male and female roles as such (Hughes 2002, 46). Cumann na mBan emerged from the 1916 Rising a significantly more confident and assertive organization, and the Easter Proclamation guaranteed equality for women, but mainstream and radical Irish nationalism remained highly "gendered" (Pašeta 2013, 219–225). The regeneration of the historic Irish nation through force of arms was characterized very specifically as a reclamation of Irish manhood (Beatty 2016, 24, 40). Barry struggled to define her actions other than as a usurpation of a specifically "masculine" endeavor: "Oh Jim I've written pages about it and I'm sure you heard it all before. I'm sorry. I didn't notice myself. I love [sic] those three days at the end because I felt I was nearly as useful as a man and you don't know how helpless a feeling it is to be a woman when you feel you ought to be a man."[27] Moloney responded on February 5. The opening sentence was not promising: "You are a grand little girl in fact quite a dutiful little girl." In the end, though, heart on his sleeve, he went some way in redeeming himself: "I don't mind what you have been, were, or will be, I just want Kathy in all her moods; whether crazy, cross or quiet. So long as Kathy loves me I will be utterly satisfied . . . and don't forget that I won't cease loving you more than anything in this world . . . whether you turn out to be . . . crazy Kitby or remain neurotic Kathy, 'the most dangerous girl in the south of Ireland.'"[28] They were married eighteen months later, and she became Kathy Barry Moloney.

Barry and her sister Elgin remained uncompromising republicans to the end of their days. Barry refused to join Fianna Fáil, and became very critical of de Valera. She campaigned for the release of interned IRA men in 1939–1940 and supported Clann na Poblachta in 1948. Between 1926 and 1930, she bore five children. In the early 1930s, she took up a job with the Electricity Supply Board and became very active in her trade union. Due to ill health, she eventually retired in the 1950s. Barry was regularly interviewed or consulted about the Civil War in later years. Florence "Florrie" O'Donoghue (accompanied by Moss Twomey) interviewed her in 1952 for *No Other Law*, his biography of Liam Lynch (O'Donoghue 1986, 277, 301).[29] Later, in the 1960s, Dr. Joseph Brennan, another Hammam veteran, consulted Barry about the details of Brugha's death on behalf of de Valera, who was collecting and compiling information about Civil War deaths.[30] Tomás Ó Dochartaigh, a former *Ailtirí na hAiséirghe* national organizer and nephew of Cathal Brugha, interviewed her for his biography of his uncle (Ó Dochartaigh 1969, 250–251).[31] Yet the spirited, defiant woman she was—and remained—was barely visible in her only public account of the Hammam occupation, published by the *Irish Press* in 1932.

Barry's 1923 letter was written in the heady days of the independence struggle and Civil War, when women were demanding equal rights and participation in public life and when female activists were asserting themselves into both the events of the revolution and the public narratives that followed. Women's daily lives did improve in several respects after 1923, but Ireland was a much more conservative place by the 1930s, and their civil liberties in relation to work outside the home, jury service, and citizenship were legislatively curtailed (Clear 2000, 202; Pašeta 2013, 270). As Margaret Ward notes: "The argument now was that independence was won and women's contribution was no longer necessary. They should be content to return to the home and hearth" (1997, 303).

Most of the idealized public narratives of the revolutionary period published in newspapers, "fighting stories," commemorative speeches, and literature after 1923 reflected this changing context. By and large formulaic and traditional, these forums often omitted women or relegated them to a page or paragraph. While many, even most, of the IRA men who fought for Irish independence were also forgotten, a different set of dynamics governed the exclusion of the women. Even when they were mentioned, they were almost always "safely contained within the parameters of femininity" (Ryan 2001a, 13–14). It was rare for them to be accorded much autonomy. On the tenth anniversary of Cathal Brugha's death, the *Irish Press* published a commemorative account of his "glorious rush into the jaws of death." The Hammam women were given only the briefest mention, as "Terence MacSwiney's widow and Kevin Barry's sister."[32]

As ever, Barry was determined to have a say. A long letter to *Irish Press* editor Frank Gallagher—ostensibly written to correct a mistaken detail regarding which door Brugha had exited when he left the building—included a short account of the Hammam.[33] Gallagher published it. How she recounted the events, and her own involvement, stands in great contrast to her 1923 letter. It was a sign of the changed times that Barry, writing in 1932, carefully crafted her account as a tribute to Brugha's martyrdom. There was no mention of her defiant refusal to be evacuated before the men. It was all about making Brugha tea:

> ... fire now surrounded us on three sides, and on the fourth side was the lane—empty itself of Free State soldiers but covered at both ends. Mrs. MacSwiney and myself made some tea for the others. . . . It was only afterwards I realised that we had been privileged to watch a man making up his mind to immolate himself. It was only afterwards I realised the fierce fight he must have had, pacing up and down there in our sight, with everything that was human in him—the fierce light he must have seen beckoning him to death. Then he took a cup of tea, with a smile—and he ordered us out.[34]

Barry seems to have intended to write her own history of the Civil War.[35] Unfortunately, she never did give a full account of her revolutionary activities, nor did she apply for a military service pension.[36] When Barry was approached by the Bureau of Military History (BMH), they asked her for two accounts, one about the death of her brother Kevin, and the other about herself. Despite the best efforts of Jane Kissane (the BMH investigator charged with collecting statements from female activists), Barry never gave the requested second statement. The Hammam is mentioned briefly in the one she did submit, but otherwise it is dedicated almost entirely to her brother and contains an apology for mentioning herself at all: "Thinking over what has been set down, I am afraid that I seem to figure in it myself to an undue degree."[37]

Several years later, in a letter to Oscar Traynor, she said that, at the time, she simply "couldn't face" giving a statement about herself. By then she regretted not doing so and wanted to leave an account for her grandchildren: "If I had applied for a pension or a medal I should not have to bother people at this late stage for my own vanity."[38] Traynor and Barry had publicly clashed over remarks he had made relating to her mother's attitude toward the Dublin IRA's planned attempt to rescue Kevin Barry before his execution, but he nonetheless agreed to write her a reference: "The leadership of Miss Barry was of the utmost importance, not only to the positions occupied by the Dublin Brigade in O'Connell Street but also to the members of the General Headquarters Staff, who were in occupation of the Four Courts."[39] Although she never produced another account of her own, Barry did continue to intervene when she felt published accounts misrepresented the circumstances of Brugha's death.

During the Civil War and thereafter, pro- and anti-Treatyites made rival claims to ownership of the legacy of the independence struggle. Different factions within anti-Treatyite republicanism clashed similarly over the Civil War (Hanley 2003, 167–177). Commemorations of Brugha were political battlegrounds, and the site where he made his final stand immediately became a *lieu de memoire*. Brugha's funeral procession stopped in front of the ruins of the Hammam Hotel to say a decade of the rosary, and the first commemorations of his death were also held amid the rubble on O'Connell Street. When it was rebuilt in the mid-1920s, a new thoroughfare was constructed connecting Gloucester Street (now Sean MacDermott Street) and O'Connell Street. It had no official name at first, due to the suspension of Dublin Corporation in May 1924, and was soon dubbed "Cathal Brugha Street" by locals (Conboy 2011, 216–217; O'Halpin 1991, 283–302). Much to the chagrin of George A. Lyons, a pro-Treatyite former corporation member (who suggested "Brian Boru Street" as an alternative), republicans and radicals were quick to claim credit for its unofficial moniker.[40] Cathal Brugha Street became a regular meeting point for republican and radical groups in the 1920s and 1930s, including the Women's Prisoners Defence League, the Republican Congress, Sinn Féin, the Irish Communist Party, the Labour Defence League, and the Unemployed Workers' Group. In 1932, under the new Fianna Fáil government, it was formally named after Brugha.

By 1952, the thirtieth anniversary of Brugha's death, Fianna Fáil's brand of anti-Treaty republicanism had become well-entrenched state orthodoxy. While serving his second term as minister for defense, Oscar Traynor had Portobello Barracks (headquarters of the provisional government forces in 1922) rechristened "Cathal Brugha Barracks." For republicans who had remained active in Sinn Féin and the IRA, though, Fianna Fáil's claim on his legacy was a travesty. They, rather than Fianna Fáil, were the true inheritors of Brugha's choice of sacrificial death over compromise (O'Higgins 1962). The version of Brugha's death preferred by Dorothy Macardle, and most irredentist republicans, was that he had run toward the Free State troops firing his pistol and shouting "No Surrender!" (Macardle 1968, 686–687). Members of Brugha's family, by contrast, were keen to distance themselves from this sacrificial narrative, and there was little consensus among those who had actually been with Brugha in St. Thomas's Lane in 1922. Barry, Kearns, and MacSwiney all maintained that Brugha deliberately sacrificed himself (Clifford 1996, 35).[41] In 1923, Barry wrote: "Then he rushed out and turned up the lane with his revolver. The Staters couldn't be blamed for shooting him because he wanted to be shot. He wasn't trying to get away. He was trying to give his life and he succeeded."[42] Sean Geraghty also said Brugha had fired on the soldiers. Joseph Brennan witnessed Brugha bearing arms but was unsure of his intentions. Sean Brady, who had been in the lane with the last few evacuees, said a barrier was blocking their view and he doubted there had been any eyewitnesses to Brugha's death.[43] Pro-Treatyite Irish Army veterans of the Hammam surrender maintained that Brugha had been trying to slip away, not sacrifice himself (Pinkman 1998, 142–143).

The preferences of Brugha's family took precedence in mainstream public narratives from the 1960s onward. The Hammam women were either excluded altogether or were rendered as silent witnesses to his martyrdom. In April 1966, Florrie O'Donoghue gave a paper about Brugha to the Cumann Tir Chonaill, which the *Irish Times* then published in full (Shovlin 2013, 108–110).[44] He stated that "witnesses on the spot" all agreed that Brugha "did not fire" on Free State troops when he ran up St. Thomas's Lane. No mention was made of the women at all. Barry, obviously vexed, penned a reply to the paper (which she did not send) and another to O'Donoghue (which she did), pointing out a number of inaccuracies, including the omission of herself and Muriel MacSwiney.[45] O'Donoghue apologized and re-interviewed her but whatever words were exchanged between them, he made no effort to revise his account, probably because Cathal Brugha's son Ruairí was pleased.[46] "From my point of view it was excellent," he wrote, "though it did not satisfy either the extreme Republican or extreme Fianna Fáil elements i.e. those who see history in the light of [the] Civil War."[47]

By the fiftieth anniversary of Brugha's death in 1972, Kearns and Barry were both dead. MacSwiney was alive but estranged from her family and living elsewhere.[48] The wider political context had changed dramatically. In terms of fatalities, it was the worst year of the Northern Irish Troubles. A Cumann na mBan organization existed but women were no longer barred from joining republican paramilitary organizations. A newly formed "Cathal Brugha 50th Anniversary Commemoration Committee" announced that, in addition to the traditional commemorative masses, a "biographical pageant" in Brugha's honor would take place in the Olympia Theatre on July 9. Both de Valera and Taoiseach Jack Lynch were invited to attend. Inevitably, the pageant was marked by controversy. Fianna Fáil's claim on his legacy was challenged once again by republicans old and new.

In the week preceding the pageant, Seamus G. O'Kelly, an IRA veteran of long standing, wrote a letter to the *Irish Press* maintaining that Fianna Fáil had no right to dishonor Brugha, "who died in O'Connell Street with two blazing guns in his hands and the cry of 'no surrender' on his lips" (*Irish Press*, July 5, 1972). On the night, Joe Clarke, a ninety-one-year-old 1916 veteran, disrupted the performance midway, berating "Union Jack Lynch" for refusing to give hunger striking IRA members political status. Sinn Féin staged a protest outside, carrying placards that read "No Surrender!" and handing out leaflets stating that if Brugha were alive, he would be supporting them (*Irish Independent*, July 10, 1972). De Valera left early, and there were unsubstantiated reports that a bomb had been left in a car parked at the stage door (*Evening Herald* and *Irish Press*, July 10, 1972).

Directed by Noel Mannix, the production itself was two hours of unadulterated, militaristic patriotism "dedicated to all men and women who fought and died from Irish freedom." Brugha was played by his grandson and namesake. Jerry Cronin, the Fianna Fáil minister of defense, arranged for the loan of a Vicker's machine gun as well as rifles and revolvers from army stores.[49] The Wolfe Tones sang rebel songs, and there was traditional music and Irish dancing. Historical photographs and RTÉ footage of the National Anthem were projected behind the actors. Pat Leavy, Nuala Keogh, and C. Doyle played three unnamed members of Cumann na mBan. It was described by the *Irish Independent* reviewer as "very much a folk hero story," and "illustrated occasionally by extremely simple actions, which more often than not were unintentionally funny" (*Irish Independent*, July 10, 1972). When devising the scenario, Mannix had been "advised" by Sceilg, Ó Dochartaigh, and O'Donoghue. The text of the narration (read by Chris Curran) was O'Donoghue's 1966 text, which the organizing committee later published in a commemorative pamphlet.[50] None of the Hammam women were there to object.

O'Donoghue's account of Brugha's death—excluding the Hammam women entirely—is, still, mostly accepted without demur.[51] Tracing the depiction (or absence) of the women in subsequent accounts of the Hammam occupation makes clear just how vital it is, where possible, to access contemporary women's accounts of their experiences. The best source of information by far for female activists generally are their own letters, testimonies, and memoirs. Although

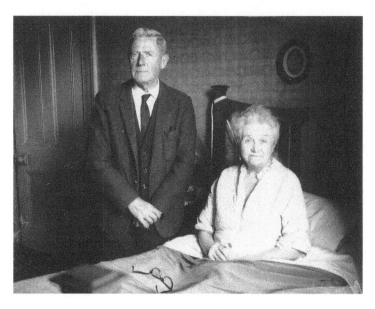

Figure 10.1. Kathy Barry Moloney and husband, Jim. Rathgar, Dublin, May 1968. (Courtesy of Louise O'Donovan.)

later personal narratives by veterans, male and female, tend to be less formulaic than idealized commemorative writing of the post-revolutionary period, the feminist impulse underpinning the actions of female activists is often missing from their later public accounts. Barry's 1923 letter demonstrates how, at the time, women insisting on their right even just to make tea and fill sandbags within earshot of artillery fire challenged the status quo.

The letters between Barry and Moloney provide insight into how gendered norms were understood at the time, and how they informed both public and personal relationships of Ireland's revolutionary generation. Despite his patronizing initial assessment of Barry's actions in the Hammam, when confronted, Moloney prized his love for her over convention. (See Fig. 10.1.) They never stopped writing to each other, and memories of their romance and the Civil War intertwined to the end. In a note to Moloney written shortly before she died, Barry wrote: "Sweetheart, all my love and thanks for all the good years since the Glen in 1923."[52] Despite having originally agreed to burn their correspondence (for security reasons), they both kept many of their Civil War letters. Several of hers were found on Moloney when he was captured after a running battle with Free State forces in the Glen of Aherlow in March 1923 (*Irish Independent*, March 9, 1923). Considered by Todd Andrews to be one of the finest characters he met in the republican movement, Moloney died in April 1981 (Andrews 1979, 297).

Nothing Barry wrote about the period subsequently matched her 1923 letter. In later years, and partly through her own doing, her contribution to the independence struggle was largely subsumed within the commemorations honoring the republican martyrs with which she was closely associated: Cathal Brugha, Liam Lynch, and her brother Kevin. She continued to intercede to protect the memory of the Hammam women, however, even if her interventions became more conventional with the passage of time. Like many republican women, Barry's Civil War had been a battle on several fronts—personal as well as political—involving confrontations with both her political enemies and her comrades and continuing long after the official ceasefire.

NOTES

1. Sackville Street was officially renamed O'Connell Street in 1924.

2. Ernie O'Malley, *Ned O'Reilly, 21/22 Sept. 1951*. Interview. From University College Dublin Archives [hereafter UCDA]. *Ernie O'Malley Notebooks* [hereafter *EOM*], P17b/126, p. 17.

3. Ernie O'Malley, *Maire Comerford, c. 1947*. Interview. From UCDA. *EOM*. P17b/87, p. 53; see also the interview with Comerford (MacEoin 1980, 35–55).

4. Frank Henderson, *Henderson to Barry, 13 July 1922*. Letter. From UCDA. *Kathy Barry Moloney Papers* [hereafter *KBM*], P94/28.

5. Countess Markievicz also took part directly in the week's fighting. Some accounts suggest that Una Gordon and Nellie Hynes might have remained in the Hammam as well. Eileen McCarvill (née McGrane), *Eileen McCarvill (née McGrane), 29 Dec. 1954*. Witness Statement. Military Archives of Ireland [hereafter MAI], *Bureau of Military History* [hereafter *BMH*], WS 1752, p. 9; Ernie O'Malley, *Ned O'Reilly, 21/22 Sept. 1951*, pp. 18–19.

6. Katherine B. Moloney, *Katherine B. Moloney, 22 Jan. 1952*. Witness Statement. From MAI, *BMH*, WS 731, p. 5; Frank Henderson, *Henderson to Barry, 11 July 1922*, and Oscar Traynor, *Oscar Traynor to Barry, 11 July 1922*. Letters. From UCDA, *KBM*, P94/28.

7. Caitlín Brugha, *Directions by Caitlín Brugha for the public funeral of her husband, 9 July 1922*. Typescript Notice. From National Library of Ireland [hereafter NLI]), *William O'Brien Papers*, Mss. 15, 687/5; *Evening Herald*, July 10, 1922.

8. *Irish World*, September 30, 1922. On September 16, the newspaper also reproduced Sceilg's "Cathal Brugha—As I Knew Him" originally published in *The Catholic Bulletin*.

9. *Irish World*, September 30, 1922; Máire Comerford, *The Dangerous Ground*. Unpublished Memoir. UCDA, *Maire Comerford Papers*, LA 18/43; Linda Kearns McWhinney, *Linda Kearns McWhinney, 6 July 1950*. Witness Statement. From MAI, *BMH*. WS 404, p. 20; See also the article about Kearns by Dorothy Macardle in *Irish Press*, June 11, 1952.

10. *The Singing Flame* was originally the final section of his acclaimed War of Independence memoir, *On Another Man's Wound* (Dublin: Rich and Cowan, 1936).

11. Among others, Garry Houlihan, Ned O'Reilly, Maurice Brennan, Tommy Merrigan, Oscar Traynor, and Madge Comer. UCDA, *EOM*, P17b.

12. Ernie O'Malley, *Ned O'Reilly, 21/22 Sept. 1951*, p. 17.

13. Katherine Barry Moloney, *Katherine Barry Moloney to Referee, Military Service Pensions, 12 Dec. 1936*. Letter. From MAI, *Military Service Pensions Project Collection*, Con Moloney: MSP34REF1359.

14. *Freeman's Journal*, March 10, 1923; *Cork Examiner*, November 10, 1923; Kathy Barry, *Irish Republican Defence Fund, c.1922–1923*. Notes and Correspondence. From MAI, *Civil War Captured Documents* [hereafter *CWCD*], IE/MA/CW/CAPT/Lot 117.

15. Moloney had previously been divisional intelligence officer of the Second Southern Division and adjutant of 4th Battalion, Third Tipperary Brigade. Arrested in March 1923, he was imprisoned in Limerick and Harepark before being transferred to Newbridge internment camp. As OC of prisoners in Newbridge, he took part in a mass hunger strike in October and November 1923.

16. Liam Lynch, *Lynch to Barry, 22 Nov. 1922 and 27 Jan. 1923*. Letters. From UCDA, *KBM*, P94/28; Kathy Barry, *Barry to Moloney, 10 Jan. 1923*. Letter. From MAI, *CWCD*, Lot 42/no. 10.

17. Jim Moloney, *Moloney to Barry, 28 Nov. 1922*. Letter. From UCDA, *KBM*, P94/71; Kathy Barry, *Barry to Moloney, 28 Nov. 1922*. Letter. From MAI, *CWCD*, Lot 42/no. 5.

18. Kathy Barry, *Barry to Moloney, 3 Dec. 1922*. Letter. From MAI, *CWCD*, Lot 42/no. 1; Jim Moloney, *Moloney to Barry, 21 Dec. 1922*. Letter. From UCDA, *KBM*, P94/71.

19. Kathy Barry, *Barry to Moloney, 20 Dec. 1922, 10 Jan. 1923, 13 Jan. 1923*. Letters. From MAI, *CWCD*, Lot 42/no. 10; Kathy Barry, *Barry to Moloney, 31 Jan. 1923*. Letter. From UCDA, *KBM*, P94/113.

20. Kathy Barry, *Barry to Moloney, 10 Feb. 1923*. Letter. From UCDA, *KBM*, P94/113.

Brigid O'Higgins (née Cole) was a professor of English at Knockbeg College in Carlow. Kevin O'Higgins was assassinated by the IRA in July 1927. She married solicitor Arthur Cox in 1940 and died in March 1961.

21. Jim Moloney, *Moloney to Barry, 27 Jan. 1923*. Letter. From UCDA, *KBM*, P94/72.

22. Jim Moloney, *Moloney to Barry, 8 Jan. 1923*. Letter. From UCDA, *KBM*, P94/71; Kathy Barry, *Barry to Moloney, 13 Jan. 1923*.

23. Kathy Barry, *Barry to Moloney, 31 Jan. 1923*.

24. Ibid.

25. Ibid.

26. Frank Henderson, *Henderson to Barry, 13 July 1922*.

27. Kathy Barry, *Barry to Moloney, 31 Jan. 1923*.

28. Jim Moloney, *Moloney to Barry, 27 Jan. 1923*. Letter. From UCDA, *KBM*, P94/71. "Kitby" was Barry's nickname. She referred to herself as "neurotic" in earlier letters.

29. Florence "Florrie" O'Donoghue, *O'Donoghue to Barry, 28 Oct. and 3 Nov. 1952*. Letters. From UCDA, *KBM*, P94/32. O'Donoghue and Maurice "Moss" Twomey were both former Cork IRA officers. The latter was active in the IRA until the late 1930s and was chief of staff from 1926 to 1936.

30. Joseph Brennan, *Brennan to de Valera, 3 Jan. 1966*. Letter. from UCDA, *Eamon de Valera Papers* [hereafter *DeV*], P150/3618.

31. The whereabouts of Ó Dochartaigh's original recorded interview is unknown.

32. *Irish Press,* July 7, 1932.

33. Kathy Barry, *Barry to Gallagher, 7 July 1932*. Letter. From UCDA, *KBM*, P94/30.

34. *Irish Press,* July 28, 1932.

35. Kathy Barry, *Barry to Gallagher, 7 July 1932*.

36. It is not clear why Barry did not apply for a pension, particularly as Jim Moloney did so.

37. Katherine B. Moloney, *Katherine B. Moloney, 22 Jan. 1952*. Witness Statement. p. 23; Jane Kissane, *Kissane to Barry, 19 Nov. 1951 and 31 Sep. 1953*. Letters. From UCDA, *KBM*, P94/31.

38. Kathy Barry, *Barry to Traynor, undated [c.1960]*. Letter. From UCDA, *KBM*, P94/33.

39. Oscar Traynor, *Reference for Kathy Barry Moloney, 12 May 1960*. Letter. From UCDA, *KBM*, P94/34.

40. George A. Lyons, *Lyons to Mulcahy, 4 Oct. 1929*. Letter. From NLI, *George A. Lyons Papers*, Mss. 33,675/A/1/83.

41. Linda Kearns McWhinney, *Linda Kearns McWhinney, 6 July 1950*. Witness Statement, p. 20; Kathy Barry, *Barry to Moloney, 31 Jan. 1923*.

42. Kathy Barry, ibid.

43. Joseph Brennan, *Brennan to de Valera, 3 Jan. 1966*, and Sean Geraghty, *Geraghty to de Valera, 9 Feb. 1966*. Letters. From UCDA, *DeV*, P150/3618; Sean

Brady, *Brady to de Valera, undated*. Letter. From UCDA, *DeV*, P150/3615. The most
recent academic account of Brugha's life does not offer a judgment one way or the
other. Fergus O'Farrell, *Cathal Brugha*, 2018, 85–86.

44. The Donegal Association was founded in 1935 and acted as a social network
for Donegal natives living in Dublin; *Irish Times*, April 26, 1966.

45. Kathy Barry, *Barry to O'Donoghue, 25 Apr. 1966* and *Barry, undated [c. 1966]*.
Letter and Note. From UCDA, *KBM*, P94/35.

46. Florence "Florrie" O'Donoghue, *O'Donoghue to Barry, 29 April 1966*.
Letter. From UCDA, *KBM*, P94/35.

47. Ruairí Brugha, *Brugha to O'Donoghue, 21 May 1966*. Letter. From NLI,
Florence O'Donoghue Papers, Ms. 31,319/2; Ruairí Brugha joined the IRA at
sixteen and was interned by de Valera in the 1940s but later became disillusioned.
He went on to become a Fianna Fáil senator, marrying Maire MacSwiney, the
daughter of Muriel MacSwiney (MacSwiney Brugha 2005).

48. Barry's obituary included a short reprise of her revolutionary activities,
including the fact that Traynor put her in charge of the women in the Hammam.
Irish Times and *Irish Press*, January 11, 1969.

49. Cathal Brugha Commemoration Committee. *A Dramatic Pageant on the
Life and Times of Cathal Brugha, 9 July 1972*. Theatrical Programme. From UCDA,
Cathal Brugha Commemoration Committee [hereafter *CBCC*], P52.

50. Cathal Brugha Commemoration Committee. *Cathal Brugha,
Commemoration 1874–1922: Cathal Brugha Anniversary Brochure, 1922–1972*.
Pamphlet. From UCDA, *CBCC*, P52.

51. Brian P. Murphy, *Murphy to Editor, September 2, 2008*. Letter. *Irish Times*.

52. Barry to Moloney, January 1, 1969, in private hands.

EVE MORRISON is currently the Canon Murray Fellow in Irish History at St.
Catherine's College, University of Oxford, and a visiting Research Fellow in the
Centre of Contemporary Irish History, Trinity College Dublin. She is a historian
of twentieth-century Irish and British history specializing in the Irish revolution
(1913–1923).

ELEVEN

—ᖴᖴ—

CURATORS OF MEMORY

Women and the Centenary of the Easter Rising

ROISÍN HIGGINS

IN 1981, THE BBC COMMISSIONED a number of dramas for its *Play for Tomorrow* series: an exploration of what life might be like in the twenty-first century. It was intended that the plays would prompt viewers to think about the long-term consequences of their actions and decisions. To provide background information for the series, the BBC held an accompanying seminar on "the future" and included speakers such as a campaign organizer for Friends of the Earth and a computer scientist. The brief for the sixty-minute plays, aimed at a contemporary audience, included the instruction that the BBC did not want six apocalyptic pieces about nuclear devastation (London *Times*, April 8, 1982). In response, Graham Reid wrote *Easter 2016*, a play set in an integrated teacher training college in Belfast. Rather than the banned mushroom cloud, Reid's play ended with the detonation of an incendiary device and one fatality. The framing of *Easter 2016* demonstrated that the most explosive material lay not in the future but at the intersection between the present and the past.

Easter 2016 was broadcast in 1982. The play reflects on the self-referential nature of Irish history, and, as the centenary of the Easter Rising approaches, several of the lecturers and students in the teacher training college suggest that it should be marked with a reenactment. Surprisingly, they decide to commemorate not the events of April 1916 but those of January 1969, when members of the People's Democracy, on their civil rights march from Belfast to Derry, were ambushed at Burntollet Bridge by loyalists. One student, Colette, questions the tutor, Conor, who is in favor of re-enacting the march:

Colette: It all seems to be getting confused Sir. You talked about an
   exhibition or essays and pictures to mark the centenary of 1916. Now

people are talking about something different, and all the emphasis is being
put on this Burntollet march.... What has that to do with the Rising?
Connor: It's a protest to assert a legitimate right that's being denied us.
Colette: The exhibition is being permitted ... why do we have to march?
John: This is the Centenary ... we want to show that the cause survives.
(Reid 1982)

The play becomes a rather confused disquisition on the use of violence by liberals who are beleaguered by militants. Nevertheless, it is an instructive example
of the way in which time becomes refracted during commemorative events.
The Easter Rising exists as both a past event and an anticipated future and carries the weight of its fiftieth anniversary into the present. Later in the play, the
security director says "1966 that's when the last lot started," echoing a belief
recorded by Prime Minister Terence O'Neill that "it was 1966 which made 1968
inevitable and was bound to put the whole future of Northern Ireland in the
melting pot" (O'Neill 1972, 87). O'Neill directly linked the fiftieth anniversary
of the Easter Rising to the outbreak of the Troubles, as though the staging of
a commemoration had the capacity to upend an otherwise stable society. This
perceived link meant that anniversaries of the Rising were seen as potentially
dangerous events. Reid is playing with the unforeseen consequences of trying
to re-create the past in contemporary society.

Reid wrote *Easter 2016* during the starkly polarized year of the Maze Prison
hunger strikes and casts the centenary of the Rising as a challenge and test for
society: asking how it will accommodate its history, and, to some extent, how
this history will continue to play itself out. These questions are pertinent too
for the recent actual centenary of the Easter Rising, which showed that it is not
possible to commemorate one event without referencing the multiple historical strands to which it has become attached. This chapter looks at the issues
that emerged when tangled histories were commemorated in Ireland in the
spring of 2016, particularly at how temporal disruption facilitated emotional
and political release.[1]

Commemorations of the Easter Rising revolve around an event that has
been fashioned to fit their purpose. It is popularly believed that the Irish
Republic came into being when Patrick Pearse read the Proclamation on the
steps of the GPO at noon on Easter Monday, April 24, 1916. The reality was
slightly different, and events unfolded in a much more chaotic way that morning. Eoin McNeill's countermanding order led to confusion and reduced the
numbers of men and women who turned out. Nonetheless, almost immediately the rebels began to craft a coherent narrative. *War News*, produced on the

second day of the Rising, recorded that "the Irish Republic was proclaimed by poster, which was prominently displayed in Dublin. . . . The G.P.O was seized at 12 noon, the Castle was attacked at the same moment, and shortly afterwards the Four Courts were occupied" (*War News*, April 25, 1916). The Republic was proclaimed by "poster," and Pearse's iconic reading was not mentioned in initial reports. Nor did Pearse stand on the steps of the GPO while reading the Proclamation as, unlike the buildings of classical Greek and Roman architecture on which the post office was based, Dublin's iconic building has no steps. The steps have been inserted by our imaginations because the design prompts our brains to see them. These minor inventions or distortions do not detract from the significance of the Easter Rising, but they do indicate something of what happens in the transition from lived event to historical memory.

One hundred years after the first day of the Rising, I was standing on the altar of St. Michan's Church in Dublin as part of the large public history gathering, "Reflecting the Rising." It was 11:30 a.m. on Easter Monday and I was due to give a half-hour talk on the meaning of the Rising in 2016. I could see the clock at the back of the church, and, as my talk progressed, I found myself telling the audience the time in ten-minute segments as we moved closer and closer to the anniversary of a moment that had not exactly happened. As the talk ended and the Angelus bell sounded, it was, in many ways, an extraordinary commemorative experience, marking a partially invented moment that had been filled with so much anticipation and meaning.

There is something very compelling about the moment when past and present are believed to touch. Rebecca Schneider, in her work on art and war, explores the ways in which reenactments trouble linear temporality, positing "that time may be touched, crossed, visited or revisited, that time is transitive and flexible, that time may recur in time" (Schneider 2011, 30). Schneider's work is concerned with historical and theatrical reenactments rather than more general commemorative practices and rituals, yet her work is suggestive for the broader field. In *Performing Remains*, she explores how "overt imitation (one descriptor of theatricality) may even be a kind of syncopation machine for the touching of time beside or across itself in the zig-zagging lived experience of history's multi-directional ghost notes" (31). Traditional histories, despite acute awareness of the significance of the past for subsequent events, proceed on a linear trajectory. Yet the emotional and political power of significant historical anniversaries indicates that there are moments of heightened awareness of the ghost notes, when the past is more visible and renders the politics of the present more vivid.

TEMPORAL LIMINALITY

Events of 2016 made the Irish past visible in different ways. *These Rooms* used the eyewitness testimonies of thirty-eight women to explore the events on North King Street, where fifteen civilians were killed by the South Stafford-shire Regiment over two days during Easter Week 1916. The piece premiered at the Dublin Theatre Festival in September 2016 and was a collaboration between Anu and CoisCéim dance company, through contemporary dance, visual art, and theater. It was funded by the Arts Council as part of its com-memorative program and performed in a *lieu de mémoire*: 85/86 Dorset Street Upper in Dublin, the birthplace of Seán O'Casey. The audience for *These Rooms* gathered in a bar that was styled to evoke the 1960s. A black-and-white television showed footage of the fiftieth anniversary of the Rising in 1966, accompanied by commentary scripted by the theater company. Owen Boss, responsible for the art installation, explained that the bar was designed realisti-cally "to enable [the audience] to acclimatise to the seismic shifts that would be witnessed within the house" (Boss 2016a). The audience believes itself to be in 1966 and slowly becomes aware that it is simultaneously encountering events that took place in 1916. Audience members are deployed as part of the unfolding drama, and the result is disorienting as both time frame and fourth wall are breached.

Performer Emma O'Kane wrote that her research for *These Rooms* focused on Teresa Hickey, the wife of Thomas and mother of Christopher, both of whom were killed in North King Street in April 1916. As part of one perfor-mance O'Kane showed a memorial card of Thomas and Christopher to a mem-ber of the audience. "Call it a coincidence, a sign or the power and might of live performance," she wrote, "but unbeknown to me I came face to face with the Grandniece of Thomas Hickey in performance. I shared a one-on-one moment with this woman. . . . Not knowing at the time that I was actually showing her a photograph of her relatives. This was a defining moment for me where the space of 100 years and the lives of the inhabitants of North King Street did not seem so distant or unfamiliar" (O'Kane 2016).

Owen Boss described *These Rooms* as a "liminal space between disciplines" (Boss 2016b), but its most striking liminality was temporal. Peter Crawley's review in the *Irish Times* asked, "How do you commemorate something that never ends?" under a headline subtitled "Bringing Unresolved History Back to Life" (Crawley 2016). Dominic Cavendish in the *Telegraph* wrote of the actors: "The numb, reeling women confide dismaying fragments of information, cling to each other and ask us for help. As we finally exit into the street, they stand rooted to the spot, staring after us, as if their grappling with grief has only just begun" (London *Telegraph*, October 8, 2016). Sarah Hemming in the *Financial Times* noted that *These Rooms* "brilliantly evokes the way grief lingers in the body and that gets you to feel, rather than think, how commemoration can be complex" (*Beyond These Rooms* 2019). The Easter Rising has a powerful affect in Ireland's cultural imagination, making it appear to some as an event without ending.[2] In *These Rooms*, the bodies in the production that hold the grief are female. It is women as witnesses who cry out from the past; it is their unresolved history that is being brought back to life.

DRESSING UP

The recovery of suppressed narratives can take place in many ways. Official commemorations often take ritualistic form, sustaining the idea that the integrity of the original event is being recaptured in an annual observance. However, each act of commemoration also reshapes and re-imagines that which is being remembered, and this creative tension is a vital element in linking past with present. Throughout its centenary, the Easter Rising was visually dominant in most major cities and towns in Ireland, drawing the event into the landscape of the present. The conjoined years 1916 and 2016 were emblazoned across a multitude of venues, including libraries, museums, galleries, shops, pubs, banks, gable walls, and trucks. The GPO Museum Witness History exhibition on Dublin's main street promised "history so close you can almost smell the smoke" and urged the public to "walk through Ireland's story. Experience it" (GPO Museum Witness History 2020). The "1916 Rise of the Rebels Bus Tour" offered its customers the opportunity to "Ride the Revolution," and Dublin Bus's official tour "Beyond Barricades" included dramatic performances with the tag line, "Take an extraordinary journey through time on the 1916 bus tour." There were thus multiple examples of the past being offered as a future experience (Schneider 2011, 19). Time was in flux and the boundaries between past, present, and future were deliberately blurred.

Dressing up (as a way of remembering the past) has become an increasingly popular aspect of Irish commemorations. On the hundredth anniversary of the Dublin Lockout's "Bloody Sunday" (August 31, 1913), thousands of people, including the Irish president, assembled on O'Connell Street in Dublin to hear an actor deliver the words of Jim Larkin while horse-drawn ambulances and police carts gathered up those who were cheering him on. Police reenactors ran at workers to simulate a baton charge. A re-enactment also took place on October 5, 2013, of the arrival in Dublin of the SS *Hare*, a food relief ship commissioned by the National Transport Workers' Federation to help feed starving Dublin workers. To mark the event, a ship sponsored by trade unions set sail from the Liverpool docks to Dublin. The centenary of the Rising officially began on the anniversary of the funeral of Jeremiah O'Donovan Rossa on August 1, 2015, and attendees at Sinn Féin's commemorative event—a reenactment of the funeral procession through Dublin city center to O'Donovan Rossa's grave in Glasnevin cemetery—were encouraged to dress up in clothes styled to look historically accurate. RTÉ's Easter Monday events—2015's *Road to the Rising* and 2016's *Reflecting the Rising*—also included many attendees who playfully arrived in period dress.

The popularity of costumes and reenactments at commemorative events reflects a more general affective turn in historical representations. Vanessa Agnew has described this type of history as that which both takes affect as its object and attempts to elicit affect so that "reenactment is less concerned with events, processes or structures than with the individual's physical and psychological experience" (Agnew 2007, 301). Agnew raises concerns about the role of popular re-enactments in properly confronting the injustices and processes of the past, arguing that they often substitute empathy for evidence and, through the collapsing of temporal boundaries, suggest historical continuities that are not only inaccurate but exploitable for ideological ends (309). In this view, affective history operates primarily as a conceit for *Gegenwartsbewältigung*, or coming to terms with the present (302). Re-enactments are, therefore, not unproblematic depictions of history but, as a way of expressing unresolved trauma, affective representations can be very powerful.

Mark Auslander has written about the Moore's Ford lynching re-enactment that has been performed annually in Walton County, Georgia, since 2005. The event commemorates the murder in 1946 of four young African Americans by a group of white Klansmen. The re-enactments were an attempt to mobilize public pressure for the reopening of the federal investigation into these deaths. An activist at the time remarked, "White folks love their Civil War re-enactments, which is mainly one big fantasy about the Lost Cause being so noble, so why not re-enact some real history for a change?" (Auslander 2013, 174). During the Moore's Ford lynching re-enactment, white participants are always careful to wear clothing that marks them as being in performance mode, while African American participants wear street clothes and make no attempt to wear period-appropriate clothing. A re-enactor told Auslander, "The thing is, we shouldn't dress up like this only happened in the past, just in the past. This thing, it happened once, but it's still happening to our people, to our young people. It just isn't over, I mean" (ibid.).

This striking example suggests some possible ways in which to understand adopting costumes in the interpretation of Irish history. On the one hand, it can be a way of performing a fantasy version of the past and imbuing it with nobility and grandeur. On the other hand, it provides a way of communing with the past that allows different versions and meanings to emerge in the present. Much depends on the power structures of the present in determining whether or not the re-enactments render visible a difficult past or provide solace from an uncertain present. Period clothing can be a way of differentiating between past and present, and of redirecting attention away from the politics of both. During the centenary of the Rising, commemoration as escapism was clearly in evidence, and, it could be argued, there was comfort for participants in a specifically Irish story told amid Ireland's growing cultural diversity and in an increasingly globalized world. David Lowenthal has reminded us that rather than enhance the here and now, the past may "replace the intolerable present altogether" (2015, 105). However, the attention paid by audiences to the details of the past indicated that there was also a search for something more and a desire to create new meanings for the present from history. It is significant that the most vigorous story to be released by this concentrated encounter with the past centered around women, and this story was given energy because it made visible inequality in the present.

In dressing up, there is both an escape from the present and a nostalgia for the past. Svetlana Boym describes nostalgia as a longing not just for place but for another time and "for unrealised dreams of the past and visions of the future which [had become] obsolete" (Boym 2001, xvi). In this sense, the commemoration of the Rising acted as a displacement for the disappointment of the present rather than a celebration of it. However, the example in Georgia shows the pain that can be present in a re-enactment in plain clothes; it shows in plain sight that the past is not over.

CURATORS OF MEMORY

Historically, Irish women tended to the memories of martyred men while their own histories were rendered increasingly invisible. Nellie Gifford Donnelly initiated the National Museum's collection of objects connected to the Easter Rising. As secretary of the 1916 research committee she contacted and negotiated with donors to build the archive and organized the first 1916 exhibition to coincide with the Eucharistic Congress in 1932 (see Joye and Malone 2015, 182–183). During the revolutionary period, Gifford, a founding member of the Irish Citizen Army (ICA), was active in the Easter Rising and later set up a recruitment bureau to find employment for Irish Volunteers. She had been attracted to the ICA because of its ethos of sexual equality and was a strong supporter of the labor movement (White and Long 2011).

Helena Molony, Winnie Carney, and Jinny Shanahan choreographed the first commemoration of the Easter Rising. On release from Aylesbury Prison on Christmas Eve 1916, the three women decided to "have a demonstration to commemorate the rebellion" on its first anniversary. They agreed the central features would be to "beflag all the positions that had been occupied in the 1916 Rising... and to get out the proclamation, and to proclaim it again, and to try to establish the position that the fight was not over and that the Republic still lives" (Helena Molony, Bureau of Military History, Military Archives, WS 391, 42). Making three flags, and with the assistance of a Glaswegian sailor called Moran and Baby Murray, a Fianna boy, they managed to raise the tricolor onto a large flagstaff at the GPO. Their efforts were so successful that it took the authorities until 6:00 p.m. to take it down, by which point a large crowd had gathered. The *Irish Times* reported that the anniversary was marked in Dublin by a good deal of excitement and gatherings, which together made up "a very considerable aggregation of persons" (*Irish Times*, April 10, 1917; see also R. Higgins 2016a, 43).

Molony and her fellow organizers also ordered facsimiles of the Proclamation using some of the typesetting from the original, which was retrieved from Liberty Hall. The plan to distribute them was abandoned because an order came, it was assumed from the Irish Republican Brotherhood, that there was to be no demonstration and that flags were not to be flown (Molony, BMH, WS 391, 46). Molony and Shanahan succeeded nevertheless in creating their own demonstration without the sanction of the trade union men, and they displayed a calico scroll outside Liberty Hall that said "James Connolly Murdered—May 12th, 1916" (ibid., 47). Molony had joined Inghindhe na hÉireann in 1903 and effectively began running it; she set up and became editor of *Bean na hÉireann* and was one of the founding members of the Fianna (McCoole 2015, 205). Yet Molony's own quite extraordinary contribution to Irish life and politics has been described as part of the "repressed memory" of the national story (McGarry 2015, 260).

The participation of women in commemorating histories that privilege the lives of men is not a uniquely Irish experience. The United Daughters of the Confederacy brought together two generations of women who tended and shaped the memory of the antebellum South in the decades after the American Civil War. Building Confederate monuments and tending the graves of the Confederate dead became an important source of social power for these women

and made some of them important public figures (Cox 2003, 12). Nevertheless, the Daughters were careful to preserve traditional definitions of womanhood while they memorialized Confederate men and promoted the history
and legacy of the Lost Cause (Cox 2003, 10, 26). In Ireland, republican women
had sought not to preserve a way of life but to push for revolutionary change.
However, their marginalization in the new dispensations of the 1920s meant
that their own histories were elided as the past was memorialized, reflecting
the present as a male space.

Derek Fraser, writing about working-class children who were evacuated
from British cities during World War II, described them as acting as messengers
carrying evidence of deprivation (Fraser 1973, 195). It is a good example of the
powerful story that can be told by the unarguably unequal body. During the
centenary of the Rising, women became more visible in their role as the messengers. During Easter Week, they had acted as dispatch riders and carriers of
weapons, food, and bandages. Their names became familiar to the public, as
historians and academics recovered the details of their lives: Margaret Skinnider, who served as a scout, dispatch rider, and sniper; Elizabeth O'Farrell,
who carried the surrender notice from the GPO and around the garrisons in the
city; and Catherine Byrne, who carried notes from the GPO to the Four Courts
in her hair bun. Women concealed weapons and messages under their clothes
and used the prejudices against their sex as a weapon, exploiting the assumption that women would not participate in military activity (see McCoole 2015;
McDiarmid 2015).

Women also acted as messengers carrying evidence into the present. They
did this through collecting and preserving evidence, like Nellie Gifford (maintaining what we might consider a traditional archive). In many ways, it is women
who have curated the memory of the Easter Rising. Before Con Colbert was
executed, he wrote a letter to Annie Cooney, with whom he was romantically
involved. Along with this final letter, he left her his watch. His prayer book he
wanted to be given to his sister Lila. Winnie Carney took jewelry from Joseph
Plunkett to give to his fiancée. Wives, mothers, sisters, and girlfriends gathered
mementos and built their unofficial archive of Easter Week.

Most strikingly, through their own stories and lives, women provided
messages for the future. The power of their intellectual, sexual, and political lives facilitated an insistence that they be heard in a way that opened
up conversations in the present. The increasing visibility of revolutionary
women in contemporary Ireland had been signaled by the campaign (spear-
headed by three young women) to name a bridge across the Liffey in Dublin, opened in 2014, after the trade unionist and member of the ICA Rosie

Hackett. Subterranean shifts in Irish society pushed through to the surface of the commemorations in the controversy over Abbey Theatre's centenary program and the subsequent Waking the Feminists movement. A gendered history of the Easter Rising created space for broader debates about the position of women in Ireland in 2016, and the complexity of individual rebel lives further enriched this discussion. The biographies of women like Rosie Hackett, Nellie Gifford, Winnie Carney, Helena Molony, and Jinny Shanahan illuminated an understanding of intersectionality. In early twentieth-century Ireland, working- and middle-class women challenged powers that sustained the status quo in a variety of ways. Their historical markings could be traced one hundred years later to articulate resistance to the ongoing silencing of female voices.

TO WHAT ARE WE LENDING POWER?

Of the Easter Rising, Helena Molony recalled: "Everyone was exalted and caught in the sweep of a great movement. We saw a vision of Ireland, free, pure, happy. We did not realise this vision. But we saw it" (McGarry 2015, 355). For Molony, it is the promise of the Easter Rising that is so compelling; the elusive, hoped-for possibility of something better. Ninety years after the event, historian of the Rising Charles Townshend wrote that it "shifted the horizons of possibility, both at the subliminal and practical level . . . the symbolic effect of the rebellion by the middle of Easter week was to burst the limits of what could be imagined" (Townshend 2006, 355). The Rising was a short-term defeat that was reframed by subsequent events as a victory, providing a compelling duality that has been reproduced in subsequent anniversaries. Official commemorations assert modern Irish society in evidence of the Rising's success, while sections of the population see the aspirations of Easter Week as proof of the failure of much that followed. This central tension means that commemorations of the Rising are significant opportunities to critique as well as to celebrate Irish society. Given this instability in the meaning and the checkered history of Easter commemorations, successive governments have understood the importance of properly framing the official message. As then minister for justice Brian Lenihan warned in 1966, "We should not make a disgrace of ourselves by having incidents that the foreign Press would gloat over and make a laugh of us. It is our duty to honour the patriots of 1916 in a proper and responsible way and see to it that there would be no incident to spoil or besmirch the name of Ireland" (*Offaly Independent*, April 9, 1966). The question, of course, remains as to what is proper and responsible.

An attempt to package the Easter Rising in a way that might "sell" it to a national and international audience caused controversy around the centenary from the outset. The launch of the video to promote the program (#IrelandInspires) in November 2014 attracted widespread criticism for its ahistorical and commercial content. Critics noted that Facebook and LinkedIn (both of which had established operations in Ireland) were referenced, but not Pearse, Connolly, or any of the Easter leaders. There were no visual mentions of the Easter Rising but instead viewers were shown a series of cultural, political, and social images promoting Ireland as a tourist destination emptied of historical context. Indeed, University College Dublin's professor of Modern Irish History, Diarmaid Ferriter, famously referred to the video as "embarrassing unhistorical shit" (*Irish Times*, November 13, 2014; January 2, 2015).

The commodification of Ireland's past was the prime subject of Rita Duffy's *Souvenir Shop* (2016), an art installation in a house on Dublin's North Great George's Street. Duffy designed the shop to echo the layout of Tom Clarke's tobacconist, recycling period furniture and fittings from a disused shop in County Cavan. The exhibition played with ideas of invention and authenticity through artifacts and messages embedded in mimicry. Curator Helen Carey explained that the genesis of the exhibition was the image management and propaganda used during World War I. Tanks became central to the machinery of trench warfare from 1916 and, to counter the possibility of public revulsion at this killing machine, the *Daily Mirror* celebrated the tank as a means to outwit the enemy. It was then reproduced during the war as handbag, teapot, and money box so that, Carey writes, the abstract image of a killing machine became a fetishized object and the audience became complicit in this management of ideas (Carey 2016, 5–9). In Duffy's *Souvenir Shop*, visitors could purchase items including Mexican candles adorned with images of the Easter leaders, bars of "Lady Lavatory" soap and "Rise Up" baking soda. In making these items available for purchase, Duffy implicated the viewer as consumer by marketing potent symbols on everyday objects that can either neutralize or lend power to something banal (ibid.). In exploring the "relationship of truth to notions of value, the market place, ideology and power relations, along with the fluid part played by the audience" (ibid.), Duffy's *Souvenir Shop* prodded some of the deepest complexities of the centenary by drawing on humor and absurdity as well as sacred commemorative tropes. The installation interrogates what historical "truth" means and the ways in which commemorative activities might shape history into "a tool in the arsenal of the status quo" (ibid.). It prompts the viewer to question what it is he or she is lending power to when participating in a national commemoration.

LONGING FOR A DIFFERENT IRELAND

Rita Duffy is a northerner who positions herself on the border, challenging boundaries. Her exploration of the ways in which the past can be marshaled to reinforce the status quo addressed perhaps the most pertinent and complicated element of the commemorations. In 2012, anticipating the centenary of the Easter Rising, I wrote that it would be a test of the credibility of those who represented power in Ireland, an indication of Irish citizenry's relationship with authority (R. Higgins 2012, 209). This observation grew out of research on the fiftieth anniversary and subsequent commemorations of the Easter Rising. Commemorations of the Rising have not only provided a vehicle through which the southern state asserts its legitimacy; they also offer an obvious event around which opposition to the government can cohere. Of the three significant movements in the early years of the twentieth century—the national movement, the labor movement, and the women's movement—the first two have traditionally been able to use the commemoration of the Rising to revisit the ideals of the original event and assail the government for the failures and lost opportunities of the intervening years. Historically, the women's movement has been much less successful in this regard.

During the fiftieth anniversary of the Rising, the authority invested in Ireland's history of struggle for independence had been drawn on to underwrite the economic policies of the Irish government, which was moving the country from protectionism to free trade. Pageants, plays, exhibitions, and statues that were commissioned for the jubilee in 1966 were all consciously or subconsciously in dialogue with this central message, endorsing or resisting the ideas that the success of independence was evidenced in the strategy of modernization (R. Higgins 2012, passim). Left-wing writers and groups in Ireland were vocal during and galvanized by the fiftieth anniversary of the Rising and used the writing of James Connolly (which had much more power during the jubilee) to challenge the policies of Fianna Fáil (R. Higgins 2016a, 33–44). Furthermore, in 1966, republicans understood the importance of maximizing the opportunity afforded by the commemoration to enliven northern nationalism and to dispel "the deadening apathy that had immobilised the people for so many years" (Liam McMillen in Ó h-Agáin 1979, 6). The golden jubilee, while not carrying responsibility for the collapse of civil order in Northern Ireland, nevertheless undoubtedly made nationalism more visible and assertive during this period. Therefore, commemorations of the Easter Rising provided a way for Irish society to raise awareness of important debates in 1966: most notably about the economy and nationalism in the north.

Feminist critiques (or indeed gendered readings of the Rising) were largely absent in 1966. Female relatives of Easter leaders (like Kathleen Clarke, Margaret Pearse, and the sisters of Seán MacDiarmada) used their influence to tend to the memories of their dead husbands and brothers, effectively privileging a militant masculine heroic ideal, rather than employing the radical potential of the revolutionary period to articulate an alternative vision. Unlike socialists and republicans, feminists did not manage to mobilize the biographies of female revolutionaries to promote their own politics or agenda. The Easter Rising operates as a conduit; the past retains multiple narratives, but agency lies in the present. In 2016, the story seemed very different. Waking the Feminists was the most effective mobilization of an ideological position during the centenary and was matched by the harnessing of women's stories from Easter Week to emphasize that the issues were of a pressing nature in this particular historic moment. What was seen as one of the most successful aspects of the centenary—the attention given to women's stories—also underlined the extent of their marginalization.

Indeed, more generally, the centenary of the Rising gave form to an often inarticulate, underlying anger with the politics of the present, including—and unsurprisingly after the 2008 financial crisis—the handling of the economy. The general election in the Republic of Ireland in February 2016 provided no party with an overall majority and was the first time the combined vote of the two main parties was less than 50 percent. As a result, no political party had an overall majority, and, for the period of the centenary commemorations, Enda Kenny acted in a caretaker role until a new government could be formed. This meant that no political party was in a strong position to capitalize on commemorations of the Rising and it also indicates that, despite the prevailing narrative around the centenary, the Republic was not at ease with itself. Paul Muldoon and Shaun Davey's *One Hundred Years a Nation* (which premiered at the commemorative concert in Collins Barracks, *A Nation's Voice*) does not make direct reference to the Easter Rising but does address the Celtic Tiger in Muldoon's libretto: "now Finn MacCool gave way to cool / our very monks lived by the rule / of gombeen financiers / for a great stag may be dragged down / by flimflam and stagflation" (Muldoon 2016b, 17). The piece expresses a sense of public anger over what has been squandered, the failures of the nation laid bare. Davey, as composer, explained, "As the description of the troubled century unfolds the choir becomes an army, marching in step with the narrator. For the 'Celtic Tiger' the music takes off in a jazzy gallop, which transforms into a restless dark score as the text describes corruption and greed of the recent past" (Davey 2016, 22). Poet Tom French added his interpretation of the commemoration in "1916," published in May 2016: "1916 is currently unable to come to the phone. / Please listen to the following options and select one. / If you are livid, incandescent, or apoplectic with rage, / please press 1 now . . ." (French 2016, 93).

It is possible to read the centenary, as many did, as a reaffirming moment in Ireland's history during which a plurality of narratives was heard, representing the country's "growing maturity as a nation" (Paul Colton, Bishop of Cork, Cloyne, and Ross, quoted in *Irish Times*, March 30, 2016). The contribution artists made to the commemorative program prompted Fintan O'Toole to wonder whether there had ever been "an official celebration of a state's foundations so far from chauvinism or complacency or self-congratulation?" O'Toole saw the public's ability "to poke fun at itself, acknowledge its own idiocies and lament its own murderous tendencies" as evidence of profound cultural maturation (*Irish Times*, October 29, 2016). Yet, there may be both complacency and self-congratulation among those who have cultural, political, and social power in Ireland about the fact that they did not, overall, lose control of the narrative of the centenary; that, once underway, it did not unsettle the comfortable (unlike the original event). The discourses of resistance, secreted in and exploding out of artistic endeavors, were reactions to the way in which Irish society operates and yet—as Duffy suggested—they could be marshaled, as part of the centenary, to operate in the interests of the status quo. Maurice Manning, chair of the government's historical advisory committee, told the audience at the Parnell Summer School that the committee had refused "point blank" to use the northern peace process as a frame of reference: "We were into commemoration. We were into history. We were not into politics," he was reported to have said (*Irish Times*, August 10, 2016). The three things are impossible to disentangle, and the impulse to repress the story of the north is very telling, but what is most revealing is the invisibility to Manning of a political dimension, the belief that the centenary could transcend the embedded interests and influences in society.

O'Toole was certainly right in his view that in 2016 "most people [were] capable of holding more than one thought about the Rising in their heads at the same time" (*Irish Times*, October 29, 2016). Moreover, the centenary commemorations represented two different things simultaneously: they were an expression of national pride and evidence of the failure of contemporary politics; the manifestation of deep disillusionment with the present and a search for something different. The Easter Rising contained a multitude of sometimes conflicting messages, and commemorations of 1916 reveal the polarities of Irish society and identity. The collision of past, present, and future, perceived during significant anniversaries, often magnifies elements within society, so that a moment of shared national experience also underlines the fault lines and divisions, asserting inclusion while rendering invisible those who do not participate. The incorporation of women into the historical narrative was a victory that made more vivid their lack of autonomy in contemporary Ireland. The complicated nature of the centenary meant that while appearing to represent a celebration of Irishness it also represented a longing for a different Ireland; a search for an alternative future in the aspirations of the revolutionary past.

NOTES

1. I was involved in the centenary as an academic and audience member so these experiences inevitably suffuse my observations.

2. There are echoes of the sentiments of Gael Linn when proposing a film to mark the fiftieth anniversary of the Easter Rising: "At an anniversary, however, they leap into prominence and are recognised as a living reality. The Easter Rising is for us such an event, and it is the constant reality of 1916 running through our lives today that we wish to express" (see R. Higgins 2012, 174).

ROISÍN HIGGINS is Reader in Modern History at Teesside University and has written extensively on commemorations of the Easter Rising, including her award-winning book *Transforming 1916: Meaning and Memory of the Fiftieth Anniversary of the Easter Rising* (2012). Roisín lectured in the United States, Australia, Europe, and across Ireland during the centenary in 2016, was historical adviser on the commemoration zone of the GPO Museum Witness History permanent exhibition, and was one of the curators for the public history project *National Treasures*, a collaboration between RTÉ, the National Museum of Ireland, and the Broadcasting Authority of Ireland. The television series to accompany the project was broadcast on RTÉ throughout April 2018.

TWELVE

—꩜—

EXHIBITING ÉIRE

Representations of Women in the Easter Rising Centenary Commemorations

MAEVE CASSERLY

WILLIAM BUTLER YEATS AND LADY Augusta Gregory's 1902 play *Cathleen Ní Houlihan* famously contains a symbolic and personified representation of Ireland in the title character. Choosing to embody the Irish nation as a female figure—sometimes called Éire, sometimes Hibernia, Cathleen Ní Houlihan, or *An Sean-Bhean Bhocht* (the poor old woman)—was not unique to Gregory and Yeats or to theater; indeed, it was not unique to Ireland. This practice was well established in Europe in eighteenth- and nineteenth-century debates about national identity, and figures like Marianne, Germania, or Britannia were familiar to the general public (Anderson 2006; Hobsbawm and Ranger 1983). Yeats and Gregory's plot relied on this understanding of and familiarity with the feminine national symbol, Cathleen, and the way in which her transformation from the strange "old woman" to a beautiful young queen personified an Ireland in chains emerging as a free Republic. Like many of his contemporaries, Yeats regarded Ireland as "manifestly gendered, and that gender was feminine" (Stevens, Brown, and Maclaran 2000, 410). Stevens et al. argue that "Ireland has struggled with its 'feminine' identity throughout its history." The dichotomy between male and female identities is "embedded in colonial and postcolonial constructions of Irishness" and continues to manifest itself in contemporary representations of Ireland and Irish identities (405). In this argument, the feminine identity of Ireland is related to its role as a subservient colony in the British Empire, which led to a problem for Irish nationalists of the nineteenth century who continued to identify their country as "feminine" and who thus took up a "compensatory and exaggerated masculinity" (406). Stevens et al. point, in particular, to Eamon de Valera's infamous quote about female revolutionaries: "Women are at once the boldest and most unmanageable revolutionaries"

(409). One hundred years on, as Ireland looked toward the centenary of the Easter Rising, did this gendered perspective on the country remain in place? How did contemporary artists, historians, politicians, and public institutions choose to represent modern Ireland? A number of commemorative activities confronted gender issues: the notion and promotion of a "shared history" as well as the cultural demobilization of Ireland in a post-conflict society. These themes frame an analysis of the representation of national identity in various examples of commemorative practice and two key case studies discussed in this chapter. These case studies do not make up the whole of the decade of centenaries output in 2016 but rather offer contrasting representations of contemporary Irish identity through the Éire motif and allow us to reflect on the means by which depictions of Éire comment on and mirror the role of women in Irish society.

The centenary commemorations of the Easter Rising, seen by many as a foundational moment of the current Irish state, were highly anticipated. Previous commemorations provided decisive moments in Irish political, social, and cultural heritage, measuring the achievements of the Irish state against the ideals of the Proclamation and proving a litmus test to gauge Ireland's view of itself at a particular moment. In their seminal analysis of the 1966 commemorations of the Rising, Mary E. Daly and Margaret O'Callaghan posit that "1916 has been the key site of memory in twentieth-century Ireland," the blueprint from which the national narrative can be written and rewritten (Daly and O'Callaghan 2007, 3). Regarding our understanding of the function of memory and commemoration within this national narrative, historian John Gillis notes that "we are constantly revising our memories to suit our current identities" (Gillis 1996, 3). The Easter Rising commemorations, therefore, offer a key case study around which to analyze the makeup of Ireland's "identity" in 2016. Debates over women's rights and a call for greater gender equality, instigated by a variety of historians, artists, community groups, and institutions, emerged as themes within the centenary commemorations, demonstrating that history and commemoration were not a peripheral part of Irish society in 2016 but key in defining how the nation sees itself.

The beginning of 2016 saw a number of journalists reflecting on the state of the nation one hundred years on from the Rising, with several articles explicitly addressing the position of women in contemporary Ireland. In *The Guardian*, Olivia O'Leary, a noted journalist and political affairs presenter, wondered, "Why, 100 Years after the Easter Rising, Are Women Still Fighting?" (2016), concluding that the promise for gender equality enshrined in the Proclamation had not yet been fulfilled. *Irish Times* columnist and activist Una Mullally, in "Why Women Have Risen to the Top in 1916 Lore" (2016), argued that the emphasis on women in the 1916 narrative was a "catch-up" on the male-dominated history that had previously held court. Not everyone was in favor of this turn. Victoria White, columnist with the *Irish Examiner*, wrote, "I am sick, sore and tired of hearing about the women of 1916. Women's role in the 1916 Rising was marginal" (2016). White objected to what she described as overwhelming and perhaps inaccurate attention being given to women's role in the Easter Rising. As early as 2015, historian of modern Ireland Anne Dolan raised this issue of historical accuracy and integrity regarding the Rising commemorations in response to an ahistorical promotional video, *Ireland Inspires*, launched by the Irish state in the lead up to the 2016 commemoration program. Dolan argued that *Ireland Inspires* clearly demonstrated the gap between history and commemoration, since the video was more of a tourism gimmick than a piece of historical promotion or education. But, as Dolan asked, "when has commemoration ever truly been about history?" (2015).

Because commemoration functions to define contemporary identities, it is crucial to examine commemorations of the Easter Rising within the political and social context of Ireland in 2016. Public history projects such as exhibitions and reenactments as well as historical dramas and state parades have all been shaped and influenced by the goals and motivations of the actors behind them. We need only to examine earlier Rising commemorations to see the influence of contemporary politics on the way in which the past is presented. Taoiseach Seán Lemass and his Fianna Fáil government saw the fiftieth jubilee of the Rising "as an opportunity to showcase a modern prosperous state to a wider world" and to unite the country after a bitter Civil War (Daly and O'Callaghan 2007, 8). The 1966 commemorations, therefore, were executed on a scale never seen before to produce a moment of "unrestrained triumphalism," which many have argued to be the catalyst of the Troubles in Northern Ireland and a factor in the subsequent resurgence of IRA military activity (R. Higgins 2012, 1). "Societies, like individuals, remember in order to forget," Roisín Higgins notes (19). If the aim of the 1966 commemorations was to present the world with a modern Ireland in order to forget the Civil War, economic hardship, and cultural stagnation, then was an objective of the 2016 state commemorations to remember the "forgotten" women of the Rising in order to forget the role the state had played in sidelining these women from Irish society since the Rising? For instance, what Victoria White perceived as an apparent overemphasis on women's roles in the Rising and the revolutionary period could be seen as the result of a political strategy to make up for the debacle, for example, of the Abbey Theatre's commemorative *Waking the Nation* program, which saw the state-funded national theater include the work of only one female playwright, sparking outrage and the Waking the Feminists movement (see O'Connell, this volume).

Throughout the decade of commemorations and in 2016, in particular, a proliferation of projects saw an increased interest in narratives beyond the standard ones seen in textbooks on modern Irish history (McGreevy 2017). The Waking the Feminists movement was one example that focused on the role of women and "herstory" in the centenary year of the Easter Rising. Others explored themes of class and sexuality to reveal "hidden" or "forgotten" histories of the past. Many of these projects, whether academic research, exhibitions by cultural institutions, or community-led initiatives, looked beyond well-known figures such as Patrick Pearse and James Connolly; a newfound appetite for local history and women's history was apparent. The Stoneybatter and Smithfield People's History project, for instance, organized a parade and plaque to commemorate civilians killed in the North King Street massacre, an event rarely included in history books on the Rising until now (Stoneybatter and Smithfield People's History Project 2016). The 1916 Sackville Street Art Project was another alternative take on the narrative of the Easter Rising: an exhibition consisting of 262 model homes representing the 262 civilians killed during the fighting in Easter Week. The project was initiated by ceramic artist Ciara O'Keefe, who issued an open call to schools, youth groups, and individuals to participate. The idea behind the Kildare County Council–funded project, O'Keefe explained, "was that 2016's civilians would make a piece for 1916's civilians, so it would just be ordinary people remembering ordinary people" (Sackville Street Art Project 2016). Where possible, participants provided a brief historical profile of the civilian that their art project commemorated. This kind of historical research into the revolutionary period has become easier to conduct since the recent release and digitization of key archival resources such as the 1901 and 1911 censuses online; the database of military service pension claims; the Bureau of Military History; and the Decade of Centenaries collections by the National Library of Ireland. Through this democratization of information, primary material became accessible to a much wider contingent of interested groups and individuals than the traditional academic scholar. State funding to remove the paywall from access to the census and increased commemoration budgets for authorities to stage exhibitions in their localities allowed many people—who previously did not have the access to or even knowledge of the existence of historical documents—to conduct research themselves and to draw conclusions of their own about this period in Irish history.

An emphasis on creating historical empathy was a key part of many of the commemoration activities, even if the events receiving attention differed across the island: the Northern Irish commemorative focus on World War I and the 1916 Battle of the Somme was in contrast to commemorative activities in the Republic of Ireland, which were dominated by the story of the Rising. Creating historical empathy was a particularly important function of commemorative activities in Northern Ireland, where the more recent history of the Troubles remains a potent and often divisive part of everyday life. Many of the commemorative activities and exhibitions created empathy through a focus on the impact of events such as World War I on the ordinary lives of individuals from local communities in Northern Ireland and by presenting multiple narratives side by side, for instance, both nationalist and unionist involvement in shared experiences such as the Battle of the Somme or the suffrage movement.

A good example of this tendency to focus on shared experiences and universal themes was #MakingHistory, a World War I exhibition. Curated by Creative Centenaries, based in Derry / Londonderry's Nerve Centre, "Northern Ireland's leading creative media arts centre" (Nerve Centre 2019), the exhibit was launched in June 2016 in the Ulster Museum. #MakingHistory placed particular emphasis on the role of women in the war effort, both at home in their communities and at the front. This exhibition effectively explored the daily life of people in 1916—even creating tweets using direct quotes from contemporary figures like Maud Gonne and the Chancellor of the Exchequer—and accommodated multiple narratives of 1916 that still make up an important part of community identity. #MakingHistory was perhaps too accommodating, however, and missed an opportunity to reinforce the wider point of the destruction World War I wrought on so many lives and communities. The exhibition did tackle themes of violence head on with some of the modern art installations that complemented the manuscript and ephemera material, such as Eamonn O'Doherty's Iron Pram for Derry. The piece, dating from 1991 and restored in 2013, reflects the lasting resonance and imagery of themes from World War I as well as responds to contemporary violence in Derry through an image associated with domestic life and the role of women as mothers and caregivers. #MakingHistory also explored the opportunities that war gave to women for roles outside the home, as through the manuscripts of nurse Olive Swanzy, whose sketchbooks gave a detailed perspective on her life at the front. The role of women as nurses, munitions factory workers, or volunteers in charities like the British Red Cross has been central to the ways in which the lives of women during 1916 and World War I are explored in #*MakingHistory* and other exhibitions, such as *Doing Their Bit*, a 2018 exhibition by Dublin City Council, and *World War Ireland* by the National Library of Ireland, which ran from 2014 to 2019. These "safe options" presented women in roles that were easy to accept, but other pieces tried to challenge this representation, with a stronger focus on the agency of women as well as their bodily experience of World War I and the Rising.

All of the above examples of commemoration occurred against the backdrop of significant social and cultural events that highlighted the ways in which women's issues are of central concern in contemporary Ireland. Throughout 2016, debates continued to rage over the campaign to repeal the Eighth Amendment to the Constitution of the Republic of Ireland, which recognized the "rights of the unborn" as being equal to the mother and prevented legislation for abortion. Movements like Waking the Feminists were key in bringing issues of inequality to the fore, as have been continued fights for government redress by former residents and survivors of institutions known as mother and baby homes.[1] It is in this context that a diverse number of memory choreographers—that is, memory and public history practitioners such as museum curators and state committees—chose to tackle contemporary politics or pursued particular agendas in their commemorative versions of Ireland (B. Conway 2010).

The *Women of 1916 and Irish Revolution* project was an important example of a public history initiative to emerge from newly available archive material and to reveal the importance of the political and social context of women's issues. This project, a collaboration between Richmond Barracks, academics, and local women's groups, created a commemorative quilt remembering the seventy-seven women detained in Richmond Barracks after the Easter Rising (Richmond Barracks 2020c). Each of the seventy-seven women was assigned to a member of a local women's group, who then created a quilt panel based on the woman's life and contribution to the Rising. The project website emphasized that many of the detained women were forgotten figures in Irish history; the aim of the quilt was to "start a conversation" between the women of 1916 and those living in the area in the present (Richmond Barracks 2020). Many of the panels, however, were just names, as any further information on the women's lives was difficult to find. This in itself demonstrates that even with the release of information like the 1901 and 1911 censuses, archives may still have gaps about the lives of "ordinary" people.

Other examples of commemorative performances that engaged with the experience of women and the female body in the modern Irish state include *Embodied at the GPO*. Performed in April 2016 as part of the Dublin Dance

Festival, *Embodied at the GPO* staged dances by seven female dancers and choreographers in the General Post Office and the GPO Museum Witness History Visitor Centre—opened in 2016 as a new permanent visitor attraction in part of the General Post Office on O'Connell Street—with the aim of confronting the wording of the Proclamation read outside the GPO in 1916 (Dublin Dance Festival 2020). The performance was a significant female occupation of a site of Irish history usually considered a male-dominated *lieu de mémoire*: the headquarters of the Rising leaders. In September 2016, performance artists Jesse Jones and Sarah Browne staged another example of a piece that reflected the troubled relationship between women and the female body in modern Ireland. *The Touching Contract* was staged in the Pillar Room of the Rotunda Maternity Hospital, the first lying-in hospital in the British Isles and thus another significant site of public memory in an urban space. *The Touching Contract* was one of four pieces that formed *In the Shadow of the State*, a project that investigated "the role of the nation state in the regulation of the female body, tracking the everyday institutions of the state," particularly the Irish state's control over access to an abortion in the Republic of Ireland (The Arts Council 2020). In these pieces, issues of consent and control over the female body were explored through the artists' interaction with the audience.

TWO CASE STUDIES OF 1916 COMMEMORATIONS: *THE SOUVENIR SHOP* AND *REVOLUTION 1916*

Two exhibitions launched in 2016—*The Souvenir Shop* and *Revolution 1916: The Authentic Exhibition*—provide a study in contrasts in terms of the ways that commemorative activity has deployed and represented women. Both prominently featured women in their narratives of the Easter Rising and, like previously mentioned commemorative events, were based in urban Dublin. Neither of these exhibitions were in traditional museum settings, nor were their creators and curators from traditional, state-run historical museum backgrounds. *The Souvenir Shop* was funded by the Irish Arts Council, curated by independent visual arts curator Helen Carey, and created by visual artist Rita Duffy. *Revolution 1916* was curated by Bartle D'arcy, longtime member of Sinn Féin and coordinator of the party's commemoration program (Minihan 2015; Treacy 2016). The nontraditional exhibition spaces of *Revolution 1916* and *The Souvenir Shop* are in close proximity to one another: according to Google Maps, North Great George's Street and the Ambassador Theatre are divided by a mere five-minutes' walk. But the two exhibition sites are a world apart. *Revolution 1916*'s Ambassador Theatre, at the top of O'Connell Street, was where the (all-male) Irish Volunteers formed in 1913; it is located beside the Garden of Remembrance, marking the Irish revolutionary dead, in an area with substantial tourist footfall. O'Connell Street is the boulevard of Ireland national memory: it is where huge processions marched for the funerals of Daniel O'Connell, Charles Stewart Parnell, and Jeremiah O'Donovan Rossa; it was the site of "Big" Jim Larkin's rousing speech to a roaring crowd during the 1913 Dublin Lockout. Symbolically, it is the heart of the Easter Rising, with the General Post Office as the rebel's headquarters during the majority of the fighting. *Revolution 1916* would also have been in direct competition with one of the Irish government's key capital investments for 2016, the GPO Museum Witness History Visitor Centre mentioned above. *The Souvenir Shop*, on the other hand, was set, peripherally, in a crumbling tenement house on North Great George's Street, in the heart of what had been fashionable Georgian Dublin in the eighteenth century. Apart from the presence of the James Joyce Centre,[2] North Great George's Street retains little of the grandeur of its former heyday, and pales in comparison to the grand boulevard of O'Connell Street, though a new insight into the cultural heritage of the area has since changed with the opening of the Tenement Museum at 14 Henrietta Street in 2018.

The location of an exhibition can profoundly influence the historical narrative with which it seeks to identify. The journey to reach the space, whether by foot, public transport, or car, makes an impression on visitors before they arrive at their destination. Status can be implied by the area in which an exhibit is located, and there is a message of historical inheritance in both sites: the narrative of the Ambassador is one of visibility, grandeur, and significance and is male dominated, whereas an unremarkable former tenement building tells a tale of invisibility; it is humble and marked by women's experience of the domestic sphere. These issues and their subsequent impact on the representation of women in these exhibitions are explored in what follows.

The Souvenir Shop, on 13 North Great George's Street, opened on the calendar centenary of the Easter Rising, April 24, 2016, and ran until June 15. It was one of the major projects commissioned by the Arts Council of Ireland to mark the centenary of the Rising under the banner ART: 2016. *The Souvenir Shop* was at once an exhibition space, an art gallery, and a shop in which visitors were able to purchase fine works of contemporary art, which were sold alongside tongue-in-cheek representations of iconic figures in history. The exhibition was created by Northern Irish artist Rita Duffy, who was born in Belfast in 1959 and grew up in Northern Ireland during the Troubles. Duffy is now based in County Fermanagh, one of the six counties of Northern Ireland and one that borders the Republic. Duffy has worked as an artist-in-residence with Cavan County

Figure 12.1. *The Souvenir Shop* by Rita Duffy. (Courtesy of Rita Duffy.)

Council, a border county on the Republic side, and thus has a cross-border perspective on Irish history and the Irish present. In *The Souvenir Shop*, Duffy examined the shifting meanings and commodification of icons, gestures, and symbols associated with the revolutionary movement, and how these images, objects, and themes of the 1916 Easter Rising can become "souvenirs." Duffy's "shop" referenced the tobacconist's once owned by Tom Clarke, one of the seven signatories of the Irish Proclamation, which was itself both a shop and a meeting place for political and revolutionary discussion. Duffy's project also had a dual function, as both a shop and an art installation: it was filled with foodstuffs, goods, and medicines available to buy alongside images of the Rising and its heroes woven into everyday objects. (See Fig. 12.1.)

To create the hundreds of "souvenirs" sold in the shop, Duffy collaborated with the County Cavan Guild of the Irish Countrywomen's Association and the Cavan Arts Office. Concentrating on traditional domestic skills, Irish Countrywomen's Association members nationwide made "Carson's No Surrender" marmalade, "Free State" jam, and hemmed a range of tea towels featuring prints designed by Duffy. One print showed a sewing kit that illustrated how to sew Northern Ireland back to the Republic of Ireland to "Unite Ireland." Irish Countrywomen's Association members also knitted a range of dolls designed by Duffy: an Irish World War I nurse; a Black and Tan soldier;

Figure 12.2. Rise Up Baking Soda, *The Souvenir Shop* by Rita Duffy. (Courtesy of Rita Duffy.)

an Orangeman; and an injured soldier with his guts in his pocket (which could be put back in place). The partnership with the Irish Countrywomen's Association began in 2015 at the National Ploughing Championships (a nationwide agricultural competition) when Duffy met with the president of the Cavan branch of the Irish Countrywomen's Association, Anna Rose McCormack (Cavan Arts 2017). Duffy then presented her idea for *The Souvenir Shop* as a way for women to take part in the Rising commemorations and to celebrate their role of "nourishing the nation" (Cosstick 2016). The items produced by the Association women included knitted tea cozies with eyes for "surveillance on the kitchen table," Black and Tan boot polish, Rise Up Baking Soda, Birth of a Nation Salve, Lip Locker lip balm, and Irish Imperial Mints (Duffy 2016). These items, sold in the scenario of an ordinary shop, begin a complex and

Figure 12.3. Free State Jam, *The Souvenir Shop* by Rita Duffy. (Courtesy of Rita Duffy.)

multilayered dialogue around memory and value, which fundamentally questions public attitudes toward violence, commemoration, and national identity (Cosstick 2016). (See Figs. 12.2–12.3.)

In addition to the shop items, *The Souvenir Shop* exhibited commissioned artworks by Duffy, mainly focusing on women and their experience of the Rising. Displayed in the backroom, Duffy's large oil paintings hung on the walls surrounding cases containing delicately painted glass and ceramic works, also by Duffy. Just as the front-of-shop items suggested how important events and figures could be turned into souvenirs, the ceramic works, glass, and oil paintings suggested how everyday items like those found in the shop space could be transformed into artworks. The oil paintings were particularly illustrative of this process, with pieces featuring shirts, armchairs, uniforms, and aprons allowing Duffy to explore the significance of each in Irish memory. One prominent painting was dedicated to a bloody shirt lying limply on a wooden chair, referencing James Connolly's bloodstained shirt, an iconic item displayed in the National Museum of Ireland at Collins Barracks, which he wore while tied to a chair before his execution by firing squad. In another painting, the nostalgic ideal of "Dancing at the Crossroads," made famous by de Valera's 1943 speech, is parodied in a frenzied depiction of young Irish rebels dancing together while the city is destroyed around them (Wulff 2008, 12). But it was

Figure 12.4. Nurse, *The Souvenir Shop* by Rita Duffy. (Courtesy of Rita Duffy.)

Duffy's stark painting of a bloody-handed nurse, hung prominently over a dis-used fireplace, that emerged as the embodiment of Duffy's understanding of the Rising and clarified her sense of women's experience in it. (See Fig. 12.4.) Duffy's nurse, "as everywoman, is faint and fading except for the starkness of her bloodied hands" (Carey 2016). Duffy reasoned that "to be a nurse somehow or another was sensible . . . sutures, bandaging, weaving, and sewing offer both healing and making qualities that speak to the instrumental role that women have played publicly and privately in Ireland in the last century" (J. Keating 2016, 22). Duffy hoped this exhibition would "give voice to the silent, unspoken army of women who have literally had to put the pieces back together" (ibid.). By producing handicrafts like sewing and knitting, the members of the ICA echoed the sentiments expressed by Duffy who likened these handicraft skills to a woman's role of healing and bandaging the Irish nation.

In *The Souvenir Shop*, as in her previous work, Duffy uses irony and humor to confront difficult issues. During her opening remarks at the exhibition launch Duffy explained that she was trying to convey a sense of the commodifica-tion of the memory of the Rising by selling items like "Padraig Pearse Pasta Sauce," antique teacups and saucers newly branded with the Cumann na mBan logo, and tinned peas labeled "Peas Process." Selling and displaying objects of skewed meanings juxtaposed against original function allowed for an explora-tion of the complex relationship between historical truth and notions of value, the market place, ideology and power relations, as well as the fluid part played by the audience, who explicitly participate by consuming and purchasing the "souvenirs" and, by implication, the narratives that they represent. Duffy exam-ines the ways in which commemorative activity embeds and continues legacies, turning history into a tool in the arsenal of the status quo, or challenging it. Duffy's exhibition invites people to see the Rising and its legacy from a fresh and often irreverent angle. Through her artwork, particularly her paintings in the backroom, Duffy raises serious questions about attitudes to violence, commemoration, and the role of women in society. The nurse embodies these questions and is a healing figure in *The Souvenir Shop*; her role is to put Ireland, torn apart by war and rebellion, back together.[3]

Only a few streets away, *Revolution 1916: The Original and Authentic Exhi-bition*, "took over" the Ambassador Theatre, Dublin, from early February to October 2016. As the subtitle indicates, *Revolution 1916* claimed to be the stand-out exhibition on the Easter Rising because of the amount of original material on display (Sinn Féin 2015a). There was some confusion among the public over the declared involvement of Sinn Féin in the running of the exhibition (Brophy 2015). Several complaints to the Advertising Standards Authority of Ireland revealed that the postal and email contact details for the exhibition were Sinn Féin addresses. However, when interviewed by the *Irish Times*, a spokesperson from Sinn Féin stated that "there isn't a link between it and Sinn Féin. . . . There are party members involved and it is an event that Sinn Féin supports but it would be wrong to say it is being run by Sinn Féin" (Pope 2016). An introduction to the exhibition catalog was written by Gerry Adams, then leader of Sinn Féin, detailing the objectives of the exhibition curators and the political message, but apart from this connection with the Sinn Féin Party, little other information was available either online or in the exhibition catalog about the producers of the exhibition and their political background.[4] The exhibition received media attention as early as February 2015, when Adams and Sinn Féin were accused of running a "counter-event" centenary program in competition with Fine Gael government-run commemorations (Brophy 2015). A downloadable brochure from the launch of the program in 2015 clearly stated that Sinn Féin viewed the centenary commemorations as an opportunity to highlight its own political agenda and put the party forward as the inheritors of the Rising leaders: "We need to apply the principles of the Proclamation to our own time. For Sinn Féin that means . . . national reconciliation and an end to Partition. We want to build a New Republic. With these commemorative events we invite people to join with us—not alone in remembering the past but in shaping the new Ireland" (Sinn Féin 2015b).

The historical and political context of Sinn Féin's republican politics and its centenary program's competition with the state-run commemorations may not have been obvious to exhibition visitors. But one agenda made very clear was the duty of the exhibition to highlight for the visitor the role of women in Irish history, using one figure in particular, Molly O'Reilly. The exhibition claimed that "teenager Molly O'Reilly is a pivotal part of the overall history of this period" because "she raised the Irish flag over Liberty Hall a week prior to the Rising, and throughout she acted as an emissary between City Hall and . . . the GPO" (Clayton-Lea 2016). Adams gives a brief biography of O'Reilly in his online blog, *Léargas*, emphasizing her early republican and socialist credentials in connection with key events in Irish nationalist history: the Dublin Lockout, the Irish Citizen Army, and her siding with anti-Treaty members of Cumann na mBan. O'Reilly was "an exceptional woman; a courageous woman; a strong woman," and she remained a "stalwart of the republican struggle" until her death; it is because of this that O'Reilly was chosen as the central figure in *Revolution 1916* (Adams 2015). However, since the rest of Adams's blogpost goes on to highlight the role of the (all-male) Irish Volunteers in the Rising and the various weaponry and paraphernalia from the Volunteers that visitors would see at *Revolution 1916*, Molly O'Reilly's positioning seems tokenistic. Adams was critical of the Fine Gael and Labour Party coalition government's "amnesia" and "bungling approach" to the Rising centenary, which he saw as an important opportunity for inclusivity and to not be the monopoly for any one group: "The 100th anniversary of the Easter Rising will be marked, and in a big way, by ordinary people across this island with the support and leadership of Irish republicans, whether or not the Irish Government is involved" (Adams2015). In this context, what was the purpose of O'Reilly?

The exhibition catalog argues that "history sometimes doesn't include everyone it should" before explicitly stating that one key example was "Dubliner" Molly O'Reilly, who had been "forgotten about or sidelined." The exhibition saw itself as having a role in bringing Molly O'Reilly out of the shadows: "She is much more than a footnote, as *Revolution 1916* will confirm." The exhibition "is very much aware of how important a part women played in the Easter Rising" (Clayton-Lea 2016). It is apparent in the catalog's wording that there was a moral obligation for this exhibition to tell the "transformative tale of the young O'Reilly," who became politicized at a young age when assisting in soup kitchens and who went on hunger strike when imprisoned for political activism (ibid.). Molly's perspective is at the heart of the exhibition, as "the visitor will experience the Rising through Molly's eyes" (Adams 2015).

Interestingly, despite obvious differences in curation style, tone, and motivation, a familiar language of Irish nationalist iconography is utilized in both *Revolution 1916* and *The Souvenir Shop*. It is used particularly well in *Revolution 1916* to link the "forgotten about or sidelined" Molly O'Reilly into the well-established birth of a nation story, known to many Irish people, which begins with the Rising in 1916. Flags, symbols, colors, and ritual performances associated with the Easter Rising are all important narrative tools in telling the "hidden histories" of Molly O'Reilly in *Revolution 1916* and the experiences of the nurse in *The Souvenir Shop*. The iconography of Irish nationalism presented in *The Souvenir Shop* and *Revolution 1916*, specifically regarding the nurse and Molly O'Reilly, is worth analyzing in terms of how well these female figures are adopted into the predominantly male narrative of the Easter Rising. Symbolism, the use of "stable image[s] on which new elements are intermittently imposed" (B. Conway 2010, 17), is very important in both of these exhibitions. A prominent statue of O'Reilly on the exhibition's first floor, by artist Stuart Dunne, depicted her hoisting the flag, reminding visitors of her key role but also recalling other classic images of the female personification of a nation: Hibernia above the GPO, the Statue of Liberty on Ellis Island, and the bare-breasted Marianne in Eugène Delacroix's *Liberty*

Leading the People hoisting the flag to lead her troops into battle. The use of iconography—the transformation of Molly O'Reilly into a figure of Ireland itself—is clear, but the exhibit also pushes beyond this. Iconography is also combined with the ritual elements of performed commemorations like wreath laying, parade marches, or flag ceremonies, which represent a particular form of continuity that allows for the transmission of the past into the present. Paul Connerton has outlined the ways in which symbols and images of the past are conveyed and sustained by ritual performances, arguing that performative memory is also bodily memory (Connerton 2014). *Revolution 1916* drew on this process of performative memory when, every day at noon, an actor dressed as Padraig Pearse read the Proclamation aloud, reenacting the famous moment that marked the start of the Rising in 1916. The social function of these rituals is a transference of ownership to each new generation so that the passage of time serves to reinforce, rather than erode, behaviors and beliefs (Bryan 2016, 30). This ritual performance was an important legitimizing factor, especially since *Revolution 1916*'s subtitle described it as *The Original and Authentic Exhibition* of the Easter Rising during the centenary year. (See Fig. 12.5.)

With so many commemorative projects, parades, and exhibitions concentrated in Dublin city, their proximity—as is particularly evident in the nearness of *The Souvenir Shop* and *Revolution 1916*—meant that they were in competition for a limited audience and visibility not only with each other but also with a number of other big-ticket centenary projects in the area, including the state-funded GPO Museum Witness History Visitor Centre. The industry of commemoration is a zero-sum game: there is only a certain amount of audience interest, media time, and spending money (integral to the viability of sites with entry fees) before the market becomes oversaturated and an audience begins to suffer from "commemoration fatigue" (Rothberg 2009). Memory choreographers such as curators or politicians can adopt "framing devices" to advance narratives such as "forgotten or hidden histories" to distinguish their particular exhibition or museum from other cultural institutions (B. Conway 2010, 9). The "forgotten figure" framing device, for instance, is a very important narrative tool in *Revolution 1916* and the story of Molly O'Reilly.[5] O'Reilly's story is unique to *Revolution 1916*, and bringing her story to light is part of the exhibit's appeal or "unique selling point." Parallels can be drawn between the use of O'Reilly in *Revolution 1916* and the way in which Labour Youth and the Irish Labour Party used the "forgotten figure" of Rosie Hackett during their centenary commemorations of the 1913 Dublin Lockout. Labour historian Padraig Yeates argues convincingly that the exaggeration of Rosie Hackett's role in

Figure 12.5. Molly O'Reilly statue, *Revolution 1916*. (Courtesy of Stuart Dunne.)

the Dublin Lockout of 1913 was a political tool to garner support for the Labour Party in 2013 (Yeates 2017). O'Reilly, saved from obscurity by *Revolution 1916*, was deployed in the same way by Sinn Féin in the 2016 commemorations. Positioning itself as the inheritor of the Rising leaders and remembering the role of ordinary people like O'Reilly, Sinn Féin differentiated itself from the Fine Gael/Labour government in its story of Easter Week. The inclusion of the Long Kesh/Maze hunger strike in an area at the end of the exhibition drew the direct link. In a general election year, this may well have been a political strategy to encourage new votes by positioning Sinn Féin as representing ordinary people as well as the women's movement—embodied in their elevation of O'Reilly to a central role in *Revolution 1916*.

Another element that differentiated *Revolution 1916* and *The Souvenir Shop* from other centenary exhibitions was the nature of the material that they displayed. As both exhibitions were situated in non-traditional exhibition spaces, the display of material culture of the Rising (and to a lesser extent of the 1981 Maze/Long-Kesh hunger strikes) played an important role in legitimizing their curatorial narrative (Godson and Brück, 2015). *Revolution 1916* claimed to hold the largest collection of material relating to 1916 from the Irish Volunteers Commemoration Association. It particularly emphasized the presence of an original copy of the Proclamation as well as the Mauser rifle used by Tom Clarke during the Rising. *The Souvenir Shop*, on the other hand, did not have the same claim to legitimacy through artifacts linked to historical figures or events and works of art. Instead, the items on display were handicrafts made by Irish Countrywomen's Association members in 2015 and 2016. However, these "ordinary" items conveyed an important message—through humor, wordplay, and clever use of nationalist clichés, Duffy's collaboration with the Irish Countrywomen's Association members made it possible to turn everyday items historically associated with the domestic woman's realm into something sinister, subversive, and rebellious. The Irish flag, among other relics and sacred cows, was distorted and mocked. *Revolution 1916*, on the other hand, revered the flag—it was the key item that distinguished Molly O'Reilly from other women. Molly is wrapped in the Irish flag in Stuart Dunne's painting, and raises the flag in the large statue of her with its strong echoes of Hibernia figures that line O'Connell Street and mark other public buildings in Dublin.

In an age of consumerism, history has become commodified in both of these exhibitions. Whether this was through the fetishization of guns, uniforms, or weapons in *Revolution 1916* or through the complicit act of the visitor purchasing items in *The Souvenir Shop*, the role of the audience as a consumer was key to the function of both exhibitions (J. Steele 2003, 100). It cannot be denied that memory and public history are part of an industry of supply and demand. Whether the exhibition is an outright shop or has the "exit via the gift shop" policy, both confirm a consumer-driven ethic that informs history, memory, and commemoration in contemporary Ireland.[6]

Many of the items that were for sale in the *Revolution 1916* gift shop highlighted the overtly militaristic narrative of the exhibition and indicated an attitude toward violence that could be interpreted as glorified. The plethora of paraphernalia in *Revolution 1916*, particularly the badges and uniforms, or the stark, bloody hands of the nurse in *The Souvenir Shop*, connect the visitor to an individual's bodily experience of the Rising. The contrast between the experience of the male and female body, and, consequently, the depiction of these bodies, is also apparent in both exhibitions: both link the male body with martyrdom and the female body with the idea of nationhood and national healing. In Duffy's oil painting of James Connolly's bloody shirt in *The Souvenir Shop*, the shirt is draped over an empty chair. Connolly's body is nowhere to be seen; his bloodstained shirt is all that is left to remind us of his sacrifice. The faces of other male martyrs such as Padraig Pearse, who espoused the theory of "Blood Sacrifice," and the smiling young face of the 1981 hunger striker Bobby Sands are depicted on Mexican Church candles lit in memory of the dead. In *Revolution 1916*, a large area is dedicated to re-creating Pearse's cell, which visitors enter to experience the confined space where he spent his final hour; after leaving Pearse's cell the visitor then enters the Stonebreaker's Yard in Kilmainham Gaol where Rising leaders were executed. Visitors can even sit on a model of the chair that James Connolly was strapped to before he was shot. The area following the Rising leaders' final experiences is an art exhibition by artist and activist Robert Ballagh on the 1981 Maze/Long Kesh hunger strikers to mark the thirty-fifth anniversary of the hunger strikes in 2016. Recent depictions of these men in films like Steve McQueen's *Hunger* (2008) show the emaciated, gaunt bodies of the hunger strikers and demonstrate the consequences of war on the male body (Coomasaru 2016). Ballagh's paintings, however, are based on smiling photographs of the men in the prime of their health. Compared to the raw and often uncomfortable depictions of the impact of the starvation on the bodies of the men involved in films like *Hunger*, Ballagh's paintings come across as a sanitized portrayal of the men's experience. The only connection with the real bodily experience of the men is through a small number of artifacts on display connected to their time in prison, including a shirt worn by Kieran Doherty, who died after seventy-three days of protest (Treacy 2016), in an echo of Connolly's famous shirt.

The exhibitions' attitudes toward the female body and its relationship to violence are quite different. *Revolution 1916*'s Molly O'Reilly is iconic, militant, and sometimes powerful, but she is also static. The majority of women are depicted in artistic works such as portraits, statues, and murals. The female body is removed from everyday experience and the implicit message of the exhibition is that the female body is sacred. This message is in contrast with that of *The Souvenir Shop*, where the bodily experience of the bloody-handed nurse is a recurring motif throughout. There is little real material culture in *Revolution 1916* to represent the female experience of the Rising. The guns, paraphernalia, medals, and flags, which make up the largest part of the exhibition artifacts, were donated by the Irish Volunteers Commemoration Association, a society that remembers the all-male militant group. In *The Souvenir Shop*, the bloody-handed nurse is the predominant body through which the visitor experiences the Rising; she is often holding her hands up or clasping them in despair or surrender. The result is a sense of violence being critiqued rather than celebrated, cited for its impact on culture as opposed to glorified as an ideal.

CONCLUSION

In recent decades, Irish memory of the revolutionary period has been complicated by the inclusion of Irish participation in World War I in the national narrative, especially since the 2014 centenary commemorations. Irish memory is also being challenged by a growing number of investigations that question the authority of the state, as into the Tuam Mother and Baby Home, the publication of the Ryan Report, and seen too in the debates about Irish laws on abortion. Victoria White may have been tired of hearing about the women of the Easter Rising, but it is essential to keep telling these stories, challenging the dominant narrative, and bringing in the "marginal." This challenge will be even more crucial as the Irish people and state continue to confront the complex, confusing, and often traumatic memory of the Irish War of Independence and the Irish Civil War, remnants of which remain in local and national politics. Evidence indicates that audiences in general are not in fact "sick, sore and tired" of hearing about women. Projects such as this volume, recent conferences on Women in the Irish Revolution at the Royal Irish Academy, and national and local commemorative projects marking the centenary of women's suffrage in Ireland show that there is still a wealth of research to be done and books to be written.

Yeats and Gregory's *Cathleen Ní Houlihan* has been replaced by contemporary embodiments of Éire that include the complex figures of Molly O'Reilly and Duffy's bloody-handed nurse. These reconfigured versions of Irish womanhood in the 1916 centenary events are interesting illustrations of the ongoing eagerness to engage with women's history in Ireland today. A final example of the contemporary interrogation of Éire in the Easter Rising narrative comes in Emma Donoghue's contribution to *Signatories*, a University College Dublin project of commissioned monologues that brought the audience into the innermost thoughts of the seven signatories of the Proclamation and nurse Elizabeth O'Farrell. Each historical figure was assigned to a contemporary Irish writer, who then presented an artistic response to the character; the monologues premiered at Kilmainham Gaol in 2016, where the executions of the Easter Rising leaders took place. Writer Thomas Kilroy gave an insight into Padraig Pearse's last hours before his execution, while Joseph Mary Plunkett recalled hearing his three friends being shot beside him in Joseph O'Connor's piece. Novelist and screenwriter Emma Donoghue's monologue, written for nurse Elizabeth O'Farrell, stood out in dealing with the complex memory of a woman's role in the Rising. Patrick Mason, the director of *Signatories*, described Donoghue's monologue as a "dream journey" into O'Farrell's old age, "retracing her courageous criss-crossing of the city to deliver Pearse's surrender note" (Mason 2016). The final passage of Donoghue's monologue explores the airbrushing of the nurse out of history in the well-known photograph of the surrender of the rebel leaders to General Lowe. Challenging this dominant narrative, Donoghue gives O'Farrell back her voice: "I take up my position on the far side of the Commandant. Not to be seen, at the moment of humiliation. Not to give the enemy the satisfaction.... Why should I be remembered.... None of the bullets were mine, in the end. What did I do that I had to live so long, men's faces blurred in my head, but the smell of blood still fresh? The weight of memory, like a gravestone over my head" (Donoghue 2016, 12). Although the photograph is known to have been doctored, in this version of history, O'Farrell also makes a conscious decision to hide herself from the record of the surrender. Donoghue's monologue returns O'Farrell's agency and makes it apparent to the audience that O'Farrell actively chose how she wanted to be remembered.

In memory studies and public history it is important to incorporate an analysis of "event driven" commemoration alongside a consideration of the importance of "silent transformations" over longer periods of time, such as the death of a language or gender role perception (Cronin 2016, 28–29). Commemoration expresses shared public points of reference, comprising both an official and an unofficial historiography; it is represented in varied forms by political systems, cultural institutions, or grassroots community initiatives. Like memory, it is not an eternal or stable entity; its components vary over time and space, the result of changing systems and processes of negotiation. Thus, commemoration practices give an account of the contemporary perception of past events rather than of the events themselves, expressing the mutual influence of past and present in sociocultural contexts. In the case of the 2016 commemorations, we see a clear shift—perhaps the result of a "silent transformation"—toward the inclusion of women not just in the narratives of Ireland's revolutionary period but in a new type of narrative that challenges the glorification of male violence in service of a passive figure of feminine Ireland. In many of the recent commemorations of the revolutionary period, *Cathleen Ní Houlihan* is no longer persuading the young men of Ireland to fight for her as she did in Yeats and Gregory's iconic play. Cathleen or Éire has followed the advice of another "unmanageable revolutionary," Countess Markievicz, who famously suggested "dress[ing] suitably in short skirts and strong boots, leav[ing] your jewels and gold wand in the bank, and buy[ing] a revolver" (in Margaret Ward 1989, 46–47). Éire need not persuade young men to help her; she is now going out to fight for herself.

NOTES

1. Further information on these institutions is available at http://www .mbhcoi.ie/MBH.nsf/page/index-en, accessed April 18, 2019.

2. Number 35 was saved from demolition because of its connection with James Joyce. Professor Denis J. Maginni who ran a Dance Academy here was a well-known and colorful character in Dublin and appears several times in James Joyce's *Ulysses*. Maginni's Academy was rescued from demolition by Senator David Norris, a Joycean scholar who lives on the same street, and was subsequently turned into The James Joyce Centre.

3. Duffy followed *The Souvenir Shop* with another textile project in August 2017, "Soften the Border," in reaction to the Brexit Leave vote in June 2016. In collaboration with Cavan County Council, Duffy worked with local groups across Ulster to knit a range of "soft furnishings" from recycled material. Together the women produced dolls representing border dwellers and refugees.

4. The website of the company lists two directors: Brian Dowling and Teresa Quinn, with a company address in Prussia Street in Dublin 7 (information from SoloCheck at Solocheck.ie, accessed 2018). Bartle D'Arcy is listed as the exhibition's Artistic Director/Curator in the credit page of the exhibition catalog (Clayton-Lea 2016).

5. For more on the "forgotten figure" narrative in Irish history and literature, see Kelleher 2003.

6. Another interesting example of a consumer-driven commemoration souvenir was the launching of a Molly O'Reilly doll in 2016 by the toy company Treasured Dolls (McGreevy 2016). The doll, available to buy from the Tallaght-based company's website, is dressed in an Irish Citizen Army uniform. In the product description, Treasured Dolls states that Molly was "an extraordinary girl; she helped those in need, stood strong and fought for what she believed in. Treasured Dolls salutes Molly O'Reilly and the brave girls of 1916" (Treasured Dolls 2018).

MAEVE CASSERLY is a PhD student at University College Dublin funded by the Irish Research Council Employment-Based Scheme, jointly supervised by Professor Mary E. Daly and Dr. Emilie Pine. Her doctoral research considers public engagement with history through centenary commemorations during the Irish Decade of Centenaries, with a main focus on engagement with women's history during 2016–2018. Maeve's doctoral research is informed by her work as a heritage practitioner in the Irish cultural heritage sector. She was Dublin City Council Historian-in-Residence (2017–2020) and has worked in the Exhibitions, Learning, and Programming Department of the National Library of Ireland since 2015. She was the recipient of a Creative-Ireland Museums Fulbright Fellowship for 2020 at the Harry Ransom Center at the University of Austin, Texas.

—ɯɯ—

WAKING THE FEMINISTS

Gender "Counts"

BRENDA O'CONNELL

AS EMER O'TOOLE OBSERVES, IRISH theater has historically been considered a "mirror [held] up to the nation" (2017, 134). Theater scholar Patrick Lonergan, highlighting the absence of female playwrights from the Irish literary canon, notes that Sean O'Casey's *The Plough and the Stars*, first performed in 1926 at the Abbey Theatre, "established that the function of the Abbey [Theatre] in an independent Ireland would be to analyse the nation's sense of itself"; the play famously "provoked a series of protests that were based on the belief that national theatre is worthy of serious debate and contestation" (cited in ibid.; Lonergan 2014). This legacy of Ireland's national theater was unwittingly invoked by the announcement of the Abbey's 2016 artistic program—titled *Waking the Nation* and announced in October 2015—which provoked a level of protest unseen in Irish theater since O'Casey's provocative play.

Waking the Nation was part of the countrywide centenary of the 1916 Easter Rising and the Proclamation of the Irish Republic. The centenary year of 2016 was a highly mediatized event, comprising parades, re-enactments, and speeches, including a clear emphasis on the role that women played in the Easter Rising, evident even in a major drama on national television.[1] The plays of the *Waking the Nation* program were, in contrast, all by men, with just one work by a female playwright.[2] It subsequently emerged that from 1995 to 2014, of the 320 plays produced at the Abbey, only 36 plays written by women made it to the Abbey stage. Yet women were crucial in the early formative years of the Abbey Theatre. It was funded by Annie Hourniman and partly managed by Lady Augusta Gregory, who wrote twenty-eight plays for the theater, drawing from the same cultural nationalist themes of myth, history, and rural Irish life as in the writing of Yeats and Synge. Indeed, Lady Gregory was so highly regarded that the play *Cathleen Ni Houlihan*, co-written by herself and Yeats, premiered at Abbey-precursor the Irish Literary Theatre's first night in 1902. Lady Gregory's contemporaries, Maud Gonne, Alice Milligan, Constance Markievicz, and Eva Gore-Booth were also writing and producing plays at this time. However, after Irish independence, women's rights were sacrificed, with this sacrifice written into the controversial 1937 constitution, *Bunreacht na hEireann*, which highlighted the special place of women within the home. The female revolutionaries of 1916 were largely written out of history, and one hundred years later, at the announcement of the *Waking the Nation* program, playwrights such as Lady Gregory were also being written out, alongside a refusal to acknowledge contemporary women playwrights. This exclusion of women from the Abbey's program provoked a swift reaction on social media, led by Lian Bell, a Dublin-based freelance theater maker. In response to Bell's inquiry about the wisdom of this selection and the notable absence of female playwrights, then Abbey director Fiach Mac Conghail replied, in what became a famous tweet, "Them's the breaks" (@fmacconghail, October 29, 2015).

The program and Mac Conghail's initial response caused an immediate uproar. *Irish Times* journalist and activist Una Mullally, among the first to write about the program, wondered whether it was "time for another riot" (Mullally 2015). Also writing for *The Irish Times*, Peter Crawley commented that "instead of commemorating 1916 we are reflecting on, perhaps, the failed potential of 1916. . . . If gender equality was one such potential, it may be disappointing to find just one woman writer on the programme announced so far" (Crawley 2015). It was not only disappointment but anger that was felt, in fact, and, following an invitation from a chastened Abbey Theatre, a public meeting was arranged by Bell and her team, calling themselves "Waking the Feminists," now known by the hashtag #WTF; the movement gained worldwide attention, including postings of support on social media by high-profile actors Meryl Streep, Debra Messing, and Wim Wenders. The subsequent grassroots campaign, which ran from November 2015 to November 2016, called for equality for women across the Irish theater sector, and included men and women. Writers, directors, managers, actors, designers, choreographers, technicians, programmers, producers, artists, and audience members were encouraged to speak out for equality. The campaign also encouraged and supported those individuals to speak out and to interrogate what stories are told, who is entitled to tell those stories, who makes those decisions, and who is represented.

The initial meeting was designed to showcase women's stories: chaired by Irish senator Ivana Bacik, the event saw thirty presenters speak for ninety seconds each. As O'Toole notes, the fact that the protestors sat in a semi-circle

Figure 13.1. Waking the Feminists meeting, the Abbey Theatre, November 12, 2015. (Courtesy of Fiona Morgan Photography.)

and spoke from the "centre of the hallowed stage from which they have been so excluded" was a powerful statement in itself (E. O'Toole 2017, 139). The women, from diverse socioeconomic backgrounds, spoke with conviction and sometimes with anger. Playwright Gina Moxley detailed the reluctance that women have of speaking out for fear of being viewed as "difficult to work with" (my notes). Director Laura Bowler noted that when only half the world is listened to, "you only get half the story" (E. O'Toole 2017, 138). Playwright Rosaleen McDonagh, from a Traveller background and with a disability, reminded the audience about the need for inclusion within feminist movements. Director Catriona McLaughlin noted that "being fair takes work," while black Irish playwright Mary Duffin revealed that any chance of having her work staged would involve casting her characters as white actors (139). What emerged was a picture of the extraordinary difficulties female theater makers have endured in trying to have their work produced in Ireland's national theater and beyond. (See Fig. 13.1.)

As Mac Conghail stepped down as director of the Abbey a year later, in December 2016, he noted that

> putting on a play is a political act. . . . It's the Abbey Theatre's job to create work that challenges and reflects Irish society. That ideal was challenged late

last year. The Waking the Feminists movement pointed out that our Waking
the Nation season did not represent gender equality. An urgent conversation
began online, and we welcomed the debate, hosting a public meeting . . .
to give voice to the call to redress the gender inequality that exists across
the arts industry. The board of the Abbey Theatre is committed to the
development of a comprehensive policy and detailed implementation plan
to ensure that the Abbey Theatre leads the way in achieving a much-needed
cultural shift towards gender equality in the Irish theatre sector. (Abbey
Theatre's Annual Report 2015)

The historic public meeting at the Abbey, the fastest-selling "show" in its history, was just the beginning of that "cultural shift towards gender equality." The
response to #WTF has been wide reaching and irreversible, as there is a new
awareness of how power is exercised on Irish stages. This chapter traces the
development and impact of #WTF, a grassroots movement that has resulted
in significant shifts in Irish theater: a networking and activist organization
formed by mothers in theater; a recently published commissioned report on
gender in Irish theater; academic work focused on the recovery of Irish women
playwrights; and a timely reworking of the plays of Teresa Deevy, an acclaimed
playwright. That these events all unfolded in the centenary year of Irish independence meant that Ireland was granted another glimpse of itself in that "mirror [held] up to the nation," one that spoke clearly of the need to address blatant
inequalities.

At the first #WTF meeting at the Abbey, theater maker Tara Derrington
stood apart from the crowd, brandishing a sign with the words: "Where are the
DISAPPEARED women of the Arts? . . . At the school gates now." Photogra-
phers noted Derrington's solo stand and her image circulated extensively in the
media. On the day that the #WTF rally received international attention, the
seeds of MAM—Mothers Artists Makers (@Mam Ireland)—were thus sown.[3]
MAM functions as an advocacy organization for approximately 350 female
feminist theater practitioners across Ireland who felt disenfranchised from
the theater on becoming mothers. The irregular working hours and demands
of theater work are particularly difficult for mothers; as Derrington puts it, the
"logistics of reality" make working in any capacity almost impossible. Suddenly, she tells Sara Keating, "you're not put forward any more, you're not
considered, and your confidence is just drip, drip, dripping away until you end
up believing you're just not capable" (S. Keating 2016). Derrington *is* a capable
artist: arriving in Ireland in the late 1990s after training in England, she was
successful as a director of interactive theater and started her own company.
After the birth of her second child, the cost of childcare forced her to opt out

Figure 13.2. Tara Derrington, Waking the Feminists meeting, the Abbey Theatre, November 12, 2015. (Courtesy of Photocall Ireland.)

of theater work altogether. However, at "One Thing More" (November 14, 2016), a second #WTF event held at the Abbey to mark the anniversary of the initial meeting and to assess the year's progress, Derrington, now an invited speaker, highlighted the absence of motherhood from the initial agenda. Now, with the support of the Abbey as well as other Irish theaters who host MAM workshops—FringeLab, The Project Arts, The Lyric, Fishamble, Smock Alley, and the O'Reilly Theatre—these artist mothers are becoming visible once more.[4] Alongside regular meetings and the provision of networking and artistic support, MAM is seeking Irish governmental grants and support for theater artist childcare, advocating for artists-in-residence in Irish university theater departments and studio spaces where children are freely welcomed, as well as devising plans for symposia.[5] Sarah FitzGibbon describes the MAM movement as having "small boots, but taking big strides" (Spencer Hewitt 2016). (See Fig. 13.2.)

The #WTF meetings revealed the violent erasure not just of women playwrights who were simply "fired" from the canon, in Sara Keating's term (2015), but also the "firing" of contemporary female theater makers who happen to be mothers. As an advocacy group, MAM draws attention not just to the absence of mothers in Irish theater work, of course, but also to historical questions of how mothers and motherhood are treated in Ireland. The group works to highlight the mostly female issues of domestic isolation, marginalization, and the disproportionate impact of parenting on the income of mothers, in this case those who work in theater. In a survey of their 350 members, they reported that over half lost all their income and 95 percent suffered reduced income as a direct result of having children. The MAMs believe that one of the main factors that contribute to gender imbalance in theater is the swift exodus of women after childbirth. Derrington argues that the "One Thing" unresolved in today's feminism is motherhood. Central to MAM's mission is the need to heal this division of women regarding motherhood and to unite to fight inequality in the arts sector.

Derrington's comments indicate how Irish attitudes toward motherhood and gender roles have been remarkably static, with lack of infrastructure and support making it exceedingly difficult for mothers to remain at work, particularly in the arts sector. MAM challenges the invisibility of artist mothers in Irish theater; its members include Sarah FitzGibbon, a professional theater artist who works as an education consultant to the Abbey, and actor Susie Lamb, who has argued that the narrow view of women and mothers depicted onstage is a "form of censorship" (Spencer Hewitt 2016). Lamb identifies the main obstacles to mothers in theater as "unaffordability and lack of access to childcare, exclusion of children in the rehearsal and performance space, and lack of 'pathways back in' to the professional network for professionals who take maternal time" (ibid.). Since mothers make up 54 percent of Ireland's female population, Spencer Hewitt argues that Irish theater's refusal to accommodate professional mothers "not only reduces its talent in terms of contributors, but also cuts off a huge portion of potential audience members" (ibid.).

MAM's determination to make the invisible visible materialized in a devised work, "Observe the Mothers of Theatre Marching towards the Stage," commissioned by the Abbey Theatre in 2016. The piece was a direct response to the Abbey's revival—as part of *Waking the Nation*—of Frank McGuinness's acclaimed *Observe the Sons of Ulster Marching Towards the Somme*, featuring eight male characters who march their way onto the stage. Where McGuinness's play was groundbreaking in its focus on Irish and, particularly, Ulster participation in World War I and in addressing issues of homophobia, MAM's piece similarly sought to challenge cultural norms, this time around motherhood. Performed on September 21, 2016, shortly after Ireland's national theater committed to an "eight-step gender equality initiative," MAM's theatrical response was rehearsed for six weeks by over forty women and children. Taking four sections of McGuinness's play and exploring their themes, the women added "mother" to the play's themes of "soldier, war, loyalty, identity, heroism, and sacrifice," realizing the analogy between a military battlefield and the battlegrounds of motherhood (Spencer Hewitt 2016). (See Fig. 13.3.)

The result was a performance that made visible the women—mothers, wives, sisters, daughters—who hover outside of the perspective of McGuinness's play, and whose wartime experience has historically often been ignored. In a scene named "Bonding" (as in McGuinness's play) the MAMs re-created the original "bridge scene": in McGuinness's play, the character Millen tries to coax fellow soldier Moore to cross a high rope bridge to help him overcome his terror of returning to the war. Having explored the similarities between motherhood and soldiering in their workshops, MAM's version connected the trauma of war with the female-centered experience of postnatal depression. Performer Marianne Marcote, who herself suffered from post-natal depression, played the role of Moore as a mother who cannot face her baby after childbirth (2016). Millen, played by Kathleen Warner Yeates, encourages Moore to bond with her newborn. This analogy of motherhood as a battlefield directly challenges the male-centered war themes that are the focus of McGuinness's play.

At the end of the performance, all the children joined their mothers on stage; each woman stepped forward, some with babies strapped to their bodies, stating their mother-soldier names and whether they were volunteers or were conscripted into motherhood. Abbey Theatre co-director Graham McLaren described it as "Brilliant, Brave, Beautiful, Honest, and Very, Very, Necessary" (@MCLAREN_G, September 21, 2016). In 2018, this "necessary" work took on a new significance in its analogy of motherhood as a battlefield for choice; on May 25, a fourth referendum on the controversial issue of abortion rights in Ireland took place, with the electorate asked to vote Yes or No to "Repeal the 8th Amendment," an article inserted into the Irish constitution after the first abortion referendum in 1983, which gave equal rights to life of both the mother and the unborn.[6] The referendum was on a highly emotive issue, with both sides of the campaign irreconcilable in their views on the definition of personhood and the right to bodily autonomy. In what has been termed "a quiet revolution," Ireland voted to repeal the Eighth Amendment by a resounding 66.4 percent of the voting electorate, taking both sides of the campaign by surprise at the margin in favor.[7] The fight for gender equality remains high on the agenda in Irish society.

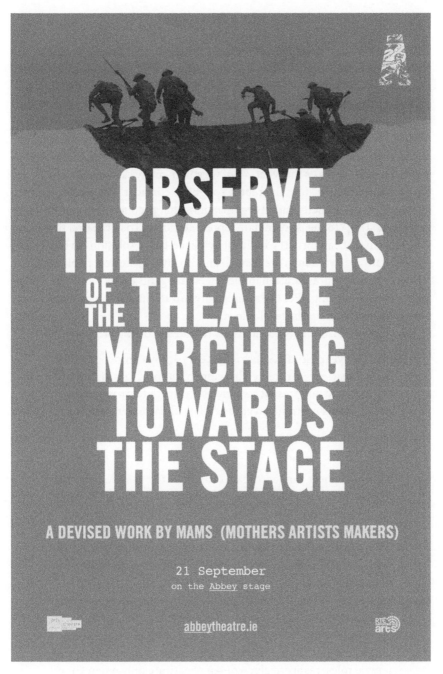

Figure 13.3. Original *Observe the Sons of Ulster Marching Towards the Somme* artwork by Zero G; artwork adapted for MAMs by Mandy Horton. (Courtesy of Mandy Horton.)

GENDER "COUNTS"

This is clearly illustrated in a 2016 report on gender in Irish theater over the past decade. Commissioned by #WakingTheFeminists and funded by the Arts Council, *Gender Counts: An Analysis of Gender in Irish Theatre 2006–2015* was officially launched on June 9, 2017. In the report, Lian Bell writes that within one year of the movement's foundation, there were "extraordinary shifts" in working practices, and a newfound openness in debating gender issues in Ireland's major arts organizations (Donohue et al. 2017, 5). She notes, however, that the report "gives us the what—but we still in many cases need to work out the why and the how" (6). The report sought to consider "the gender balance in the top Arts Council funded organisations that produce or present theatre in Ireland" (17); "to measure female representation in Irish theatre, providing information that can form the basis for evidence-based solutions to the under-representation of women in the sector"; and "to investigate how public funding relates to female representation in the selected organisations" (12). The results make for stark reading.[8] For the sampled organizations, funding amounts, and percentages of total funds, see Table 13.1.

Data analyzed from 1,155 productions revealed startling facts:

- In the ten years studied, just 8 percent of plays produced at the Gate Theatre were directed by women. In six of those ten years, the Gate did not present a single play directed by a woman.
- In 2008, all plays produced at the Abbey Theatre were by men.

The key findings of the report, which also counted 9,205 individual roles, are as follows:

- The four highest-funded organizations in the sample have the lowest female representation; the Gate and Abbey Theatres have the lowest of all.
- In the first eight sampled organizations, there is a general pattern of an inverse relationship between levels of funding and female representation: the higher the funding received, the lower the female presence.
- In six of the seven roles studied (in every role except costume designer), women are poorly represented.
- 28 percent of "authors" employed by these organizations are women.
- "Sound designer" and "costume designer" are gendered male and female roles, respectively; women constitute only 9 percent of sound designers employed.

Table 13.1. Gender Balance in Top-Funded Theater Organizations

Company Name	Funding in € Millions (2006–2015)	% of Total Funds (2006–2015)
1. The Abbey Theatre	76.6	57
2. The Gate Theatre	10.6	8
3. Dublin Theatre Festival	8.6	6
4. Druid	8.5	6
5. Project Arts Centre	8.1	6
6. The Ark	6.4	5
7. Rough Magic Theatre Company	6.2	5
8. Dublin Fringe Festival	3.7	3
9. Barnstorm Theatre Company	2.8	2
10. Pan Pan Theatre	2.8	2

- The highest female representation occurred in the Ark, Rough Magic Theatre Company, and Dublin Fringe Festival. In 2011, 77 percent of actors at the Ark were female; notably, the Ark is a cultural organization for children.
- The gap to achieving gender parity ranges between 41 and 8 percentage points in the roles studied.

The overall percentage of female representation in each category studied is as follows:

Directors	37%
Authors	28%
Cast	42%
Set Designers	40%
Lighting Designers	34%
Sound Designers	9%
Costume Designers	79%

As a direct result of #WTF and the report's findings, the Abbey Theatre established a Gender Equality Committee, which developed an eight-step set of guiding principles to be enshrined for the future; other theaters are working collaboratively to establish gender equality guidelines for the industry.[9] Heather Humphreys, then minister for Culture, Heritage and the Gaeltacht, suggested that all Irish cultural institutions implement their own gender policies by 2018.

Bell notes that institutions who do not reflect this push are increasingly "taken to task by their audiences" (Donohue et al. 2017, 5). Immediately following their gender guidelines policy, the Abbey Theatre devised its innovative "5x5" (#Abbey5x5) series, which invites "communities who feel marginalised and silenced" to submit an idea or project that they wish to develop. The theater selected five projects, awarded through an online submission process, that were allowed five days of theater space and technical assistance and awarded €5000 per project. This program, which gained a lot of attention on social media, is another direct response to the Abbey's commitment to "creating an environment that promotes equality and dignity" (Abbey Theatre 2020).[10]

We are now witnessing a sea change in programming and equal-employment opportunities across the arts sector that reflects a deeper understanding of gender and unconscious bias. One of the most significant examples of this shift occurred in April 2017, when British-born theater director Selina Cartmell was appointed director of the Gate Theatre, founded in 1928 by Hilton Edwards and Michael Mac Liammoir; Cartmell is not only the first ever woman to occupy the position but the third ever director of the theater. Cartmell replaced the controversial director Michael Colgan, who stepped down after thirty-three years in the position. Since taking up the role, Cartmell has focused on producing exciting work by female playwrights, rapidly reversing the Gate's abysmal record to date.[11] Shortly after Colgan's departure, however, a significant number of women working in Irish theater came forward with serious allegations against him, which reverberated around the wider arts and academic sector (Gallagher and Mackin 2017; F. Kelly 2017). The Colgan controversy has overshadowed Cartmell's initial success; in November 2017, the theater's board commissioned a report "Gate Theatre Confidential Independent Review," conducted by Gaye Cunningham, following the allegations made concerning Colgan's behavior in the years between 1983 and 2017 (Cunningham 2018). The purpose of the review was to establish if Colgan had a case to answer for with respect to "any dignity of work, abuse of power and related inappropriate behaviours and failings on the part of any person associated with the Gate and to make recommendations arising from the process" (1). The reviewer's methodology comprised face-to-face interviews, statements, and phone interviews, held over twenty days with thirty-three individuals: former and current staff, former and current board members, members of the art community, freelancers, and others.

The findings of the review, published on March 1, 2018, concluded that Michael Colgan had a case to answer in relation to "Dignity at Work" behaviors,

"Abuse of Power" and "Inappropriate Behaviours," in line with the definition of sexual harassment (Cunningham 2018, 10). On February 9, 2018, in anticipation of the report's findings, the Gate issued a formal apology to those who experienced "abuse of power and inappropriate behaviours" at the theater, where an insidious culture pervaded "which was not conducive to people speaking out freely" (Gate Theatre 2018). The stark findings of the report, while casting a shadow over the historic appointment of Cartmell as the first female director at the Gate, promises meaningful change for all those working not only at this theater but also in the wider arts and freelance community. The allegations also link Colgan with the wider #MeToo movement, initially founded in 2006 to help survivors of sexual violence, particularly black women and girls, and re-emerging with gusto in the wake of the sexual abuse allegations made against Hollywood producer Harvey Weinstein in 2017.[12] The report on Colgan, along with *Gender Counts*, forms part of a remarkable revolution in Irish theater directly linked to the centenary year of 2016 and the Abbey's *Waking the Nation* program, which continues to reverberate.

ACADEMIC RESPONSES: RESEARCH AND RECOVERY

The reverberations have been felt in the arts sector and in academic research. Academics working in the area of theater, gender studies, and related disciplines have responded quickly to #WTF. The "Irish Women Playwrights and Theatremakers" conference (June 8–10, 2017)[13] coincidentally took place the week of the launch of the *Gender Counts* report, which was discussed at the event by researchers. The conference highlighted the historical difficulties that Irish women playwrights have faced trying to have their work produced in Ireland; David Clare cited as an example the canonical novelist Maria Edgeworth (1768–1849), who resorted to having her plays performed as "home theatricals" in Edgeworthstown. Also cited was one of the most successful but forgotten Irish female playwrights of the twentieth century, Teresa Deevy (1894–1963). Deevy produced an impressive body of work for the Abbey stage in the 1930s; as a young adult she became profoundly deaf, making her success even more remarkable. However, when Ernest Blythe took control of the Abbey in the 1930s, Deevy was eventually shunned with the rejection of her play *Wife to James Whelan* in 1942.[14] Until recently, research shows that there has been an inexplicable reluctance to revive the work of successful women playwrights like Deevy and Lady Gregory, despite the fact that major Dublin theaters have continually revived male playwrights' work. The recent revival of Deevy's *Katie*

Figure 13.4. Image of
Teresa Deevy, which
the Abbey used in their
souvenir program for
the 1938 Abbey Theatre
Dramatic Festival of Plays
and Lectures, August
6–20, 1938. (Courtesy
of Abbey Theatre.)

Roche at the Abbey is a timely first step toward engagement with what Melissa Sihra calls "its remarkable legacy of women dramatists, starting surely with Lady Augusta Gregory" (Sihra 2017). Gregory, "author of over 40 plays and co-founder of the theatre, was not represented in any way" (Sihra 2009, 158) at the Abbey's 2004 centennial celebrations, when, in fact, not a single work from a female playwright was performed. (See Fig. 13.4.)

As the Irish Women Playwrights and Theatremakers conference and ongoing research demonstrates, Irish women playwrights and theater makers have experienced profound difficulties across the centuries. These women were, in Sara Keating's phrase, "fired from the canon" in three ways: through lack of production, lack of revival, and lack of publication (S. Keating 2015).[15] Melissa Sihra's work—including a notable plenary address at the Irish Women Playwrights and Theatremakers conference, titled "Beyond Token Women: Towards a Matriarchal Lineage from Lady Gregory to Marina Carr"—challenges the "tokenistic" placement of Lady Gregory in the canon;[16] Sihra argues that to redress the violent gender imbalance, we must begin "by tilting the lens, to re-establish a foundational status of Irish women in theatre" (my notes). Sihra repositions Gregory as "matrilineal origin point," a "centrifugal force" from which all Irish playwrights, both male and female, descend (my notes). After all, Sihra points out, it was in fact Gregory and not J. M. Synge who first visited the Aran Islands and who first mastered Hiberno-English as a dramatic language. Famously, it was also Gregory who predominantly wrote *Cathleen Ni Houlihan*, a seminal Irish play, for the Abbey Theatre's first incarnation, the Irish Literary Theatre. Gregory also experimented with absurdist forms and subversive humor and pioneered the act of waiting as dramatic device in *The Gael Gate* (Nakase 2017). Gregory emerges, in Sihra's research, as a highly innovative playwright who was not simply the cofounder of the Abbey Theatre but a precursor to J. M. Synge, Samuel Beckett, Tom Murphy, and Marina Carr in her stagecraft, language, and themes.

Sihra's work complements other recent academic research presented at the same 2017 conference by Cathy Leeney, who argues that ways of looking and seeing in theater are highly gendered. In her plenary address "Waking Up to Theatrical Aesthetics: Women's Way of Looking," Leeney notes that work by women is often analyzed "as if they don't know what they are doing" (my notes). As Justine Nakase writes, Leeney challenges audiences' unconscious bias toward women's theater, which is sometimes regarded as messy, the intended assumed to be error, with failure to conform to "masculine aesthetics . . . seen simply as failure" (Nakase 2017). Anna Pilz notes how Leeney's work highlights the importance of historical research as "an act of 'recovery of the roots of self,'" vital in serving to challenge and reject established narratives (Pilz 2017). In her address, Leeney ultimately challenged the audience to reevaluate their own unconscious biases in how they look at women's theater and begin to embrace those "new ways of seeing" (my notes).

Recent academic work also lays bare the fact that Ursula Rani Sarma, an acclaimed playwright, screenwriter, and poet who has collaborated with theaters in the United States and Britain, remains practically unproduced and unknown in Ireland. Rani Sarma, of Irish/Indian descent, grew up in County Clare, Ireland. Since 1999, she has written thirteen stage plays and three radio plays and has published poetry in several anthologies. Her awards include an Edinburgh Fringe award, an Irish Times/ESB Theatre award, and awards for Best New Play and Best Production for her play *The Dark Things* (2009) at the 2010 Critics' Awards for Theatre in Scotland.[17] A pattern emerges, then, of the many blind spots in Irish theater, notably how women playwrights have been hidden, as Feargal Whelan succinctly puts it, "in plain sight" (my notes). If we "tilt the lens," in Sihra's phrase, numerous instances of playwrights "hidden in plain sight" are revealed, such as Mary Balfour, Belfast's only woman playwright of the nineteenth century: David Clare notes that her 1814 play *Kathleen O'Neill* arguably acted as a prototype for many of the tropes that eventually became Irish melodrama, yet it is the plays of her contemporary Dion Boucicault, Irish dramatist and actor, that are regularly restaged.

As a result of the Irish Women Playwrights and Theatremakers conference, a two-volume publication on women playwrights is being produced to address their inexcusable erasure from the Irish dramatic canon. The impressive list of authors, some of whom will be unfamiliar to readers, will go some way toward rebalancing that "firing from the canon" of women playwrights, "tilting the lens" in favor of "women's way of looking."[18] Academic researchers and archivists play a pivotal role in recovering lost histories and lost voices: over the three days of presentations and performances, a new picture of Irish theater began to emerge, one in which women are not just present but central to its development. As Melissa Sihra concluded, in order to be forgotten, women must first be acknowledged. And women refuse to be forgotten anymore (Nakase 2017). As theatergoers and academic researchers, we must also show up for women's work, particularly the revivals of neglected playwrights such as Teresa Deevy, whose work is finally being fruitfully researched and restaged in Ireland and abroad.

TERESA DEEVY'S RETURN TO THE ABBEY AND PEACOCK THEATRES

In 2017, partly in response to the previous year's events, the Abbey Theatre presented a major revival of neglected playwright Teresa Deevy's most successful play, *Katie Roche* (August 26 to September 23). The theater also published a research pack on the play, compiled by Dr. Marie Kelly (M. Kelly 2017). Kelly notes that this new production is "enormously significant in the context of recent local and world events that have pushed issues of inequality and mobility unprecedentedly to the fore. Katie stands for those on the margins, those without place and voice" (5). She writes that the play celebrates "the astonishing forces of human indefatigability and self-determination in circumstances of oppression and disempowerment" (6). At the same time, on the Peacock stage, Amanda Coogan presented a performance art-based interpretation of Deevy's play *The King of Spain's Daughter* (September 19–23). The Irish Coogan, born hearing to deaf parents and whose first language is Irish Sign Language, engages with silence as a radical act in her work. In collaboration

TERESA DEEVY.

" Katie Roche," by which play Miss
Teresa Deevy is represented in the Festival
programme, was selected for publication
in the collection of the best plays of its
year in the English language. That this
play represents its author worthily, and at
her best, will not be doubted, as it is almost
a summary of everything which she has
treated in her other plays. Miss Deevy
is concerned mainly with the presentation
of psychological problems on the stage,
and to the study of these problems she
brings a mind that has more than a tinge
of mysticism. The conflict of dream with
reality, of the soul with its environment,
is her theme, and it is embodied in people
who are easily recognisable as normal
ordinary citizens. There is no straining
after the abnormal, and the language is
that of everyday life in one of the smaller
provincial cities of Ireland. Miss Deevy
lives in Waterford.

Figure 13.5. Biography supplied for Deevy in the official 1938
souvenir program. (Courtesy of Abbey Theatre.)

with Dublin Theatre of the Deaf, *Talk Real Fine, Just Like a Lady* presented an immersive audience experience echoing Deevy's deafness and her challenges to church and state. The current directors of the Abbey, Graham McLaren and Neil Murray, who replaced Mac Conghail, acknowledged the political importance of the choice to program Deevy: "The Abbey Theatre is committed to elevating the work of women in Irish Theatre. *Katie Roche* is a brilliant play from the Irish canon. Welcoming Teresa's work back to our stage is just one way we hope to correct the issues of gender inequality that we see in our own society today" (3). In what appears to be a "Deevy moment," the Mint Theater Company in New York also produced four of Deevy's short plays, collectively titled *Suitcase Under the Bed* (July 21 to September 30, 2017).[19] All of these revivals and reworkings of Deevy's oeuvre reinstate her as an artist of universal and enduring appeal, painstakingly long after this accolade is due. (See Fig. 13.5.)

Deevy has been described as "one of the most undeservedly neglected and significant Irish playwrights of the 20th century" (Bank 2011, vii). Between 1930 and 1936, in a period of remarkable output, Deevy had six of her plays produced on the Abbey stage, beginning in 1930 with *The Reapers* and ending in 1936 with *Katie Roche*. Overall, Deevy wrote over twenty-five plays in her short career of over a decade or so. Her 1932 play *Temporal Powers* was highly lauded by Frank O'Connor, who wrote that "nothing since the *Playboy* has excited me so much. It's a grand thing to think that Ireland is stepping into the limelight once more" (Sihra 2017). In 1939, Deevy's *Holiday House* was accepted by the Abbey under contract but was never staged. In 1942, her last new work *Wife to James Whelan* was rejected by Ernest Blythe, managing director of the Abbey from 1941 to 1967. Deevy's dramatic focus on outspoken women who challenged the stifling effects of marriage and patriarchy was far too radical both for her time and for the notoriously conservative Blythe. The environment in which Deevy wrote had radical implications for women, whose role was consistently diminished by the new Irish State: this period drafted legislation such as the 1927 Juries Bill, which meant that women had to apply for jury duty; the 1932 public service marriage bar, which denied women the right to work after marriage; and, most damagingly, the 1937 constitution, which considered women's role best served as unpaid full-time workers within the home. Deevy was an outspoken critic of these censorship laws, and her plays reflect this in female characters who challenge their social milieu and demand autonomy, which, ultimately, was the death knell for her career.

Christopher Morash notes that to understand Deevy's work, we need to place her "in the context of the generation of Irish writers who came before her"

(2011, ix). She was born in 1894, just three years before the Irish Literary Theatre (which became the Abbey Theatre) was formed by Lady Gregory, Edward
Martyn, and W. B. Yeats. When Deevy entered University College Dublin, she
was one of the first female students, just a few years before the Easter Rising in
1916. In 1913, she contracted Ménière's disease and became profoundly deaf. As
lipreading was not taught in Ireland at that time, she moved to London, where
she became fascinated with theater and the work of Ibsen, Chekhov, and Shaw.
She grew up, then, alongside the formation of the Abbey and the new Irish
State. Following her rejection by Blythe, and apart from one performance of
her work *Light Falling* in October 1948, produced by the Abbey Experimental
Theatre and directed by Jack MacGowran, Deevy left the environs of the Abbey
and the stage and began to write for radio, a remarkable feat for a woman who
was profoundly deaf. As her nephew Kyle Deevy mused, it is a "source of wonder that she wrote at all" (Friel 1995, 125).

Katie Roche premiered at the Abbey Theatre in 1936, directed by Hugh Hunt,
starring Eileen Crowe as Katie. The play was subsequently revived on seven
occasions, before the major revival in 2017.[20] The 1975 Abbey staging of *Katie*
has been described by Anthony Roche as "an isolated incident," as there were
virtually no other productions of female playwrights at that time (Roche 1995,
143). In the 1994 revival on the Peacock stage, the director Judy Friel noted that
"when Patrick Mason, the Artistic Director of the Abbey Theatre, gave me the
plays of Teresa Deevy to read I was surprised simply by the existence of another
female Irish playwright in the first half of the century apart from Augusta
Gregory ... I found no published letters, no biographies" (Friel 1995, 117). Caroline Byrne, who directed the 2017 revival, also admitted to her "shame" that
when asked to consider directing *Katie* for the Abbey, she was familiar with
neither the play nor the playwright (M. Kelly 2017, 36).

Katie focuses on the title character, an illegitimate young woman who works
as a domestic servant for Amelia Gregg and serves as the love interest of two
men: Michael, a local suitor whose mother objects to Katie on the basis of her
illegitimacy, and Amelia's older brother Stan, an architect. Katie, impulsive in
a culture that discourages women from being outspoken and strong, accepts
Stan's proposal as she accepts most things that are thrown at her, adapting
and changing as necessary. The relationship is unsuccessful, as Katie quickly
realizes the restrictions of married life. Stan, unable to control his exuberant
young wife and her passionate desire to be his equal, disappears to the capital
city, upon which Katie resorts to religion. Michael, her ex-lover, pointedly
tells Katie that her life seems more restricted now that she is married. Stan
returns, and, upon realizing that Katie is still attracted to Michael and fearing

Figure 13.6. Set design for *Katie Roche*. (Courtesy of Ros Kavanagh.)

the potential of this relationship, he decides to take Katie away from her home forever, facing an unknown and fearful future. The contrast between Katie's interior longings and her reality is stark and encapsulates many aspects of Irish women's experiences not only from the 1930s, when the play is set, but in the twentieth century.

For the 2017 production, Caroline Byrne, together with Morna Regan and Joanna Scotcher, merged the original three acts of the play into a one act, with no interval. Byrne wanted to create a sealed experience for the audience with no interruption, so that the audience could fully commit to Katie's journey from what Fiona Becket describes as "voice to voicelessness" (M. Kelly 2017, 9). The set is a gritty mix of glass, marble, and soil. Byrne explained that the decision to use glass resulted from a conversation with Chris Morash, who described an image of Deevy taken from a letter where she is seated behind a glass panel in a radio station lipreading actors as they were recording one of her plays. Morash suggested that this image represented Deevy's life: as an outsider, constantly facing barriers because of her deafness, yet the keen observer of the minutiae of life. The soil, which covers most of the set, represents how "mucky, how messy, how fertile, and how expressive Katie is"(39). The marble which lurks underneath the soil points to Katie's potential, which is eventually stifled. (See Fig. 13.6.)

Figure 13.7. Caoilfhionn Dunne as Katie Roche. (Courtesy of Ros Kavanagh.)

Morash argues that Deevy's success lies in "her ability to create characters with fully realized private lives that are partly obscured from the audience (and from the other characters)" (Morash 2011, xiv). Her characters have private hopes and dreams that, as Una Kealy writes, "are written into the narrative of cultural history, countering the fact that real-life women's histories were often dismissed or diminished in other State sponsored histories of Irish life" (M. Kelly 2017, 9). Deevy's women, like Katie, struggle within their domestic milieu, but they cannot escape it; her theater is one of "subtext, of subtle demonstrations of attitudes rather than proclamations and declarations" (ibid.). At the center of her plays is the plight of young women who long for a more expansive sense of selfhood. Drawing on her own experience as a deaf woman, Deevy's work is subtle and paradoxical; her use of silence exposes and breaks her characters' voicelessness, thereby revealing experiences hidden away in the bodies, places, and conventions of Irish life and people. Eibhear Walshe notes that Deevy is one of only four Irish women, along with Lady Gregory, Christine Longford, and Maura Laverty, whose work was consistently staged by the Abbey and Gate Theatres between 1890 and 1980 (54). Her 2017 restaging at the Abbey is, therefore, a move toward both acknowledging Ireland's legacy of mostly forgotten women dramatists and addressing gender inequality both onstage and in Irish society. (See Fig. 13.7.)

WHAT NEXT?

In a lecture marking the end of her three-year term as inaugural Laureate of Irish Fiction, acclaimed novelist Anne Enright drew attention to the gender imbalance in the review pages of Irish newspapers. Noting the way in which men praise books and plays by other men, she argued that men's failure to fully engage with work written by women results in a "spiral of male affection" that "twists up through our cultural life, lifting male confidence and reputation as it goes" (Conroy 2017). Alongside the failure to produce the work of women playwrights in Ireland, Enright noted that for ten years in a row, until 2016, the One City, One Book initiative, which each year promotes a single book across Dublin, chose books written by men. Significantly, the book choice for 2018 was *The Long Gaze Back* by Sinéad Gleeson, an anthology of thirty new short stories by Irish women writers (eight of whom are now deceased and twenty-two living). The International Dublin Literary award, a prestigious award with a €100,000 prize for a novel written in English and sponsored by Dublin City Council, has been won for the last seventeen consecutive years by a man; in 2018 there was, for the first time, a preponderance of female nominees shortlisted.[21]

However, given the extraordinary impact of the #WTF movement, Enright notes that there is a new momentum. In light of the deluge of allegations of sexual harassment and bullying in the workplace made against Michael Colgan at the Gate Theatre, and globally, the allegations made against American producer Harvey Weinstein and the resulting #MeToo movement, there was another robust response from the theater community in Ireland. On March 21, 2018, an event, "Speak Up & Call It Out: Dignity in the Workplace. Establishing a Code of Behaviour for Irish Theatre," was hosted at Liberty Hall. This initiative was led by the Irish Theatre Institute and supported by the Department of Culture, Heritage and the Gaeltacht (Irish Theatre Institute 2020). The one-day event brought members of the Irish theater community together to discuss and identify pathways to cultural change in behavior across the sector. The initiative will introduce a "robust and workable Code of Behaviour to protect Irish theatre practitioners, makers and presenters" (ibid.), including the elimination of the abuse of power that has pervaded the sector to build a safe environment for all theater workers. This response, which is directly linked to the centenary of the Irish republic and the Abbey's *Waking the Nation* program, is the latest in a series of domino-effect outcomes in the Irish arts sector. The *Gender Counts* report has statistically revealed the extent of gender inequality in Irish theater. Although the founders of #WTF stepped down in 2016 to re-focus on their own art practices, their extraordinary achievement continues to be acknowledged:

on March 21, 2018, Lian Bell, #WTF co-founder, won a Tonic Award in London for a "brave and creative campaign to effect positive change in regard to representation of women in Irish theatre" (Falvey 2018). The Tonic Awards, established in 2017, celebrate women's achievements in theater and support the goal of greater gender equality in the sector.[22] The award was presented to Bell by award-winning Irish Indian author Ursula Rani Sarma, mentioned earlier as a playwright practically unproduced in Ireland. Sarma acknowledged Bell's intervention as having decided that it was time for a revolution when she said that "to say it was a movement isn't enough. We were all part of something that was bigger than our individual experiences" (Falvey 2018). Considering the responses outlined here, the revolution has begun.

NOTES

1. *Rebellion* was a €6 million budget, five-part drama series about the birth of modern Ireland. The story is told from the perspective of various fictional characters, including three young women who lived through the political events of the 1916 Easter Rising.

2. *Waking the Nation* featured work by David Ireland, Sean P. Summers, Phillip McMahon, Shakespeare, Tom Murphy, Frank McGuinness, and Sean O'Casey; there was one play dealing with Israel and Palestine by Mutaz Abu Saleh, and a staged reading of an adaptation by Jimmy Murphy. The only work by a female playwright was a monologue for children written by Ali White.

3. After a meeting held on International Women's Day in 2016, MAM was officially formed by Derrington, Fiona Browne, Cerstin Mudiwa, Emma Lowe, Susie Lamb, Oonagh McLaughlin, Charlotte Harrison, Melanie Clarke Pullen, Kate Harris, Sarah Fitzgibbon, and others.

4. Michelle Brown, mentor and founder of the Mothership Project, gave MAM crucial advice: "If you feel invisible, meet in places that make you feel visible" (Spencer Hewitt 2016).

5. MAM advises "5 Family Friendly Practices Towards Gender Balanced Irish Theatre": sympathetic scheduling, children in the work space, family friendly staff training, and childcare facilities.

6. On September 7, 1983, the first referendum on abortion was held in Ireland. The Irish State sought to legislate for the Eighth Amendment of the Constitution of Ireland: "The State acknowledges the right to life of the unborn and, with due regard to the equal right to life of the mother, guarantees in its laws to respect, and, as far as practicable, by its laws to defend and vindicate that right" (Article 40.3.3). It was approved by 67 percent to 33 percent of the voters, with a 53.6 percent turnout. On November 25, 1992, a further referendum, proposing three

amendments, was put to the Irish people: the Twelfth Amendment, seeking to exclude the risk of suicide as grounds for a legal abortion in Ireland was rejected; the Thirteenth Amendment, proposing that the prohibition would not limit the freedom of travel abroad to seek an abortion was approved; the Fourteenth Amendment, which was also approved, proposed that information regarding abortion services abroad would be legalized. In 2002, a third referendum, seeking to legislate into the constitution the right to an abortion in Ireland in the case of the threat to the life of a woman, but not in cases where there was a threat of suicide, was narrowly defeated.

7. There was a 64.13 percent voter turnout, with 66.4 percent voting Yes and 33.6 percent voting No. Only one county, Donegal, voted against the proposal.

8. All data quoted in this section is taken directly from the report, *Gender Counts: An Analysis of Gender in Irish Theatre 2006–2015.*

9. The Abbey first appointed Sarah Durcan, leading #WTF spokesperson, to the board and then declared their eight "guiding principles on gender equality." The principles are: to amend the theater's mission statement and other key documents to reflect the goal of gender equality; to make gender equality a "key board priority and responsibility" with immediate effect; to commit to continued gender equality at "board level"; to achieve gender equality in "all areas of the artistic programme," to be measured every five years starting in 2017; to pursue gender equality in play commissioning; to deliver workshops for "all employees, examining issues of gender equality in the workplace"; to create a yearly program for second-level students with "a view to raising awareness of the career opportunities for women"; and, finally, to report progress made by gender equality "initiatives" in the Abbey's annual report (Abbey Theatre's Annual Report 2020).

10. In 2017, women who wrote or directed work at the Abbey/Peacock included Noelle Brown, Michele Forbes, Cora Bissett, Annabelle Comyn, Amanda Coogan, Teresa Deevy, Emma Donoghue, Lurlene Duggan, Lisa Dwan, Sarah Finlay, Tara Flynn, Stacey Gregg, Orla O'Loughlin, Dael Orlandersmith, Jane Madden, Caitriona McLaughlin, Frances Poet, Annie Ryan, and Maeve Stone. The theater's 2018 program featured new and adapted work by female playwrights: Deirdre Kinahan made her belated debut at the Abbey with two productions, *The Unmanageable Sisters*, a new version of Michel Tremblay's *Les Belles Soeurs*, and *Rathmines Road*, which deals with the timely subject of sexual assault. Acclaimed playwright Marina Carr's *On Raftery's Hill* (2000) was directed by Caitriona McLaughlin; Gina Moxley collaborated with choreographer Liv O'Donoghue and filmmaker John McIlduff in *The Patient Gloria*; Louise O'Neill's novel *Asking for It* dealt with sexual assault and was adapted for the stage by Maedhbh McHugh and Annabelle Comyn; and Tara Flynn wrote and starred in *Not A Funny Word*, a monologue about the highly

contentious issue of abortion rights in Ireland. This work was staged off-site at the Complex in Smithfield, Dublin.

11. Selina Cartmell has directed work ranging from Greek tragedy and Shakespeare to contemporary international and Irish drama. Her productions have been nominated for thirty-five Irish Times Theatre Awards, winning ten, including three for best director. She directed three award-winning productions for the Gate, *Catastrophe, Festen,* and *Sweeney Todd,* described in *The Guardian* as "a new dawn for the theatre" (Gate Theatre History 2020). In 2017, plays by women at the Gate included the award-winning *Tribes* by Nina Raine and *The Red Shoes,* adapted by Nancy Harris. In 2018, featured work was directed by Selina Cartmell, Annabelle Comyn, and Elizabeth Freestone (Gate Theatre Information 2020).

12. The story first came to light in a *New York Times* article on October 5, 2017, with actresses such as Rose McGowan and Ashley Judd among the first to come forward. Weinstein was subsequently sacked by the board of his company, charged with rape and several other counts of sexual abuse against two women in New York, and, on February 24, 2020, convicted of sexual assault and rape.

13. The conference was organized by Dr. David Clare, Dr. Fiona McDonagh, and Dr. Aideen Wylde and hosted by the Department of Drama and Theatre Studies, Mary Immaculate College, University of Limerick.

14. Clare points to the unfortunate fact that since the early 1980s, playwrights such as Lucy Caldwell, Anne Devlin, Stella Feehily, Deirdre Kinahan, Ailis Ni Riain, Lynda Radley, Ursula Rani Sarma, Christina Reid, Abbie Spallen, and Lisa Tierney-Keogh have debuted their work in London, Edinburgh, and New York, while being mostly ignored in their home country of Ireland (Clare 2017).

15. Alongside Christine Longford and Teresa Deevy, Keating names other playwrights such as Geraldine Cummins, Suzanne Day, Eva Gore-Booth, Dorothy McArdle, and Alice Milligan, whose work should be revisited and restaged.

16. In the recently published *Oxford Handbook of Modern Irish Theatre,* edited by Nicholas Grene and Chris Morash (2016), Lady Gregory is awarded a mere eight lines for her work with the Abbey, while Oscar Wilde, Brian Friel, and Tom Murphy get two dedicated chapters each.

17. Rani Sarma's plays, which have been translated and produced extensively, include: *Touched* . . . (2002), *Blue* (2002), *The Magic Tree* (2008), and *The Dark Things* (2009).

18. *Irish Women Playwrights, Volume One: 1716–1992:* Mary Davy's *The Northern Heiress* (1716), Frances Sheridan's *The Discovery* (1763), Elizabeth Griffin's *The Platonic Wife* (1765), Maria Edgeworth's *The Double Disguise* (1786) and *The Knapsack* (1801), Mary Balfour's *Kathleen O'Neill* (1814), Alice Milligan's *The Daughter of Donagh* (1900), Lady Gregory's *The Rising of the*

Moon (1903) and *Grania* (1912), Cummins and Day's *Fox and Geese* (1917), Mary
Manning's *Youth's the Season* . . . ? (1932), Teresa Deevy's *The King of Spain's
Daughter* (1935), *Katie Roche* (1936) and *A Wife to James Whelan* (1942), Elizabeth
Connor's *Mount Prospect* (1940), Maura Laverty's *Tolka Row* (1951), Mairead
Ni Ghrada's *An Triail* (1964), Christina Reid's *Tea in a China Cup* (1983), Ann
Devlin's *Ourselves Alone* (1985), and Patricia Burke Brogan's *Eclipsed* (1992). *Irish
Women Playwrights, Volume Two: 1993–2016*: Emma Donoghue's *I Know My Own
Heart* (1993), Marie Jones's *Yours, Truly* (1993), Gina Moxley's *Danti-Dan* (1995),
Marina Carr's *By the Bog of Cats* (1998) and *Woman and Scarecrow* (2006), Ursula
Rani Sarma's *Blue* (2000), Abbie Spallen's *Pumpgirl* (2006), Stella Feehily's
O Go My Man (2006), Lizzie Nunnery's *Intemperance* (2007), Anne Devlin's
The Forgotten (BBC radio 4, 2009), Amy Conroy's *I Heart Alice Heart I* (2010),
Deirdre Kinahan's *Moment* (2011), Lynda Radley's *Futureproof* (2011), Nancy
Harris's *Our New Girl* (2012), Stacey Gregg's *Shibboleth* (2015), and Celia de
Freine's *Luise* (2016).

19. Mint's artistic director Jonathan Bank uncovered Deevy's papers on a visit
to her family home in Ireland in 2010, which resulted in "The Deevy Project" and
the donation of the original papers to Maynooth University, where her archive is
preserved.

20. The play was revived at the Abbey in the following years: in 1937 and
1938, directed by Hugh Hunt, starring Eileen Crowe as Katie; in 1949, 1953, and
1954, directed by Ria Mooney, starring Maire Ni Dhomhnaill as Katie; in 1975,
directed by Joe Dowling, starring Jeananne Crowley as Katie, and, in 1994, on
the Peacock stage, directed by Judy Friel, starring Derbhle Crotty as Katie.

21. Of the ten novels shortlisted, six were written by women and four by men;
for the 2019 award, half of the shortlisted nominees were women.

22. Caryl Churchill, Katie Mitchell, and Lyn Gardner are among those who
have been recognized for their work in gender equality by the Tonic Awards.

BRENDA O'CONNELL received her PhD from Maynooth University on the topic
of *Motherhood, Female Ageing and Samuel Beckett*. Her research interests include
gender and sexuality, motherhood, psychoanalysis, aging, performance art, and
Irish theater. She has published on Samuel Beckett and female aging as well as
Beckett and performance art and has forthcoming publications on Queer Ageing
in Irish theatre and Beckett and Politics.

FOURTEEN

—ጢ—

"NO COUNTRY FOR YOUNG WOMEN"

(Re)producing the Irish State

SINÉAD KENNEDY

THE YEARS FROM 1912–1922 WERE pivotal in the emergence and formation of the Irish State, encompassing momentous political change in Ireland, Britain, and beyond. This period of transformation included the campaign for Home Rule, World War I, and the War of Independence (1919–1921), culminating in the foundation of the Irish Free State in 1922. Campaigns and movements for social reform, in particular the movement for suffrage and the Dublin Lockout of 1913, corresponded with and energized these political events. One of the central events of the decade was, of course, the Easter Rising, during which approximately sixteen hundred volunteers, men and women, mounted a rebellion and occupied buildings across Dublin. Standing outside the General Post Office (GPO), Patrick Pearse proclaimed, "in the name of God and of the dead generations from which she receives her old tradition of nationhood," an independent Irish Republic. The centenary of the 1916 rebellion against British rule has thus far been the most central and significant occasion of the "decade of centenaries," 2012–2022, an official state-sponsored and -funded program of events. Then Taoiseach Enda Kenny launched the government's 1916:2016 Centenary Programme with a statement on the significance of the Easter Rising to the history of the Irish state: "There are some moments in history when a seed is sown and the old order changes forever. Easter 1916 was such a moment and, from the very early days of this State, it has been the moment we have chosen

---

Chapter title taken from Olivia O'Leary's radio column on Drivetime, RTÉ, April 23, 2013. Accessed January 10, 2018. Available at http://www.rte.ie/radio1/drivetime/programmes /2013/0423/385234-drivetime-tuesday-23-april-2013/?clipid=1064550.

to commemorate as marking the birth of our sovereign Nation" (Kenny 2016). Reproduced in various official and state materials, this statement frames the narrative of the 2016 centenary events in terms of the heterosexual (re)production of the body politic.[1] The language of reproduction is clearly utilized—the sowing of seed, birth—to describe the emergence of the Irish state. In the context of the brutal history of the Irish state's regulation of women's reproductive capacities and the incarceration of those who failed to conform to the constitutionally prescribed heteronormative ideal, this language cannot be considered neutral: what it suggests, in fact, is that there is a need and an opportunity, particularly within the period of the decade of centenaries, to reflect on the state's emergence and to interrogate its role in regulating women's bodies.

This chapter argues that the interconnected terms of production (the performance of creation) and reproduction (the performance of re-creation) have an important resonance when considered within the framework of the Irish body politic. While much attention has been drawn to the erasure from history of the role that women played in the 1916 Rising and the subsequent war for independence, it is not enough to simply rewrite or reinscribe women back into history; we need to deconstruct the history itself. As historian Elizabeth Fox-Genovese writes: "Women's history challenges mainstream history not to substitute the chronicle of the female subject for that of the male, but rather to restore conflict and ambiguity and tragedy to the centre of the historical process: to explore the varied and unequal terms upon which genders, classes and races participate in the forging of a common destiny" (Fox-Genovese 1982, 29). Such a feminist and materialist approach allows us to address fundamentally different questions: What image of the Irish state emerges when it is considered from the perspective of the female body? How do women navigate a state that conceives as central to its raison d'être the control and regulation of the female body and its reproductive capacities? By exploring how the containment of the female body became central to the project of national identity formation, this chapter argues that the female body came to represent the repressed histories and political desires of the Irish state by forcing women to live their lives invisibly, regulated to the margins, elided from the historical narrative, existing in what visual artists Sarah Browne and Jesse Jones have termed "the shadow of the State" (2016).

CONTEXTS

What does it mean to commemorate the revolutionary project of the 1916 Rising—originally a nationalist and a socialist movement with elements of a feminist project—at a moment in Irish history when the most radical and egalitarian aspects of the project seem, for so many sections of society, consigned to the "dustbin of history"? Heather Laird reminds us in her study of commemoration that what and who gets commemorated, at least at an official level, "tend to be those that have been categorised as events and assigned a key role in a history of writing that . . . is always and inevitably selective" (Laird 2018, 10). The centenary year of the Easter Rising also, for example, marked the twentieth anniversary of the closing of the last Magdalene laundry in Ireland, yet there was no official state commemoration of this event—despite the state acknowledging the central role that it occupied in the incarceration of women in these religious-run institutions.[2] The decision to commemorate the 1916 Rising to the neglect of other anniversaries presents an opportunity to interrogate the nature of that state, particularly in relation to gender, and to explore how and why the promises offered in the Proclamation of 1916 were quickly extinguished.

In the national imagination, the 1916 Proclamation is understood as "the" foundational moment of the Irish State, a text explicitly addressed to both Irish men and Irish women. The Proclamation proclaims a vision of egalitarianism:

> The Irish Republic is entitled to, and hereby claims, the allegiance of every Irishman and Irishwoman. The Republic guarantees religious and civil liberty, equal rights and equal opportunities to all its citizens, and declares its resolve to pursue the happiness and prosperity of the whole nation and of all its parts, cherishing all the children of the nation equally, and oblivious of the differences carefully fostered by an alien Government, which have divided a minority from the majority in the past.
>
> Until our arms have brought the opportune moment for the establishment of a permanent National Government, representative of the whole people of Ireland and elected by the suffrages of all her men and women, the Provisional Government, hereby constituted, will administer the civil and military affairs of the Republic in trust for the people. (Clarke et al. 1916)

Over a century later, the radical promise of this document continues to radiate, but it is useful to remember that the document clearly reflected the broader democratic, socialist, and feminist ideas at play in republicanism in 1916. Senia Pašeta, in her work on feminism and nationalism, notes that feminists of the period consistently "highlighted" and "insisted" on this "guarantee of the equality," maintaining that it must be central to the newly proclaimed Republic (Pašeta 2013, 191–192). Furthermore, Pašeta contends that historians have "largely underestimated the impact on the thinking of some of the key republicans of that era of the women's movement" and the women with whom these men associated in everyday political, cultural, and social life (Pašeta 2013, 193). However, as feminists would soon discover, their aspirations would be one of the first casualties of the Irish Free State that emerged from the detritus of the War of Independence with Britain.

In the struggle for definition and identity for the fledgling partitioned Irish State, there was, unsurprisingly, a deliberate, ideologically driven attempt to define Ireland as "not England." This led to a search for distinguishing marks of Irish identity, in which Catholicism and women's reproductive sexuality would become key. This was not inevitable but rather the political logic of the counterrevolutionary forces that came to dominate within the Irish state following the Civil War. Breda Gray and Louise Ryan suggest that, in their desire to "create a new imagined community within the boundaries of the twenty-six-county state," the leaders of the new state fashioned a seamlessly homogeneous society that closed off internal challenges and contradictions even as they represented society as pure and untainted by external corruption (Gray and Ryan 1998, 126–127). The state adopted Catholicism as one of its principle regulating ideologies, which also served to confer upon it a necessary legitimacy as a new postcolonial state. A number of legal measures designed to erase women from public life were introduced, including the Jury Bills of 1924 and 1927, the Civil Service Amendment Act of 1925, and the Conditions of Employment Act of 1935. Through the banning of abortion,[3] divorce (1925), and the sale and importation of contraception (1935), women's sexuality was channeled into childbearing within marriage and family life in the home. The results of these measures meant, Maryann G. Valiulis notes, that "women's political, economic and reproductive rights" were "so severely curtailed so as to make it clear and explicit that women were . . . barred from claiming for themselves a political subjectivity, a public identity" (Valiulis 1992, 43). Within the 1937 constitution, the institutions of marriage and family enjoyed a privileged position. The section of the constitution titled "The Family" (Article 41) states:

1. 1° The State recognises the Family as the natural primary and fundamental unit group of Society, and as a moral institution possessing inalienable and imprescriptible rights, antecedent and superior to all positive law.
   2° The State, therefore, guarantees to protect the Family in its constitution and authority, as the necessary basis of social order and as indispensable to the welfare of the Nation and the State.
2. 1° In particular, the State recognises that by her life within the home, woman gives to the State a support without which the common good cannot be achieved.

2° The State shall, therefore, endeavour to ensure that mothers shall not be obliged by economic necessity to engage in labour to the neglect of their duties in the home.

The family imagined in these articles is highly gendered, where the "special" role of women within the private home is elevated as an ideal. Ruth Riddick has observed that the terms *woman* and *mother* are understood here as interchangeable in the Irish constitution, demonstrated by the rhetorical shift in the constitution from 2.1 to 2.2 (Riddick cited in Conrad 2001, 156). This section of the constitution is clearly influenced by Catholic social teaching as outlined in the papal encyclicals *Rerum Novarum* (1891) and *Quadregesimo Anno* (1931), both of which elucidate Catholicism's teaching on the "natural" function of women as wives and mothers (see Beaumont 1997, 564). Considered as totality, these legislative and constitutional designated gendered roles implied that women's key role is to reproduce and, indirectly, to reproduce the nation.[4]

This regulatory framework for sexuality was certainly not unique to Ireland, and, in some ways, it was not dissimilar to post-war ideological efforts visible in many European countries to recenter women lives back within the domestic sphere. Sociologist Tom Inglis contends that "Irish prudery" around sexuality can be located within the "wider context of Victorian attitudes to women, marriage and the family." But, he notes, what is significant is "how long this Victorian regime lasted and how deeply it seeped into the minds and bodies of the Irish" (Inglis 2005, 11). It is equally important to acknowledge how that sexuality, and women's sexuality in particular, became an ideological bulwark for the Irish state, which was Catholic but also capitalist. The regulation of sexuality became one of the key ideological devices through which the new postcolonial Irish state dissociated itself from the revolutionary struggles central to its foundation, including significant socialist and feminist movements (see Margaret Ward 1983, 219–247). Michael G. Cronin (2012) argues that for a newly formed state born out of counterrevolutionary struggle, the regulation and control of sexual behavior created a sense of social stability for a state in flux. This regulatory ideal of sexuality became a way of extending the hegemony of the newly empowered Catholic middle classes, who emerged as the bearers of this stability and morality (Cronin 2012, 52). It was society's most marginalized transgressing bodies—poor, infant, and female—that were incarcerated into a nexus of church-state institutions that included Magdalene laundries, mother and baby homes, industrial schools and reformatories, and psychiatric hospitals: "The confined and abused body of the young working-class woman or orphan silently but powerfully affirmed the healthy respectability of their youthful middle-class compatriots pursuing fulfilment and happiness outside, while serving as an equally powerful warning that the privileges of middle class youth were always provisional and that maintaining healthy respectability required constant and anxious endeavour" (Cronin 2012, 7–8). We now know that this vision of the stable, traditional family so cherished by Catholic Ireland rested upon a particularly brutal system of containment in which women and their children were considered "little more than a commodity for trade amongst religious orders" with the full knowledge and complicity of the state (Ó Fátharta 2015). While the effects of this regime were most profoundly experienced by those who either failed or refused to conform to the heteropatriarchal norm, the culture of containment contaminated the whole of society, so that even those who appeared empowered by the system were "also held hostage by it, trapped within the family cell" (Conrad 2001, 3–4).

Ongoing debates within Irish cultural studies, James M. Smith observes, have reconsidered how the project of national identity formation in the decades following political independence utilized the heteropatriarchal family and the Catholic Church's ideal of sexual morality in ways that were particularly oppressive for Irish women (Smith 2007, 137). Ireland's status as a postcolonial state is central to understanding this project. Postcolonial nationalism promoted Catholicism as a signifier of Irishness; women were constructed as mothers and childbearers, dedicated to reproducing the next generation of the Irish nation, located either within the private home or in "homes" controlled by religious orders with women. This constructed version of womanhood became elevated as a symbol of Ireland's moral and cultural distinctiveness over its former colonial master, Britain. The postcolonial theorist Ashis Nandy, in his study *The Intimate Enemy* (1984), argues that the colonial relationship is inevitably and profoundly gendered. Colonialism generates a gendered power relationship that constructs the colonizing power as masculine and dominant and the colonized as feminine and passive. Yuval-Davis's work on gender and nationalism goes further by incorporating the question of reproduction into the frameworks of gender and nationalism, contending that, when women are marginalized, it is "women who reproduce nations biologically, culturally and symbolically" while simultaneously remaining "'hidden' in the various theorizations of nationalist phenomena" (Yuval-Davis 1997, 7). Ruth Fletcher has deployed Yuval-Davis's work to highlight how Irishness has been gendered and racialized through the regulation of women's reproductive capacities, though Fletcher develops this argument to illustrate how reproductive activities "change the contours of the nation and the agendas of nationalisms as much as they respond to them" (R. Fletcher 2005, 370). In order to understand this, she argues, we need to consider how nation, gender, reproduction, and racism intersect in particular ways at particular moments. The intersection of these issues is evident in the more recent history of the abortion debate in Ireland, when reproductive politics became a site for struggle over definitions of Irishness.

REPRODUCTION AND THE CONSTITUTION

In Ireland, understandings of reproduction have been burdened not only by the weight of the Irish/British distinction but by a particular version of Irishness as race/ethnicity that is enshrined into a constitution that implicitly conceives Irishness as Catholic, settled, and white. The body of the pregnant woman and the fetus that she carries become the vehicle for the production of a national culture. Writing in an American context, Lauren Berlant argues that it is a woman's body that "bears the burden of keeping these gendered, racial, class, ethnic and national identities stable and intelligible . . . an identity machine for others, producing children in the name of the future, in service to the national culture whose explicit ideology of natural personhood she is also helping to generate" (Berlant 1997, 85). So too in Ireland women's reproducing bodies would become, both in early and contemporary debates around the foundation of the state, the "medium through which competing national origin stories that focus on Irish national identity and cultural self-determination . . . are imagined and expressed" (Oaks 1998, 133). The fetus is a potential citizen, a sign of the reproduction of the nation. One of the key tropes in Irish nationalist antiabortion discourse is the innocent fetus that, like the Irish nation, is under threat from corruptive outside forces. Feminist scholar and activist Ailbhe Smyth has argued that Ireland is often conceived of in "extreme-right ideology and politics" as the last bastion in the battle to preserve the purity and sanctity of the traditional family: "In this scenario, Ireland plays the heroic role of the tiny beleaguered State staunchly defending the Faith of Our Fathers (and the invisibility of our mothers) by holding out against the global wave of depravity which threatens to engulf it, and thus (somewhat illogically) Ireland shines as a beacon for all those in need of salvation. . . . Those—especially women—who go the way of all flesh and 'choose' divorce, contraception, or abortion are therefore traitors to both Church and State" (Smyth cited in Conrad 2001, 156). It is women's agency that threatens the reproduction of the national patriarchy and must, therefore, be contained, Conrad argues, both within the "heterosexual familial paradigm" and through limiting their reproductive choices (Conrad 2001, 161).

The year 1983 saw the introduction of a constitutional ban on abortion following a bitterly divisive referendum campaign. That ban would remain in place for thirty-five years. Abortion was already illegal in Ireland under the 1861 Offences Against the Person Act, which had been incorporated into Irish law following independence. The act specifically criminalized a woman who attempted to procure an abortion for herself with a life sentence of penal servitude (Farrell 2013, 82–83). The object of the Pro-Life Amendment Campaign (PLAC), then, was not to ban abortion; it was already illegal and feminist activists were still fighting for access to contraception and had given limited attention to legalizing abortion (see L. Connolly 2003). The so-called "pro-life" amendment was, instead, a political and ideological battle designed to stem the tide of what the Catholic right felt was an encroaching assault by liberal and secular values on Irish society (see O'Reilly 1992). Ireland was, as a result, the first country in the world to give the fetus constitutional status, although the move was reflective of wider arguments for fetal personhood that were happening internationally at the time. For Berlant these kinds of laws render the pregnant woman increasingly invisible as she "becomes the child to the fetus, becoming more minor and less politically represented than the fetus, which is in turn made more *national*, more central to securing the privileges of law, paternity and other less institutional family strategies" (Berlant 1997, 85).

The campaign to introduce what became the Eighth Amendment was led by a number of conservative Catholic groups fearing that the growing support for more liberalization in Irish society could lead to abortion becoming legal in Ireland at some point in the future. The first call for a constitutional amendment appeared in a leaflet produced by a fundamentalist Catholic lay group called the Irish Family League, headed by John O'Reilly, which specifically targeted the *McGee* (1974) Supreme Court judgment—which found that married couples had a right to privately make family planning decisions—by stating that the matter of contraception was far too important to be left to the Supreme Court (Hesketh 1990, 163–168). O'Reilly went on to establish PLAC in January 1981. From the outset the ideology behind the campaign was much broader than just contraception and abortion. One of the campaign's first fronts was to oppose the formation of a multi-denominational primary school in Dublin, arguing that such a school fundamentally challenged the Catholic dominance of the Irish education system. They also began public campaigns against "immoral" TV shows and family planning clinics and were vehemently opposed to the establishment of the first Dublin Rape Crisis Centre. However, it was around the issue of abortion that it quickly became clear that they could maximize support for traditional values. PLAC sought to enshrine Catholic teaching on abortion in the constitution and thereby ensure a "backlash" against what they viewed was the increasing advance of a liberal social agenda (Hug 1999, 146–148).

The Eighth Amendment, which became Article 40.3.3 of the constitution, read: "The State acknowledges the right to life of the unborn and, with due regard to the equal right to life of the mother, guarantees in its laws to respect, and, as far as practicable, by its laws to defend and vindicate that right." The amendment subordinated the life of a pregnant woman to that of the fetus she was carrying, rendering abortion illegal in Ireland in all circumstances except where there was a "real and substantial risk" to the life of the pregnant woman.[5] The amendment was, Senator Ivana Bacik has argued, "uniquely misogynistic, in that it expressly sets up the right to life of both the pregnant woman and the foetus that she carries in conflict—anticipating that a time would come when somebody would have to decide between them" (Bacik 2013, 22). While Article 40.3.3 would be further amended in 1992 by the Thirteenth and Fourteenth Amendments, it remained—along with the 1861 Offences Against the Person Act—the core legal provision relating to abortion. Between 1980 and 2016, over one hundred seventy thousand[6] Irish women would travel abroad, largely to Britain, in order to access abortion. The consequences of the Eighth Amendment's introduction were thus profound for Irish women for the next three decades.

It was not until 1992 and the case of *Attorney General v. X* that the courts would have to make a specific judgment about abortion and the constitution. The X case involved a fourteen-year-old rape victim, known in court proceedings only as "Miss X," whose family decided to bring her to Britain for an abortion. The Gardaí were contacted by the girl's parents to see if fetal tissue could be submitted as evidence against her rapist. When the Gardaí sought legal clarification on admissibility from the attorney general, Harry Whelehan, he responded by seeking an injunction against Miss X and her parents, prohibiting them from leaving the jurisdiction. The case was famously depicted on the front page of the *Irish Times* by the cartoonist Marty Turner: Miss X appears as a young girl with a teddy bear standing on a fenced-in map of the twenty-six counties of the Republic of Ireland. The caption, drawing on nationalist iconography, reads "the introduction of internment in Ireland . . . for 14 year old girls. . . ." (See Fig. 14.1.) As Ruth Fletcher has argued, in "depicting the X case decision in terms of Ireland's virtual imprisonment of a young vulnerable child, the cartoon criticises the Irish state in terms that used to be reserved for the British state when it imprisoned Northern Irish republicans without trial" (Fletcher 2005, 384).

Miss X's parents appealed to the Supreme Court, arguing that their daughter was suicidal at the prospect of continuing the pregnancy, but Justice Costello upheld the injunction, arguing that the risk posed to Miss X's life by requiring her to continue the pregnancy was "much less and of a different order of

Figure 14.1. Cartoon: "17th February 1992 ... the introduction of internment in Ireland ... for 14 year old girls ..." (Courtesy of Martyn Turner.)

magnitude" than the risk to the life of the unborn (cited in McDonagh 1992, 89). Costello further held that Miss X's right to travel, guaranteed by Irish and European law, must yield to the right to life of the unborn (McDonagh 1992, 91). The judgment was then appealed to the Supreme Court, who lifted the injunction by a majority of four to one. All five Supreme Court justices held that a woman had a constitutionally protected right to an abortion if there was a "real and substantial" risk to her life and this, they ruled, included a risk of suicide. However, two of the five judges ruled that Article 40.3.3 did not permit a woman to travel abroad for an abortion in circumstances where it would not be legal within the borders of the state. Therefore, as James Kingston observed, the case of Miss X "demonstrated that while Article 40.3.3 did not contain an absolute prohibition on abortion, it did require the State to provide protection of the right to life of the unborn by ensuring that pregnant women did not travel out of the jurisdiction" (Kingston 2001, 31). The response of the government to the X case judgment reveals the official hypocrisy that has long characterized the state's attitude to women who need access to abortion; women living in Ireland would be allowed to access abortion, just as long as those abortions did not happen on the island of Ireland.

The strategy adopted to address the problems highlighted by the X case was explicitly one of containment. Instead of introducing a referendum to remove the Eighth Amendment, the state proposed to confine the anger around it in two ways: first, the state sought to introduce a new constitutional amendment that would exclude risk of suicide as grounds for obtaining an abortion in Ireland and, second, the state attempted to constitutionally protect a woman's right to travel abroad to access abortion even if it was unlawful in Ireland. The proposals also included an amendment that would provide a constitutional right to access information on abortion services that were available abroad. Three simultaneous referenda were held in November 1992: the electorate rejected the proposal that would exclude suicide as grounds for an abortion in Ireland and endorsed constitutional changes protecting a woman's freedom to travel for an abortion and to access abortion information in Ireland.[7] A further attempt to remove suicide from the constitution would be attempted again in 2002 and would, again, fail. It is worth noting that, until 2018, the electorate was never afforded the opportunity to liberalize abortion laws in Ireland, but, on the two occasions they were asked to further restrict access, they refused.

While the X case illuminated, yet again, the tempestuous relationship between state nationalism and women's bodies, the 2002 "Baby O" case would reveal the hollow and hypocritical nature of the state's protection for "unborn" life. David Theo Goldberg argues that all modern nation states need to be understood as racial states attempting to construct homogeneity (Goldberg 2001). Irishness, as we have seen, is both gendered and racialized through abortion law, but over the course of the twentieth century the nature of this gendered and racialized discourse has shifted away from functioning as an opposition to Britishness toward a more explicit ideology that values and privileges the reproduction of some women over others. The Celtic Tiger economy of the 1990s saw dramatic levels of economic growth in Ireland which, for the first time in its history, began to experience significant inward migration. In this period, there is a notable shift in discourse around Irish identity as migrant women's birth practices began to be constructed as threatening to the integrity of Irish citizenship. Both Eithne Luibhéid and Ruth Fletcher have connected the case of Miss X with a 2002 deportation case involving a woman referred to in court proceedings as Ms. O. Ms. O, a thirty-two-year-old Nigerian citizen, appealed her deportation to Nigeria to the High Court and later to the Supreme Court on the grounds that she was pregnant. Her legal representatives argued that her deportation contravened Article 40.3.3, which guarantees the "right to life of the unborn." The Nigerian infant mortality rate was ninety per thousand births (compared with just seven per thousand in Ireland) and, therefore, could be constituted as a threat to the life of her "unborn" child (Luibhéid 2013, 125). The Supreme Court rejected her appeal, but the judgment and the arguments utilized by the state to ensure her deportation illustrated the racialized nature of Ireland's "pro-life" position. The state's presentation of its case initially denied that Baby O was a person or had a right to a legal personality, although it later revised this position, arguing instead that the rights of the unborn were indistinguishable from the rights of the pregnant woman (Luibhéid 2013, 139). This position, Ruth Fletcher argues, is in direct contrast to the state's position in the X case, "where the 'unborn's' rights were deemed capable of limiting women's rights," and where the state made an "explicit representation of the 'unborn' as a distinct legal entity" (Fletcher 2005, 391–392). The Supreme Court ruled in the Baby O case that the state had the right to deport individuals who had been refused refugee status and that, in this context, the "unborn" was not entitled to special rights. However, as Luibhéid correctly argues, this was not the only interpretation of Article 40.3.3 available to the court: Article 40.3.3 could have been interpreted as entailing a "positive duty on the part of the State" to enable all women to carry their pregnancies to term (2013, 140). Not only did the Supreme Court decline to interpret the Eighth Amendment in this manner but it failed to explain, given the presence of the Eighth Amendment, why there was no duty of care to a minimum standard during pregnancy (Luibhéid 2013, 140–141). Consequently it is impossible not to concur that there is "a racial stratification of foetal protection" in Ireland, with some fetuses deemed more worthy of protection than others (Fletcher 2005, 395).

Many of the most high-profile cases around the Eighth Amendment and childbirth have involved migrant women of color: Savita Halappanavar, Ms. Y, and Aisha Chithira. Migrants account for 39 percent of all maternal deaths in Ireland, even though migrants only constitute 24 percent of all women giving birth (P. Cullen 2015). The Eighth Amendment assumes mobility: that women have both the means and the ability to travel. Until abortion was legalized on January 1, 2019, at least nine women traveled daily to Britain to avail of abortion services.[8] This option is unavailable to many migrant women for a combination of economic reasons and visa restrictions. Asylum seekers and undocumented women cannot travel in all but exceptional circumstances, while for many others visa restrictions make it impossible to travel urgently. Some communities report being scared to access pregnancy care due to the racism they experience in Irish society, and some migrants do not have Personal Public Service (PPS) numbers, meaning that health care is expensive or unavailable to them (see MERJ 2018). Through Ms. O's pregnant body, the Irish State "redrew and restabilised" the line between national and nonnational women, harnessing women's bodies for "racialised strategies of immigration controls" (Luibhéid 2013, 143). Two years after the Ms. O case, in 2004, the Irish state would introduce a further constitutional amendment to remove the automatic entitlement to citizenship for any child born in Ireland, which would signal a shift in "Irishness" from a cultural to a biological property. Through the control of Ms. O's pregnant body, the state's utilization of women's reproductive capacities for racialized strategies for nation building was revealed. Women not born in Ireland and their children would have their opportunities for citizenship foreclosed and the state's deportation policies reinforced, while the reproductive capacities of Irish women would be exploited for building a nation that was becoming defined in ever more exclusory terms. The hollow racist and misogynist nature of the state's protection for the "unborn" has been revealed in a number of key legal cases around the Eighth Amendment highlighted by abortion rights activists, whose campaign to repeal the Eighth Amendment gained political and moral urgency following the death in 2012 of Savita Halappanavar, who developed septicemia after being denied an abortion during a miscarriage. When Halappanavar challenged this, she was told that a termination could not be carried out because Ireland was a "Catholic country" (Cullen and Holland 2013). Halappanavar became a galvanizing figure during the "Repeal the Eighth" campaign that led to the vote of May 25, 2018, with a memorial to her appearing in Dublin and messages left that included apologies: "Sorry we were too late, but we are here now. We didn't forget you" (Specia 2018).

INTERROGATING THE STATE

While challenges to the state's stance on reproductive rights and abortion have come through court cases like the ones briefly discussed above, in recent years there have been many other platforms through which protest has occurred. Since its establishment in 2013, and when women began calling more vocally for a repeal of the Eighth Amendment, the performance-based project Speaking of IMELDA has done important work in interrogating the Irish state's intimate relationship with gender and reproduction. Speaking of IMELDA is a London-based direct action feminist performance and protest collective "comprised largely, although not exclusively, of Irish women living in London." Through their performances they "purposefully play with the insidious and hypocritical culture of silence and shame" that exists around abortion in Ireland (Speaking of IMELDA 2020). Their performances reference earlier forms of abortion support activism for Irish women traveling to Britain, thus acting as uncomfortable acts of commemoration of pasts that officialdom does not acknowledge. IMELDA is an acronym for "Ireland Making England the Legal Destination for Abortion discourses while actively continuing their labours" (Speaking of IMELDA 2015a); "Imelda" was also the code word for abortion employed by the Irish Women's Abortion Support Group (IWASG; Rossiter 2009), used in the 1980s, when access to abortion information was heavily censored, to protect women who might be using a public or family telephone to make arrangements to travel (McTiernan 2015). The IMELDAs dress in red for their performances, just as members of the IWASG wore red skirts when meeting women who traveled from Ireland for abortions at airports or train stations so that they would be recognizable. Participants understand their performances as operating "against the secrecy and denials that maintain the rigid policing of women's bodies. In retrieving the tropes, aesthetics and histories of feminist activists in the past, we operate against the silencing of feminist activism in dominant discourses while actively continuing their labours" (Speaking of IMELDA 2015a). The IMELDAs have staged a number of provocative actions in Britain and Ireland, including wearing red and wheeling suitcases through crowds at the 2014 St. Patrick's Day parade in London, asking directions to abortion clinics. In a performance titled "Knickers for Choice," they polished the brass and granite of the Irish embassy building with their underwear and requested that their supporters tweet photos of knickers with pro-choice slogans in public places. In October 2013, when then Taoiseach Enda Kenny was invited as a guest of honor to a London dinner celebrating Irish emigrants, the IMELDAs greeted Kenny by chanting "12 women a day!" a reminder of the number of women who were traveling from Ireland to England for abortions, and presented him with a pair of knickers, asking him to repeal or remove the Eighth Amendment (Enright 2015).

One of their most provocative performances was at Dublin's GPO during the 2015 "Road to the Rising" event in O'Connell Street, a historical re-enactment of life in 1915 Dublin initiated by the national television broadcaster RTÉ in advance of the centenary of the 1916 Rising, and part of the Decade of Centenaries commemorative program. The IMELDAs chained themselves to the

GPO and, echoing the male signatories of the 1916 Proclamation, read their own "Pro-Choice Proclamation":

> Irish men and Irish women,
> And all who live in Ireland,
> In the name of the freedom promised to us on these steps
> Ninety-nine years ago,
> We call on the government of Ireland
> To fulfil our international obligation,
> As highlighted by the UN Human Rights Committee,[9]
> To provide access to safe legal abortion in Ireland.

> Just like those who stood on these steps
> Ninety-nine years ago,
> We declare the right of all people in Ireland to ownership of their own
> bodies,
> And to control their own destinies.
> We applaud and stand in solidarity with
> The vibrant pro-choice movement all around the country.
> Ireland is Rising!
> To tell the politicians
> The time to repeal the eight amendment is now!

> (Speaking of IMELDA 2015b)

This alternative proclamation directly echoed the tone and liberatory language of the original, declaring "the right of all people in Ireland to ownership of their own bodies." The performance sought to highlight the manner in which the bodies of women living in Ireland "are territorially controlled as if they are national property" (Speaking of IMELDA 2015a). Coming at what amounted to a dress rehearsal for the centenary of the Easter Rising, and at the *lieu de mémoire* that is the GPO, the IMELDAs' protest highlighted the difficulties with state and official commemorative practices that wish to celebrate the past and assume that it is safely removed from the culture of the present. The IMELDAs' simultaneous engagement with both past and present refuses the typical representations of Ireland's enervating past that permits present-day detachment from and complacency about the nation's history—responses Joe Cleary argues are synonymous with experiencing "a lucky escape 'from all that'" (Cleary 2000, 108). Imagining the past as stagnant and repressive typically affirms the current social formation of Irish society. The work of the IMELDAs reminds us that Ireland's past, for significant sections of society, is still very much the present.

If the Decade of Centenaries was envisioned, at least in part, as a celebratory consideration of Ireland's past and the state's achievements, it was certainly not envisioned as providing an important stage for the campaign to achieve one of the most important referendums in the history of the state: the referendum to remove the Eighth Amendment. This campaign for a once-in-a-generation opportunity to address the question of abortion in Ireland and to interrogate the lived reality of a constitutional article that equates a pregnant woman's life with that of her fetus was one of the key political questions of 2016, a ghostly presence haunting many of the key commemorative events that year. While many of the commemorative acts of the decade retrieved women from the margins of history, and while much important scholarly work has redressed the silences on women's role in Irish history, it was the resounding endorsement of "repeal" of the Eighth Amendment on May 25, 2018, that might, in retrospect, take its place as one of the most significant events within the decade's context: on that day, 66.9 percent of the population voted in favor of repealing the Eighth Amendment in a historic vote. While we must be careful not to overstate the vote's significance for the increasingly economically divided and alienated society that is twenty-first-century Ireland, it can serve to show that historic and meaningful change is possible. Perhaps the vote to repeal will serve as a small first step toward building the genuinely egalitarian society Pearse alluded to outside the GPO more than one hundred years ago, a commemorative act that surpassed pageantry and was itself a proclamation.

NOTES

Author acknowledgment: I am grateful to Leeann Lane and Mary McAuliffe for reading and commenting on this essay.

1. I am grateful to Mary McAuliffe for drawing my attention to this.

2. A conference at University College Dublin, 1916 Home 2016, was organized by Mary McAuliffe and Emilie Pine to mark this event. The conference interrogated wider questions of how we commemorate the history of women and how their bodies were treated during the revolutionary period and, later, by the Irish State. More information available at http://www.irishhumanities.com/events/1916-home-2016/.

3. Abortion was illegal before independence under the 1861 Offences against the Person Act, and this act was incorporated into Irish law following independence.

4. Despite the narrow roles ascribed to them, women did continue to assert their citizenship rights and were not, as Caitriona Beaumont's important work has shown, simply "brain-washed" into submission by Catholicism (see Beaumont 1997).

5. In the 1992 X case judgment, the majority opinion of the Irish Supreme Court (C. J. Finlay, Egan McCarthy, and J. J. O'Flaherty) held that a woman had a right to an abortion under Article 40.3.3 if there was "a real and substantial risk" to her life. This right did not exist if there was a risk to her health but not her life; however, it did exist if the risk was the possibility of suicide. See *Attorney General v. X*, [1992] IESC 1; [1992] 1 IR 1.

6. These statistics, based on data collected by the UK Department of Health Statistics, refer to women resident in Ireland who traveled to both England and Wales to access safe abortion services. These numbers are underestimates, however, as they do not include women who travel to Scotland or to other countries in Europe. They also fail to include women who do not provide their Irish address to clinics or hospitals in England and Wales, often in order to protect their confidentiality.

7. The Twelfth Amendment proposed that the possibility of suicide was not a sufficient threat to justify an abortion; this was rejected by a 65.35 percent majority. The Thirteenth Amendment proposed that the prohibition of abortion would not limit freedom of travel from Ireland to other countries where a person might legally obtain an abortion; this was supported by a 62.39 percent majority. The Fourteenth Amendment proposed that Irish citizens have the freedom to pursue and learn about abortion services in other countries; this was supported by a 59.88 percent majority. Voter turnout for the three referendums was 68.1 percent.

8. Abortion Statistics UK Department of Health Statistics. This figure is based on the average number of women who traveled to England and Wales giving Irish addresses in 2018. More information available at https://www.gov.uk/government/collections/abortion-statistics-for-england-and-wales.

9. In July 2014, during the fourth periodic review of the state under the International Covenant on Civil and Political Rights (ICCPR), the UN Human Rights Committee (HRC) criticized Ireland's abortion laws and urged legislative and constitutional change to bring these laws in-line with human rights standards.

SINÉAD KENNEDY teaches in the Department of English at Maynooth University, where she received her PhD. She is coeditor of *The Abortion Papers Ireland: Volume 2* (2015), and is currently finishing a book on the cultural history of Ireland's Eighth Amendment. She was the cofounder with Ailbhe Smyth of the Coalition to Repeal the Eighth Amendment and the head of research for Together for Yes, the national civil society campaign to remove the Eighth Amendment in 2018.

FIFTEEN

—ɯ—

REMEMBERING THE HOME AND THE NORTHERN IRISH TROUBLES

ELI DAVIES

THE BOUNDARIES OF PUBLIC AND private, fluid in any political context, have been particularly unsettled in Northern Ireland from the time of partition. Adam Hanna, introducing his study of Northern Irish poetry and domestic space, provides a neat précis of the material and symbolic importance of houses in the region's political and public life from its very inception. "The creation of the six counties as a separate political entity had been made possible by the census-driven determination of its border," he writes, pointing out that it was through these calculations that the majority protestant state was formed, making individual houses "a unit that either underwrote or called into question the existence of the polity." Hanna references the sectarian house burnings of the early 1920s, briefly describes the struggles for housing justice by the national-ist community in the 1960s, and emphasizes the involvement of homes in the violence that sparked the Troubles (2015, 2–3). Housing and houses continue to occupy a hugely political role in the post-conflict landscape of the north of Ireland, demonstrating segregation and territorial claim through physical fea-tures such as peace lines and murals on gable ends. Sectarian attacks on homes, while far less frequent than during the conflict, also continue. As Brionie Reid writes, "In Northern Ireland the textures of the intercommunal conflict have had distinct effects on understandings of the house; its private and personal status has been compromised repeatedly" (2007, 934).

The role of houses and housing, in symbolic, territorial, and political senses, has thus long been a focus for activists, scholars, and commentators discuss-ing Northern Ireland and its history. In a present that has recently marked the fiftieth anniversaries of the start of the civil rights movement in North-ern Ireland as well as the start of the Troubles, I aim to draw attention to the importance of what has happened *inside* houses during the Troubles, as homes and sites of daily life, an area that is talked about far less and is difficult to mark or commemorate. The home was and is a site of violence, not only from the outside via army raids and paramilitary murders but also from *within* in the form of partner-on-partner domestic violence and abuse. Furthermore, homes were—and continue to be—a site of other, less visible, activity, all of it gendered to greater or lesser degrees: physical and emotional labor, feeding and caring for people, political awakenings and discussion, supporting politically active family members, the daily psychological toll of simply living in a war zone. How do these experiences fit with how we remember, narrate, and memorialize the Troubles? How have they been excluded and how do we insert them into historical narratives? This chapter posits that the home is a site of conflict, integral *to* the conflict. It looks at how and why the home has been omitted from public narratives about the Troubles, examining its presences and absences in commemorative landscapes and the ways that it has been fetishized by political discourse.

1968 IN 2018

The house and housing played an important role in the formation of the civil rights movement in Northern Ireland. A key and widely acknowledged event in the sparking of the civil rights movement was the June 20, 1968, protest in the Tyrone village of Caledon, at which nationalist MP Austin Currie led the squatting of a house in protest at Dungannon Council's discriminatory housing policies. This direct action raised the profile of the fight against anti-Catholic discrimination in the North and drew attention to the issue of housing injustice. August 24 saw a march from Coalisland to Dungannon, followed by the Derry march on October 5, which was blocked and baton-charged by the Royal Ulster Constabulary and is widely seen as the beginning of the broader conflict. On most timelines of the conflict, including in the Ulster Museum and in the wider commemorative calendar, the Coalisland–Dungannon march and the Derry march are the significant dates singled out as "the beginning of civil rights." As part of commemorations in 2018, there was a Social Democratic and Labour Party–organized conference on housing in Northern Ireland to mark the fiftieth anniversary of Caledon in June, while the main fiftieth anniversary celebrations—the Civil Rights Festival—took place in Derry around the anniversary of the Derry march, in October. During such anniversary periods, it is as interesting to look at the stories that do not get remembered as those that have been included in commemorative events and exhibits. In mainstream retellings of the civil rights story certain individuals are seen as crucial to this historical moment: Austin Currie, Gerry Fitt, Bernadette Devlin McAliskey, and John Hume. The permanent civil rights display in the Ulster Museum is, for example, notable for its unquestioning hagiography in this regard. In such displays, Devlin McAliskey is usually the sole prominent woman; as Chris Reynolds points out, "In the collective memory of this period, the widespread participation of women has been distilled into [this] single figure" (2019, 57).

Rebecca Graff-McRae identifies "silence" as an important object of study in relation to Northern Irish commemoration. For Graff-McRae an examination of silence is part of a feminist methodology: "How can gender politics be excavated, traced and made visible in spite of the apparent impartiality of memory?" (2010, 3; 2016). Graff-McRae's ideas can be used in conjunction with Guy Beiner's recent work on "social forgetting," in which he investigates the "realms of forgetting" in Irish cultural memory and argues that "new terminology and conceptual frameworks are required in order to help us find our bearings and to try and understand the denizens of these strange places" (2018, 5). In the spirit of studying such silences and "realms of forgetting," discussions certainly did take place throughout 2018 about the participation of women in 1968, with several events devoted to exploring women's importance in the civil rights struggle. In Belfast, for example, there was a panel event at City Hall coinciding with a civil rights exhibition, and the Public Records Office Northern Ireland hosted a one-day conference examining the role of women in this period in honor of the late civil rights activist Inez McCormack. During the Civil Rights Festival, at Derry's Playhouse, an evening of women writers' reflections on 1968 took place, while the city's Void Gallery exhibited *The Long Note* by film artist Helen Cammock (October to December). Cammock's work tells the stories of women involved in the movement with the stated aim of unearthing voices that were less heard in the histories of the civil rights movement in Derry (2018).

There is still much to be done, however, to fully integrate women's stories into the political histories of the north. In contrast to the above events, the Ulster Museum scheduled a panel event on civil rights and unionism in September 2018 that included no women speakers; the museum was forced to cancel the event after a significant social media backlash. This in turn opened up further vital discussions on social media and beyond about the representation of women in the story of Northern Ireland. Reynolds reminds us of the role of commemoration in reexamining the past in Northern Ireland and argues that "Northern Ireland's 1968 is a pertinent example of the possibilities on offer to reassess and even recalibrate memories of such seminal moments" (2018, 64). While it seems it is becoming increasingly publicly unacceptable to exclude women from commemorative programs, or at least less acceptable to do so without facing significant vocal criticism, the possibilities referred to by Reynolds are still too often missed: there is much work to be done to take full account of the reality of women's lives in these stories. Such a process is necessary to make visible the workings of gender in society in the north and to challenge what Eilish Rooney calls the "invisibility of women and gender in explanations of the conflict" (2007).

High-profile commemorative events raise questions about what in the past is deemed worthy of remembering; the example of the Homeless Citizens' League (HCL), an organization whose formation and actions predated the events of 1968, is certainly one that deserves the attention of feminist excavation and is an example of how women's histories can get swallowed up by more prominent male narratives. The HCL was a hugely significant example of women's organizing; not only does it fit into broader histories of women's political activism in the north[1] but its actions "gave way to a larger critique of systematic government discrimination against the Catholic community" (Keenan-Thomson 2010, 61) and led to the formation of the Campaign for Social Justice, a key organization in the early days of the civil rights campaign headed by Patricia and Conn McCluskey, both of whom are frequently name-checked for their role in the politics of this period. (The website of the Civil Rights Commemoration Committee does acknowledge the HCL in its timeline of key events, which begins in 1963 with its formation [Northern Ireland Civil Rights 2020]; there was also discussion of the HCL's role at several Civil Rights Festival events.)

The league was formed in Dungannon in 1963 when local women Angela McCrystal, Susie Dinsmore, and Anne Dunlop were driven by the poor quality and overcrowding of their homes to take action to highlight the problem of homelessness in their community and protest their plight to the council. These women had been following events in Alabama and all have since spoken openly about being inspired by the civil rights movement led by Martin Luther King Jr. and the involvement of women in these protests (see Shannon 1995; Keenan-Thomson 2010). They began their campaign by informally surveying those living in their area about housing needs and by organizing several demonstrations at the Dungannon Council offices. Frustrated by the cautious, more reformist approach of the organizing committee headed by Patricia McCluskey, these women went over its head and eventually organized a squat of prefabricated houses due for demolition in the Fairmount Park area of the town. The squat grew to 120 people and went on for several weeks, drawing high-profile media attention in the process and ending with the council agreeing to extend a housing scheme to cover new families (Keenan-Thomson

2010, 76–78). Catherine B. Shannon argues that the relative obscurity of the HCL's actions—"the very first protests against discriminatory housing policies by Unionist dominated local government"—is a "glaring example of women being written out of the history of the 'Troubles'" (1995, 238). Aside from the accounts of Keenan-Thomson and Shannon, there remains very little written about this campaign, though, in 2018, around the time of the civil rights fiftieth anniversary commemorations, the story of the HCL was explored by a BBC radio documentary (*Stories in Sound* 2018) and in an *Irish Times* article (McClements 2018), albeit relatively briefly.

The BBC's *Stories in Sound* explores the formation of the HCL and its influence on later civil rights protests. Bernadette Devlin McAliskey, an iconic figure from the civil rights era as a result of her public political activism, speaks in the capacity of a childhood friend of the McCluskeys' daughter Darine. She gives an account of her friendship with Darine and of the McCluskeys' position in the community, noting that "the reason we went there was a very high political ethical reason . . . they had coffee" (*Stories in Sound* 2018). Her comment, though made humorously, gestures to a more serious point about the inner life of houses, the minutiae of daily life, the moments of eating, drinking, and shared experiences that take place inside a home and that sustain political life.

The documentary also includes accounts by McCrystal, Dinsmore, and Dunlop describing what drove them forward and how they organized their actions. The descriptions of the protests, both by the women themselves in this documentary and by critics elsewhere, foreground the physical features of motherhood: "all of us with our prams," noted McCrystal in the documentary. Tara Keenan-Thomson writes of "this unusual march populated by women, children and babies in strollers" (2009, 209), echoing Catherine B. Shannon: "These demonstrations featured mothers dressed in their Sunday best, pushing baby prams with many toddlers in tow" (1995, 239). Conn McCluskey similarly describes the marches' "sad but impressive turnouts, the women in their Sunday best, children walking and in prams" (in Keenan-Thomson 2009, 214).

The prams and children are used in these different accounts as markers of what made the protestors distinctive, the symbols of motherhood made visible as they took to the streets to protest against housing injustice. There is a note of pride in the women's accounts, while McCluskey's account appears to use the prams almost as something with which to dismiss the women's cause. Shannon sees the display as part of the expression of the women's "assertiveness on this fundamental right to adequate housing," which "was in stark contrast to the irredentist rhetoric and abstentionist profile that had characterised the local nationalist councillors as well as the six Nationalist members at Stormont for years" (1995, 239). Keenan-Thomson, in contrast, takes a more pessimistic view, arguing that the form of the marches demonstrates that the women had "internalized a class-based and patriarchal interpretation of their position in Northern Irish politics" in which housing was only a women's issue by virtue of their role as wives and mothers (2009, 222).

Shannon outlines further instances of everyday political activism undertaken by women in the early days of the conflict: the devising of homemade gas masks from nappies soaked in lemon juice, vinegar, and water as the police attacked communities with tear gas; Eileen Doherty's conversion of her William Street flat into a makeshift cafeteria during the Battle of the Bogside; the banging of dustbin lids to warn of the army approaching; and the women who in July 1970 traveled to the lower Falls Road area in Belfast from other parts of the city during the British Army curfew "with supplies of badly needed bread and milk for their friends and relatives" (Shannon 1995, 243). Though from some perspectives these acts could be seen as largely auxiliary, solidifying women's status as confined to the domestic sphere, there is a certain radicalism on show here. There has been a limited space allowed for such activities in the public memorializing of conflict in Northern Ireland; images and footage of women kneeling outside terraces as they bang lids, for example, have become particularly iconic and are used in exhibitions, murals, and documentaries. Arguably, however, this is tokenistic and an example of what Sara McDowell describes as a process in which "the multiple experiences of women in Northern Ireland continue to be either obscured or male-defined" (2008, 338). All of the above examples of protest suggest the domestic life of women, but objects are brought out onto the streets, used in acts of resistance, and private spaces are made into explicit sites of political refuge, solidarity, and support. They show us, in Shannon's words, "what ordinary women have done, individually, collectively, and usually outside the official and public patriarchal structures, to protect and to minimise the impact of political violence on their families and communities" (1995, 242). As such, the highly gendered divisions between the home and the street are blurred and demonstrate that the "discrete categorizing of space into public and private, and the assumed privacy of the house are untenable" (B. Reid 2007, 935).

This militant show of domesticity and motherhood can, of course, be found in other contexts. In Argentina, high-profile protests by the Madres of the Plaza de Mayo brought out onto the streets an explicitly politicized form of motherhood. During the country's military dictatorship, women began a campaign of weekly marches in the square outside the presidential office, demanding information about the whereabouts of their children who had been "disappeared" by the regime. A crucial aspect of the protest was the "performance of mothers as activists" (Taylor 1997, 185), achieved through, for example, the white head-scarves they wore, which were originally made from children's cloth nappies.[2] Diana Taylor comments on the radicalism of the Madres' protests, pointing out that "traditionally, mothers have been idealized as existing somehow beyond or above the political arena" (Taylor 1997, 185). The positioning of motherhood and the home beyond the realm of politics was fundamentally challenged by the Madres of the Plaza de Mayo, as it was by the women of the Homeless Citizens' League. This "engagement with the everyday fabric" (McDowell and Switzer 2011, 86) is an example of what de Certeau calls "making do" and creatively using the structures of everyday life for the purposes of resistance (1988, xv). Further, in making these symbols of domesticity visible, the women invite us to turn our attention to the home and to make it part of stories of conflict and fights against injustice.

WHOSE COMMEMORATION?

The contentions of commemoration are sewn into the very fabric of Northern Ireland. How do we commemorate what happened in the home and make it part of the story of the Troubles? Where is the language for this? How do we commemorate the past at all when so much remains contentious about what that past actually is? Exploring the genealogy of commemoration in the run-up to the fiftieth anniversary of the Easter Rising in 1966, Margaret O'Callaghan points out that "acts of unionist political and cultural commemoration were inscribed in the public and private spaces of Northern Ireland from its foun-dation" (Daly and O'Callaghan 2007, 87). In their exploration of the role of heritage in Northern Ireland, Elizabeth Crooke and Tom Maguire point out how commemoration of unionist identity was embedded in the very structures of government: "In the first decades of the new Northern Ireland, unionist identity was consolidated around the creation of buildings for governance, statues and rituals" (2018, 4). In this climate, commemoration became a way for groups to express an affiliation either with the unionist founding myth of the state or with the "rebellious" nationalist/republican narrative. The strug-gles over the anniversary in 1966 exacerbated this split, with battles taking place between unionists and republican leaders over ownership of various sites of remembrance. In those cases, commemoration centered on cemeter-ies, Gaelic Athletic Association (GAA) grounds, and town halls (R. Higgins 2012, 91), arguably very specific types of spaces that sanction particular public male identities. The use of memorials to publicly lay claim to "a side" became more pronounced and highly charged during the conflict itself, with events and spaces often becoming sites or targets of violence. Since the end of the Troubles the "two tribes" narrative is still very much in evidence in the commemorative landscape, while efforts to go beyond these binary versions and commemorate all victims collectively have, as McDowell and Switzer write, "been fraught with controversy" (2011, 82).

In many instances, commemorations in Northern Ireland are given a specific flavor by the everyday contexts in which they occur—in streets, on the gable ends of houses, and on blocks of apartments—which in turn makes these spaces into "a venue for conflict of another kind" (McDowell and Switzer 2011, 82). In their exploration of the "intensively memorialized" landscape in Derry's Bogside, McDowell and Switzer describe the stories, struggles, and power dynamics embodied by these practices. They outline the ways in which big symbolic narratives interact with, and in some cases obstruct, more prosaic, everyday occurrences: the maintenance and improvement of properties by the Housing Executive, for example (2011, 92). McDowell and Switzer's work thus points to something that is often overlooked in discussions of murals in Northern Ireland: that they are painted on houses, places of residence, in which people's everyday lives take place. The physical edifice of the home, in this landscape, embodies a kind of tension between public and private stories. The home projects signs of collective resistance and identity into the public world through flags and murals (B. Reid 2007, 943), becoming a symbolic object in the landscape. In the process, however, the domestic, emotional, and physical labor that takes place inside is concealed by these commemorative functions. There is very little documented, for example, about the views and experiences of those who live inside such houses.

It is not only the experiences of women in the home that are not seen in historical narratives, of course. The stories told on the outside of these houses have various tropes in common, with the imagery used in both republican and loyalist murals often militaristic and hypermasculine (McDowell 2008, 336). In her study of the gendered nature of Northern Irish commemoration, McDowell quotes several women who object to the violent and male-dominated nature of the images that define their physical surroundings and points out that the "one female narrative" present during her study of murals in the Lower Shankhill was a commemoration of the life of Princess Diana. Queen Elizabeth II is another female frequently used in loyalist imagery, the monarch being of central importance to the loyalist story. Women are used for particular rhetorical purposes in these cultural narratives: Mother Ireland is a symbolic figure to be fought for, while the Queen, and Princess Diana, are figures to be loyal to. Often women are presented as victims, without agency. In recent years, there has been a growing amount of research on women activists during the Troubles, pointing out how their actions were overshadowed and blocked by patriarchal power structures (see Aretxaga 1997; Corcoran 2004; Potter and MacMillan 2008). When women's roles as activists or combatants *are* commemorated, they are often used in the service of bigger male narratives, as Graff-McRae and Rooney show, or presented as exceptional cases, not the norm (Margaret Ward 1989, 1). In the case of the 1981 hunger strikes, Emilie Pine points out that the memorializing of the male strikers began before they had even died, and since their death the imagery of these male faces and bodies has "become shorthand for the sacrifice they made and the armed conflict they died in the name of" (Pine 2010, 103). This iconography is still much in evidence throughout republican areas in Northern Ireland.

These are all examples of what Rooney calls a preoccupation with the "arena of 'power politics,' with the personalities, political parties and armed groups involved" (Rooney 2007) gesturing to broader difficulties with representing women in the region's history. This is a discourse in which certain types of activities are hailed as worthy of attention while others are not, and in which concerns about gender, including the emotional work performed by women both during and after the conflict, do not figure.

Margaret Ward writes that "women in Northern Ireland have been vital in maintaining some semblance of 'normality' throughout years of devastating conflict" (Ward 2005, 4; see also McWilliams 1997, 78). Such normality was sustained by a great deal of emotional work performed by women in the home, through, for example, feeding and caring for family members and supporting imprisoned relatives. A report produced by the Women's Resource and Development Agency (WRDA) in 2007, when Ward was director of the organization, highlighted the absence of women's voices in post-conflict Northern Ireland and drew attention to the range of domestic experiences that have affected women during and after the Troubles. Through interview and testimony, the report put forward the accounts of women who are ignored in the service of or overshadowed by those "power politics" narratives. The experience of "worry," for example, recurred in women's accounts in relation to male relatives. One woman, the daughter of a male republican activist, described the counseling she was getting to help her deal with her past and the anger she felt toward her father for being "able to fight for country but not for me" (WRDA 2007, 12).

In Northern Ireland, this emotional work is stripped of its political dimensions by sentimentalized narratives about the home. When such work *is* referenced in mainstream political discourse, it is often in fetishized or idealized forms. Politicians might thank their partners in public, for example, as when Gerry Adams paid gushing tribute to his wife Colette in his final speech to the Ard Fheis as Sinn Féin leader in November 2017: "Finally, my thanks to Colette. I have been very lucky. We are now married forty-seven years. There have been ups and downs—the Prison Ship Maidstone, Belfast Prison, Long Kesh, the H-Blocks and years of life on the run. But love has prevailed over everything life has thrown at us" (Adams 2017). Adams acknowledges in slightly vague terms the strain his republican activity exerted on his marriage but, ultimately, resorts to the clichéd phrase "love has prevailed." The rhetoric here, by no means atypical of such a speech, largely elides any sense of the work—the discussion and negotiation—all this must surely have generated in his and Colette's relationship. Aretxaga points out that republican women's responses to the incarceration of their husbands was often far more ambivalent than is commonly acknowledged in such rhetoric. Despite this, however, and despite "the serious emotional and material hardship" faced by these women, "the ideology of unconditional love was, and still is, projected onto the wives" (Aretxaga 1997, 119).

Some of these tendencies in nationalist culture can be traced back to the figures of Mother Ireland and the Virgin Mary, both, in different ways, symbols of maternal suffering (Aretxaga 1997, 108). In loyalist culture, there exist powerful stereotypes around the "proper" role of women in domestic life, as wives and mothers, which downplay or oversimplify their political agency (see R. Ward 2002; Potter 2008; McEvoy 2009). One way to puncture these sentimentalized versions of women's lives is by paying an uncompromising attention to the specific material realities of women in their homes, not as idealized wife and mother figures but as individuals with a variety of concerns—intellectual, emotional, economic, political, and psychological.

Jeanette Ervine gives an insight into some of the gendered labor that sustained male political activity, this time from a wife's perspective and in much more granular, less idealized form. Here, she is interviewed for an RTÉ documentary in 2010; she talks about her husband David's membership in the UVF, and the conversations they had when he was released from prison: "I was angry with him because I felt that I never would have made a decision that would have affected both our lives so profoundly. I would never have done that to him, and I felt that he shouldn't have done it to me. . . . I made it clear to him—if it ever happened again—that I wouldn't be standing by him. I wouldn't put my children and myself through that" (cited in Parr 2018, 206). Ervine's account shows the physical and emotional toll that her husband's paramilitary activity had on her and her children; she explicitly describes the anger she felt and the conversations she had with him about this. Her version of events here is a corrective to the simplified and sentimentalized narratives offered by those such as Adams and throws light on some of the hidden experiences of women in positions such as hers.

A PLACE APART

None of this is to essentialize the gendered binaries of public and private; rather it is to unearth the labor that male public political cultures in Northern Ireland have exploited and depended on. Making these spaces visible, as shown in the example of the Homeless Citizens' League, is a radical act. Susan Fraiman's study of domesticity makes a striking case for why we must pay attention to the home: "The point, of course, is to stress that domesticity doesn't just lie there, isn't a given, can't be taken for granted. Someone (probably female) does it. Someone (feminized if not female) produces several meals a day, a place to sleep, a degree of cleanliness and order, and perhaps a touch of beauty" (Fraiman 2017, 24). Efforts have been made by feminists to explicitly politicize this plane of domestic labor; one of the most prominent in Britain was led by Selma James in the 1970s, in which she drew attention to the dependency of male political and economic activity on women's work in the home and demanded "Wages For Housework" (James 1972). In an examination of the home as a site of resistance in African American political struggle, bell hooks stresses that it is possible to critique the gendered binaries of public and private at the same time as recognizing women's work in the domestic sphere: "Contemporary black struggle must honor this history of service just as it must critique the sexist definition of service as women's 'natural' role" (1991, 384). While one must be careful not to draw crude parallels between the plight of African American and Irish women, hooks provides us with a useful vocabulary and framework with which to address the status of working-class women in Northern Ireland and the political significance of their activity in the home.

Women's domestic lives have been set aside as a "discursive 'place apart'" (Rooney 2008, 461). In this context, the woman is a symbol and object to be paid tribute to but not to be seen in any real sense. Making visible the labor that takes place within the home asserts its position as a political space. I have already outlined some of the challenges of inserting the home into the story of conflict in Northern Ireland, relating to tribal narratives and the masculinist nature of commemoration. When analyzing the contexts in which women's experiences in the home are or are not seen, it is also useful to think about how historical events are understood and constructed through cultural remembrance and commemoration.

In his recent study of "social forgetting" in Ulster, Guy Beiner warns against reading commemorative practices too literally: "Studies of cultural memory too readily assume that any representation of the past—whether appearing in writing or as a monument—is an indication of memory. Yet, memory is not actually stored in these lifeless artifacts. Historical remembrance is generated by the interactions of readerships and audiences with such representations" (2018, 33). Beiner invites us to interrogate what such representations do, and what histories they conceal, and to think more broadly about the ways they function in the memory landscape for the people who interact with them. This analysis can be applied to the examples already mentioned: the murals, exhibits, and politicians' tributes, which arguably provide monolithic versions of the past, centered around particular individuals, and "forgetting" other stories and experiences in the process.

As Crooke and Maguire write, public stories have been informed by the struggles for power between the two "polarised identities" in Northern Ireland, which has led different groups to "suppress many of the distinctions within their own communities to maintain their hegemony . . . ignoring or recuperating very different forms of heritage or insisting on the primacy of specific interpretations of the past within their communities" (Crooke and Maguire, 2018, 6). We have seen that these specific interpretations often exclude women, and women in the private sphere especially, and reveal what McDowell calls "a past and present shaped and defined overwhelmingly by men" (2008, 336). In an essay published in 2018, Laura McAtackney draws on and updates some of McDowell's themes in relation to gendered commemorative practices in post-conflict Northern Ireland, examining the role of "bottom up" community memorials and exploring some more recent attempts to include women in the commemorative landscape. One such attempt was a sculpture titled *Mother, Daughter, Sister* unveiled in 2015 on Belfast's Sandy Row, in front of a loyalist mural commemorating King William of Orange and the Battle of the Boyne. The sculpture was the result of efforts by the Arts Council of Northern Ireland (ACNI) to reconfigure stories told about the past and "add . . . women to public space" and came about through workshops between artist Ross Wilson and local women "exploring themes of identity, reconciliation and peace" (ACNI in McAtackney 2018, 167).

While, as McAtackney says, "it is evident that the women of the community played a central role in conceiving the sculpture," she highlights that the anonymity of this female figure as a result of its symbolic function "follows a noticeable trajectory in representing women in conflict in a way that elides their experiences and roles" (2018, 167). Further, she argues that its setting means that the King William mural behind it is "effectively the frame and backdrop... and as such can only undercut the latter's role and intended meaning" (ibid). McAtackney's issues with *Mother, Daughter, Sister* point to broader problems with commemorative practices in Northern Ireland: namely the distillation of stories and experiences into singular figures, narratives, or objects and the viewing of women's stories through the lens of male experience. Though the figure of Bernadette Devlin McAliskey has clearly not been anonymized in the way that the woman in this sculpture is, it could be argued that she serves a similar symbolic function in many representations of 1968–1969. There is an absence of specificity in such representations that glosses over the daily realities of women's lives. In 1989, Margaret Ward described this absence of women from public historical consciousness thus: "Because women have been so marginal in the consciousness of researched events, their significance has remained hidden within historical records, waiting for the understanding of someone who wants to know what women did, what they thought, and how they were affected by the upheavals of the past century" (1989, 2).

To enable such specificity, it is necessary to broaden our ideas of the past and think in terms of pluralized "histories" rather than one singular "history," an idea advanced in the Irish context by, among others, Beiner (2018, 5) and also by Helen Cammock, the artist behind *The Long Note* (Cammock 2018). In these versions, history becomes about more than singular iconic events or individuals and can also focus on everyday, localized struggles. Such democratic histories could be used to bring the stories of women's lives in domestic spaces into discussions of conflict in Northern Ireland.

WHOSE JUSTICE?

As we have seen, the cultural narratives surrounding events of the Troubles in Northern Ireland provide limited reference points for talking about the experiences of women, particularly in the home. In this context the actions of the HCL, in inserting domestic symbols and private lives into public protest, are radical, unsettling as they do such rigid frameworks of understanding conflict and demanding that we turn our attention to the home. In redirecting our attention, we must think about the home's gendered politics and power dynamics and, in particular, inequality, concerns that are very much present in contemporary Northern Ireland. One condition of the more representative, pluralistic history called for by those such as Beiner and Cammock is the acceptance of such issues. Here, the received truths around certain hegemonic community narratives on both "sides" may have to be questioned and those hitherto perceived as "heroes" may have this status taken away.

A denial of the home as a political space means a denial of the significance of what takes place inside it. Activities that take place in the home are many and varied, of course, but they include issues such as domestic violence, struggles with mental health, and economic hardship. Feminist commentators and activists in the voluntary sector continue to point out the endurance of these problems in the lives of women. In their 2016 *Women's Manifesto*, for example, the WRDA pointed to the high rates of domestic violence reported to the Police Service of Northern Ireland in 2014–2015 and expressed concerns about underreporting of such crimes and the low rate of prosecutions (Women's Resource and Development Agency 2016). Monica McWilliams wrote in 1997 about the specific ways that women had been affected by domestic violence during the Troubles (McWilliams, 1997), and there are powerful personal testimonies about this in the WRDA's 2007 report. All of these accounts highlight the particular problems with reporting such crimes for women, especially in nationalist communities, where trust in the police was—and in some cases continues to be—very low, but also because perpetrators in both communities may well have been powerful political or paramilitary figures. With regard to mental health, tranquilizer use was notoriously widespread during the conflict—in 1980 Ward and McGivern reported that there were 35 million tranquilizers consumed every year in the province, with twice as many women using them as men (1980, 67)—and mental health problems in post-conflict Northern Ireland continue to have gendered manifestations (see Mental Health Society 2016). These examples demonstrate the impact of the conflict on the safety of women and on their emotional, psychological, and physical well-being "behind closed doors." To turn our attention to the home and make these experiences part of conflict memory inevitably raises difficult questions about gendered power relations.

The idea of justice is crucial when thinking about how memory and commemoration works and in whose interests. Graham Dawson connects memory and commemoration in Northern Ireland to campaigns such as the Bloody Sunday Justice Campaign and the Border Victims' Group; in these contexts, he examines the power of "shared/common memories" to be "woven together into a narrative which is both widely held and publicly expressed," in turn having political impact and affecting change (Dawson 2007, 53). A 2017 roundtable exchange between memory studies scholars and artists on the subject of "Moving Memory" for an *Irish University Review* special issue raised related themes.

In this discussion, Dawson's work and his concept of "reparative remembering" were raised, with Ann Rigney observing that "suffering has dominated public memory culture since at least World War One." Rigney suggested that "memory studies has been largely invested in salvaging, highlighting, and analysing different forms of historical injustice" ("Moving Memory" 2017, 238). If we think about the experiences of women outlined above and how they have been "brushed under the carpet," in the words of one of the WRDA report's participants (2007, 16), it becomes clear that these notions of suffering and injustice do not yet apply in any widespread sense to what happens to women in the home in Northern Ireland. These issues have been the object of study of feminist commentators during and after the conflict but have yet to take hold in popular consciousness.

This is, in part, due to the "two traditions" approach both in understanding the conflict and in thinking through its resolution; in this approach, identities that exist in intersection either with or outside of sectarian identities are squeezed out of Troubles narratives. It is an analysis that overlooks the ways in which such traditions "are not merely cultural, they represent relations of power and domination" (Sales 1997, 53) and in which "violence against the female has largely been overshadowed by sectarian violence" (Evans cited in Steele 2004, 107). These arguments pose a threat to masculinist narratives, especially as in some cases certain "key players" on both sides of the community may have been implicated in gendered abuses, which have, in the past, not been dealt with (Graff-McRae 2010, 8). This in turn raises questions about what counts as "justice" in post-conflict Northern Ireland (Ashe 2015). As Beiner writes, "'Dealing with the Past' is still a very heated topic in Northern Ireland and, in the absence of consensus on what to remember in public, consideration of forgetting becomes an even more loaded and sensitive issue" (2018, 33). Domestic activity exists in the context of such forgetting; it is hidden from public narratives, viewed as separate to politics or as a backdrop occasionally acknowledged, through, for example, the platitudes of politicians like Adams, and there remain few public frameworks through which experiences in the home can be understood.

CONCLUSION

Making the home integral to Northern Ireland's story poses many challenges in the current political landscape. From a social justice perspective, to bring domestic experience into remembrance practices necessarily raises difficult questions about sexism, gendered power relations, and the economic position of women, showing the "forms of concealment that constitute and govern public discourse" (Rooney 2007, 3). It also invites us to interrogate the nature of public memory, how it is constructed, in whose interests and for what purposes. The private nature of experiences in the home does perhaps inescapably clash with what we commonly understand as commemoration, linked as it is with a "group" story, cause, or campaign. But we should welcome the chance to rethink our ideas of how and what we remember. As Pine points out, "if the Irish past is still a contested space . . . the act of contestation can be a positive force, helping us to know our past better" (2010, 2). It has become commonly recognized that the stories we tell about the past are a reflection of our concerns in the present: perhaps by telling some of these stories of the home these concerns can be forced into public consciousness. Describing the work of domesticity publicly valorizes this work; by seeking out domestic accounts and listening to them, we can make this a part of what is important in the past and present of Northern Ireland.

NOTES

1. For more on women's housing activism, see Keenan-Thomson (2010), on the Springtown protests in Derry, and Ward and McGivern (1980), on the Turf Lodge Flat and Maisonettes Action Committee.

2. A further instance of militant motherhood can be found in the protests organized by journalist and community activist Jane Jacobs against the plan by city planner Robert Moses to put a road through Washington Square, available at https://www.thevillager.com/2017/06/flashback-to-the-50s-and -heroic-moms-protest/, accessed March 18, 2019.

ELI DAVIES is a writer and PhD researcher at Ulster University, exploring the relationship between gender, memory, literature, and the Troubles in Northern Ireland. She completed an M.Phil. in Irish Literature at Trinity College Dublin in 2003 and between then and 2016 worked as an adult education teacher, writer, and editor. She has written on popular culture, literature, and politics for various publications and is coeditor of *Under My Thumb: Songs That Hate Women and the Women Who Love Them*, an anthology of women's music writing published by Repeater.

SIXTEEN

—w—

HONEST COMMEMORATION

Reconciling Women's "Troubled" and "Troubling" History in Centennial Ireland

LINDA CONNOLLY

IRELAND IS IN THE THROES of a decade of commemoration. The process of commemorating the tumultuous revolutionary events that led to the establishment of the Irish state a century ago has incorporated government sponsorship of events, public debate, cultural interventions, and exciting new academic scholarship on the period of revolution. The outputs of the first stage of the government's official Decade of Centenaries program 1912–1916—including conferences, books, studies, concerts, documentaries, public events, and drama—were most impressive (Decade of Centenaries, 2020a). The national commemoration of the Easter Rising of 1916, for instance, was notable for its sensitive and rich cultural content. In the arena of scholarship, access to new historical sources including those available free and online (such as the Bureau of Military History collection) as well as academic engagement projects (such as the Women of the South Project in the Farmgate Café in Cork's English Market (Women of the South 2016) have inspired a new generation of interdisciplinary scholars to study the Irish Revolution and generated a new conception of "public history."[1] The second phase of the program, for 1917–1922, covers the War of Independence, the Civil War, and the partition of the island in the state's formation, north and south. This stage also included a series of events to mark the hundred-year anniversary of votes for women in 2018 (Vótáil 100, 2018). Building on earlier work (such as Margaret Ward 1995), new academic scholarship on the achievement of votes for women and the critical role women played in the Irish revolutionary period has emerged in the decade of centenaries (Pašeta 2013; McDiarmid 2015). The Irish government's Vótail 100 program also commemorated women's participation in institutional politics in the course of the past century in a number of events and a pop-up museum representing women's history through ephemera, which was curated by Sinéad McCoole.

However, disturbing scandals and historical abuses in women's lives have also come to light in Ireland in the past twenty years and in the midst of these initiatives. Recent research has addressed the neglected question of the violence women experienced (including forced hair cutting/shearing and sexual assault) in the period covering the War of Independence and the Civil War—addressing the thorny question of violence against women perpetrated by members of the national army (L. Connolly 2019). The violence of the revolution was not just a war between men, and this new research consolidates a more complete picture of women's experience during and after the revolution. Traumatic stories of incarceration and institutional abuses that were also prevalent in the period of revolution have emerged, primarily through public inquiries, investigative journalism, and survivor testimony in more recent decades. O'Sullivan and O'Donnell (2012) provide an overview of the incarceration of tens of thousands of men, women, and children during the first fifty years of Irish independence. Psychiatric hospitals, mother and baby homes,[2] Magdalene laundries, and reformatory and industrial schools formed a network of institutions of "coercive confinement" that was integral to the emerging state. Historical injustices that were perpetrated in state-funded, religious-run institutions in Ireland and concealed at the time have been documented in a number of state inquiries and reports, including the Ryan Report of 2009, the McAleese Report of 2013, and the Report of the Commission of Inquiry into the Mother and Baby Homes of 2019. In a move indicative of the impact of this documentation, in 2013, as a result of the McAleese Report, the Irish government apologized to the women who were incarcerated in Magdalene laundries that existed until the late twentieth century.[3]

As Shelton notes, "History is replete with episodes of genocide, slavery, torture, forced conversions, and mass expulsions of peoples" (2019). States and societies throughout the world are regularly asked to account for historic abuses and provide redress to victims, with some of these historical injustices involving events occurring a century or more ago. In Ireland, this applies to the large-scale system of institutionalization and to the traumatic legacies of the past that continue to exist—outside of the official state commemoration program—in present-day narratives of survivors of injustice who are reflecting on and participating in political and legal actions seeking redress and retribution. This chapter provides a critical overview of the commemoration process in Ireland, examining the role of women's history and feminism in the decade's events. After considering the relationship between "history" and commemoration and outlining key issues in Irish women's history, this essay proposes an alternative approach to commemoration concerned with historical accountability and truthful remembering capable of including profound injustices and abuses of power that occurred in their own time and that are a disruptive element of the present. The concept of historical accountability can be understood in different ways, including in terms of "giving an account" of oppression, violence, or brutalization by conducting methodologically sound, evidence-based research, and as "being accountable" in scholarship to groups or individuals ignored, eclipsed, and excluded from generalized accounts of society and the collective memory of nations. The analysis provided in this chapter suggests that historical accountability should be a more central consideration in a program of national commemoration claiming to address difficult questions about the past.

THE DECADE OF CENTENARIES: COMMEMORATION OR HISTORY?

The relationship between academic history writing and commemoration has been subject to a degree of scrutiny both during the decade of centenaries and more generally in the interdisciplinary field of memory studies (Frawley 2010–2012, 2014; Pine 2010, 2020; Beiner 2018). The public commemoration of the 1916 Rising was one of the first major events in the state's program. Numerous public commentators during 2016 attempted to both define the role of the commemoration of the 1916 Rising from the perspective of "professional history" and interpret the Rising itself, assessing its origins, impact, and revolutionary scale, in particular. The prominent public role of academic history writing and historians during the decade of commemorations is palpable. Rankean historiography, which seeks to ground history writing in unimpeachable facts based on sources close to the event or person whose history was being written, is still an important principle in Irish history writing. If the relevant sources cannot be found, then scholars cannot write "scientific history." As R. Higgins argues (2012), however, there is a clear disjunction between commemoration / commemorative practice and this interpretation of history. Similarly, as Edward Madigan writes, "We should remind ourselves at the outset that historians, academic or otherwise, hold no monopoly on the interpretation of the past, and that there are many ways in which we can learn about and confront the events our ancestors lived through . . . while there should ideally be as much interaction between history and commemoration, we should recognize emphatically that they are not the same thing" (Madigan 2013, 1–2). Undoubtedly the integrity of "the past," which professional historians are trained to reconstruct primarily through the prism of texts, archival sources, and oral history, counts for a great deal so that, among other things, the politics of the present is not flagrantly employed to provide a completely distorted view of what actually happened in 1916, the subsequent revolutionary years, and post-independence decades.

Evidence-based research is clearly essential to reconstructing historical experience. The craft of analyzing data and evidence, however, always brings to bear an interpretation that is framed by the author's standpoint and theoretical disposition. As Tom Dunne (1992) has suggested, history writing produces a particular kind of text, one shaped as much by the politics of the writer as by established conventions in regard to evidence and debate.

Alongside greater acknowledgment that the writing of Irish history has always been selective, the danger of historians creating "myths" for political ends in moments of commemoration has also been rehearsed, including in John Regan's text *Myth and the Irish State* (2014). Regan's text provided a critical interpretation of a select range of historiographical debates and "myths" that have shaped and divided the canon of Irish history over time, focusing in particular on the role of the Troubles in Northern Ireland as a key political fault line. However, a myth that historical arguments about the past only take place between men and historians more interested in the masculine attributes of the state must not be perpetuated either. There is much further charged debate to be had about the "rights and wrongs of our history" (the title of a robust 2014 review of Regan's book in the *Irish Times* by Diarmaid Ferriter), but this includes in relation to the difficult position of women in Irish history, which gets negligible mention in Regan's text.

Historiography combines the study of historians and historical method. The writing and construction of Irish history throughout the twentieth century was undoubtedly selective, partial, incomplete, and ideological in relation to women's history and gender inequality: a history that was predominantly about one gender was clearly deficient. E. H. Carr, in the 1961 George Macaulay Trevelyan lectures on the theme "What Is History?" sought to undermine the idea that historians enjoy a sort of unquestionable objectivity and authority over the history they study. Likewise, feminist scholars and historians challenged this view by critiquing the gender bias of mainstream histories, which was (and still is) reflected in the absence of women in senior positions in the profession. The exclusion of women from key tomes and anthologies in other disciplines seeking to define canons (such as the *Field Day Anthology of Irish Writing*) was also a source of contention in Irish studies at this time. Carr, in common with feminist scholars, challenged the idea that the privileged historian was in any sort of commanding position, "like a general taking a salute" (Carr 1961). Feminist scholars embarked on the critical task of recovery work in women's history from the 1980s and gradually claimed their rightful place in understanding and elucidating the past.

Alongside the historian's critique of a tendency to create false myths about the past for present political ends in contemporary politics (Regan 2014), a number of other "dangers" associated with historical writing at a time of commemoration have been pointed out in public interventions, including by Anne Dolan and Ronan Fanning. As part of a series of articles in the *Irish Times* on the decade of centenaries, in "Commemorating 1916: How Much Does the Integrity of the Past Count?" Dolan examined the "limited role" (2015) of professional history by pointing out the gap and distinction between commemoration—as a broader social and political process of the wider national collectivity, the state—and the scholarly principles and task of "history" as practiced and envisaged by prominent professional historians. Dolan, echoing R. Higgins's earlier analysis (2012), argued: "But when has commemoration ever truly been about history? The memorial events for the 50th anniversary of the Easter Rising told us more about 1966 than they did about 1916, and 2016's efforts are not likely to be different" (Dolan 2015).

Ronan Fanning, in the same series, cautioned against debunking established (or perhaps the *establishment's?*) views of the past at a time of remembrance by engaging in what he termed *endless "whatifism"*: "There is a real risk that the commemoration of the Rising will degenerate into a self-indulgent exercise in whatiffery: that the recognition of the importance of what happened in 1916 will be diluted by the unhistorical obsessions of the crystal-gazers with what might have happened if the Rising had not taken place" (Fanning 2015). But the role of scholars at a time of widespread public commemoration is not *just* to look back, remember, and assess the relative magnitude of events as they actually took place, or to protect an "established" view while never asking "what if" questions. The past is not *pure* or resolved once it has been written up. Public commemorations also raise questions about the impact of unequal power, experience of marginalized groups, and selective memory. Guy Beiner (2018), for example, has explored the nature and impact of "social forgetting"— where communities apparently attempt to obscure, erase, and otherwise leave behind certain events from their past. In addition, historical interpretation cannot stand still or be sealed in an airtight vault once it has been written by its preliminary masters and professoriate. There are too many unanswered and airbrushed questions in Irish history writing thus far to arrive at such a safe/assured view—and too many state inquiries into historical injustices and abuses that require much more evidence/excavation. A key problem is that women would never have been written into Irish history had "what if" questions not been asked by pioneering women's historians and feminist scholars (and indeed local historians outside academic institutions) from the 1980s on (Margaret Ward 1995). One entirely valid question, for instance, is *what* would Irish history look like *if* women had been properly included in the prevailing narrative of twentieth-century professional history writing: should a history that managed for such a long time to effectively exclude and minimize half the population not be fundamentally rewritten, rethought, and *revised*?

The rewriting of women into Irish history in recent decades was not just ideology as originally implied; it was, rather, a necessary *scholarly* corrective to the received history being incomplete, gender biased, and partial. In addition, methodological and ethical issues concerning accountability arose. Why were women's lives and experience excluded from the historiography of the Irish revolution (a key focus of the decade of centenaries) and assessment of its aftermath for such a long period of time? The occlusion and exclusion of women from the dominant historical narrative was perhaps, instead, an inevitable consequence of the gendered bias of arguments about historical purity and authority (Fanning 2015) and, undoubtedly, not enough "whatifism," especially if we shift our focus to historical accountability and a history of some of the more profound *injustices* evidenced in Irish women's lives. As Cheryl Glenn writes, "Writing women (or any other traditionally disenfranchised group) into the history of rhetoric, then, can be an ethically and intellectually responsible gesture that disrupts those frozen memories in order to address silences, challenge absences, and assert women's contributions to public life" (2000, 387). Beyond commemorating the Irish revolution and the establishment of the Republic as a set of political institutions and as a "Free State," an excision of deeply troubling silences and secrets buried in Irish women's lives and collective experience is occurring. State-led commemorations clearly link past and present narratives in a manner that is not benign or purely ceremonial and this requires further elucidation in relation to gender and historical injustices at the current conjunction.

COMMEMORATION AND WOMEN

As was the case in many other "revolutions," an elite class of men both took the credit for the revolution that deposed British rule in the Republic and assumed state power in its aftermath. Women had played critical roles as revolutionaries before independence. Yet the Catholic Church and new Irish State created a social and political order in which women were explicitly and progressively marginalized in public life and in the law after 1922—a marginalization duplicated in the main content of historical scholarship right up to the 1980s in Ireland. By the 1980s, however, a new wave of women's history writing and feminist theory in effect flourished alongside the vociferous revisionist and nationalist debates that divided Irish studies (L. Connolly 2004).

Recovery work conducted since the 1980s has generated important analysis into previously neglected questions in women's lives. As women's historians and other scholars have by now widely documented (Beaumont 1999; Connolly 2003), one of the travesties of the post-independence period of nation building was the marginal role the church and state afforded to women as full and equal citizens in a range of arenas, despite their significant achievement of the vote in 1918. Historical scholarship in recent decades has widely demonstrated that (some) women were to varying degrees afforded an active public role in the revolutionary process in 1916 but were systematically marginalized in the private sphere in the decades after independence. As Beaumont (1999) has demonstrated, even though women in the post-independence era were acutely marginalized by church-state policies, laws, and censorship, they were also active agents in that same history—including in the private sphere of home and in the public realm of activism, work, and politics. The 1937 constitution stated, and still states, that women by their "life" (as opposed to by their "work") in the home give to the state a support without which the common good cannot be achieved. A cool and dispassionate historical interpretation of this clause suggests that it simply reflects the social order of the day. Women were in reality confined to the sphere of the home and family; feminists of the time were "exceptional" and marginal women who did not reflect the overall experience of Irish women. Some even argue that the 1937 clause actually gave value to the stem family model on which Irish society was premised[4] and in which women occupied a central (even powerful) role as mothers—ergo the fundamental role of history was seen and accepted as describing society as it was.

But to describe society within a generalization as to *how it was* is to first create an ideological version of the past that presumes society is always built on consent and social order. In addition, such a move fails to dissect the underlying power dynamics on which society is structured and the resistances, differences, and conflicts within it. Describing a society in this way also failed to address the silences and oppressions of twentieth-century Ireland, examples of which later rocked Irish society in the 1980s and 1990s vis-à-vis the scale of institutional abuses and scandals that came to light.

The marginalization of women in the public sphere of paid work and politics in Irish society in the decades after independence was not the only issue airbrushed from the official historical narrative for decades. In recent years, it has become apparent that serious forms of abuse arising from institutionalized social control of women's sexuality and reproduction, including in coercive institutions, was also elided. Ireland has been rocked by the revelation of past institutional abuses, including in relation to the widespread institutionalization of unmarried pregnant women and their children in mother and baby homes that recorded excessive infant mortality rates, unorthodox burial practices, and high adoption rates. The *lessons of the past* should have real currency and importance in contemporary Ireland, not least in the arena of women's rights, at a time when the state has hosted a major centennial commemoration to mark one hundred years of female suffrage. A welcome outcome of the commemorative events, apart from the generation of burgeoning and exciting new literature on the revolution itself, should include, for example, critical reflection about gender issues, equal citizenship, and the kind of society Ireland is and has become one hundred years after suffrage was extended to women.

The stories of enforced institutionalization and mistreatment of "fallen" women in mother and baby homes, Magdalene laundries, and other institutions in Ireland throughout the twentieth century have been buried in largely unavailable records. In recent years, a litany of state inquiries and commissions has exposed the harsh reality of life in these institutions *retrospectively* through powerful survivor testimony and other academic evidence. Mandated by the Irish state beginning in the eighteenth century, they were operated by various orders of the Catholic Church after independence until the last laundry closed in 1996. In 1993, an order of nuns in Dublin sold part of their Magdalene convent to a real estate developer. In order to develop the site for new housing, the remains of 155 inmates, buried in unmarked graves on the property, were exhumed, cremated, and buried elsewhere in a mass grave, triggering a public scandal in Ireland.

Focusing on the ten Catholic Magdalene laundries operating between 1922 and 1996, *Ireland's Magdalen Laundries and the Nation's Architecture of Containment* (Smith 2007) provided the first detailed history of women entering these institutions in the twentieth century. Smith described how the Magdalene laundries were workhouses in which many Irish women and girls were effectively imprisoned because they were perceived to be a threat to the moral fiber of society. Because the religious orders have not opened their archival records, Smith argues that Ireland's Magdalene institutions continue to exist in the public mind primarily at the level of *story* (cultural representation and survivor testimony) rather than *history* (archives and documents). The importance of interdisciplinary research using other methods, apart from traditional historical methods, was underlined in Smith's work and has been implemented in subsequent memory studies and oral history projects. Pioneering interdisciplinary work has resisted any impulse to write up the objective history of institutions as confined to the distant past and is as concerned with addressing manifestations of injustice, abuse of power, and reparation in the present. Pine, for instance, explores how recent cultural explorations of Ireland's history of institutional abuse have focused on buildings as ways of creating a commemorative space and ensuring through active spectatorship this abuse never happens again (2019).

Theoretically, the received understanding of the past century in Ireland can also be enhanced by more considered attention to sociological concepts such as "total institutions" (Goffman 1961) and Michel Foucault's conception of "disciplinary institutions" (1977). For Deleuze, following on from Foucault, discipline "cannot be identified with any one institution or apparatus, precisely because it is a type of power, a technology, that traverses every kind of apparatus or institution, linking them, prolonging them, and making them converge and function in a new way" (Deleuze 1988, 26). The cultural shift that for Foucault led to the predominance of incarceration of the body and the power over it directly applies to Ireland's history of institutionalization, where women considered sexually transgressive, "fallen," or a moral threat were institutionalized in large numbers, with their children removed from them (voluntarily and involuntarily) and adopted out in mother and baby homes. Disciplinary power and punishment is reflected in a series and web of interconnected institutions that existed in local communities and were sustained by the state.

The Commission of Investigation into Mother and Baby Homes and Certain Related Matters is the most recent Irish judicial commission of investigation, established in 2015 by an order of the Irish government. The commission was set up in the wake of individually researched claims by local historian Catherine Corless that the bodies of up to eight hundred babies and children may have been interred in an unmarked mass grave located in a sewer in the Bons Secours Mother and Baby Home in Tuam, County Galway. The remit of the commission also covered investigation into the records of and the practices at an additional thirteen mother and baby homes, including alleged adoption of children from these institutions without mothers' consent. Originally scheduled to issue a final report by February 2018, the commission was granted an extension and reported in April 2019. Profound injustices of the past experienced by Irish women will, therefore, continue to reemerge in the present and in the future through the medium of state inquiries, survivor testimony, and schemes to provide redress.

There are many questions to be asked about historical abuses and inequality in contemporary Ireland, some of which have been played out in the courts—a century after diverse groups of women both in Dublin and outside it assisted in the uprising of 1916, which had a clear vision of equality and gender at its ideological core. "The past" also continues to be intertwined with the state and society's record on women's reproductive rights in the arena of health, bodily autonomy, obstetrics, and motherhood. Twentieth-century scandals in relation to Irish maternity hospitals and many instances of systems failure in maternal health (including the death of Savita Halappanavar in a Galway hospital) are rooted in an institutional culture that historically has exercised systemic authority over women's bodies and reproduction, including in mother and baby homes. As feminist scholars have widely demonstrated, many suffrage campaigners in 1918 recognized the significance of achieving the vote but quickly moved on to a range of other campaigns and causes with unrelenting commitment. The important task of commemorating and remembering the granting of the vote for women, in centennial Ireland, should also consider Irish suffragists' continued desire for change beyond the vote and their unfinished cause, which continued in an active women's movement that has sustained and challenged patriarchy ever since (L. Connolly 2003).

Where does history begin and accountability end in a context where so many practices that damaged mothers and pregnant women persist in legal cases, state inquiries, redress schemes, and hospital scandals? The past is also frequently invoked as a central factor in cases of abuse that were excised from more recent state inquiries and court cases in contemporary Ireland. The "context of the times" was, for example, used in a 2015 case as an argument to deny adequate compensation to Irish victims of symphysiotomy, a painful medical alternative to caesarean sections that predominated in Ireland to encourage high fertility rates (McDonald 2015). A purely Rankean argument—that historians have a true capacity and the authority to represent the past "as it actually happened"—was deployed to suggest that doctors and nurses were merely operating in an era of profound Catholicism. This argument was also used in the courts to justify lesser compensation in the present for elderly women who were physically and psychologically damaged by a procedure long phased out in other Western countries (L. Connolly 2016). In the example of the case of symphysiotomy in the courts, historiography à la Ranke was invoked in the hearings by lawyers to shape a legal outcome. The "context of the time" argument thus successfully served the state and reflected in the legal case a close

relationship between established principles in "objective" historical scholar-
ship and institutional *power*. Historical abuses belong in their time (Catholic
Ireland of the 1940s–1980s), yet the UN Human Rights Committee report,
following the July 2014 questioning of an Irish government delegation led by
Minister for Justice Frances Fitzgerald about Ireland's compliance with the
International Covenant on Civil and Political Rights, stated that the "perpetrators" of symphysiotomy should be punished and prosecuted (Holland 2014).
On symphysiotomy, which was brought to the committee's attention for the
first time, it said: "The State party should initiate a prompt, independent and
thorough investigation into cases of symphysiotomy, prosecute and punish the
perpetrators, including medical personnel, and provide an effective remedy to
the survivors of symphysiotomy for the damage sustained, including fair and
adequate compensation and rehabilitation, on an individualized basis. . . . It
should facilitate access to judicial remedies by victims opting for the ex-gratia
scheme, including allowing a challenge to the sums offered to them under the
scheme" (in Holland 2014). The justification of this practice as historically
appropriate in the past, therefore, took precedence over an interpretation of
this practice as historically unjust, outdated, and damaging to women—which
it was.

The construction of gender and, more specifically, motherhood through
the lens of a historically acceptable church-state model of power has been vividly demonstrated in other scandals that have mired the state and wider body
politic and have incorporated the denial of basic human rights such as consent,
knowledge, and bodily integrity in life and death. Outside of the issues of the
mother and baby homes, numerous reproductive tragedies rooted in traditions
that stigmatized pregnancy outside marriage have dominated Irish political
debate since the 1980s. The death, in 1984, of fourteen-year-old Anne Lovett in
childbirth alongside her stillborn baby in a grotto in County Longford was a
profoundly tragic event. Moreover, Joanne Hayes, a single mother, was falsely
accused of a double infanticide in a tribunal of inquiry into what became known
as the "Kerry Babies" case in the same year.

From the 1970s on, reproductive rights entered the arena of national politics
with vigor. A battle for women to establish reproductive and bodily autonomy
by accessing legal contraception and abortions has been sustained for over four
decades. A referendum passed in 1983 was intended to copper-fasten a ban on
abortion in Ireland and to protect the right to life of the unborn at all costs in
Irish law and medical practice. Subsequently, it also became apparent that there
was an intention to deny women information on abortion elsewhere and the
right to travel to the UK for an abortion. The reference to women's "life" in the

Eighth Amendment to the Irish constitution was, however, later brought into sharp focus when a woman's life and death vis-à-vis motherhood and pregnancy was literally the subject of a Supreme Court case (Ms. P) conducted in the days before and after Christmas day 2014, concerning a brain dead pregnant mother who was left on a life support machine against her family's wishes.

In the period since the Eighth Amendment was introduced, numerous such individual women impacted by reproductive injustices have been the subjects of a range of litigation in both Irish and international courts (see Connolly forthcoming). The X case in 1992 involved the attorney general obtaining an injunction to stop a suicidal fourteen-year-old girl who was raped from traveling to the UK for an abortion. In the case of *A, B and C v. Ireland* in 2010, the European Court of Human Rights found that Ireland had violated the European Convention on Human Rights by failing to provide an accessible and effective procedure by which a woman can have established whether she qualifies for a legal abortion under Irish law. A number of cases related to whether an abortion was permissible in cases of fatal fetal abnormalities were also taken. Irish abortion law received worldwide attention when Savita Halappanavar died in 2012. She requested and was denied an abortion while suffering from septicemia during a miscarriage. The case of Ms. P in December 2014 particularly demonstrated the chaos that evolved from a combination of the long-standing lack of clear legislation to define the right to life of the mother with the lack of clarity about the rights of the unborn (Carolan 2016). The construction of a long-standing problematic version of gendered citizenship and women's bodies was confirmed by the Supreme Court to deny women and their families autonomy, consent, and dignity in the arena of maternal death prior to childbirth. P, a clinically dead pregnant woman, was kept on a life support machine to deleterious effect because of the Eighth Amendment to the constitution. The case of Y, who was an asylum seeker, underlined the additional problems the Eighth Amendment caused for women who were effectively barred from traveling outside Ireland in time for a termination or who were too sick to travel. In light of the problems being caused by the existence of the Eighth Amendment in obstetrics and the care of pregnant women, the constitutional and legislative abortion provisions were subsequently tabled and discussed at a series of Citizen's Assembly meetings in 2016 and 2017 and at a government-appointed committee in 2017, which recommended substantial reform. In a situation where the Eighth Amendment was increasingly representing a threat to women's maternal health during difficult pregnancies and miscarriages, the government ultimately proposed the thirty-sixth amendment of the constitution, which was passed in a referendum on May 25, 2018.

Such injustices of the past do not belong "in the past," therefore; they are continually emerging and reemerging in the present, having been buried, denied, and silenced.

CONCLUSION: WHAT IS IRELAND REMEMBERING?

For Irish women, 2018 was a very important year: the Eighth Amendment to the constitution was repealed and the granting of votes for women was marked in an official state-sponsored centenary. These events, exactly one hundred years apart, indicate social progress in key arenas of women's rights—votes and greater reproductive choice were fought hard for in feminist campaigns over years. And yet, as Fintan O'Toole has stated, "dark elements of our past" are also forces in our present (2019). Inconvenient truths in the case of institutionalized women disrupt any received sense of a linear historical narrative, where the past is definitely behind us, the present is what is being experienced, and the future is something yet to come.

Remembering and marking the centenary of votes for women in 2018 has been important in and of itself. However, the centenary of suffrage also raises many additional critical questions from the perspective of women. Women's social and political rights have a complex history in Ireland. Texts written by the historians and scholars of the Irish women's movement have cataloged in detail the achievements, difficulties, and legacy of a long campaign fought for Irish women's right to equal citizenship in several domains (see L. Connolly 2003; Ryan and Ward 2018). The persistence of gender inequality is evident, however, in several arenas including in the glaring underrepresentation of women in senior academic positions in Irish universities today. The percentage of female professors of history in Ireland is, for instance, notoriously low. Approximately 87 percent of all professors of history in Irish universities were men in 2018, yet women comprise a third of all the academic staff listed in history departments.[5] Women also remain vastly underrepresented in the Dáil and currently suspended Northern Irish Assembly, including at cabinet level, despite the introduction of gender quotas in the Republic to address a century-long problem of a very low percentage of women in politics. The fact that "change" has been so slow in academia, politics, and the media, for instance, suggests that although suffrage was significant at the time, as suffrage campaigners of the era themselves recognized, it was just one aspect of an otherwise unfinished cause. The holding of one referendum in 2018 along with the postponing of another (to repeal or replace the 1937 constitutional clause that defines women's role in Ireland as primarily in the home) sharply represents the interplay of past and present, and the tension between tradition and modernity that infuses women's rights in contemporary Ireland.

The process of "remembering" the past through the lens of women's lives has real political currency and human rights implications in contemporary Ireland. The centennial commemoration in 2021 of a violent and traumatic Civil War will clearly be difficult (Dolan 2003). The function of commemoration, though, is in part to ensure that other shameful aspects of the state's history be neither forgotten nor erased. The question of *what* Ireland is commemorating likewise begs the question of *how* it should be commemorating, including in arenas that are not included in the official decade of centenaries agenda. As David Fitzpatrick has noted, historical accountability arises in this context: "Commemoration, like good history, should help us to understand what forces impelled people to commit courageous as well as terrible acts. Though the outcome of such investigations is often contentious and morally unsettling, it is preferable to a bland recitation of general blamelessness" (2013b, 127). The history of trauma in Ireland is embedded in a bloody revolution in the early twentieth century and a later war in Northern Ireland. But widespread trauma was likewise generated in religious-run institutions that were ubiquitous and a core element in the state's formation and development. The unequal and at times barbaric treatment of women in Ireland in the last century in several arenas has created a fallout and fault line that must also be remembered, conceptualized, and addressed in the decade of centenaries if the state and society is to arrive at a full, mature, and honest appraisal of its past, *inclusively understood.*

NOTES

1. Public history is defined in different ways in historical literature. In general, it represents an aim to deepen and empower public connection with the past; see, for instance, Ashton and Kean 2009.

2. In 2014, the horrific reality of Ireland's state-funded, church-run mother and baby homes came to light when local historian Catherine Corless discovered a mass grave at a home located in Tuam. Approximately thirty-five thousand women went through Ireland's nine mother and baby homes between 1904 and 1996, where it is estimated six thousand babies and children died.

3. "I, as Taoiseach, on behalf of the State, the Government and our citizens deeply regret and apologise unreservedly to all those women for the hurt that was done to them, and for any stigma they suffered, as a result of the time they spent in a Magdalene laundry. The McAleese report shines a bright and necessary light on a dark chapter of Ireland's history" ("Enda Kenny's State

Apology to the Magdalene Women," February 2013, accessed on June 19, 2019, available at https://www.youtube.com/watch?v=Q9qf--0IavQ).

4. The stem family is "a three-generational structure which functioned to retain its original location (land and/or house) by means of dispersing most younger members, while preserving the main family stem by a principle of single inheritance" (Gibbon and Curtin 1978, 429).

5. A baseline online survey I performed in January 2018 of 136 (non-retired) academic staff currently named on Irish history department websites revealed that only three out of a total of twenty-three professors listed (at the Irish Higher Education Authority–recognized A and B Professor levels) were women.

LINDA CONNOLLY is Professor of Sociology at the Maynooth University Social Sciences Institute and author of a number of books, including *From Revolution to Devolution: The Irish Women's Movement*. She is currently working on a research project on gender-based violence in the Irish revolution.

REFERENCES

Abbey Theatre. 2020. Dublin. Accessed May 10, 2020. Available at www.abbey
theatre.ie.

Abbey Theatre's Annual Report. 2015. Abbey Theatre's Annual Report. Accessed June
8, 2020. Available at https://www.abbeytheatre.ie/wp-content/uploads/2017/03
/AbbeyTheatre_AnnualReport2015-1.pdf.

———. 2020. Abbey Theatre Annual Report. Dublin. Accessed May 10, 2020.
Available at https://www.abbeytheatre.ie/annual-reports/.

Adams, Gerry. 2015. "REVOLUTION 1916: Molly O'Reilly and the Rising." *Léargas
Blogspot by Gerry Adams.* December 19. Accessed May 15, 2018. Available at http://
leargas.blogspot.ie/2015/12/revolution-1916-molly-oreilly-and-rising.html.

———. 2017. Ard Feis Presidential Address. November. Accessed February 27, 2019.
Available at http://www.sinnfein.ie/contents/47265.

Agnew, Vanessa. 2007. "History's Affective Turn: Historical Reenactment and Its Work
in the Present." *Rethinking History: The Journal of Theory and Practice* 11 (3): 299–312.

Aiken, Síobhra. 2018. "'Ní Cathair Mar a Tuairisgí': (Mis)Representing the American
City in the Literature of the Gaelic Revival?" *Éire-Ireland* 53 (3): 93–118.

———. 2020a. "'The Women Who Had Been Straining Every Nerve': Gender-
Specific Medical Management of Trauma in the Irish Revolution (1916–1923)."
In *Trauma and Identity in Contemporary Irish Culture,* edited by Melania Terrazas
Gallego, 133–158. Bern: Peter Lang.

———. 2020b. "'Sinn Féin Permits . . . In the Heels of Their Shoes': Cumann na mBan
Emigrants and Transatlantic Revolutionary Exchange." *Irish Historical Studies* 44
(165): 1–25.

amNY. 2017. "Flashback to the '50s and Heroic Moms' Protest." June 15. Accessed May
10, 2020. Available at https://www.thevillager.com/2017/06/flashback-to-the-50s
-and-heroic-moms-protest/.

Anderson, Benedict. 2006. *Imagined Communities: Reflections on the Origins and Spread of Nationalism*, rev. ed. London: Verso.

Andrews, C. S. ("Todd"). 1979. *Dublin Made Me.* Dublin: Mercier.

———. 1982. *Man of No Property: An Autobiography.* Dublin: Mercier.

An Fiolar. 1958. Golden Jubilee issue of *An Fiolar.* Roscrea, County Tipperary: Mount St. Joseph College.

Aretxaga, Begoña. 1997. *Shattering Silence: Women, Nationalism and Political Subjectivity in Northern Ireland.* Princeton, NJ: Princeton University Press.

Armour, Noel. 2004. "Isabella Tod and Liberal Unionism in Ulster, 1886–96." In *Irish Women's History*, edited by Alan Hayes and Diane Urquhart, 72–87. Dublin: Irish Academic Press.

Arrowsmith, Aidan. 2012. "Imaginary Connections? Postmemory and Irish Diaspora Writing." In *Memory Ireland: Diaspora and Memory Practices*, edited by Oona Frawley, 12–23. Syracuse, NY: Syracuse University Press.

Arts Council, The. 2020. "Art: 2016. In the Shadow of the State." The Arts Council, Dublin. Accessed June 7, 2020. Available at http://www.artscouncil.ie/Art-2016/In-the-Shadow-of-the-State/.

Ashe, Fidelma. 2015. "Gendering Demilitarisation and Justice." *British Journal of Politics and International Relations* 17 (4): 665–680.

Ashton, Jenna C., ed. 2017. *Feminism and Museums: Intervention, Disruption and Change*, Vol. 2. Edinburgh, UK: MuseumsEtc.

———. 2018. *Feminism and Museums: Intervention, Disruption and Change*, Vol. 2. Edinburgh, UK: MuseumsEtc.

Ashton, Paul, and Hilda Kean, eds. 2009. *People and Their Pasts: Public History Today.* London: Palgrave Macmillan.

Assmann, Aleida. 2008. "Canon and Archive." In *Cultural Memory Studies: An International and Interdisciplinary Handbook*, edited by Astrid Erll and Ansgar Nünning, 97–108. Berlin: Walter de Gruyter.

Atkinson, Diane. 1997. *Funny Girls: Cartooning for Equality.* London: Penguin Books.

Atwood, Margaret. 1985. *The Handmaid's Tale.* Toledo, Ohio: McClelland and Stewart.

Aughey, Arthur. 1989. *Under Siege: Ulster Unionism and the Anglo-Irish Agreement.* London: Palgrave Macmillan.

Auslander, Mark. 2013. "Touching the Past: Materializing Time in Traumatic 'Living History' Reenactments." *Signs and Society* 1, no. 1 (Spring): 161–183.

Bacik, Ivana. 2013. "Legislating for Article 40.3.3°." *Irish Journal of Legal Studies* 3 (3): 18–35.

Bank, Jonathan, John P. Harrington, and Christopher Morach, eds. 2011. *Teresa Deevy Reclaimed*, Vol. 1, *Temporal Powers, Katie Roche, Wife to James Whelan.* New York: Mint Theater.

Barber, Fionna. 2016. *Constructing Constance (and Some Other Women)*. Drogheda, County Louth: Highlanes Gallery and Drogheda Arts Festival.

Barry, Aoife. 2015. "A Massive Same-Sex Marriage Mural Appeared Overnight in Dublin City." TheJournal.ie. April 11. Accessed May 10, 2020. Available at https:// www.thejournal.ie/marriage-equality-mural-dublin-2042322-Apr2015/.

———. 2016. "This Amazing Mural of 1916 Women Just Appeared in Dublin City Centre: It Shows Three Women Who Were All Involved in the Rising." TheJournal .ie. March 8. Accessed May 10, 2020. Available at https://www.thejournal.ie /mural-women-1916-dublin-georges-st-2647818-Mar2016/.

BBC *Voices 16*. 2016. "A Typewriter and a Gun." Accessed May 10, 2020. Available at https://www.bbc.co.uk/programmes/articles/19ytB8NQdgzxg95sDMdDhb2 /winifred-carney.

Beatty, Aidan. 2016. *Masculinity and Power in Irish Nationalism, 1884–1938*. New York: Palgrave Macmillan.

Beaumont, Caitríona. 1997. "Women, Citizenship and Catholicism in the Irish Free State, 1922–1948." *Women's History Review* 6 (4): 563–585.

———. 1999. "Gender, Citizenship and the State in Ireland, 1922–1990." In *Ireland in Proximity: History, Gender, Space*, edited by Scott Brewster, Virginia Crossman, Fiona Becket, and David Alderson, 94–108. London: Routledge.

Beckett, Ian F. W. 2007. *The Great War 1914–1918*. Harlow: Longman.

Beiner, Guy. 2007. *Remembering the Year of the French: Irish Folk History and Social Memory*. Madison: University of Wisconsin Press.

———. 2018. *Forgetful Remembrance: Social Forgetting and Vernacular Historiography of a Rebellion in Ulster*. Oxford: Oxford University Press.

Berger, John. 1973. *Ways of Seeing*. London: Pelican Books.

Berlant, Lauren. 1997. *The Queen of America Goes to Washington City: Essays on Sex and Citizenship*. Durham, NC: Duke University Press.

Beyond These Rooms. 2019. Art Installation. November. ANU and CoisCéim. Collins Barracks, National Museum of Ireland—Decorative Arts and History, Dublin. Accessed May 10, 2020. Available at https://theserooms.ie/book/.

Bielenberg, Andy. 2013. "Exodus: The Emigration of Southern Irish Protestants during the Irish War of Independence and the Civil War." *Past and Present*, no. 218, 199–233.

Black, Catherine. 1939. *King's Nurse—Beggar's Nurse*. London: Hurst and Blackett.

Bond, Lucy, and Jessica Rapson, eds. 2014. *The Transcultural Turn: Interrogating Memory Between and Beyond Borders*. Berlin: De Gruyter.

Boss, Owen. 2016a. "Art Installation." *These Rooms*. Accessed January 12, 2018. Available at http://theserooms.ie/room01/.

———. 2016b. "Introduction: Working Together." *These Rooms*. Accessed January 12, 2018. Available at http://theserooms.ie/room04/.

Bourke, Angela. 2004. *Maeve Brennan: Homesick at the New Yorker*. New York: Counterpoint.

Bowman, Timothy. 2007. *Carson's Army: The Ulster Volunteer Force, 1910–22*. Manchester, UK: Manchester University Press.

———. 2014. "Ireland and the First World War." In *The Oxford Handbook of Modern Irish History*, edited by Alvin Jackson, 603–620. Oxford: Oxford University Press.

Boyce, David G. 2002. "'That Party-Politics Should Divide Our Tents': Nationalism, Unionism and the First World War." In *Ireland and the Great War: "A War to Unite Us All,"* edited by Adrian Gregory and Senia Pašeta, 190–216. Manchester, UK: Manchester University Press.

Boyce, David G., and Alan O'Day, eds. 2006. *The Ulster Crisis*. London: Palgrave Macmillan.

Boym, Svetlana. 2001. *The Future of Nostalgia*. New York: Basic Books.

Brearton, Fran. 2000. *The Great War in Irish Poetry: W. B. Yeats to Michael Longley*. Oxford: Oxford University Press.

Brennan, Niall. 1966. "The Easter That Ireland Bled." *The Age*, April 9, p. 13.

Brewer, John. 2016. "How to Mark the Easter Rising in Northern Ireland." *The Conversation*, April 5. Accessed June 10, 2020. Available at https://theconversation .com/how-to-mark-the-easter-rising-in-northern-ireland-53189.

Brockes, Emma. 2018. "Me Too Founder Tarana Burke: 'You Have to Use Your Privilege to Help Other People.'" *The Guardian*, January 15. Accessed May 22, 2018. Available at https://www.theguardian.com/world/2018/jan/15 /me-too-founder-tarana-burke-women-sexual-assault.

Brophy, Daragh. 2015. "The Rising: Sinn Féin Is Booking Out the Ambassador Theatre for Most of 2016." The Journal.ie, February 6. Accessed June 7, 2020. Available at https://www.thejournal.ie/sinn-fein-1916-1923915-Feb2015/.

Brown, Heloise. 1998. "An Alternative Imperialism: Isabella Tod, Internationalist and 'Good Liberal Unionist.'" *Gender and History* 10, no. 3 (November): 358–381.

Browne, Sarah, and Jesse Jones. 2016. "In the Shadow of the State." Derry, Liverpool, London, and Dublin, March 12 to November 20. Accessed June 20, 2019. Available at https://www.artangel.org.uk/project/in-the-shadow-of-the-state/.

Brundage, David. 2016. *Irish Nationalists in America: The Politics of Exile, 1798–1998*. Oxford: Oxford University Press.

Bryan, Dominic. 2016. "Ritual, Identity and Nation: When the Historian Becomes the High Priest of Commemoration." In *Remembering 1916 The Easter Rising, the Somme and the Politics of Memory in Ireland*, edited by Richard Grayson and Ferghal McGarry, 24–42. Cambridge: Cambridge University Press.

Burnell, Tom. 2017. *26 County Casualties of the Great War*. 15 vols. Scotts Valley, CA: CreateSpace Independent.

Butler Cullingford, Elizabeth. 1996. *Gender and History in Yeats's Love Poetry*. Syracuse: Syracuse University Press.

Cammock, Helen. 2018. Interview with Helen Cammock on RTÉ. *Arena*, October 3. Accessed May 1, 2019. Available at https://www.rte.ie/radio/radioplayer/rteradiowebpage.html#!rii=b9_21443200_1526_03-10-2018_.

Carey, Helen. 2016. "It Is Still Great Theatre." *The Souvenir Shop by Rita Duffy Exhibition Catalogue*, 5–9. Belfast: Nicholas and Bass.

Carolan, Mary. 2016. "Judgment on Brain-Dead Pregnant Woman Wins Award. Decision to Allow Switching-Off of Life Support Honoured for 'Promoting Gender Equality.'" *Irish Times*, April 11. Accessed June 20, 2019. Available at https://www.irishtimes.com/news/crime-and-law/judgment-on-brain-dead-pregnant-woman-wins-award-1.2606884.

Carr, E. H. 1961. *What Is History?* Cambridge: Cambridge University Press.

Cavan Arts. 2017. "The Souvenir Project by Rita Duffy." Accessed May 15, 2018. Available at http://www.cavanarts.ie/Default.aspx?StructureID_str=3&guid=707.

Century Ireland. 1913. "Postal Boxes Attacked by Suffragettes in Dublin." December 17. Accessed August 19, 2016. Available at http://www.rte.ie/centuryireland/index.php/articles/postal-boxes-attacked-by-suffragettes-in-dublin.

Christianson, Sven-Ake, and Elizabeth Loftus. 1991. "Remembering Emotional Events: The Fate of Detailed Information." *Cognition and Emotion* 5, no. 2 (March): 81–108.

Clare, David. 2017. "Fired from the Canon: Waking the Feminists, the Conference." *Irish Times*, May 16. Accessed May 15, 2018. Available at https://www.irishtimes.com/culture/books/fired-from-the-canon-waking-the-feminists-the-conference-1.3084729.

Clarke, John. 2017. "Kathleen Fox Interview." *Footprints* (December): 1–8.

Clarke, Thomas J., Sean MacDiarmada, Thomas MacDonagh, P. H. Pearse, Eamon Ceannt, James Connolly, and Joseph Plunkett. 1916. "1916 Proclamation of Independence: The Provisional Government of the Irish Republic to the People of Ireland." Accessed May 13, 2018. Available at https://www.taoiseach.gov.ie/eng/Historical_Information/State_Commemorations/Proclamation_of_Independence.html.

Clayton-Lea, Tony. 2016. *Revolution 1916: Exhibition Catalogue*. Dublin: Seminal Merchandising.

Clear, Catriona. 2000. *Women of the House: Women's Household Work in Ireland, 1926–1961: Discourses, Experiences, Memories*. Dublin: Irish Academic Press.

———. 2008. "Fewer Ladies, More Women." In *Our War: Ireland and the Great War*, edited by John Horne, 157–170. Dublin: Royal Irish Academy.

Cleary, Joe. 2000. "Modernisation and Aesthetic Ideology in Cotemporary Irish Culture." In *Writing the Irish Republic: Literature, Culture, Politics 1949–1999*, edited by Ray Ryan, 105–129. London: Palgrave.

Cleary, Phil. 2000. "Marie Cleary Arrested in Upper Dorset Street." Accessed March 22, 2019. Available at http://www.philcleary.com.au/history_civil_war_maire_cleary.html.

Clifford, Angela, ed. 1996. *Muriel MacSwiney: Letters to Angela Clifford*. Belfast: Athol Books.

Coleman, Marie. 2018. "'There Are Thousands Who Will Claim to Have Been 'Out' during Easter Week': Recognising Military Service in the 1916 Easter Rising." *Irish Studies Review* 26 (4): 488–509.

Collins, Vanessa. 2013. "'A One-Battalioned Mind': Albert Thomas Dryer (1888–1963): Identity, Culture and Politics." Unpublished MA thesis, University of Melbourne.

Colum, Pádraic. 1905. *The Land: A Play in Three Acts*. Dublin: Maunsel Press.

———. 1916. *Three Plays: The Fiddler's House, The Land, Thomas Muskerry*. Boston: Little, Brown.

———. 1926. *The Road Round Ireland*. New York: Macmillan.

Comerford, James J. 1980. *My Kilkenny Days: 1916–22*. Kilkenny: Dinan.

Comerford, Máire. 1990. "Lasamar ár dTinte," *Agus*, 1981–1990.

Commasaru, Edwin. 2016. "Emancipating Machismo: Masculinity, Murals and Memorialising Hunger Strikes." *Irish Times*, May 5. Accessed June 7, 2020. Available at https://www.irishtimes.com/culture/books/emaciating -machismo-masculinity-murals-and-memorialising-hunger-strikes-1.2636109.

Conboy, Séamus. 2011. "Changing Dublin Street Names, 1880s to 1940s." *Historical Record* 64, no. 2 (Autumn): 205–225.

Condon, Denis. 2008. "Politics and the Cinematograph: The Boer War and the Funeral of Thomas Ashe." *Field Day Review* 4:132–145.

Connell, Joseph E. A. 2017. *Michael Collins: 1916–22*. Dublin: Wordwell.

Connerton, Paul. 2014. *How Societies Remember*. Cambridge: Cambridge University Press.

Connolly, James. 1904. "Some Plays and a Critic." *United Irishman*, May 7.

Connolly, Linda. 2003. *The Irish Women's Movement: From Revolution to Devolution*. Dublin: Lilliput Press.

———. 2004. "The Limits of 'Irish Studies': Culturalism, Historicism, Paternalism." *Irish Studies Review* 12 (2): 139–162.

———. 2016. "Symphysiotomy Report Begets More Questions." *Irish Examiner*, November 29. Accessed June 20, 2019. Available at https://www.irishexaminer .com/viewpoints/analysis/symphysiotomy-report-begets-more-questions-432728 .html.

———. 2019. "Towards a Further Understanding of the Violence Experienced by Women in the Irish Revolution." Maynooth University, County Kildare. MUSSI Working Paper, no. 7. Accessed June 11, 2020. Available at http://mural .maynoothuniversity.ie/10416/.

———. 2020. "Why Was Repeal Passed? A Long-Term View." In *After Repeal: Rethinking Abortion Politics*, edited by Kath Browne and Sydney Calkin, 36–52. London: Zed Books.

Connolly O'Brien, Nora. 1981. *We Shall Rise Again*. London: Mosquito.

Conrad, Kathryn. 2001. *Locked in the Family Cell: Gender, Sexuality, and Political Agency in Irish National Discourse.* Madison: University of Wisconsin Press.

Conroy, Catherine. 2017. "Anne Enright: 'There Is So Much Mediocre Work by Men Around.'" *Irish Times,* September 15. Accessed May 15, 2018. Available at https://www.irishtimes.com/culture/books/anne-enright-there-is-so-much-mediocre-work-by-men-around-1.3222337?mode=sample&auth-failed=1&pw-.

Conway, Brian. 2010. *Commemoration and Bloody Sunday: The Work of Memory.* New York: Palgrave Macmillan.

Conway, Martin A. 1997. "The Inventory of Experience: Memory and Identity." In *Collective Memory of Political Events: Social Psychological Perspectives,* edited by James W. Pennebaker, Dario Paez, and Bernard Rimé, 21–45. Mahwah, NJ: Lawrence Erlbaum.

Conway, Martin A., Qi Wang, Kazunori Hanyu, and Shamsul Haque. 2005. "A Cross-Cultural Investigation of Autobiographical Memory: On the Universality and Cultural Variation of the Reminiscence Bump." *Journal of Cross-Cultural Psychology* 36 (6): 739–749.

Coogan, Tim Pat. 2015. *Wherever Green Is Worn: The Story of the Irish Diaspora.* London: Head of Zeus.

Corcoran, Mary. 2004 "'We Had to Be Stronger': The Political Imprisonment of Women in Northern Ireland, 1972–1999." In *Irish Women and Nationalism: Soldiers, New Women and Wicked Hags,* edited by Louise Ryan and Margaret Ward, 114–131. Dublin: Irish Academic Press.

"Corrosive Fluid in Dublin Letter Boxes." 1913. *Irish Times,* December 20, p. 4.

Cosstick, Vicky, 2016. "Laundered Diesel and Black and Tan Boot Polish: The Rising Gets an Artful Injection of Mischief." *Irish Times,* April 5. Accessed May 15, 2018. Available at https://www.irishtimes.com/culture/art-and-design/laundered-diesel-and-black-and-tan-boot-polish-the-rising-gets-an-artful-injection-of-mischief-1.2595376.

Cousins, James H., and Margaret E. Cousins. 1950. *We Two Together.* Madras, India: Ganesh.

Cox, Karen L. 2003. *Dixie's Daughters: The United Daughters of the Confederacy and the Preservation of Confederate Culture.* Gainesville: University Press of Florida.

Crawford, Elizabeth. 2000. *The Women's Suffrage Movement: A Reference Guide, 1866–1928.* London: Routledge.

———. 2008. *The Women's Suffrage Movement in Britain and Ireland: A Regional Survey.* London: Routledge.

———. 2018. *Art and Suffrage: A Biographical Dictionary of Suffrage Artists.* London: Francis Boutle.

Crawley, Peter. 2015. "Abbey Theatre to 'Interrogate Rather Than Celebrate' Easter Rising." *Irish Times,* October 28. Accessed May 15, 2018. Available at https://www

.irishtimes.com/culture/stage/abbey-theatre-to-interrogate-rather-than-celebrate
-easter-rising-1.2408870.

———. 2016. "These Rooms Review: Bringing Unresolved History Back to Life."
Irish Times, September 30.

Cronin, Michael. 2016. "From Vivid Faces to Frozen Masks? Remembering to
Forget in Late Modern Ireland." *Lacunae, APPI International Journal for Lacanian
Psychoanalysis*, 12 (Easter): 21–36.

Cronin, Michael G. 2012. *Impure Thoughts: Sexuality, Catholicism and Literature in
Twentieth Century Ireland*. Manchester, UK: Manchester University Press.

Crooke, Elizabeth, and Thomas Maguire. 2018. "Introduction: Negotiating Heritage
after Conflict: Perspectives from Northern Ireland." In *Heritage after Conflict:
Northern Ireland*, edited by Elizabeth Crooke and Thomas Maguire, 1–15. London:
Routledge.

Crowe, Catriona, Mary Cullen, and Anthea McTiernan, eds. 2012. "How Irish
Women Won the Vote." *Irish Times Century Series*, October 17.

Crowley Ford, Anne. 2014. *When I Am Going: Growing Up in Ireland and Coming to
America, 1901–1927*, edited by Daniel Ford. Cork: Kilnahone Press.

Crozier-De Rosa, Sharon, and Vera Mackie. 2019. *Remembering Women's Activism*.
Oxon: Routledge.

Cullen, Paul. 2015. "New Report Reveals Sharp Rise in Number of Maternal
Deaths." *Irish Times*, February 21. Accessed May 12, 2018. Available at https://
www.irishtimes.com/news/health/new-report-reveals-sharp-rise-in-number
-of-maternal-deaths-1.2111831.

Cullen, Paul, and Kitty Holland. 2013. "Midwife Manager 'Regrets' Using 'Catholic
Country' Remark to Savita Halappanavar." *Irish Times*, April 10. Accessed May 10,
2019. Available at https://www.irishtimes.com/news/health/midwife-manager
-regrets-using-catholic-country-remark-to-savita-halappanavar-1.1355895.

Cullen Owens, Rosemary. 1984. *Smashing Times: A History of the Irish Women's
Suffrage Movement, 1889–1922*. Dublin: Attic.

———. 2007. *A Social History of Women in Ireland, 1870–1970*. Dublin: Gill and
Macmillan.

———. 2012. "A New Battlefield." *Irish Times*, October 17, p. 20.

Cunningham, Gaye. 2018. "Gate Theatre Confidential Independent Review."
Gate Theatre. Accessed May 15, 2018. Available at https://www.irishtimes.com
/polopoly_fs/1.3419457.1520499809!/menu/standard/file/Gate%20Report%20I
%20March.pdf.

Curry, James. 2012. *Artist of the Revolution: The Cartoons of Ernest Kavanagh (1884–
1916)*. Cork: Mercier.

Cusack, Geraldine O'Connell. 2003. *Children of the Far-Flung*. Dublin: Liffey.

Daly, Mary E., and Margaret O'Callaghan, eds. 2007. *1916 in 1966: Commemorating
the Easter Rising*. Dublin: Royal Irish Academy.

Davey, Shaun. 2016. "Composer's Note." *A Nation's Voice Glór an Phobail*. Dublin: Arts Council and RTÉ.

Dawson, Graham. 2007. *Making Peace with the Past? Memory, Trauma and the Irish Troubles*. Manchester, UK: Manchester University Press.

Decade of Centenaries. 2012a. *Decade of Centenaries Programme*. "About." Dublin: Department of Culture, Heritage, and the Gaeltacht. Accessed May 10, 2020. Available at https://www.decadeofcentenaries.com/about/.

———. 2012b. "8 April 2012: 96th Anniversary Commemoration of Easter Rising." Accessed May 10, 2020. Available at https://www.decadeofcentenaries.com /easter-commemoration-laying-of-wreath/.

———. 2020. "Official Commemoration." Dublin: Department of Culture, Heritage, and the Gaeltacht. Accessed May 10, 2020. Available at https://www .decadeofcentenaries.com/category/official-commemoration/.

Decade of Centenaries School Project Competition. 2020. "The 'Decade of Centenaries' Irish History Competition for Primary and Post-Primary Schools 2020." University College Cork, Ireland, School of History, Department of Education and Skills. Accessed May 10, 2020. Available at https://www.education .ie/en/Schools-Colleges/Information/Curriculum-and-Syllabus/Decade-of -Centenaries-History-competition-Entry-Requirements.pdf.

Decade of Centenaries: Second Phase Guidance, 2018–2023. Expert Advisory Group on Centenary Commemoration. 2018. Dublin: Department of Culture, Heritage, and the Gaeltacht.

Decade of Commemorations. 2012. British-Irish Parliamentary Assembly, Committee A: Sovereign Matters. Doc. No. 191, October 2012. Accessed May 10, 2020. Available at http://www.britishirish.org/assets/BIPA-Commemorations-Report-FINAL.pdf.

de Certeau, Michel. 1988. *The Practice of Everyday Life*. Berkeley: University of California Press.

De Cesari, Chiara, and Ann Rigney, eds. 2014. *Transnational Memory: Circulation, Articulation, Scales*. Berlin: De Gruyter.

Deleuze, Giles. 1988. *Foucault*. Minneapolis: University of Minnesota Press.

De Valera, Eamon. 1918. *Ireland's Case against Conscription*. Dublin: Maunsel Press.

Diner, Hasia R. 1983. *Erin's Daughters in America: Irish Immigrant Women in the Nineteenth Century*. Baltimore: John Hopkins University Press.

Dirrane, Bridget, Rose O'Connor, and Jack Mahon. 1997. *A Woman of Aran: The Life and Times of Bridget Dirrane*. Dublin: Blackwater.

Dolan, Anne. 2003. *Commemorating the Irish Civil War: History and Memory, 1923–2000*. Cambridge: Cambridge University Press.

———. 2015. "Commemorating 1916: How Much Does the Integrity of the Past Really Count?" *Irish Times*, January 2. Accessed May 15, 2018. Available at https://www .irishtimes.com/opinion/commemorating-1916-how-much-does-the-integrity-of -the-past-count-1.2052868.

Donner, Henriette. 1997. "Under the Cross—Why VADs Performed the Filthiest Tasks in the Dirtiest War: Red Cross Women Volunteers, 1914–1918." *Journal of Social History* 30, no. 3 (Spring): 687–704.

Donoghue, Emma. 2016. "Nurse Elizabeth O'Farrell." In *Signatories*, edited by Lucy Collins, 1–14. Dublin: University College Dublin Press.

Donohue, Brenda, Ciara O'Dowd, Tanya Dean, Ciara Murphy, Kathleen Cawley, and Kate Harris. 2017. *Gender Counts: An Analysis of Gender in Irish Theatre, 2006–2015.* Dublin: Arts Council. Accessed May 15, 2018. Available at https://www.dropbox.com/s/gawewk3dq43rqnd/Gender_Counts_WakingThe Feminists_2017.pdf?dl=0.

Dooley, Terence. 2001. *The Decline of the Big House in Ireland: A Study of Irish Landed Families, 1860–1960.* Dublin: Wolfhound.

Dorney, John. 2017. *The Civil War in Dublin: The Fight for the Irish Capital, 1922–1924.* Newbridge, County Kildare: Irish Academic Press.

Downes, Lawrence. 2016. "Martyrs with Guns and the Easter Rising." *New York Times*, March 25. Accessed May 15, 2018. Available at https://www.nytimes.com/2016/03/27/opinion/sunday/martyrs-with-guns-and-the-easter-rising.html.

Doyle, Tom. 2008. *The Civil War in Kerry.* Dublin: Mercier.

Dryer, Albert. 1956. "History of the Movement in Australia for Independence of Ireland, 1915–1925." August 21. Military Archives of Ireland, Bureau of Military History, W.S. 1526.

Dublin City Council. 2014. "Announcement of Restoration of Richmond Barracks, Inchicore for 1916 Commemorations." October 2. Accessed May 15, 2018. Available at http://www.dublincity.ie/announcement-restoration-richmond-barracks-inchicore-1916-commemoration.

———. 2020. "Doing Their Bit: Irish Women and the First World War." Accessed May 10, 2020. Available at http://www.dublincity.ie/doing-their-bit-irish-women-and-first-world-war.

Dublin Dance Festival. 2020. "Press Release: Embodied at the GPO." Dublin Dance Festival 2016 News, Dublin. Accessed June 7, 2020. Available at https://www.dublindancefestival.ie/news/article/press-release.-embodied-at-the-gpo.

Duffy, Rita. 2016. *The Souvenir Shop by Rita Duffy Exhibition Catalogue.* Belfast: Nicholas and Bass.

Dunn, Cathy. 2017. "May O'Carroll—Cumann na mBan, the GPO and Sydney." October 25. Accessed January 27, 2020. Available at http://irishassociation.org.au/sydney-irish-histories/may-ocarroll-cumann-na-mban-the-gpo-and-sydney/.

Dunne, Tom. 1987. "A Polemical Introduction: Literature, Literary Theory and the Historian." In *The Writer as Witness: Literature as Historical Evidence,* edited by Tom Dunne and Charles Doherty, 1–9. Cork: Cork University Press.

———. 1992. "New Histories: Beyond Revisionism." *Irish Review* 12:1–12. Cork: Cork University Press.

Edkins, Jenny. 2003. *Trauma and the Memory of Politics*. Cambridge: Cambridge University Press.

Embassy of Ireland, Australia. 2020. "2016 News and Events." Accessed May 10, 2020. Available at https://www.dfa.ie/irish-embassy/australia/news-and-events/2016/#feb.

Enright, Mairéad. 2015. "The Importance of Women-y Fringe-y Excesses of Irish Pro-Choice Activism." *Irish Human Rights Blog*. Accessed April 30, 2018. Available at http://humanrights.ie/gender-sexuality-and-the-law/the-importance-of-the -women-y-fringe-y-excesses-of-irish-pro-choice-activism/.

Falvey, Deirdre. 2018. "Waking the Feminists Campaign Wins a Tonic Award in London." *Irish Times*, March 21. Accessed May 15, 2018. Available at https://www.irishtimes.com /culture/stage/waking-the-feminists-campaign-wins-a-tonic-award-in-london-1 .3434845.

Fanning, Ronan. 2015. "Commemorating 1916: There Is a Risk It Will Degenerate into a Self-indulgent Exercise in Whatiffery." *Irish Times*, January 3.

Farrell, Elaine. 2013. *"A Most Diabolical Deed": Infanticide and Irish Society, 1850–1900*. Manchester, UK: Manchester University Press.

Fell, Alison. 2018. *Women as Veterans in Britain and France after the First World War*. Cambridge: Cambridge University Press.

Fell, Alison, and Christine Hallett. 2013. *First World War Nursing: New Perspectives*. New York: Routledge.

Ferriter, Diarmaid. 2010. *The Transformation of Ireland, 1900–2000*. London: Profile Books.

———. 2014. "Picking a Fight over the Rights and Wrongs of Our History." *Irish Times*, April 5. Accessed May 22, 2018. Available at http://www.irishtimes.com /culture/books/picking-a-fight-over-the-rights-and-wrongs-of-our-history-1 .1747128.

Finnane, Mark. 2013. "Deporting the Irish Envoys: Domestic and National Security in 1920s Australia." *Journal of Imperial and Commonwealth History* 41 (3): 403–445.

Finnegan, Margaret. 1999. *Selling Suffrage: Consumer Culture and Votes for Women*. New York: Columbia University Press.

Fitzgerald, Karen. 2018. "A Suffragette in the Family: Laura Geraldine Lennox." Paper presented at the Centenary Seminar "Protest through Print: Women's Suffrage and Print Media." National Print Museum. September 14.

Fitzpatrick, David, ed. 1986. *Ireland and the First World War*. Dublin: Trinity History Workshop.

———. 1996. "Militarism in Ireland, 1900–22." In *A Military History of Ireland*, edited by Thomas Bartlett and Keith Jeffery, 379–406. Cambridge: Cambridge University Press.

———. 2001. "Commemoration in the Irish Free State: A Chronicle of Embarrassment." In *History and Memory in Modern Ireland*, edited by Ian McBride, 184–203. Cambridge: Cambridge University Press.

REFERENCES

———. 2013a. "Protestant Depopulation and the Irish Revolution." *Irish Historical Studies* 38 (152): 643–670.

———. 2013b. "Historians and the Commemoration of Irish Conflicts, 1919–23." In *Towards Commemoration: Ireland in War and Revolution, 1912–1923*, edited by John Horne and Edward Madigan, 126–133. Dublin: Royal Irish Academy.

———. 2018. "Ireland and the Great War." In *The Cambridge History of Ireland*, Vol. 4, *1880 to the Present*, edited by Thomas Bartlett, 223–257. Cambridge: Cambridge University Press.

Fitzpatrick Dean, Joan. 2014. *All Dressed Up: Modern Irish Historical Pageantry*. Syracuse, NY: Syracuse University Press.

Flanagan, Frances. 2015. *Remembering the Revolution: Dissent, Culture, and Nationalism in the Irish Free State*. Oxford: Oxford University Press.

Flannery, Michael. 2001. *Accepting the Challenge: The Memoirs of Michael Flannery*, edited by Dermot O'Reilly. New York: Cló Saoirse—Irish Freedom Press.

Fletcher, M. H. 1989. *The WRNS: A History of the Women's Royal Naval Service*. London: Naval Institute Press.

Fletcher, Ruth. 2005. "Reproducing Irishness: Race Gender, and Abortion Law." *Canadian Journal of Women and Law* 17 (2): 356–404.

Florey, Kenneth. 2013. *Women's Suffrage Memorabilia: An Illustrated Historical Study*. Jefferson, NC: MacFarland.

Foster, Gavin. 2012. "'No 'Wild Geese' This Time'? IRA Emigration after the Irish Civil War." *Éire-Ireland* 47 (1): 94–122.

———. 2015. *The Irish Civil War and Society: Politics, Class and Conflict*. New York: Palgrave MacMillan.

———. 2017. "Locating the 'Lost Legions': IRA Emigration and Settlement after the Civil War." In *Atlas of the Irish Revolution*, edited by John Crowley, Donal Ó Drisceoil, and Mike Murphy, 744–747. Cork: Cork University Press.

Foster, Roy. 2003. *W. B. Yeats: A Life, Volume 2: The Arch-Poet 1915–1939*. Oxford: Oxford University Press.

———. 2014. *Vivid Faces: The Revolutionary Generation in Ireland, 1890–1923*. London: Allen Lane.

Foucault, Michel. 1972. *The Archaeology of Knowledge and the Discourse on Language*. New York: Tavistock.

———. 1977. *Discipline and Punish: The Birth of the Prison*. New York: Pantheon.

Fox-Genovese, Elizabeth. 1982. "Placing Women's History in History." *New Left Review* 133 (May–June): 5–29.

Fraiman, Susan. 2017. *Extreme Domesticity: A View from the Margins*. New York: Columbia University Press.

Fraser, Derek. 1973. *The Evolution of the British Welfare State*. London: Palgrave.

Frawley, Oona. 2005. *Irish Pastoral: Nostalgia and Twentieth-Century Irish Literature*. Dublin: Irish Academic Press.

———. 2010. "Towards a Theory of Memory in an Irish Postcolonial Context." In *Memory Ireland*, Vol. 1, *History and Modernity*, edited by Oona Frawley, 18–34. Syracuse, NY: Syracuse University Press.

———. 2011. "Introduction." In *Memory Ireland*, Vol. 1, *History and Modernity*, edited by Oona Frawley, xiii–xxiv. Syracuse, NY: Syracuse University Press.

———, ed. 2012. *Memory Ireland*, Vol. 2, *Diaspora and Memory Practices*. Syracuse, NY: Syracuse University Press.

———, ed. 2014. *Memory Ireland*, Vol. 3, *The Famine and the Troubles*. Syracuse, NY: Syracuse University Press.

French, Tom. 2016. *The Way to Work*. Loughcrew, County Meath: Gallery.

Friel, Judy. 1995. "Rehearsing 'Katie Roche.'" *Irish University Review* 25, no. 1 (Spring–Summer): 117–125.

Furlong, Sharon. 2009. "'Herstory' Recovered: Assessing the Contribution of Cumann Na mBan 1914–1923." *The Past: The Organ of the Uí Cinsealaigh Historical Society*, no. 30, 70–93.

Gallagher, Conor. 2019. "How #MeToo Is Influencing Rape Trials in Ireland." *Irish Times*, January 21. Accessed June 24, 2019. Available at https://www.irishtimes .com/news/crime-and-law/how-metoo-is-influencing-rape-trials-in-ireland-1 .3764416.

Gallagher, Conor, and Laurence Mackin. 2017. "Gate Women Put Colgan's Behaviour Centre Stage." *Irish Times*, November 4. Accessed May 15, 2018. Available at https:// www.irishtimes.com/news/ireland/irish-news/seven-women-allege-abuse-and -harassment-by-michael-colgan-1.3279488.

Garrett, Miranda, and Zoë Thomas, eds. 2019. *Suffrage and the Arts: Visual Culture, Politics and Enterprise*. London: Bloomsbury Visual Arts.

Gate Theatre. 2018. "The Board of the Gate Theatre Issues Apology." February 9. Dublin. Accessed May 10, 2020. Available at https://www.gatetheatre.ie /the-board-of-the-gate-theatre-issues-apology/.

Gate Theatre History. 2020. "Where It All Started." Dublin. Accessed May 10, 2020. Available at https://www.gatetheatre.ie/about/.

Gate Theatre Information. 2020. "Explore the Gate." Dublin. Accessed May 10, 2020. Available at http://www.gatetheatre.ie/.

Gibbon, Peter, and Chris Curtin. 1978. "The Stem Family in Ireland." *Comparative Studies in Society and History* 30 (3): 429–453.

Gibson, Rebecca, and James M. Vanderveen. 2013. "Control of Their Bodies, Control of Their Votes: Pins and Prophylactics Tell the Suffragette Story." *Indiana Archaeology* 8 (1): 56–71.

Gilligan, Donna. 2018. "Written Out of the Narrative: Tracking Down the Irish Suffrage Movement." *Irish Examiner*, November 2.

Gillis, John R. 1998. *Commemorations: The Politics of National Identity*. Princeton, NJ: Princeton University Press.

Gilmore, Leigh. 2001. *The Limits of Autobiography: Trauma and Testimony*. Ithaca, NY: Cornell University Press.

Gleeson, Sinead, ed. 2015. *The Long Gaze Back: An Anthology of Irish Women Writers*. Dublin: New Island.

Glenn, Cheryl. 2000. "Truth, Lies, and Method: Revisiting Feminist Historiography." *College English* 62 (3): 387–389.

Godson, Lisa, and Joanna Brück, eds. 2015. *Making 1916: Material and Visual Culture of 1916 Easter Rising*. Liverpool: Liverpool University Press.

Goffman, Erving. 1961. *Asylums: Essays on the Social Situation of Mental Patients and Other Inmates*. New York: Anchor Books.

Goldberg, David Theo. 2001. *The Racial State*. London: Wiley/Blackwell.

Good, Joe. 2016. *Inside the GPO 1916: A First-hand Account*. Dublin: O'Brien.

Gordon Bowe, Nicola. 2015. *Wilhelmina Geddes: Life and Work*. Dublin: Four Courts.

Gore-Booth, Eva. 1914. "Whence Come Wars? A Speech Delivered at a Meeting of the National Industrial and Professional Women's Suffrage Society, in London, December 12th, 1914." London: Women's Printing Society.

GPO Museum Witness History. 2020. Dublin: Dublin City Centre. Accessed May 10, 2020. Available at www.gpowitnesshistory.ie.

Graff-McRae, Rebecca. 2010. *Remembering and Forgetting 1916: Commemoration and Conflict in Post-Peace Process Ireland*. Dublin: Irish Academic Press.

———. 2016. "Ghosts of Gender: Memory, Legacy and Spectrality in Northern Ireland's Post-Conflict Commemorative Politics." *Ethnopolitics* 16 (5): 500–518.

Gray, Breda, and Louise Ryan. 1998. "The Politics of Irish Identity: Feminism, Nationhood, and Colonialism." In *Nation, Empire, Colony: Critical Categories of Gender and Race Analysis*, edited by Ruth Roach Pierson and Nupur Chaudhur, 121–138. Bloomington: Indiana University Press.

Grayson, Richard S., and Fearghal McGarry, eds. 2016. *Remembering 1916: The Easter Rising, the Somme and the Politics of Memory in Ireland*. Cambridge: Cambridge University Press.

Grenan, Julia. 1917. "Miss Julia Grenan's Story of the Surrender." *Catholic Bulletin* 7 (June): 396–398.

Griffith, Kenneth. 1998. *Curious Journey: An Oral History of Ireland's Unfinished Revolution*. Dublin: Mercier.

Guillemette, Antoine. 2013. *Coming Together at Easter: Commemorating the 1916 Rising in Ireland, 1916–1966*. Unpublished doctoral dissertation, Concordia University.

Halbwachs, Maurice. 1992. *On Collective Memory*. Chicago: University of Chicago Press.

Hall, Dianne. 2019. "Irish Republican Women in Australia: Kathleen Barry and Linda Kearns' Tour in 1924–1925." *Irish Historical Studies* 43, no. 3 (May): 73–93.

———. 2020. "Women of the Rising in the Australian and New Zealand Press." In *New Zealand Reactions to the Rising*, edited by Peter Kuch. Cork: Cork University Press.

Hanley, Brian. 2003. "The Rhetoric of Republican Legitimacy." In *Republicanism in Modern Ireland*, edited by Fearghal McGarry, 167–177. Dublin: University College Dublin Press.

———. 2009. "Irish Republicans in Interwar New York." *IJAS Online*, no. 1, 48–61.

Hanna, Adam. 2015. *Northern Irish Poetry and Domestic Space*. Basingstoke, UK: Palgrave Macmillan.

Hart, Peter. 2000 (1998). *The I.R.A. and Its Enemies: Violence and Community in Cork, 1916–1923*. Oxford: Oxford University Press.

Hauser, Christine. 2017. "A Handmaid's Tale of Protest." *New York Times*, June 30. Accessed May 22, 2018. Available at https://www.nytimes.com/2017/06/30/us/handmaids-protests-abortion.html.

Hesketh, Tom. 1990. *The Second Partitioning of Ireland? The Abortion Referendum of 1983*. Dublin: Brandsma Books.

Higgins, Michael D. 2018a. "Reflection by Michael D. Higgins, Uachtarán na hÉireann Tofa, on Armistice Day 2018." November 11. Glasnevin Cemetery. Accessed May 10, 2020. Available at https://president.ie/en/media-library/speeches/reflection-by-michael-d-higgins-uachtaran-na-heireann-tofa-on-armistice-day-2018.

———. 2018b. "Speech at the Launch of the *Cambridge History of Ireland*." April 30. Dublin Castle. Accessed May 18, 2018. Available at http://www.president.ie/en/media-library/speeches/speech-at-the-launch-of-the-cambridge-history-of-ireland.

———. 2018c. "Speech at the Unveiling of a Plaque Dedicated to Irish Suffragettes." June 13. Dublin Castle. Accessed May 10, 2020. Available at https://www.president.ie/en/media-library/speeches/speech-at-the-unveiling-of-a-plaque-dedicated-to-irish-suffragettes.

Higgins, Roisín. 2012. *Transforming 1916: Meaning, Memory and the Fiftieth Anniversary of the Easter Rising*. Cork: Cork University Press.

———. 2016a. "The 'Incorruptible Inheritors of 1916': The Battle for Ownership of the Fiftieth Anniversary of the Easter Rising." *Saothar: The Journal of Irish Labour History* 41:33–44.

———. 2016b. "'The Irish Republic Was Proclaimed by Poster': The Politics of Commemorating the Easter Rising." In *Remembering 1916: The Easter Rising, the Somme and the Politics of Memory in Ireland*, edited by Richard S. Grayson and Fearghal McGarry, 43–63. Cambridge: Cambridge University Press.

Hinkson, Pamela. 1991. *Seventy Years Young: Memories of Elizabeth, Countess of Fingall*. Dublin: Collins.

Hirsch, Marianne. 2012. *The Generation of Postmemory: Writing and Visual Culture after the Holocaust*. New York: Columbia University Press.

Hoagland, Kathleen. 1944. *Fiddler in the Sky*. New York: Harper.

———. 1947. *1000 Years of Irish Poetry: The Gaelic and Anglo-Irish Poets from Pagan Times to the Present*. New York: Devin-Adair Company.

Hobhouse, Emily. 1915. "Open Christmas Letter." *Jus Suffragii* 9 (4): 228–229.

Hobsbawm, Eric, and Terence Ranger, eds. 1983. *The Invention of Tradition.* Cambridge: Cambridge University Press.

Hogan, Robert, and James Kilroy. 1976. *Laying the Foundations 1902–1904.* Dublin: Dolmen.

Holland, Kitty. 2014. "'Perpetrators' of Symphysiotomy Should Be Punished, UN Says." *Irish Times,* July 24. Accessed May 22. 2018. Available at https://www .irishtimes.com/news/social-affairs/perpetrators-of-symphysiotomy-should-be -punished-un-says-1.1876896?mode=sample&auth-failed=1&pw-origin=https %3A%2F%2Fwww.irishtimes.com%2Fnews%2Fsocial-affairs%2Fperpetrators-of -symphysiotomy-should-be-punished-un-says-1.1876896.

Holmes, Rachel. 2017. "A New Feminist Statue Is a Great Idea. Shame They Picked the Wrong Feminist." *The Guardian,* April 14. Accessed June 10, 2020. Available at https://www.theguardian.com/commentisfree/2017/apr/14 /new-feminist-statue-women-suffrage-millicent-fawcett.

hooks, bell. 1991. "Homeplace: A Site of Resistance." In *Yearning: Race, Gender, and Cultural Politics,* 41–49. London: Routledge.

Horne, John, ed. 2010. *Our War: Ireland and the Great War.* Dublin: Royal Irish Academy.

Houses of the Oireachtas. 2018. "Picture of Constance Markievicz, First Woman Elected to House of Commons, Gifted to UK by Ceann Comhairle." July 19. Dublin. Accessed May 10, 2020. Available at https://www.oireachtas.ie/en/press -centre/press-releases/20180719-picture-of-constance-markievicz-first-woman -elected-to-house-of-commons-gifted-to-uk-by-ceann-comhairle/.

Hug, Chrystel. 1999. *The Politics of Sexual Morality in Ireland.* London: Macmillan.

Hughes, Christina. 2002. *Key Concepts in Feminist Theory and Research.* London: Sage.

Huyssen, Andreas. 2003. "Diaspora and Nation: Migration into Other Pasts." *New German Critique,* no. 88, 147–164.

Inglis, Tom. 2005. "Origins and Legacies of Irish Prudery: Sexuality and Social Control in Modern Ireland." *Eire/Ireland* 40, nos. 3–4: 9–37. Accessed January 17, 2019. Available at doi:10.1353/eir.2005.0022.

Irish Humanities Alliance. 2016. "1916 Home 2016." International Conference, October 27–28. University College Dublin, Dublin. Accessed June 10, 2020. Available at https://www.irishhumanities.com/events/1916-home-2016/.

Irish Theatre Institute. 2018. "Speak Up and Call It Out: Dignity in the Workplace. Towards A Code of Behaviour for Irish Theatre." Accessed May 10, 2020. Available at www.irishtheatreinstitute.ie/.

Irwin-Zarecka, Iwona. 1994. *Frames of Remembrance: The Dynamics of Collective Memory.* New Brunswick, NJ: Transaction.

Jackson, Alvin. 1989. *The Ulster Party: Irish Unionists in the House of Commons, 1884–1911.* Oxford: Clarendon.

———. 1990. "Unionist Politics and Protestant Society in Edwardian Ireland." *Historical Journal* 33 (4): 839–866.

———. 2018. "Mrs Foster and the Rebels: Irish Unionists Approaches to the Easter Rising, 1916–2016." *Irish Historical Studies* 42 (161): 143–160.

James, Selma. 1972. *Women, the Unions and Work, or . . . What Is Not to Be Done* and the Perspective of Winning. Accessed May 23, 2019. Available at http://libcom.org/library/women-unions-work-or%E2%80%A6what-not-be-done.

Janssen, Lindsay. 2018. "Diasporic Identifications: Exile, Nostalgia and the Famine Past in Irish and Irish North-American Popular Fiction, 1871–1891." *Irish Studies Review* 26 (2): 199–216.

Jeffares, Norman A., and Anna MacBride White, eds. 1994. *The Gonne-Yeats Letters.* Syracuse, NY: Syracuse University Press.

Jeffery, Keith. 2000. *Ireland and the Great War.* Cambridge: Cambridge University Press.

Johnson, Nuala. 1994. "Sculpting Heroic Histories: Celebrating the Centenary of the 1798 Rebellion in Ireland." *Transactions of the Institute of British Geographers* 9:78–94.

———. 2003. *Ireland, the Great War and the Geography of Remembrance.* Cambridge: Cambridge University Press.

Jones, Heather. 2013. "As the Centenary Approaches: The Regeneration of First World War Historiography." *Historical Journal* 56 (3): 857–878.

Jones, Mary. 1988. *Those Obstreperous Lassies: A History of the IWWU.* Dublin: Gill and Macmillan.

Joye, Lar, and Brenda Malone. 2015. "Displaying the Nation: The 1916 Exhibition at the National Museum of Ireland, 1932–1991." In *Making 1916: Material and Visual Culture of the Easter Rising,* edited by Lisa Godson and Joanna Brück, 180–193. Liverpool: Liverpool University Press.

Kantor, Jodi, and Megan Twohey. 2017. "Harvey Weinstein Paid Off Sexual Harassment Accusers for Decades." *New York Times,* October 5. Accessed May 22, 2018. Available at https://www.nytimes.com/2017/10/05/us/harvey-weinstein-harassment-allegations.html.

Kearney, Richard, and Sheila Gallagher. 2017. *Twinsome Minds: An Act of Double Remembrance.* Cork: Cork University Press.

Keating, Jennifer. 2016. "Tom Clarke, Tobacconist, Stationer. Purveyor: Irish Freedom, the Principles of Freedom and Tit-Bits." In *The Souvenir Shop by Rita Duffy Exhibition Catalogue,* 19–23. Belfast: Nicholas and Bass.

Keating, Sara. 2015. "Fired from the Canon: The Fate of Irish Female Playwrights." *Irish Times,* December 2. Accessed May 15, 2018. Available at https://www.irishtimes.com/culture/stage/fired-from-the-canon-the-fate-of-irish-female-playwrights-1.2450015.

———. 2016. "Can You Stay Centre-Stage after Having Babies?" *Irish Times*, July 5. Accessed May 15, 2018. Available at https://www.irishtimes.com/life-and-style/health-family/parenting/can-you-stay-centre-stage-after-having-babies-1.2704154.

Keenan-Thomson, Tara. 2009. "From Co-op to Co-opt: Gender and Class in the Early Civil Rights Movement." *The Sixties* 2 (2): 207–225.

———. 2010 *Irish Women and Street Politics, 1956–1973*. Dublin: Irish Academic Press.

Kelleher, Margaret. 2003. "'The Field Day Anthology' and Irish Women's Literary Studies." *Irish Review*, no. 30 (Spring–Summer): 82–94.

Kelly, Fiach. 2017. "Establish External Inquiry into Sexual Harrassment Claims at Gate, Say FF." *Irish Times*, November 5. Accessed May 15, 2018. Available at https://www.irishtimes.com/news/ireland/irish-news/establish-external-inquiry-into-sexual-harassment-claims-at-gate-say-ff-1.3280736?mode=sample&auth-failed=1&pw-.

Kelly, Marie. 2017. "Abbey Theatre Research Pack on Teresa Deevy: Katie Roche." Abbey Theatre. Accessed May 15, 2018. Available at https://3kkb1z11gox47npp d3tlqcmq-wpengine.netdna-ssl.com/wp-content/uploads/2017/10/KATIE-ROCHE_RESEARCH-PACK-2017.pdf.

Kenny, Enda. 2016. "Statement by an Taoiseach Enda Kenny at the Official State Ceremonial Event to Mark the Beginning of the Centenary Year and the Ireland 2016 Centenary Programme." January 1. Accessed January 10, 2018. Available at https://www.chg.gov.ie/president-and-taoiseach-lead-first-state-ceremonial-event-to-mark-start-of-2016-centenary-year/.

Kilkenny Great War Memorial. 2011. "About." Kilkenny, Ireland. Accessed May 10, 2020. Available at http://kilkennygreatwarmemorial.com.

Kilmainhamgaolgraffiti. 2014. "Exploring Female Experiences of Imprisonment during the Irish Civil War (1922–1923)." Accessed May 15, 2018. Available at www.kilmainhamgaolgraffiti.com.

Kinghan, Nancy. 1975. *United We Stood: The Story of the Ulster Women's Unionist Council, 1911–74*. Belfast: Appletree.

Kingston, James. 2001. *The Need for Abortion Reform in Ireland: The Case against the Twenty-Fifth Amendment of the Constitution Bill*. Dublin: Irish Council for Civil Liberties.

Laird, Heather. 2018. *Commemoration*. Cork: Cork University Press.

Leeney, Cathy. 2010. *Irish Women Playwrights 1900–1939: Gender and Violence on Stage*. New York: Peter Lang.

Lejeune, Philippe. 1975. *Le pacte autobiographique*. Paris: Seuil.

Lenehan Nastri, Kathleen. 2016. "Photo Album: Rebel Irish Girl." *Irish America Magazine* (blog), November. Accessed May 13, 2019. Available at https://irishamerica.com/2016/10/photo-album-rebel-irish-girl/.

Lennon, George G. 1971. *Trauma in Time.* Accessed May 13, 2019. Available at http://
www.waterfordmuseum.ie/exhibit/web/Display/article/317/Memoirs_Of
_George_Lennon_.html.

Letters 1916–1923 Project. 2013. Accessed May 10, 2020. Available at http://letters1916
.maynoothuniversity.ie.

Levenson, Leah, and Jerry H. Natterstad. 1986. *Hanna Sheehy-Skeffington: Irish
Feminist.* Syracuse, NY: Syracuse University Press.

Lindsey, Dorothea. 1944. "First Novel of Stature." *Cincinnati Enquirer,* June 10, p. 5.

Lisburn and Castlereagh City Council. 2018. "Rare Hunger Strike Medal
Belonging to Local Suffragette Goes on Display." September 26. Accessed
May 10, 2020. Available at https://www.lisburncastlereagh.gov.uk/news
/rare-hunger-strike-medal-belonging-to-local-suffragette-goes-on-display.

Litterine, Lynn. 1973. "From America She Watches Her Cousin's Rise in Ireland." *The
Record* (New Jersey) 4 (March): 60.

Lonergan, Patrick. 2014. "More Thoughts (and Stats) on Women Writers at the
Abbey." *Scenes from the Bigger Picture.* January 22. Accessed May 15, 2018. Available
at https://patricklonergan.wordpress.com/2014/01/22/more-thoughts-and-stats
-on-women-writers-at-the-abbey/.

Longley, Edna. 2001. "Northern Ireland: Commemoration, Elegy, Forgetting." In
History and Memory in Modern Ireland, edited by Ian McBride, 223–253. Cambridge:
Cambridge University Press.

Los Angeles, California, 1930, Census Return, Ancestry. Accessed May 10, 2020.
Available at https://www.ancestry.com/search/collections/6224/?event=
_los+angeles-ca.

Loughrey, Mark. 2016. *1916 Nurses and Midwives in the 1916 Easter Rising.* Dublin: Irish
Nurses and Midwives Organisation.

Lowenthal, David. 2015. *The Past is a Foreign Country Revisited.* Cambridge,
Cambridge University Press.

Lucy, Gordon. 1995. *The Great Convention: The Ulster Unionist Convention of 1892.*
Lurgan, County Armagh: Ulster Society.

Luibhéid, Eithne. 2013. *Pregnant on Arrival: Making the Illegal Immigrant.* Minneapolis:
University of Minnesota Press.

Macardle, Dorothy. (1937) 1968. *The Irish Republic.* London: Corgi.

Mac Eoin, Uinseann. 1980. *Survivors: The Story of Ireland's Struggle as Told Through
Some of Her Outstanding Living People.* Dublin: Argenta.

MacSwiney Brugha, Maire. 2005. *History's Daughter: A Memoir from the Only Child
of Terence MacSwiney.* Dublin: O'Brien.

Madden, Christine. 2004. "How the Abbey Is Celebrating Its Centenary." *Irish
Times,* January 16. Accessed June 21, 2019. Available at https://www.irishtimes
.com/culture/how-the-abbey-is-celebrating-its-centenary-1.1130306.

Madigan, Edward. 2013. "Introduction." In *Towards Commemoration: Ireland in War and Revolution, 1912–1923*, edited by John Horne and Edward Madigan, 1–2. Dublin: Royal Irish Academy.

Mahony, Hubert. 2015. "Iza Mahony: VAD Nurses and First World War Victim." Unpublished talk for the Kilmacud Stillorgan Local History Society, March 12.

Malcolm, Elizabeth, and Dianne Hall. 2018. *A New History of the Irish in Australia.* Sydney: NewSouth.

Mansergh, Martin. 2017. "Ulster's Solemn League and Covenant, 1912." In *Atlas of the Irish Revolution*, edited by John Crowley, Donal Ó Drisceoil, and Mike Murphy, 159–161. Cork: Cork University Press.

Maples, Holly. 2011. "Producing Ireland: A History of Commemoration and the Abbey Theatre." In *Memory Ireland*, Vol. 1, *History and Modernity*, edited by Oona Frawley, 172–183. Syracuse, NY: Syracuse University Press.

Marcote, Marianne. 2016. "You Lose Control and You Lose Your Life When You Become a Mother." *Irish Times*, February 2. Accessed May 15, 2018. Available at https://www.irishtimes.com/life-and-style/health-family/you-lose-control-and -lose-your-life-when-you-become-a-mother-1.2512336.

Martin, F. X. 1967. "1916: Myth, Fact and Mystery." *Studia Hibernica* 7:7–126.

Marwick, Arthur. 1967. *The Deluge: British Society and the First World War.* London: Penguin.

Mason, Patrick. 2016. "Director's Note." In *Signatories,* edited by Lucy Collins, xii–xviii. Dublin: University College Dublin Press.

Matthews, Ann. 2010. *Renegades: Irish Republican Women, 1900–1922.* Cork: Mercier.

———. 2012. *Dissidents: Irish Republican Women, 1923–1941.* Cork: Mercier.

Maxwell, Jane. 2018. "Violence Ridicule and Silence 1750–1937: An Inter-institutional Exhibition Plotting Irish Women's Road to the Vote in 1918." Accessed February 15, 2019. Available at https://artsandculture.google.com/exhibit /WAKykHyoPC6zKA.

McAtackney, Laura. 2011. "Peace Maintenance and Political Messages: The Significance of Walls During and After the 'Troubles' in Northern Ireland." *Journal of Social Archaeology* 11 (1): 77–98.

———. 2016. "Gender, Incarceration, and Power Relations During the Irish Civil War." In *The State and Gender Violence: International Perspectives*, edited by Victoria Stanford, Katerina Stefatos, and Cecilia M Salvi, 47–63. New York: Rutgers University Press.

———. 2018. "Where Are All the Women? Public Memory, Gender and Memorialisation in Contemporary Belfast." In *Heritage after Conflict: Northern Ireland*, edited by Elizabeth Crooke and Thomas Maguire, 154–172. London: Routledge.

McAuliffe, Mary. 2014. "2014—Centenary Year of the Formation of Cumann na mBan." April 2. Accessed March 8, 2018. Available at http://www.decadeofcenten aries.com/cumann-na-mban-centenary-commemoration-glasnevin-cemetery -wednesday-2-april-2014/.

———. 2017. "Carrying a Cross for Ireland: Thomas Ashe in Profile." *Century Ireland.* Accessed March 5, 2018. Available at http://www.rte.ie/centuryireland/index.php /articles/carrying-a-cross-for-ireland-thomas-ashe-in-profile.

———. 2018a. "'An Idea Has Gone Abroad That All the Women Were against the Treaty': Cumann na Saoirse and Pro-Treaty Women, 1922–1923." In *The Treaty: Debating and Establishing the Irish State,* edited by Liam Weeks and Mícheál Ó Fathartaigh. Dublin: Merrion.

———. 2018b. "Lá na mBan: A Day of Mass Civil Disobedience." *Irish Independent,* June 10. Accessed May 11, 2019. Available at https://www.independent.ie /irish-news/l-na-mban-a-day-of-mass-civil-disobedience-36988025.html.

McAuliffe, Mary, and Liz Gillis. 2016. *We Were There: 77 Women of the Easter Rising.* Dublin: Four Courts.

McBrinn, Joseph. 2009. "'A Populous Solitude': The Life and Art of Sophia Rosamund Praeger, 1867–1954." *Women's History Review* 18 (4): 577–596.

McCarthy, Cal. (2007) 2014. *Cumann na mBan and the Irish Revolution.* 2nd ed. Dublin: Collins.

McCarthy, Helen. 2015. "Pacificism and Feminism in the Great War." *History Today,* March 25. Accessed May 15, 2018. Available at https://www.historytoday.com /helen-mccarthy/pacifism-and-feminism-great-war.

McCarthy, Mark. 2005. *Ireland's Heritages: Critical Perspectives on Memory and Identity.* Aldershot, UK: Ashgate.

McCaughey, Patsy. 2018. *Discovering History: Junior Cycle History.* Dublin: Mentor Books.

McClements, Freya. 2018. "The Story of Northern Ireland's First Civil Rights March." *Irish Times,* August 24. Accessed May 23, 2019. Available at https:// www.irishtimes.com/news/politics/the-lost-story-of-northern-ireland-s -first-civil-rights-march-1.3605463.

McConville, Chris. 1987. *Croppies, Celts and Catholics: The Irish in Australia.* Caulfield East, Victoria, Australia: Edward Arnold.

McCoole, Sinéad. 1997. *Guns and Chiffon: Women Revolutionaries and Kilmainham Jail, 1916–1923.* Dublin: Stationary Office.

———. (2003) 2015. *No Ordinary Women: Irish Female Activists in the Revolutionary Years, 1900–1923.* Dublin: O'Brien.

———. 2015. *Easter Widows: Seven Irish Women Who Lived in the Shadow of the 1916 Rising.* Dublin: Doubleday.

McCormack, Mike. 1988. "Aunt Bridie: A Woman of Ireland." *Irish Echo,* April 2 [OBJ0036 Kilmainham Gaol Archive].

———. 2015. "Bridie Halpin: Irish Patriot." *Wild Geese* (blog). March 5. Accessed May 13, 2019. Available at https://thewildgeese.irish/main/search/search?q=bridie+halpin.

McDermott, Mary. 1923. "Letters to Editor." *Daily Herald.* May 7.

McDiarmid, Lucy. 2015. *At Home in the Revolution: What Women Said and Did in 1916.* Dublin: Royal Irish Academy.

McDonagh, Sunniva. 1992. *The Attorney General v. X and Others: Judgments of the High Court and Supreme Court. Legal Submissions Made to the Supreme Court.* Dublin: Dublin Incorporated Council of Law Reporting for Ireland.

McDonald, Dearbhail. 2015. "Symphysiotomy Test Case Fails at High Court in Blow to Survivors." *Irish Independent,* May 2. Accessed May 22, 2018. Available at http://www.independent.ie/irish-news/courts/symphysiotomy-test-case-fails-at-high-court-in-blow-to-survivors-31189524.html.

McDowell, Sara. 2008. "Commemorating Dead 'Men': Gendering the Past and Present in Post-conflict Northern Ireland." *Gender, Place and Culture* 15 (4): 335–354.

McDowell, Sara, and Catherine Switzer. 2011. "Violence and the Vernacular: Conflict, Commemoration, and Rebuilding in the Urban Context." *Buildings and Landscapes: Journal of the Vernacular Architecture Forum* 18 (2): 82–104.

McEvoy, Sandra. 2009. "Loyalist Women Paramilitaries in Northern Ireland: Beginning a Feminist Conversation about Conflict Resolution." *Security Studies* 18 (2): 262–286.

McGarry, Fearghal. 2011. "'Too Many Histories'? The Bureau of Military History and Easter 1916." *History Ireland* 19, no. 6 (November–December): 26–29.

———. 2015. *The Abbey Rebels of 1916: A Lost Revolution.* Dublin: Gill and Macmillan.

McGaugh, James L. 2000. "Memory—A Century of Consolidation." *Science* 287 (5451): 48–251.

McGaughey, Jane. G. V. 2012. *Ulster's Men: Protestant Unionist Masculinities in the North of Ireland, 1921–23.* Montreal: McGill-Queen's University Press.

McGreevy, Ronan. 2016. "1916/2016: A Miscellany." *Irish Times,* March 24. Accessed May 15, 2018. Available at https://www.irishtimes.com/culture/heritage/century/1916-2016-a-miscellany/1916-2016-a-miscellany-1.2584948.

———, ed. 2017. *Centenary: Ireland Remembers 1916/ Comóradh Céad Bliain, Tugann Éireann 1916 chun cuimhne.* Dublin: Government Publications/Royal Irish Academy.

McWilliams, Monica. 1997. "Violence against Women and Political Conflict: The Northern Ireland Experience." *Critical Criminology* 8:78–92.

Mental Health Foundation. 2016. *Mental Health in Northern Ireland: Fundamental Facts.* Accessed February 28, 2019. Available at https://www.mentalhealth.org.uk/publications/mental-health-northern-ireland-fundamental-facts.

MERJ. 2018. *We've Come a Long Way: Reproductive Rights of Migrants and Ethnic Minorities in Ireland.* Accessed May 10, 2019. Available at http://merjireland.org/index.php/resources/.

Miller, Kerby A. 1988. *Emigrants and Exiles: Ireland and the Irish Exodus to North America*. Oxford: Oxford University Press.

Minihan, Mary. 2015. "Sinn Féin Announces Plans to Commemorate 1916 Rising." *Irish Times*, March 31. Accessed June 7, 2020. Available at https://www.irishtimes.com /news/politics/sinn-f%C3%A9in-announces-plans-to-commemorate-1916-rising-1 .2159313.

Mitchell, Arthur, and Pádraig Ó Snodaigh, eds. 1985. *Irish Political Documents, 1916– 1949*. Dublin: Irish Academic Press.

Monaghan, John. 2016. "Housing Executive Provides Funds to Commemorate Family Divided by Rising and the Somme." *Irish News*, March 31. Accessed on June 5, 2020. Available at https://www.irishnews.com/news/2016/03/31/news /housing-executive-provides-funds-to-commemorate-belfast-family-divided-by -rising-and-somme-469338/.

Morash, Chris. 2011. "Teresa Deevy: Between the Lines." In *Teresa Deevy Reclaimed*, Vol. 1, *Temporal Powers, Katie Roche, Wife to James Whelan*, edited by Jonathan Bank, John P. Harrington, and Chris Morash, ix–xiv. New York: Mint Theater.

Morash, Chris, and Nicholas Grene, eds. 2016. *Oxford Handbook of Modern Irish Theatre*. Oxford: Oxford University Press.

Morris, Ewan. 2004. *Our Own Devices: National Symbols and Political Conflict in Twentieth-Century Ireland*. Dublin: Irish Academic Press.

Morrison, Eve. 2009. "The Bureau of Military History and Female Republican Activism: 1913–1923." In *Gender and Power in Irish History*, edited by Maryann Gialanella Valiulis. Dublin: Irish Academic Press.

"Moving Memory" (Roundtable). 2017. With Stef Craps, Astrid Erll, Paula McFetridge, Ann Rigney, and Dominic Thorpe; convened by Charlotte McIvor and Emilie Pine. *Irish University Review* 47 (1): 165–196.

Muldoon, Paul. 2016a. "1916: The Eoghan Rua Variations." *Irish Times*, March 26, 2016. Accessed May 10, 2020. Available at https://www.irishtimes.com/culture /books/1916-the-eoghan-rua-variations-1.2586864.

———. 2016b. "One Hundred Years a Nation." *A Nation's Voice Glór an Phobail*. Dublin: Arts Council and RTÉ.

———. 2016c. *Rising to the Rising*. Loughcrew, County Meath: Gallery.

Mulhall, James. 2016. "Street Mural of Easter Rising Women Appears Overnight in Dublin to Mark International Women's Day." *Irish Post*. March 8. Accessed May 15, 2018. Available at https://www.irishpost.co.uk/news/82360-2-82360.

Mullally, Una. 2015. "Abbey Theatre Celebrates 1916 Centenary with Only One Woman Playwright." *Irish Times*, November 2. Accessed May 15, 2018. Available at https://www.irishtimes.com/opinion/una-mullally-abbey-theatre-celebrates -1916-centenary-with-only-one-woman-playwright-1.2413277.

———. 2016. "Why Women Have Risen to the Top in 1916 Lore." *Irish Times*, March 28. Accessed May 15, 2018. Available at https://www.irishtimes.com/opinion /una-mullally-why-women-have-risen-to-the-top-in-1916-lore-1.2588986.

Murphy, Brian P. 1989. "J. J. O'Kelly, the Catholic Bulletin and Contemporary Irish Cultural Historians." *Archivium Hibernicum* 44:71–88.

———. 2012. "Telling the Story of 1916: The 'Catholic Bulletin' and 'Studies.'" *Studies: An Irish Quarterly Review* 101, no. 401 (Spring): 47–56.

Murphy, Cliona. 1989. *The Women's Suffrage Movement and Irish Society in the Early Twentieth Century*. Philadelphia: Temple University Press.

———. 2007. "'Great Gas' and 'Irish Bull': Humour and the Fight for Irish Women's Suffrage." In *Irish Women and the Vote: Becoming Citizens*, edited by Louise Ryan and Margaret Ward, 90–113. Dublin: Irish Academic Press.

Murphy, Jeremiah. 1998. *When Youth Was Mine: A Memoir of Kerry, 1902–1925*. Dublin: Mentor.

Nakase, Justine. 2017. "Women in Irish Theatre: No More Waiting in the Wings." *Irish Times*, June 20. Accessed May 15, 2018. Available at https://www.irishtimes .com/culture/books/women-in-irish-theatre-no-more-waiting-in-the-wings-1 .3126448.

Nandy, Ashis. 1984. *The Intimate Enemy: Loss and Recovery of Self under Colonialism*. New Delhi: Oxford University Press.

Nerve Centre, The. 2019. Accessed May 12, 2019. Available at https://www.nervecentre .org/content/about-us.

Newman, Vivien. 2014. *We Also Served: The Forgotten Women of the First World War*. Barnsley, UK: Pen and Sword.

NIDirect Government Services. 2020. "Suffrage." Accessed May 10, 2020. Available at https://www.nidirect.gov.uk/articles/suffrage.

NLI Web Archive. 2020. "The 1916 Rising: Personalities and Perspectives." National Library of Ireland, Dublin. Accessed May 10, 2020. Available at https://www .nli.ie/en/udlist/programme-and-events-education-post-primary.aspx?article= df2eebbd-ee4b-4c7b-beea-d489e793ea7b.

Noakes, Lucy. 2001. "Gender, War and Memory: Discourse and Experience in History." *Journal of Contemporary History* 36 (4): 663–672.

Nolan, Janet. 1989. *Ourselves Alone: Women's Emigration from Ireland, 1885–1920*. Kentucky: University Press of Kentucky.

Northern Ireland Civil Rights. 2020. "Civil Rights Timeline." Accessed May 10, 2020. Available at http://www.nicivilrights.org/about-us/.

Novick, Ben. 2002. "Propaganda 1: Advanced Nationalist Propaganda and the Moralistic Revolution, 1914–1918." In *The Irish Revolution, 1913–1923*, edited by Joost Augusteijn, 34–52. London: Palgrave Macmillan.

Oaks, Laury. 1998. "Irishness, Eurocitizens, and Reproductive Rights." In *Reproducing Reproduction: Kinship, Power, and Technological Innovation*, edited by Sarah Franklin and Helena Ragoné, 132–155. Philadelphia: University of Pennsylvania Press.

Obama, Michelle. 2016. "New Hampshire Speech." October 13. Accessed May 18, 2018. Available at https://www.theguardian.com/us-news/2016/oct/14/michelle-obama-speech-transcript-donald-trump.

O'Callaghan, Margaret. 2007. "From Casement Park to Toomebridge: The Commemoration of the Easter Rising of 1916 in Northern Ireland in 1966 in Political Context." In *1916 in 1966: Commemorating the Easter Rising*, edited by Mary E. Daly and Margaret O'Callaghan, 86–147. Dublin: Royal Irish Academy.

O'Carroll, Íde. (1990) 2015. *Models for Movers: Irish Women's Emigration to America.* Dublin: Attic.

O'Carroll, Leora. 2019. *Maureen O'Carroll: A Musical Memoir of an Irish Immigrant Childhood.* Sydney: Self-published.

Ó Ceallaigh, (Sceilg) Seán. 1922. "Cathal Brugha—As I Knew Him." *Catholic Bulletin* 12 (August): 485–496.

———. 1942. *Cathal Brugha.* Baile Átha Cliath: M. H. Macanghoill agus mhac Teoranta.

O'Connor, J. F. 1989. *An Irish Civil War Exile.* New York: Vantage.

O'Connor, Séamus. 1970. *Tomorrow Was Another Day: Irreverent Memories of an Irish Rebel Schoolmaster.* Dublin: Anvil Books.

Ó Dochartaigh, Tomás. 1969. *Cathal Brugha: A Shaol is a Thréithe.* Baile Átha Cliath, Foilseacháin Naisiúnta Teoranta.

O'Doherty, Michael Kevin. 1999. *My Parents and Other Rebels: A Personal Memoir.* Donegal: Errigal.

O'Donoghue, Florence. (1954) 1986. *No Other Law: The Story of Liam Lynch and the Irish Republican Army, 1916–1923.* Dublin: Anvil Books. Originally published in Irish Press.

Ó Drisceoil, Donal. 2012. "Keeping Disloyalty within Bounds? British Media Control in Ireland, 1914–19." *Irish Historical Studies* 38 (149): 52–69.

Ó Duigneáin, Proinnsíos. 2002. *Linda Kearns: A Revolutionary Irish Woman.* Nure, Manorhamilton, County Leitrim: Drumlin.

O'Faolain, Julia. 1980. *No Country for Young Men.* London: Penguin Books.

———. 2013. *Trespassers: A Memoir.* Faber and Faber.

O'Faoláin, Seán. 1953. "Love among the Irish." *Life Magazine*, March 16, p. 140.

O'Farrell, Elizabeth. 1917. "Miss Elizabeth O'Farrell's Story of the Surrender." *Catholic Bulletin* 7 (April–May): 266–270, 329–334.

O'Farrell, Fergus. 2018. *Cathal Brugha.* Dublin: University College Dublin Press.

O'Farrell, Patrick. 1986. *The Irish in Australia.* Sydney: University of New South Wales Press.

———. 2005. "A. T. Dryer and the Irish National Association, Sydney, 1915–16." In *Passing the Torch: The Aisling Society of Sydney, 1955–2005*, edited by Peter Walter Gray, 63–86. Sydney: Aisling Society.

Ó Fátharta, Conall. 2015. "Special Investigation: Government Already Knew of Baby Deaths." *Irish Examiner*, June 3. Accessed June 8, 2020. Available at https://www.irishexaminer.com/ireland/special-investigation-government-already-knew-of-baby-deaths-334260.html.

Ó'Grádá, Cormac. 2001. "Famine, Trauma & Memory." *Béaloideas* 69: 121—143.

Ó Grianna, Séamus [Máire]. 1959. *Tarngaireacht Mhiseóige*. Dublin: Oifig an tSoláthair.

Ó h-Agáin, Deasún. 1979. *Liam McMillen: Separatist Socialist Republican*. Dublin: Sinn Féin.

O'Halpin, Eunan. 1991. "The Civil Service and the Political System." *Administration* 38 (4): 283–302.

O'Higgins, Brian. 1962. *Wolfe Tone Annual 1962: Cathal Brugha, Salute to the Soldiers of 1922*. Dublin: Brian O'Higgins.

O'Kane, Emma. 2016. "The Hickey Family." *These Rooms*. Accessed January 12, 2018. Available at http://theserooms.ie/the-hickey-family/.

Oldfield, Sybil, ed. 2003. *International Woman Suffrage: Jus Suffragii, 1913–1920*, Vol. 2. London: Routledge.

———, ed. 2005. *This Working Day World: Women's Lives and Culture(s) in Britain, 1914–1945*. London: CRC.

O'Leary, Maeve. 2016. "The Story of Lucy Agnes Smyth and Thomas F Byrne—Both Garrisoned in the GPO during Easter Week 1916." *Tintean*, March.

O'Leary, Olivia. 2016. "Why, 100 Years after the Easter Rising, Are Irish Women Still Fighting?" *The Guardian*, March 25. Accessed May 15, 2018. https://www.theguardian.com/commentisfree/2016/mar/25/100-years-after-easter-rising-irish-women-still-fighting-gender-equality.

Olivier, Laurent. 2011. *The Dark Abyss of Time: Archaeology and Memory*. Lanham, MD: Rowan and Littlefield.

O'Malley, Ernie. 1936. *On Another Man's Wound*. Dublin: Rich and Cowan.

———. (1978) 2012. *The Singing Flame*. Cork: Mercier. Originally published by Anvil Books.

O'Neill, Marie. 1987. "Katharine Tynan Hinkson: A Dublin Writer." *Dublin Historical Record* 40 (3): 82–93.

———. 2000. *Grace Gifford Plunkett and Irish Freedom: Tragic Bride of 1916*. Dublin: Irish Academic Press.

O'Neill, Terence. 1972. *The Autobiography of Terence O'Neill*. London: Rupert Hart-Davis.

O'Reilly, Emily. 1992. *Masterminds of the Right*. Dublin: Attic.

O'Sullivan, Eoin, and Ian O'Donnell, eds. 2012. *Coercive Confinement in Ireland: Patients, Prisoners and Penitents*. Manchester, UK: Manchester University Press.

O'Sullivan, Janet. 2016. "Press Release from Abortion Rights Campaign: Huge Cross-Party Show of Support for Repeal of 8th Amendment as Politicians Pledge to Secure Abortion Rights." September 20. Accessed May 15, 2018. Available at https://www.abortionrightscampaign.ie/2016/09/20/press-release-from -abortion-rights-campaign-huge-cross-party-show-of-support-for-repeal-of-8th -amendment-as-politicians-pledge-to-secure-abortion-rights-in-ireland/.

O'Sullivan, Niamh. 2007. *Every Dark Hour: A History of Kilmainham Jail.* Dublin: Liberties Press.

O'Toole, Emer. 2017. "Waking the Feminists: Re-imagining the Space of the National Theatre in the Era of the Celtic Phoenix." *Lit: Literature Interpretation Theory* 28 (2): 134–152.

O'Toole, Fintan. 2013. "Beyond Amnesia and Piety." In *Towards Commemoration: Ireland in War and Revolution, 1912–1923,* edited by John Horne and Edward Madigan, 154–161. Dublin: Royal Irish Academy.

———. 2019. "Enough Shame about the Past. What We Need Is Guilt." *Irish Times,* April 23. Accessed June 20, 2019. Available at https://www.irishtimes.com/opinion /fintan-o-toole-enough-shame-about-the-past-what-we-need-is-guilt-1.3867461.

Ouditt, Sharon. 1994. *Fighting Forces, Writing Women: Identity and Ideology in the First World War.* London: Routledge.

Overlack, Peter. 1997. "Easter 1916 in Dublin and the Australian Press: Background and Response." *Journal of Australian Studies* 54–55:188–193.

Parkhill, Trevor. 2014. *The First World War Diaries of Emma Duffin: Belfast Voluntary Aid Nurse.* Dublin: Four Courts.

Parkins, Wendy. 1997. "Taking Liberty's, Breaking Windows: Fashion, Protest and the Suffragette Public." *Continuum* 11 (3): 37–46.

Parr, Connal. 2018. "Ending the Siege? David Ervine and the Struggle for Progressive Loyalism." *Irish Political Studies* 33 (2): 202–220.

Pašeta, Senia. 2013. *Irish Nationalist Women, 1900–1918.* Cambridge: Cambridge University Press.

Patrick, Sheila. 1954. "Where Fiddle, Harp, Trombone, Trumpet and Irish Laughter Mingle." *Australian Women's Weekly,* January 20: 11–13.

Pearce, Susan. 1995. "Archaeology as Collection." *Museum Archaeologist* 22:55–72.

Pearse, Patrick. 1903. "Gleo na gCath." *An Claidheamh Soluis* 25 (April): 3.

———. 1915 (2013). "Graveside Panegyric for O'Donovan Rossa," in *Collected Works of Padraic H. Pearse: Political Writings and Speeches.* Dublin, 1916. Republished by Éire-Gael Society.

Pennell, Catriona. 2012. *A Kingdom United: Popular Responses to the Outbreak of the First World War in Britain and Ireland.* Oxford: Oxford University Press.

———. 2017. "Choreographed by the Angels? Ireland and the Centenary of the First World War." *War and Society* 36 (4): 261–271.

Pethica, James. 2016. "'Easter, 1916' at Its Centennial: Maud Gonne, Augusta Gregory and the Evolution of the Poem." *International Yeats Studies* 1, no. 1 (December): 30–48.

Pickles, Eric. 2015. "The Valiant Troops of the World Wars Celebrated This Commonwealth Day." Accessed May 15, 2018. Available at https://www .gov.uk/government/speeches/the-valiant-troops-of-the-world-wars -celebrated-this-commonwealth-day.

Pinkman, John A., and Francis E. Maguire, eds. 1998. *In the Legion of the Vanguard.* Cork: Mercier.

Pilz, Anna. 2017. "Numbers, Narratives, and New Perspectives." *Irish Women's Writing (1880 –1910) Network.* July 6. Accessed May 15, 2018. Available at https:// irishwomenswritingnetwork.com/2017/07/06/inspirations-from-the-irish -women-playwrights-and-theatremakers-conference/.

Pine, Emilie. 2010. *The Politics of Irish Memory: Performing Remembrance in Contemporary Irish Culture.* London: Palgrave Macmillan.

———. 2019. "We Have a Culture of Not Listening to Abuse Survivors. Sealing Witnesses' Testimony for 75 Years Is Highly Detrimental to National History." *Irish Times,* May 14. Accessed June 20, 2019. Available at https://www.irishtimes .com/opinion/we-have-a-culture-of-not-listening-to-abuse-survivors-1.3891074.

———. 2020. *The Memory Marketplace.* Bloomington: Indiana University Press.

Pope, Conor. 2016 "Advertising of 'Sinn Féin-Backed' 1916 Exhibition Criticized." *Irish Times,* April 3. Accessed June 7, 2020. Available at https://www.irishtimes .com/culture/heritage/advertising-of-sinn-f%C3%A9in-backed-1916-exhibition -criticised-1.2597028.

Potter, Michael, and Ariel MacMillan. 2008. *Unionist Women Active in the Conflict in Northern Ireland.* Report for Training for Women Network. Accessed May 17, 2019. Available at https://www.twnonline.com/images/stories/researchPDF /uniWomenActivConfNI.pdf.

"Pro-choice Campaigners Dress as *The Handmaid's Tale* Characters in Protest outside Dáil." 2017. breakingnews.ie, September 20. Accessed May 22, 2018. Available at https://www.breakingnews.ie/ireland/pro-choice-campaigners-dress-as-the -handmaids-tale-characters-in-protest-outside-dail-806704.html.

Purvis, June. 2017. "A Suffragist Statue in Parliament Square Would Write Emmeline Pankhurst Out of History." *The Guardian,* September 27. Accessed June 11, 2020. Available at https://www.theguardian.com/commentisfree/2017/sep/27 /suffragist-statue-parliament-square-emmeline-pankhurst-millicent-fawcett.

Raughter, Rosemary. 2018. "The Suffragettes and the Chief Secretary: An 'Amusing Scene' on Greystones Pier." Greystones Archeological and Historical Society. Accessed December 2018. Available at www.countywicklowheritage.org.

Redmond, Jennifer. 2019. *Moving Histories: Irish Women's Emigration to Britain from Independence to Republic.* Oxford: Oxford University Press.

Regan, John. 2014. *Myth and the Irish State.* Dublin: Irish Academic Press.

Reid, Brionie. 2007. "Creating Counterspaces: Identity and the Home in Ireland and Northern Ireland in Environment and Planning." *Society and Space* 25:933–950.

Reid, Gerald. 1982. *Play for Tomorrow: "Easter 1916."* BBC Written Archives 50/ LDPD/624E,J.

Reid, Richard, Jeff Kildea, and Perry McIntyre. 2020. *To Foster an Irish Spirit: The Irish National Association of Australasia 1915–2015.* Sydney: Anchor.

Remembrance NI. 2018. "First World War Nurses." February. Accessed May 10, 2020. Available at https://remembranceni.org/2018/02/26/first-world-war-nurses-2/.

Revolution 1916. 2016. *Revolution 1916: The Original and Authentic Exhibition.* Ambassador Theatre, Dublin. February to October 2016. Accessed May 20, 2018. Available at https://www.anphoblacht.com/contents/25591.

Reynolds, Chris. 2019. "Transnational Memories and Gender: Northern Ireland's 1968." In *Women, Global Protest Movements, and Political Agency: Rethinking the Legacy of 1968,* edited by Sarah Colvin and Katherina Karcher, 50–66. London: Routledge.

Reynolds, Paige. 2007. *Modernism, Drama, and the Audience for Irish Spectacle.* Cambridge: Cambridge University Press.

Richmond Barracks. 2020a. "A List of Women Who Were Detained at Richmond Barracks after the 1916 Rising." RichmondBarracks.ie. Accessed May 10, 2020. Available at http://www.richmondbarracks.ie/women-1916/women-detainees -list/.

———. 2020b. "The Women of 1916 and the Irish Revolution." Accessed May 10, 2020. Available at http://www.richmondbarracks.ie/category/women-1916/.

———. 2020c. "Women and 1916—Commemoration Quilt." Richmond Barracks, Dublin City Council Culture Company, Dublin. Accessed June 7, 2020. Available at http://www.richmondbarracks.ie/women-1916/commemoration-quilt/.

Roche, Anthony. 1995. "Woman on the Threshold: J. M. Synge's 'The Shadow of the Glen,' Teresa Deevy's 'Katie Roche,' and Marina Carr's 'The Mai.'" *Irish University Review* 25 (1): 143–162.

Rolley, Katrina. 1990. "Fashion, Femininity and the Fight for the Vote." *Art History* 13 (1): 47–71.

Rooney, Eilish. 2007. "Intersectionality in Transition: Lessons from Northern Ireland." *Web Journal of Current Legal Issues* (5). Accessed June 11, 2020. Available at https://www.researchgate.net/publication/292747562_Intersectionality_in _transition_Lessons_from_Northern_Ireland.

———. 2008. "Critical Reflections: Documenting Gender and Memory." *Women's Studies International Forum* 31:457–463.

Roper, Esther, ed. (1934) 1987. *Prison Letters of Countess Markievicz.* London: Virago.

Rossiter, Ann. 2009. *Ireland's Hidden Diaspora: The "Abortion Trail" and the Making of the London Irish Underground, 1980–2000.* London: Iasc.

Rothberg, Michael. 2009. *Multidirectional Memory: Remembering the Holocaust in the Age of Decolonization.* Stanford, CA: Stanford University Press.

Ryan, Louise, ed. 1996. *Irish Feminism and the Vote: An Anthology of the Irish Citizen Newspaper 1912–1920*. Dublin: Folens.

———. 2001a. "Splendidly Silent: Representing Irish Republican Women, 1919–1923." In *Re-presenting the Past: Women and History*, edited by Ann-Marie Gallagher, Cathy Lubleska, and Louise Ryan, 23–43. London: Longman.

———. 2001b. "Irish Female Emigration in the 1930s: Transgressing Space and Culture." *Gender, Place and Culture* 8 (3): 271–282.

———. 2002. *Gender, Identity and the Irish Press, 1922–1937: Embodying the Nation*. Lewiston: Edwin Mellon.

———. 2004. "'In the Line of Fire': Representations of Women and War (1919–1923) through the Writings of Republican Men." In *Irish Women and Nationalism: Soldiers, New Women and Wicked Hags*, edited by Louise Ryan and Margaret Ward, 45–61. Dublin: Irish Academic Press.

———. (1996) 2018. *Winning the Vote for Women: The Irish Citizen Newspaper and the Suffrage Movement in Ireland*. Dublin: Four Courts.

Ryan, Louise, and Margaret Ward, eds. 2004. *Irish Women and Nationalism: Soldiers, New Women and Wicked Hags*. Dublin: Irish Academic Press.

———. (2007) 2018. *Irish Women and the Vote: Becoming Citizens: New Edition*. Dublin: Irish Academic Press.

Sackville Street Art Project. 2016. "1916 Sackville Street Art Project." March 28. Accessed May 10, 2020. Available at https://1916.rte.ie/event/oconnell-street/1916-sackville-street-art-project/.

Sales, Rosemary. 1997. *Women Divided: Gender, Religion, and Politics in Northern Ireland*. London, Routledge.

Saunders, Max. 2008. "Life-Writing, Cultural Memory, and Literary Studies." In *Cultural Memory Studies: An International and Interdisciplinary Handbook*, edited by Astrid Erll and Ansgar Nünning, 321–332. Berlin: Walter de Gruyter.

Schneider, Rebecca. 2011. *Performing Remains: Art and War in Times of Theatrical Reenactment*. London: Routledge.

Scrivner, Ellen, and Martin A. Safer. 1988. "Eyewitnesses Show Hypermnesia for Details about a Violent Event." *Journal of Applied Psychology* 73:371–377.

Sewell, Jessica. 2008. "Tea and Suffrage." *Food, Culture and Society* 11 (4): 487–507.

Shannon, Catherine B. 1995. "Women in Northern Ireland." In *Chattel, Servant or Citizen: Women's Status in Church, State and Society*, edited by Mary O'Dowd and Sabine Wichert, 238–247. Belfast: Institute of Irish Studies.

Shaw, George Bernard. 1914. "Common Sense About the War: A Supplement to the *New Statesman*." *New Statesman* 4, no. 84 (November 14).

Sheehy Skeffington, Hanna. 1975. "Reminiscences of an Irish Suffragette." In *Votes for Women: Irish Women's Struggle for the Vote*, edited by A. D. Sheehy Skeffington and Rosemary Owens, 12–26. Dublin: Arlen House.

Sheehy Skeffington, Micheline. 2017. Accessed February 14, 2019. Available at https://www.dublincity.ie/councilmeetings/documents/s14805/Hanna

%20Sheehy%20Skeffington%20Application%20Form%20amended%20wording .pdf.

Shelton, Dinah L. 2019. "Historical Injustices." *Encyclopedia of Genocide and Crimes against Humanity.* Encyclopedia. Accessed June 11, 2019. Available at https:// www.encyclopedia.com/international/encyclopedias-almanacs-transcripts -and-maps/historical-injustices.

Sheppard, Alice. 1994. *Cartooning for Suffrage.* Albuquerque: University of New Mexico Press.

Sherman, David. 1996. "Monuments, Mourning and Masculinity in France after World War I." *Gender and History* 8:82–107.

Shovlin, Paul. 2013. *When Push Comes to Shove: A Memoir.* Morrisonville: Lulu.

Sihra, Melissa. 2009. "Interchapter III: 1970–2005." In *Women in Irish Drama: A Century of Authorship and Representation,* edited by Melissa Sihra, 151–159. Basingstoke, UK: Palgrave Macmillan.

———. 2017. "Power of Silence: Teresa Deevy Returns to Abbey." *Irish Independent,* August 27. Accessed May 15, 2018. Available at https://www.independent.ie /entertainment/theatre-arts/power-of-silence-teresa-deevy-returns-to-abbey -36067284.html.

Sinn Féin. 2015a. "Sinn Féin Launches Programme of Events to Mark Centenary of 1916 Rising," Sinn Féin. February 6. Accessed June 7, 2020. Available at https:// www.sinnfein.ie/contents/33261.

———. 2015b. "Sinn Féin National Launch Commemorative Events," Sinn Féin. Accessed June 7, 2020. Available at https://www.sinnfein.ie/files/2015 /SinnFein2016BrochureWeb.pdf.

Smith, James M. 2007. *Ireland's Magdalen Laundries: And the Nation's Architecture of Containment.* Notre Dame, IN: University of Notre Dame Press.

Souvenir Shop, The. 2016. Accessed May 23, 2018. Available at http:// souvenirshop19162016.com/home.html.

Speaking of IMELDA. 2015a. "Dirty Work Still to Be Done: Retrieving and Activating Feminist Acts of Resistance." *Contemporary Theatre Review.* Accessed May 12, 2018. Available at http://www.contemporarytheatrereview.org/2015/margaretta-darcy/.

———. 2015b. "Pro-Choice Proclamation." Accessed May 12, 2018. Available at https://youtu.be/DIVS1HbOMBM.

———. 2020. "About Speaking of IMELDA." Accessed May 10, 2020. Available at https://www.speakingofimelda.org/.

Specia, Megan. 2018. "How Savita Halappanavar's Death Spurred Ireland's Abortion Rights Campaign." *New York Times,* May 27.

Spencer Hewitt, Rachel. 2016. "Where Are the Disappeared Women of the Theatre?" *HowlRound,* December 17. Accessed May 15, 2018. Available at http://howlround .com/where-are-the-disappeared-women-of-the-theatre.

Spender, Dale. 1982. *Women of Ideas and What Men Have Done to Them.* London: Pandora.

Steele, Jane. 2003. "'And behind a Wicked Hag Did Stalk': From Maiden to Mother, Ireland as Woman through the Male Psyche." In *Irish Women and Nationalism: Soldiers, New Women and Wicked Hags*, edited by Louise Ryan and Margaret Ward, 96–131. Dublin: Irish Academic Press.

Steele, Karen. 2010. "Gender and the Postcolonial Archive." *New Centennial Review* 10, no. 1 (Spring): 55–61.

Stevens, Lorna, Stephen Brown, and Pauline Maclaran. 2000. "Gender, Nationality and Cultural Representations of Ireland." *European Journal of Women's Studies* 7 (4): 405–421.

Stewart, A. T. Q. 1967. *The Ulster Crisis. Resistance to Home Rule, 1912–14*. London: Faber and Faber.

Stoneybatter and Smithfield People's History Project. 2016. "1916–2016 North King Street Massacre—A Community Remembers." Facebook Event, April 2016. Accessed January 22, 2018. Available at https://www.facebook.com/events /691800420962581/.

Stories in Sound: In the Footsteps. 2018. BBC Ulster, August 19. Accessed February 15, 2019. Available at https://www.bbc.co.uk/programmes/m00006sl.

Strachey, Ray. 1931. *Millicent Garrett Fawcett*. London: J. Murray.

Summerfield, Penny. 1998. *Reconstructing Women's Wartime Lives: Discourse and Subjectivity in Oral Histories of the Second World War*. Manchester, UK: Manchester University Press.

Swain, Hedley. 2007. *An Introduction to Museum Archaeology*. Cambridge: Cambridge University Press.

Switzer, Catherine. 2007. *Unionists and Great War Commemoration in the North of Ireland 1914–39: People, Places and Politics*. Dublin: Irish Academic Press.

———. 2013. *Ulster, Ireland and the Somme: War Memorials and Battlefield Pilgrimages*. Dublin: History Press.

Taillon, Ruth. 1999. *When History Was Made: The Women of 1916*. Belfast: Beyond the Pale.

Taylor, Diana. 1997. *Disappearing Acts: Spectacles of Gender and Nationalism in Argentina's "Dirty War."* Durham, NC: Duke University Press.

Thom, Deborah. 1998. *Nice Girls and Rude Girls: Women Workers in World War I*. London: I. B. Tauris.

———. 2017. "Gender and Work." In *Gender and the Great War*, edited by Susan R. Grayzel and Tammy M Proctor, 46–66. Oxford: Oxford University Press.

Tickner, Lisa. 1987. *The Spectacle of Women: Imagery of the Suffrage Campaign, 1907–1914*. London: Chatto and Windus.

Tiernan, Sonja, ed. 2015. *The Political Writings of Eva Gore-Booth*. Manchester, UK: Manchester University Press.

Toal, Ciaran. 2014. "'The Brutes': Mrs Metge and the Lisburn Cathedral Bomb, 1914." *History Ireland* 6, no. 22 (November–December). Accessed June 3, 2019.

Available at http://www.historyireland.com/volume-22/brutes-mrs-metge-lisburn-cathedral-bomb-1914/.

Tonge, Jonathan. 2014. "Women in the DUP: 'The Backbone of the Party.'" In *The Democractic Unionist Party: From Protest to Power*, edited by Jonathan Tonge, Maire Braniff, Thomas Hennessey, James W. McAuley, and Sophie Whiting, 191–221. Oxford: Oxford University Press.

Toolen, Tom. 1982. "Staging William's World: Poet's Friend Helps Dramatize His Life." *The Record* [New Jersey], October 28: C1, C19.

Tornquist-Plewa, Barbara, Niklas Bernsand, and Marco La Rosa, eds. 2017. *In Search of Transnational Memory in Europe*. Kansli, Luxembourg: Lund University Press.

Townshend, Charles. 2004. "Religion, War and Identity in Ireland." *Journal of Modern History* 76 (4): 882–902.

———. 2006. *Easter 1916: The Irish Rebellion*. London: Penguin Books.

Travers, Pauric. 1995. "'There Was Nothing for Me There': Irish Female Migration, 1922–71." In *Irish Women and Irish Migration*, edited by Patrick O'Sullivan, 146–167. Leicester, UK: Leicester University Press.

Treacy, Ciara. 2016. "Sinn Féin Exhibition on 1916 Jumps to Tribute to the Provisional IRA." *Irish Independent*, April 2. Accessed June 7, 2020. Available at https://www.independent.ie/irish-news/1916/sinn-fein-exhibition-on-1916-jumps-to-tribute-to-the-provisional-ira-34592414.html.

Treasured Dolls. 2018. "Collections, Molly O'Reilly." Accessed January 22, 2018. Available at https://www.treasureddolls.ie/products/molly.

Trew, Johanne Devlin. 2016. *Leaving the North: Migration and Memory, Northern Ireland 1921–2011*. Oxford: Oxford University Press.

Tynan, Katharine. 1915. *Flower of Youth*. London: Sidgwick and Jackson.

———. 1919. *The Year of the Shadow*. London: Houghton Mifflin.

Ulster-Scots Community Network. 2012. *Understanding the Ulster Covenant*. Belfast: Ulster-Scots Community Network. Accessed 11 June 7, 2020. Available at https://www.creativecentenaries.org/ulster-covenant.

University of Sheffield. 2018. "Millicent Fawcett: A Statue to Suffrage." Research Impact Stories. Accessed May 10, 2020. Available at http://researchstories.group.shef.ac.uk/impact/a-statue-to-suffrage/.

Urquhart, Diane. 1994. "'The Female of the Species Is More Deadlier Than the Male?' The Ulster Women's Unionist Council, 1911–40." In *Coming into the Light: The Work, Politics and Religion of Women in Ulster, 1840–1940*, edited by Janice Holmes and Diane Urquhart, 93–123. Belfast: Institute of Irish Studies, Queen's University Belfast.

———. 1996. "In Defence of Ulster and the Empire: The Ulster Women's Unionist Council, 1886–1940." *Galway Women's Studies Centre Review*, no. 4, 31–40.

———. 2000. *Women in Ulster Politics, 1890–1940: A History Not Yet Told*. Dublin: Irish Academic Press.

————, ed. 2001. *The Minutes of the Ulster Women's Unionist Council and Executive Committee, 1911–40*. Dublin: Irish Manuscripts Commission.

————. 2007. *The Ladies of Londonderry: Women and Political Patronage*. London: I. B. Tauris.

UWUC Year Book. 1920. Belfast: Ulster Women's Unionist Council.

Valiulis, Maryann Gialanella. 1992. "Defining Their Role in the New State: Irishwomen's Protest against the Juries Act of 1927." *Canadian Journal of Irish Studies* 18 (1): 43–60.

Vótáil 100. 2018. "Houses of the Oireachtas Commemorated the 100th Anniversary of the Parliamentary Vote for Women in Ireland." Accessed May 10, 2020. Available at https://www.oireachtas.ie/en/visit-and-learn/votail-100/.

Walker, Nadeane. 1944. "The Irish Disillusion." *Fort Worth Star Telegram*, May 21, p. 17.

Walsh, Fionnuala. 2017. "'We Work with Shells All Day and Night': Irish Female Munitions Workers during the First World War." *Saothar, Journal of the Irish Labour History Society* 42:19–30.

————. 2020. *Irish Women and the Great War*. Cambridge: Cambridge University Press.

Ward, Margaret. 1991. *The Missing Sex: Putting Women into Irish History*. Dublin: Attic.

————. 1995. "Conflicting Interests: The British and Irish Suffrage Movements," *Feminist Review* 50:127–147.

————. (1989) 1995. *In Their Own Voice: Women and Irish Nationalism*. Dublin: Attic.

————. (1983) 1995. *Unmanageable Revolutionaries: Women and Irish Nationalism*. Dingle, County Kerry: Brandon Books; reprinted by London: Pluto.

————. 1997. *Hanna Sheehy Skeffington: A Life*. Cork: Attic.

————. 2005. "Gender, Citizenship and the Future of the Northern Ireland Peace Process." *Éire-Ireland* 40 (3–4): 1–22.

————. 2016. "Hanna and Frank Sheehy Skeffington." In *The Shaping of Modern Ireland*, edited by Eugenio Biagini and Daniel Mulhall, 221–234. Dublin: Irish Academic Press.

————. 2017. *Hanna Sheehy Skeffington: Suffragette and Sinn Féiner—Her Memoirs and Political Writings*. Dublin: University College Dublin Press.

Ward, Margaret, and Marie-Thérèse McGivern. 1980. "Images of Women in Northern Ireland." *Crane Bag* 4 (1): 66–72.

Ward, Mary. 2018. "Puritanism and Protest: How Handmaid Fashion Started a Movement." *Sydney Morning Herald*, March 24. Accessed May 22, 2018. Available at https://www.smh.com.au/lifestyle/fashion/puritanism-and-protest-how-handmaid-fashion-started-a-movement-20180321-p4z5hx.html.

Ward, Rachel. 2002. "Invisible Women: The Political Roles of Loyalist and Unionist Women in Contemporary Northern Ireland." *Parliamentary Affairs* 55:167–178.

———. 2006. *Women, Unionism and Loyalism in Northern Ireland: From "Tea-makers" to Political Actors.* Dublin: Irish Academic Press.

Whelan, Bernadette. 2015. "Women on the Move: A Review of the Historiography of Irish Emigration to the USA, 1750–1900." *Women's History Review* 24 (6): 900–916.

Whitaker, Anne-Maree. 1996. "Irish War of Independence Veterans in Australia." In *Irish-Australian Studies: Papers Delivered at the Eighth Irish-Australian Conference, Hobart 1995*, edited by Richard Davis, Jennifer Livett, Anne-Maree, and Peter Moore, 413–420. Sydney: Crossing.

———. 2016a. "Linda Kearns and Kathleen Barry's Irish Republican Fundraising Tour, 1924–25." *Journal of the Australian Catholic Historical Society* 37 (2): 208–211.

———. 2016b. "Margaret Fleming: Irish Rebel to Sydney Schoolteacher." *Descent* 46 (4): 182–185.

———. 2018. "The Irish Women's Club: Cumann na mBan in Sydney 1919–1935." Paper delivered at 23rd Australasian Conference of Irish Studies, November, University of Sydney.

White, Lawrence William, and Patrick Long. 2011. "Donnelly, Helen Ruth ('Nellie') Gifford." *Dictionary of Irish Biography.* Revised February 2011. Accessed May 19, 2018. Available at http://dib.cambridge.org/viewReadPage.do;jsessionid=F1CE6 5D48FC3B0A207487CEF2CF9E428?articleId=a3464.

White, Victoria. 2016. "True Heroines of 1916 Forgotten in Attempt to Feminise the Rising." *Irish Examiner*, March 31. Accessed May 15, 2018. Available at https://www .irishexaminer.com/viewpoints/columnists/victoria-white/true-heroines-of-1916 -forgotten-in-attempt-to-feminise-the-rising-390207.html.

Whitehouse, Harvey. 1995. *Inside the Cult: Religious Innovation and Transmission in Papua New Guinea.* Oxford: Clarendon.

Wilk, Gavin. 2014. *Transatlantic Defiance: The Militant Irish Republican Movement in America, 1923–45.* Manchester: Manchester University Press.

Wills, Clair. 2009. *Dublin 1916: The Siege of the GPO.* London: Profile Books.

Winter, Jay. 1995. *Sites of Memory, Sites of Mourning.* Oxford: Oxford University Press.

"Women of Ireland to Watch Handmaid's Tale to Escape Grim Reality." 2018. waterfordwhisperers.ie, May 1. Accessed May 22, 2018. Available at http:// waterfordwhispersnews.com/2018/05/01/women-of-ireland-to-watch -handmaids-tale-to-escape-grim-reality/.

Women of the South. 2016. "Radicals and Revolutionaries." March to November 2016. Farmgate Café, English Market, Cork. Accessed May 10, 2020. Available at http://farmgatecork.ie/womenofthesouth/.

Women's Resource and Development Agency (WRDA). 2007. *Talking about the Troubles and Planning for the Future.* Accessed March 1, 2019. Available at http:// cain.ulst.ac.uk/issues/women/docs/mclaughlin08womenconflict.pdf.

———. 2016. *Women's Manifesto.* Accessed February 27, 2019. Available at http://review .table59.co.uk/wrda/wp-content/uploads/2016/12/Womens-Manifesto-2016.pdf.

Woollacott, Angela. 1994. *On Her Their Lives Depend: Munitions Workers in the Great War.* Berkeley: University of California Press.

Wulff, Helena. 2008. *Dancing at the Crossroads: Memory and Mobility in Ireland.* New York: Berghahn Books.

WWI Ireland. 2014. "Learning Resources." Accessed May 10, 2020. Available at http://www.nli.ie/wwi/.

Yeates, Padraig. 2017. "The Cinderella Centenary." In *The Dublin Lockout, 1913*, edited by Pádraig Yeates and Conor McNamara, 161–184. Dublin: Irish Academic Press.

Yeats, W. B. 1917. *The Wild Swans at Coole.* Dublin: The Cuala Press.

———. 1919. *The Wild Swans at Coole.* London: Macmillan.

———. 1997. *The Major Works.* Edited by Edward Larrissy. Oxford: Oxford University Press.

———. 2002. *The Collected Letters of W.B. Yeats.* Edited by John Kelly. Oxford: Oxford University Press (Intelex Electronic Edition).

Young, James E. 2009. "Regarding the Pain of Women: Questions of Gender and the Arts of Holocaust Memory." *PMLA* 124 (5): 1778–1786.

Yuval-Davis, Nira. 1997. *Gender and Nation.* London: Sage.

Yuval-Davis, Nira, and Floya Anthias. 1989. *Woman-Nation-State.* London: Macmillan.

ARCHIVAL RECORDS

Adjutant General IRA. 1923. Letter from Adjutant-General to Adjutant North Mayo Brigade. August 4. University College Dublin (U.C.D.) Archives, Moss Toomey Papers, p69/167 (10).

Aiken, Frank. 1924. Letter from IRA Chief of State to Máire Ní Chomatúin. January 9. U.C.D. Archives, Moss Toomey Papers, p69/37 (124).

———. n.d. [Lámh Dhearg] "Emigration." Frank Aiken Papers, U.C.D. Archives, p104/2561.

Bates, Richard Dawson. 1917. Letter to Theresa Londonderry. January 3. Public Records Office of Northern Ireland (PRONI), D/2846/1/1/8/65.

Brennan, Michael. Military Archives of Ireland (M.A.I.) Bureau of Military History/ Witness Statement (WS) 1,068,29.

Bulfin, Catalina. 1976. Letter to Bridie Halpin (with envelope). October 27. [OBJ0033.01+02 Kilmainham Gaol Archive]

Cable, W. G. H. 1934. Letter to the Department of Defence [re: Mary O'Carroll]. October 31. M.A.I. Military Service Pensions Collection, MSP34REF10326.

Campbell, Margaret. M.A.I. Military medal file (MD34701).

Census of Ireland. 1911. Susan Manning and Elizabeth Duggan. "Religion—Militant Suffragette." Accessed May 10, 2020. Available at http://www .census.nationalarchives.ie/reels/nai000137861/.

Comerford, Máire. 1956. Draft introduction to a book entitled *The Dangerous Ground*. U.C.D. Archives, Máire Comerford Papers, LA18/1.

———. n.d. Letter from Máire Comerford to Molly Flanagan Woods. Molly Flannery Woods Papers, Burns Library, Boston College, MS.1995.034. Incoming Correspondence: C, 1918–1945, Box 1.

Commonwealth War Graves Commission. 2020. Record for Mary Doherty. Accessed June 11, 2020. Available at https://www.cwgc.org/find-war-dead/casualty/624622 /doherty,-mary-agnes/.

"Conscientious Objectors Information Bureau Reports 1917–19." 1917–1919. Working Class Movement Library, Manchester, UK, ORG/NCF/1/C.

Cosgrove, Polly. 1923. Letter to Bridie Halpin at NDU Internment Camp. Dated July 19, 1923. [OBJ0027.01–3 Kilmainham Gaol Archive]

Cumann na mBan Nominal Rolls M.A.I., CMB/1-165.

Daly, Patrick G. 1953. Witness Statement. March 21. M.A.I. Bureau of Military History/WS 814.

Davin, Mary Agnes. 1936. Sworn Statement made before Advisory Committee. June 26. M.A.I. Military Service Pensions Collection, MSP34REF16824.

Diary, North Dublin Union. M.A.I., CW/P/06/04–1923.

Douglas, Nora. M.A.I. Military pension file (MSP34REF35989; MSP34E615).

DRPEB. 1924. Dublin Republican Prisoners Employment Bureau. Request to attend for Employment. [OBJ0030 Kilmainham Gaol Archive]

Dryer, Albert. Witness Statement. M.A.I. Bureau of Military History/WS 1526.

Dunne, James. 1957. Witness Statement. February 4. M.A.I. Bureau of Military History/WS 1571.

Ferrick, Ellie. ca. 1926. Letter from Ellie Ferrick to Mary MacSwiney. U.C.D. Archives, Mary Mac Swiney Papers, p48a/123 (12–13).

Fitzgerald, James. 1954. Witness Statement. August 30. M.A.I. Bureau of Military History/WS 999.

Forkan, Phyllis. Witness Statement. M.A.I. Bureau of Military History/WS 210.

Hackett, Rosie. Witness Statement. M.A.I. Bureau of Military History/WS 546, 10–11.

Halpin, Bridie. 1923a. Autograph Book. [OBJ0023 Kilmainham Gaol Archive]

———. 1923b. Letter to Leo Halpin. Dated September 25, 1923. [OBJ0026 Kilmainham Gaol Archive]

———. 1923c. Detention Order for Eileen Colgan / Bridie Halpin signed by Richard Mulcahy on August 8, 1923.

Healy, Michael. Witness Statement. M.A.I. Bureau of Military History/WS 1064.

Intelligence Department, M.A.I. 1924. Correspondence regarding prisoners. February 1. CW/P/05/08–1924.

"Irish Girls." Inghinidhe na hÉireann handbill, M.A.I., CD119/3/1.

Join an Irish Regiment Today. 1914. Central Council for the Organisation of Recruiting in Ireland, National Library of Ireland (Department of Ephemera), WAR/1914–18/58.

Leonard (née Fleming), Margaret. 1934–1939. Letters to Secretary of the Minister of Defence, December 1, 1934; January 23, 1939; December 17, 1939. M.I.A. Military Service Pensions Collection, MSP34REF45593.

Lytle, Mary. 1934. Letter to the Department of Defence. August 30. M.A.I. Military Service Pensions Collection, MSP34REF58239.

MacBride, Maud Gonne. 1949. Letter to Bridie Halpin. Dated November 25. [OBJ0032.01–03 Kilmainham Gaol Archive]

MacCarthy, John M. 1953. "General Order Issued by Óglaigh na hÉireann, 19 June 1920." In Witness Statement. July 30. M.A.I. Bureau of Military History/WS 883.

Martin, W. H. 1918. *Killyleagh Women's War Work and Patriotic Effort and Roll of Honor.* October. [PRONI D3524/2/1]

McCarthy, Patrick J. 1915. "Report on Anti-militarist Meeting Held at Beresford Place by Patrick J. McCarthy Constable 36G, 23 May 1915." National Archives, Kew, Colonial Office Record Series, Vol. 1, Dublin Castle Special Branch Files, CO 904/215/408.

Minute book of Lurgan Women's Unionist Association. May 13, 1911. [PRONI, D/3790/4, D/1098/1/2]

"Minutes of the Cumann na mBan Convention." 1918. Ceannt and O'Brennan Papers, 1851–1953 (September 28–29, 1918) National Library of Ireland, MS 41,494/1/2.

Molony, Helena. 1907–1914. Witness Statement. M.A.I. Bureau of Military History/WS 391, Helena Molony, Secretary Inghini na hEireann, 1907–1914.

———. 1924. Letter to IRA Chief of Staff. November 9. U.C.D. Archives, Moss Toomey Papers, p69/37 (112).

Murphy, Fintan. Witness Statement. M.A.I. Bureau of Military History/WS 373.

New York, Passenger and Crew Lists, 1820–1957, Ancestry. Accessed May 10, 2020. Available at https://www.ancestry.com/search/collections/7488/.

"The Nora McKenna Story." 2000. File on Nora Brosnan (McKenna). Kilmainham Gaol Collection 20MS-1D46-27.

O'Carroll, Eileen Markievicz. 1935. Letter to Mr. Dixon [re: Mary O'Carroll]. August 21. M.A.I. Military Service Pensions Collection, MSP34REF10326.

O'Carroll, May Gahan. File. Kilmainham Gaol Collection 20MS-1B53-10.

———. M.A.I. Military Service Pension File (MSP34REF10326).

O'Driscoll, Seán. 1936. Letter from to the Department of Defence [re: Katty Hicks (née O'Driscoll)], April 21. M.A.I. Military Service Pensions Collection, MSP34REF16920.

O'Mullane, Bridget. 1950. Witness Statement. November 13. M.A.I. Bureau of Military History/WS 450.

Prisoners Location Book. 1922–1924. M.A.I., CW/P/01/01–1923–1924.

PRONI. 2016. Launch of Con and Eva Exhibition at PRONI (May 18, 2016). Accessed June 5, 2020. Available at https://www.communities-ni.gov.uk/news /launch-con-and-eva-exhibition-proni.

PRONI Ulster Covenant. 2020. Accessed May 20, 2020. Available at https://apps .proni.gov.uk/ulstercovenant/Search.aspx.

Sheehy Skeffington, Hanna. 1910. Letter to Frank Sheehy Skeffington. July 24. National Library of Ireland, Sheehy Skeffington MS 40,466/4.

Shighle Humphreys Papers. U.C.D. Archives, p106/1226[1].

UK Incoming Passenger Lists, 1878–1960. Ancestry. Accessed May 20, 2020. Available at https://www.ancestry.co.uk/search/collections/1518/.

UK Outward Passenger Lists, 1890–1960. Ancestry. Accessed May 20, 2020. Available at https://www.ancestry.com/search/collections/2997/.

Ulster Women's Unionist Council (UWUC). 1913. Annual Report. [PRONI, D/2688/1/3]

———. 1913. Executive Committee Minutes, January 16. [PRONI, D/1089/1/1]

———. 1914. Executive Committee Minutes, May 14. [PRONI, D/1098/1/2]

———. 1917. Advisory Committee Minutes, January 2. [PRONI, D/2688/1/7]

———. 1918. Executive Committee Minutes, June 18. [PRONI, D/1098/1/2]

———. 1918. Minutes, June 18. [PRONI, D/1098/1/3]

———. 1920. Annual Report. [PRONI, D/2688/1/3]

———. 1931. Executive Committee Minutes, January 26. [PRONI, D/1098/1/2]

US Census Records. 1930. Accessed May 10, 2020. Available at https://www.ancestry .com/search/collections/6224/.

INDEX

Abbey Theatre, 8, 214, 222–223; Gender
 Equality Committee, 251; *Katie Roche*
 (Deevy), 253–254, 256–261; MAM
 (Mothers Artists Makers), 245–249;
 Speaking of IMEDLA, 279–281; *Waking*
 the Nation, 4–5, 16, 242–247, 253, 262
abortion, 226, 239, 263–264n6, 270, 273–282,
 283nn6–9; *Attorney General v. X*, 275–278;
 Eighth Amendment (Irish constitution)
 and, 18, 59–61, 225, 248, 274–275,
 277–282, 311–312; Pro-Life Amendment
 Campaign (PLAC), 274; #Repealthe8th
 movement, 60
Academic Manel Watch Ireland (Twitter
 movement), 3
Adams, Gerry, 233–234
Addams, Jane, 113
Aiken, Frank, 90, 92, 191
Ambassador Theatre, 226–227, 232
Anglo-Irish Treaty, 28, 34, 91
anti-conscription movement, 107–123; anti-
 war publications, 115–116; commemoration
 of, 121–123; cooperation of British and
 Irish movements, 120–121; extending
 military conscription to Ireland, 117–118;
 International Congress of Women
 and, 111–113; Irish Anti-Conscription
 Committee, 118; No Conscription
 Fellowship, 113–115, 116; pro-militant age,
 110–111; *Tribunal, The* (journal), 115–116;
 Tribunal, The (pamphlet), 116; women

and World War I in Britain and Ireland,
 108–109
anti-nostalgia. *See* nostalgia and
 anti-nostalgia
Apprentice Boys and Unionist Clubs, 49
Arbour Hill Garrison Chapel, 28, 136
Arnold-Foster, H. O., 42
Ashe, Thomas, 23–25, 38n3, 138
Asquith, H. H., 55n11, 117, 152–153
Assmann, Aleida, 88, 93
Atwood, Margaret, 17
Augusta, Lady Gregory, 4, 5, 8–9, 220, 239–
 243, 249, 253–255, 261
Auslander, Mark, 210
Australia, 74–86; Connolly Club, 79;
 emigration to, 94, 98, 100–101; Hands
 Off Ireland Organization, 74, 78; Irish
 Amateur Athletics Association in
 Melbourne, 79; Irish in Australia in
 1916, 75–78; Irish National Association
 (INA), 78, 81, 83; newspapers, 77–81, 85;
 1916 commemorations, 78–79; Waverley
 Cemetery commemoration, 74, 78, 79, 83;
 women veterans of the Irish revolutionary
 period, 79–84
Aylesbury Prison, 180, 212

Bacik, Ivana, 123, 243, 275
Ballagh, Robert, 238
Barry, Elgin, 189, 195
Barry, Kathleen, 77, 78, 80

Ó Dochartaigh, Tomás, 195, 199
O'Doherty, Eamonn, 224
O'Doherty, Kitty, 92
O'Donoghue, Florence "Florrie," 195,
    198–199
O'Donovan Rossa, Jeremiah, 38n3, 138, 210,
    227
O'Faolain, Eileen, 105
O'Faolain, Julia, 105
O'Faolain, Seán, 90
O'Farrell, Elizabeth, 13, 28–35, *30, 31,* 36,
    38n8, 39n9, 39n11, 79, 213, 239–240
Ó Fearghaíl, Seán, 183–184
Offences Against the Person Act (1861),
    274, 275
O'Flanagan, Michael, 80
O'Hegarty, P. S., 26, 34
O'Kane, Emma, 208
O'Kelly, J. J., 26, 80
O'Kelly, Seamus G., 199
O'Leary, Maeve, 74, 84
O'Leary, Olivia, 221
O'Loughlin, Fiona, 123
O'Malley, Ernie, 190–191, 192
O'Neill, Eoin, 206
O'Neill, Lawrence, 118
O'Neill, Terence, 206
O'Neill, Timothy, 69
O'Rahilly, Nannie, 25
O'Rahilly, The, 25
Orange Order, 51–52
O'Reilly, John, 274
O'Reilly, Molly, 233–237, 238, 239, 241n6
O'Reilly, Ned, 191, 193
O'Toole, Emer, 242, 243–244
O'Toole, Fintan, 3, 218, 312

Pankhurst, Adela, 122
Pankhurst, Christabel, 109, 114, 179, 186
Pankhurst, Emmeline, 109, 114, 186
Pankhurst, Sylvia, 185–186
Parliament Act of 1911, 43, 55n11
Pearse, Margaret, 62–63, 72, 77, 217
Pearse, Mary Margaret, 28
Pearse, Padraig, 232, 235, 238, 239–240
Pearse, Patrick, 7, 13, 27, 28–29, 32–33, 76, 90,
    138, 206–207, 215, 223, 267, 282
Pennell, Catriona, 125

Pethick-Lawrence, Emmeline, 113, 169
Pickles, Eric, 107, 122
Pine, Emilie, 14, 104, 292, 299, 308
Piper, Tom, 138
Playboy of the Western World (Synge), 4
Plough and the Stars, The (O'Casey), 5, 242
Plunkett, Joseph, 25, 76, 213, 239
Plunkett, Mimi, 92
Power, Albert, 173
Power, Jennie Wyse, 27, 173
Praeger, Sophia Rosamund, 152, *162,* 163–164
Price, Leslie, 36
Primrose League, 43, 54n6, 55n15
Prison Ship Maidstone, 293
Pro-Life Amendment Campaign (PLAC),
    274
Public Record Office Northern Ireland
    (PRONI), 182

Queen Mary Army Auxiliary Corps, 125,
    134, 135

Rebellion (RTÉ drama), 36, 263n1
Redmond, John, 75, 108, 145, 153, 164, *165*
Redmond, William, 75
Regan, John, 303
Regan, Moira, 76
Regan, Morna, 260
Reid, Briony, 284
Reid, Graham, 205–206
#Repealthe8th movement, 60
Report of the Commission of Inquiry into
    the Mother and Baby Homes, 17, 301
Report of the Commission to Inquire into
    Child Abuse (Ryan Report), 16, 239, 301
Representation of the People Act, 48–49,
    171–172, 174, 177, 178–179
*Revolution 1916: The Original and Authentic
    Exhibition* (exhibition), 226–227, 232–239
Reynolds, Chris, 286–287
Reynolds, J. J., 25
Richmond Barracks, 3, 58–59, 63, 225
Róisín Dubh, 89
Rooney, Eilish, 287, 292
Roper, Esther, 110
Royal Irish Academy (RIA), 3–4, 239
Ryan, Dora, 154
Ryan, Louise, 28, 72–73, 150–151, 270